Gödel, Putnam, and Functionalism

Gödel, Putnam, and Functionalism

A New Reading of *Representation and Reality*

Jeff Buechner

A Bradford Book
The MIT Press
Cambridge, Massachusetts
London, England

For information on quantity discounts, email special_sales@mitpress.mit.edu.

Set in Stone Serif and Stone Sans on 3B2 by Asco Typesetters, Hong Kong. Printed and bound in the United States of America.

Library of Congress Cataloging-in-Publication Data

Buechner, Jeff.
Gödel, Putnam, and functionalism : a new reading of 'representation and reality' / Jeff Buechner.
    p. cm.
Includes bibliographical references and index.
ISBN 978-0-262-02623-9 (hardcover : alk. paper)
1. Realism. 2. Putnam, Hilary. Representation and reality. 3. Gödel, Kurt.
4. Functionalism (Psychology) 5. Mind-brain identity theory. 6. Computers.
I. Title.
B835.B865   2007
128'.2—dc22   2007000278

10 9 8 7 6 5 4 3 2 1

Contents

Preface

Hilary Putnam's *Representation and Reality* articulates four important theses: the use of Gödel's incompleteness theorems to refute computational functionalism (and how to avoid the simple logical error committed by John Lucas and Roger Penrose), a precise formulation of a triviality thesis (which Frankie Egan has called the hardest problem for cognitive science), a multi-realization argument against computational functionalism, and an argument that there are no computable partitionings of the set of computational multi-realizations of an arbitrary intentional state (which forecloses against the possibility of local computational reductions). Although I think that all four theses ultimately fall, I hope that what I do here will motivate others to re-examine Putnam's magnificent book. The importance of Putnam's four theses, the fact that few philosophers had critically examined all of them, the fact that there appeared to me to be difficulties for each, and Putnam's philosophical artistry were my primary motivations for writing this book.

Putnam is one of the great philosophers of the past hundred years. His depth, originality, ingenuity, and common sense, his moral and political views, and his kindness and generosity have been inspirational to me and to many others in the profession. His philosophical powers and imagination are legendary. He has revolutionized several distinct areas in philosophy. He has written important papers in philosophy of mind, in metaphysics, in philosophy of language, in ethics, in literary criticism, in philosophical logic, in philosophy of mathematics, in philosophy of physics, in mathematical logic, and in other fields. In 1965 he invented computational learning theory, which today figures in molecular biology, in homeland security, in linguistics, in theoretical computer science, in statistics, and in epistemology.

I first came under Putnam's spell when I took his "Decidability and Undecidability" course in the Mathematics Department at Harvard

University. Anything that he writes is a must-read for me. Over the years, along with the rest of the philosophical community, I have witnessed the evolution of his thought and have seen him, sometimes with great courage, shed old views and take on new ones. Writing this book has kept me in almost constant touch with his ideas, and this has given me the greatest pleasure and intellectual satisfaction.

This book began as a doctoral dissertation in the Philosophy Department at Rutgers University. I had thought about the ideas in *Representation and Reality* for several years. In June 2002, I began to see in that work various difficulties. By December of that year, I had a working manuscript. I defended on February 27, 2003. Doing my graduate work at Rutgers, the best place in the world for philosophy of mind and psychology, had a salutary and transformative influence on my ability to do philosophy. Rutgers is not just a place where great philosophy is done; it's also a place where great philosophers are kind, decent, caring people. Without their kindness, decency, and care, my dissertation—and thus this book—would never have been finished. My style is to work alone, and I am fortunate that my dissertation committee allowed me to do that. I am also lucky that some of the very best people in our profession—Frankie Egan (my adviser), Barry Loewer, Brian McLaughlin, and Zenon Pylyshyn—served on the committee. Other people at Rutgers whom I happily remember (and with many of whom I still happily discuss philosophy) are Bob Matthews, the late Bob Weingard, Peter Klein, Dick Foley (before NYU took him from us), Rob Bolton, Ernie LePore, Howard McGary, Martin Bunzl, Doug Husak, Steve Stich, Brian Loar, Vann McGee (before he left for MIT), Jeff McMahan, and Jerry Fodor.

I submitted the dissertation to The MIT Press in mid 2004. It was accepted for publication in February 2005. In the summer of 2005 I did a substantial revision. In the summer of 2006, though hampered by illness, I revised it yet again. My manuscript editor, Paul Bethge, was enormously helpful in spotting grammatical miscreants and backwater locutions and usage and thoroughly tactful in urging me to banish them. My editor, Tom Stone, helped me in many ways, large and small, personal and impersonal, always with great cheer and efficiency.

A profound influence on me has been my teacher and good friend Saul Kripke. I have studied with Kripke since the fall of 1986 and have never ceased being amazed at his raw philosophical powers. Kripke's seminars are unlike anyone else's. You always walk away feeling that this is the best philosophy has to offer. After he retired, I assembled and archived all of his unpublished writings, a task that was extraordinarily rewarding. Listening to Saul's jokes, anecdotes, and intellectual banter over dinner is a great source of pleasure.

Another profound influence on me has been the philosopher Alan Berger. After a bad accident in the summer of 1997 (I was hit by a pickup truck while jogging and was thrown 65 feet), Berger called me daily during the five weeks I was in a hospital recuperating. He talked philosophy with me. This was important for my self-confidence, because I was worried that head injuries sustained during the accident would adversely affect my ability to do good philosophy. He gave me an outstanding tour through Quine's "Truth by Convention" and through several of Saul's early ideas on the nature of logic. Alan is a good friend who does great philosophy.

The love and trust which the Philosophy Department at Rutgers/Newark bestowed upon me helped immeasurably toward finishing the dissertation and in substantially revising it. Thank you, Anna Stubblefield, Nancy Holmstrom, Raffaella DeRosa, Michael Rohr, and Pheroze Wadia. I experienced your moral goodness and philosophical acumen almost as an enchantment. Dale Howard, my co-teacher in a special critical thinking course for students on academic probation at Rutgers/Newark convinced me in 2002 that I had something important to say and that it would be easy for me to say it. My late father had a keen interest in science and in some areas of philosophy; he would certainly have enjoyed reading this book. My late mother did not share those interests, but that one of her children was about to publish a second book (the first was a critical thinking textbook) made her happy. I have had many pleasant hours of philosophical conversation with Jerry Dolan (*The* Boss), Herman Tavani, and Lloyd Carr, masters of the Nashua Circle. In the summer of 2005, I participated in the Dartmouth Summer Faculty Institute on the Human Genome Project. Ron Green and Aine Donovan, Co-Directors of the Dartmouth Ethics Institute, fostered my new-found interest in bioethics, and I thank them for their warmth, hospitality and philosophical conversations.

During the last two years, I have had the good fortune of working closely with Harvey Feder, former Associate Provost of Rutgers/Newark, who spent 2005–2006 at the Prudential Center for Business Ethics. The Center funded me for two years, and I am grateful to them (especially Oliver Quinn and Harold Davis) for that and for many other things. Harvey is a magician at getting projects done and at stimulating people to do their most creative work. Harvey and I, along with Bob Nahory (a former Bell Labs laser physicist, now a media restoration guru at the Rutgers/Newark Institute for Jazz Studies) and Barry Komisaruk (who has made major discoveries in the psychology and physiology of the human sexual response), put together a

Summer Institute in Bioethics for students in Newark's public high schools. Thanks to Merck and the Prudential Center for funding it and to Bob and Barry for great friendship.

Ed Hartman (now putting together a business ethics program at the NYU Stern School of Business) has been nothing less than my savior, both because he rescued me from a great loss and because he taught me to see the virtue in virtue ethics. Ed has as deep an understanding of the *Nicomachean Ethics* as anyone could possibly have and knows how to skillfully apply its insights to the full spectrum of ethical problems. He is one of the most decent people in the world, and I count myself quite fortunate indeed to have his friendship.

But the person who has helped me most is Karen Chaffee. She is a chemist, but her interests also include philosophy, literature, biology, politics, physics, sociology, education, anthropology, and much else. She read *Representation and Reality* so as to be able to discuss my manuscript with me while I was revising it for the first time. Her incisive criticism, philosophical and scientific good sense, and wonderful friendship made the book much, much better than it would have been without her help. Words can help to express my gratitude, but they can go only so far. Whatever there is beyond words, it is there to show the full extent of my gratitude. Thanks, Karen, for sharing your ideas with me.

Dedication

In memory of my mother and father.
For Karen.

Gödel, Putnam, and Functionalism

Introduction

Hilary Putnam was a primary architect, in the late 1950s, of the philosophical view about the nature of the human mind known as *functionalism*.[1] It is the response of a (then) scientific materialist to the demise of mind-body identity theories. The view that the human mind is a computer is called *computational functionalism*, and Putnam is credited with inventing it. But by the early 1970s he had doubts about functionalism, and about computational functionalism in particular. In papers written between 1972 and 1988, he devised arguments illustrating tensions in computational functionalism, though during that time he published no systematic attack. That came in 1988, when he published his masterly refutation *Representation and Reality*.[2]

In *Representation and Reality* (henceforth abbreviated *R&R*) Putnam expounds four powerful arguments against computational functionalism. The first involves using Gödel's incompleteness theorems to refute the view that there is a computational description of human reasoning and human rationality. What is special about this argument is that it avoids the simple logical error to which previous arguments using the theorems succumbed. Putnam's second argument shows that any computational description whatsoever can be attributed to any physical system. A cup of coffee in front of you is now computing market predictions for this afternoon. This is the triviality argument. Although this kind of argument had been known for at least 20 years before *R&R*, for the first time there is a rigorous formal proof of the claim that any physical object computes any computable function. The third argument shows there are infinitely many computational realizations of an arbitrary intentional state. This is a powerful multi-realization argument against computational functionalism. The fourth argument closes the door on any attempt to answer a multi-realization argument by showing that local reductions are possible. The argument shows there can't be local computational reductions, for there is no computable partitioning of the infinity of computational realizations of an arbitrary intentional state into a single, or a small set of, packages (or equivalence classes).

There are important inferential connections between the four arguments. Both the Gödel argument and the triviality argument are used in the argument against local computational reductions. The Gödel argument is also needed in the multi-realization argument. In this book I critically examine each of these arguments and all of their connections with one another. This is the first time that a systematic and exhaustive examination of the arguments in *R&R* has been undertaken in the literature. Although my view is that none of these arguments succeed, my hope is that this book will open up a new discussion of *Representation and Reality*, a great book by one of the world's greatest philosophers.

A Brief History of Functionalism

Functionalism is an important doctrine in twentieth-century philosophy because it provides an answer to deep and timeless questions about the human mind. Pitched at a general level, these questions can be understood by non-philosophers: What makes a mind a mind? What is the nature of thinking? What is the nature of pain? In virtue of what are pains different from thoughts?

The early history of functionalism is complex owing to differences in kinds of functionalism. Several figures played pivotal roles in bringing it to prominence. One such figure is Hilary Putnam, for whom functionalism fills the void created by the demise of mind-body identity theories. In the late 1950s Putnam argued that mental properties, such as pains, are not reducible to physical properties. Consider the panoply of creatures that experience the mental state of being in pain. This mental property is physically realized in creatures on Earth with markedly different physical brains. Moreover, if there are creatures elsewhere in the universe who experience pain, it might be physically realized in physical substances that are not carbon based.

Thus, a mental state, such as being in pain, can be physically realized in multiple physically distinct ways in different kinds of physical organisms, in a single kind of organism, and even in a single individual instance of a kind of organism at different times in its life. In human beings, mental properties are physically realized in neural tissue. In a being from another star system, they might be physically realized in patterns of light. How does this show that the mind is not identical with the physical brain? To see how, we need to know what is meant by a scientific reduction. The history of science is filled with examples of successful scientific reductions of one phenomenon to another. For instance, heat is reduced to mean molecular motion, and light is reduced to electromagnetic waves. The guiding idea behind a scientific reduction is that the reduced phenomenon is identical with the reducing phenomenon. Heat (the reduced phenomenon) is identical with mean molecular motion (the reducing phenomenon). It *is* mean molecular motion. There are additional constraints on a successful scientific reduction. One is that the laws of the reduced phenomenon are obeyed (usually approximately) by the reducing phenomenon. Another is that whatever effects the reduced phenomenon explains are also explained (usually approximately) by the reducing phenomenon. A third constraint is that there is a law-like relation between the reduced phenomenon and the reducing phenomena. This means that there is no physically possible state of affairs in which the reduced phenomenon exists without the reducing phenomenon. For instance, there is a law-like relation between light and electromagnetic waves, so there is no physically possible state of affairs in which there is light but there are no electromagnetic waves. A fourth constraint is that the reducing phenomenon is a natural kind: a kind of thing that occurs naturally in Nature, such as oxygen or trees.

If A is identical with B, it is not also identical with C unless B and C are identical. Suppose A is a pain state, B is the brain of a human being, and C is the brain of a squid. B is not identical with C. But A is physically realized in B and is physically realized in C. Is it identical with B, or with C? For a theory of mind-body identity to be meaningful, A must be identical with a particular physical state. But why not say that A is identical with several different physical states? For instance, why don't we say that A is identical with 'B or C'? This is logically true if A is identical with one of B or C. If there are many—perhaps infinitely many—ways in which a pain state can be physically realized, then we have to say that A is identical with a disjunction 'B or C or D or E or ... or Z'. But this is not the model of a scientific reduction of one thing to another. For starters, the disjunction 'A or B or C or ...' is not a natural kind. It is a motley of different kinds of brains. It is not something we think occurs naturally in Nature; rather, it is something that is an artificial construct. Even if each brain is by itself a natural kind, their disjunction is not.

It makes no sense to say that light is identical with electromagnetic waves or with something different from electromagnetic waves. Which one is it identical with? It is a cheat to say "either of them," since we want to know which one it is. If it is in principle impossible to say which one it is, then we do not have a scientific reduction of light. But this is the situation with mind-brain identity theories. Moreover, there are no law-like connections between the multiple physical realizations of mental properties in distinct physical substances, and so there is no law-like relation between the reduced (mental) property and the reducing (physical) properties.

The preceding paragraphs illustrate a multi-realization argument. Suppose that someone claims that A is scientifically reducible to B. If it is shown that A is physically realized in B, in C, and in multiple other kinds of things, then A is multi-realized. But if A is multi-realized, it is not reducible to one kind of thing. It contradicts the definition of a scientific reduction to say that A is reducible to multiple kinds of distinct things that are not lawfully related. Thus, A is not reducible to B if it is multiply realized in other kinds of things (C, D, etc.). By this kind of multi-realization argument, which Putnam himself engineered, mind-body identity theories were refuted.

Mind-body identity theorists did not passively watch their theory be destroyed.[3] They countered the multi-realization argument by restricting the kinds of beings in whom mental states occur. The brain of a squid is significantly different from the brain of a human being. Since the interest of a mind-brain identity theory is to specify the nature of the *human* mind, why not eliminate non-human beings that have physical brains unlike the human brain from the reduction of minds to brains? Indeed, even if a non-human being has a physical brain similar to that of a human being, why not eliminate those beings too? We are less interested in the nature of non-human minds than in the nature of human minds. Local scientific reductions restrict the class of objects that are either reduced or in the reducing class. The mind-body identity theorists restricted the kinds of minds to human minds and thus restricted the kinds of brains to human brains.

Defenders of functionalism—the theory that replaced the mind-body identity theory—responded with a new multi-realization argument for the local reduction. They claimed that human brains physically differ from one human to the next. Moreover, there are significant physical differences between the brains of men and those of women. Is a pain state reducible to A or B or C or . . . , where A is the brain of a certain man, B is the brain of a certain woman, C is the brain of a certain man different from the A-brain and the B-brain, and so on. The mind-body identity theorists countered this move. They claimed that the physical brains of human beings have enough in common that so they could be put into a small number of equivalence classes. An equivalence class is a set of objects all of which are sufficiently similar to count as being the same kind of object. All the brains in an equivalence class are the same kind of physical brain.

There is one kind of move functionalists did *not* make in response to the mind-body identity theorists' move of partitioning physical brains into equivalence classes: they did not claim that "generic" mental states, such as being in pain, differ from one person to the next and differ for different kinds of pains. This move banks on the possibility that different kinds of pains might be physically realized in the same kind of brain, while the same kind of pain in different individuals is physically realized in different brains. This would complicate the task of partitioning brains into equivalence classes. But it would also complicate the description of the reduced phenomena. The confrontation between mind-body identity theorists and their opponents is now at a standstill. There are few adherents of mind-body identity theories among philosophers. The consensus view is that functionalism is the best reductive account of the human mind. There are many philosophers who opt for a non-reductive account but still maintain that the mind depends on the brain. This philosophical position is known as *non-reductive physicalism*. But what is functionalism?

Functionalism—a philosophical doctrine about the nature of the mind— is the response of philosophers to the demise of mind-brain identity theories. Philosophers did not return to the Cartesian dualist view that the mind is a non-material substance and the brain is a physical substance. They did not dispute the view that the mind depends on the brain. But the brain was not the place to look in answering the question "What is the nature of the mind?" How the mind is physically realized in the brain can't provide an answer to that question. That much was made clear by the multi-realization argument against mind-brain identity theories. The philosophical view that replaced mind-brain identity theories was that the answer to the question lies in how the mind is organized and how it functions.

Functionalism made a bold move: it focused on the causal roles and causal functions that minds of any kind exemplify. Causal roles do not have to be picked out at the level of description of the brain. That neuron A causes neuron B to fire may not be the appropriate level of description for describing causal roles. The physical brain has a physical organization. Its physical components have causal roles and causal functions. The level of description chosen determines different kinds of functionalist theories. The point is that causal roles and causal functions appear in *any* mind. Suppose that the level of description chosen for describing causal roles and functions is the human brain. If that is so, then beings with minds that are physically realized in a different kind of brain or in a different chemistry than one that is carbon based may not have those causal roles and functions. If they do not, either these beings do not have minds after all or the level of description for describing causal roles and functions must be changed.

Functionalism looks for essential functional properties: causal roles and causal functions that all beings with minds possess. This condition constrains the choice of an appropriate level of description for causal roles and functions. Two different choices underlie the two major types of functionalism: computational functionalism and causal-theoretical functionalism.[4] There are family resemblances between the two types, and there is substantial cross-cutting among more specific kinds of functionalism falling under them.

Orthogonal to this division is a twofold distinction between analytic (or *a priori*) functionalism and scientific functionalism (or psycho-functionalism). The latter distinction concerns whether functional states are empirically verified to be true (scientific functionalism) or are true as a matter of definition (analytic functionalism). Most cognitive scientists eschew analytic functionalism for scientific functionalism. It would be hard for a cognitive scientist to swallow, for example, the view that seeing the edges of objects is, by definition, computing the second derivative of light-intensity changes in light-intensity arrays. Similarly, it is absurd to say that any mental state is, by definition, a computational state.

Computational functionalism takes the human mind to be a "computer" program. Its appropriate level of description for computational functionalism is an information processor. The best model of information processing is the computer. The program of the human mind, whatever it is, answers the question "What is the nature of the human mind?" Similarly, if angels (though non-material) have minds, the nature of an angel's mind is that it is a program. The same is true of the minds of frogs. The nature of a frog's mind is a program. Putnam first conceived of the idea that mental states can be functionally characterized as a computing machine. He also conjectured what kind of computational model underlies the program of the human mind.[5] Moreover, that minds were computing machines gave a respectability to computational functionalism, insofar as the technology of computing machines was on the rise in industry and in the public eye in the late 1950s.

The other functionalist theory is causal-theoretical functionalism. It conceives of the human mind as a causal network in which input states, mental states, and output states are causally connected. Mental states (and mental kinds, such as pains) are distinguished from one another by the network of causal relations in which they are situated. For instance, the mental kind pain is individuated by its causes, its effects, and its relations with other mental states. Change any single element in the network and the character of the mental state changes too. Typically, folk psychology provides the theory of the set of causal connections and how each state is described. Folk psychology is what ordinary folk believe about the human mind.[6] Folk psychology characterizes it as having beliefs and desires. We act upon our desires, using as guides to action our beliefs about the world outside our heads and the world inside our heads. Causal-theoretical functionalism is riddled with internal problems. A severe difficulty is that when Jack is in pain and he believes that it is raining, he is in a different mental state than when he is in pain and he believes it is not raining. But surely the state of being in pain is the same regardless of one's beliefs about the weather. That is not to say that one's beliefs about the weather could not affect the quality of the pain state, or even that they could not cause a pain state to come into existence. On the other hand, individuating a mental state in terms of the entire network of one's beliefs and desires leads to absurdity. But what are appropriate restrictions on the size and the parts of the network necessary for individuating mental states? Computational functionalism did not have to answer this hard question. It also did not have to take folk psychology to be the final arbiter of the causal network.

Not everyone was happy with computational functionalism. The idea that the human mind is nothing more than a computer was another blow to our self-esteem. We lost our privileged place in the heavens with the Copernican revolution, our privileged status in the animal kingdom with the Darwinian revolution, and our dignity with the Freudian revolution. If thought, talk, and rationality could just as well occur in hand-held computers, there is little left that makes human beings special. In the 20 years after the inception of functionalism, various criticisms were directed against each of its several versions.

Gödel's Incompleteness Theorems and Computational Functionalism

An important criticism of computational functionalism was made by the Oxford philosopher J. R. Lucas, who borrowed his idea from an unpublished talk the great logician Kurt Gödel gave at Brown University in 1951.[7] Lucas used Gödel's incompleteness theorems to argue that minds cannot be computing machines. The theorems describe limitations in computing machines that Lucas thought human minds transcends. To appreciate how the Gödel theorems apply to the question of whether the nature of the mind is that it is a computing machine of some kind, one must realize that mathematical reasoning formalized in a system of logic establishes its conclusions with mathematical certainty. But how do we know that mathematical reasoning establishes its conclusions with mathematical certainty? We know it when we can break down that reasoning into finitely many steps, each of which we are sure does not lead to falsehoods and which can be checked for correctness by a machine. Logic is a formal language with inference rules. If axioms of mathematics are added to it, the inferences made are mathematically certain. In fact, a finitary system of logic defines what it is for a theorem to be mathematically certain.

In the early 1930s, Gödel proved that for any system of logic suitable for reasoning about elementary arithmetic there exist arithmetical truths that cannot be proved in that system of logic, if it is consistent.[8] Since computations in a computer can be translated into logic, this limitation on logic is also a limitation on the computational abilities of computing machines. And if the nature of a human mind is that it is a computer, this limitation is also a limitation on human minds. Lucas did not think the nature of a human mind is that it is a computer. He argued that there are truths of arithmetic that human minds can recognize to be true that can't be proved true by a computer of a certain kind. If that is so, human minds are not computers of that kind.

If Lucas is right, this would refute computational functionalism. It would also be a remarkable refutation. A result in mathematical logic is used to refute a philosophical view about the metaphysics of the human mind. But Lucas's argument faced blistering criticism from philosophers, not all of whom were computational functionalists. In the mid 1980s, Roger Penrose, a notable mathematical physicist, published a book in which he revived and expanded upon Lucas's argument.[9] Penrose followed that book with another one in 1994, addressing the criticisms of his earlier book.

Putnam, in the late 1950s and in the early 1990s, exposed the fatal flaws in anti-functionalist arguments that used Gödel's incompleteness theorems.[10] Suppose that a program is proposed as the Master Program of the human mind. It is subject to the Gödel theorems, for it must be competent in elementary arithmetic, since human minds are competent in elementary arithmetic. But then there are truths in elementary arithmetic it cannot prove. However, the Gödel result obtains only if the program is not contradictory. That it is not contradictory can't be proved within the program— this is the substance of Gödel's second incompleteness theorem. If a system of logic that can express Peano arithmetic is consistent, then that truth about that system of logic cannot be proved in that system of logic.[11]

Putnam pointed out that even for a being not subject to the Gödel theorems, it might be difficult to prove a program is not contradictory. Suppose that the Master Program of the human mind is longer than all the books in the Library of Congress. No human being would be able to survey it. How would we prove it is not contradictory? Lucas and Penrose claimed that a human mind that has no computational description can "see" (Lucas) that the Master Program is correct or can "appreciate" (Penrose) that it is correct. But what exactly does the ability of seeing or appreciating consist in? Suppose that the Master Program is short. "Seeing" that it is correct cannot consist in making a finite chain of inferences with paper and pencil that requires no infinitary capacities to make any of the steps in any of the inferences. If it did, it would be a proof in a system of logic and thus subject to the Gödel theorems. But if "seeing" is not like that, then what it is like is a mystery. Now suppose that the Master Program is longer than all the books in the Library of Congress. Even if we can "see" that mathematical truths are correct in such a way that it is not merely a matter of making inferences in a system of logic, the human brain does not have the computational resources to survey such a program.[12]

Putnam argued that Penrose failed to take this possibility into account. But it is a possibility that destroys Lucas's and Penrose's use of the Gödel theorems to refute functionalism. Suppose that the Master Program is longer than all the books in the Library of Congress. If human minds have a computational description given by the Master Program, they will not be able, in principle, to prove that it is not contradictory, since they are subject to the Gödel theorems. If human minds don't have a computational description, they will not be able to prove that the Master program is not contradictory, even though they are not subject to the Gödel theorems, because it is too long to be surveyed and made comprehensible. In that case, by using the Gödel theorems, we can establish no difference between human minds with a computational description and human minds without one. Putnam took Penrose's failure to consider this possibility to be a logical error in his argument that effectively destroyed it. Nonetheless, Putnam uses the Gödel theorems in his refutation of computational functionalism. How does he avoid the simple logical error that Lucas and Penrose commit?[13] The argument appears in a short paper, "Reflexive Reflections."[14] But in that paper Putnam doesn't say how the argument avoids the error. Instead he shows that nondemonstrative reasoning is subject to the Gödel theorems. I conjecture that the error is avoided this way: Suppose that we use nondemonstrative reasoning to make a statistical estimate of the correctness of the Master Program. A finitary human mind that has a computational description and that attempts such statistical reasoning may fail because it is subject to the Gödel theorems. But a finitary human mind that does not have a computational description is not subject to the Gödel theorems. It can use nondemonstrative reasoning to establish, with less than mathematical certainty, that the Master Program is correct.

I think it is important to distinguish metaphysical from epistemic uses of the Gödel theorems in arguments against computational functionalism, in order to keep separate the kinds of claims made in those arguments. I also show the different prices that must be paid in these uses of the Gödel theorems. I exploit a sadly neglected feature of the Gödel incompleteness theorems in my discussion of Putnam's arguments using them. The Gödel theorems show that the consistency of Peano arithmetic cannot be proved *with mathematical certainty* by any finitary being. This leaves open the possibility that finitary beings prove the consistency of Peano arithmetic with less than mathematical certainty or in another epistemic modality.

Neither a finitary human mind that has no computational description nor a finitary human mind that has a computational description can prove the consistency of arithmetic with mathematical certainty. The reason why this is so is that it is reasoning in a formal system of logic that confers the epistemic modality of mathematical certainty upon what is proved in the system. Anyone who thinks that finitary human minds that have no computational description can prove the consistency of arithmetic with mathematical certainty must show how it is done. However it is done—if it can be done—it must not be by finitary steps of reasoning, none of which requires infinitary capacities, for that reasoning can be captured in a formal system of logic. But then it is subject to the Gödel theorems, and if that is so it cannot prove the consistency of arithmetic with mathematical certainty. With respect to proving either the consistency of Peano arithmetic or the truth of a Gödel sentence, the Gödel theorems cannot distinguish finitary human minds that have a computational description from finitary human minds that do not have one. This creates a serious difficulty for anyone who uses the Gödel theorems to refute computational functionalism. Both a finitary human mind that has a computational description and a finitary human mind that does not have a computational description can use methods of reasoning that prove the correctness of the Master Program, though with less than mathematical certainty or in another epistemic modality, as long as those methods of reasoning are not susceptible to the

Gödel theorems. If they are susceptible to the Gödel theorems, the same kind of difficulty that arises for proving the correctness of the Master Program (of the human mind) with mathematical certainty now arises for them. However, if the methods are not susceptible to the Gödel theorems, then both a human mind that has a computational description and the human that does not have one can use those methods. These disturbing results can be summarized as follows: Where the methods for proving the correctness of the Master Program with mathematical certainty or with less than mathematical certainty or in another epistemic modality are susceptible to the Gödel theorems, we cannot distinguish between a finitary human mind that has a computational description and a finitary human mind that does not have one. Where the methods for proving the correctness of the Master Program with less than mathematical certainty or in another epistemic modality are not susceptible to the Gödel theorems, we can't distinguish between a human mind that has a computational description and a human mind that does not have one.

The point of Putnam's theorem that nondemonstrative reasoning is susceptible to the Gödel theorems is to drive a wedge between finitary minds that have a computational description and finitary minds that don't have one. A mind that does not have a computational description engages in the kind of nondemonstrative reasoning that can establish the correctness of the Master Program, even if it is as long as all the books in the Library of Congress. But Putnam never discusses the issue of the epistemic modality of the proof. Is it known with mathematical certainty? This is a serious lacuna in the argument.

In *R&R*, Putnam says that all of our methods of demonstrative and nondemonstrative reasoning, and all methods of inquiry into the world, are susceptible to the Gödel theorems: "... if the [computational] description is a formalization of our powers to reason rationally *in toto*—a description of *all* our means of reasoning—then inability to know something by the 'methods formalized by the description' is inability to know that something *in principle.*"[15]

Suppose that ultimate computational descriptions encompassing all methods of inquiry and all justificatory procedures are susceptible to the Gödel theorems. How do human minds that have no computational description reason that Putnam's theorem is correct? If it cannot be shown correct by some method of justification, then we cannot claim to have shown that the methods it subsumes are susceptible to the Gödel theorems. Recall that a necessary condition for the First Incompleteness Theorem is that the formal system that can express arithmetic is consistent.

But if *all* methods of inquiry and justification are susceptible to the Gödel theorems, then neither a finitary mind with and a finitary mind with no computational description can prove Putnam's Theorem. This is so because all methods of inquiry and justification are subsumed by the formal system to which Putnam's Theorem applies. We cannot prove that the computational description of those methods of inquiry and justification is correct. It follows that we can't justify the inferences made in Putnam's Theorem. If that is the case, nothing prevents us from claiming all methods of inquiry and justification are not susceptible to the Gödel theorems. In that case, we can now use them to justify the inference steps in Putnam's theorem. If that is so, we now cannot use them to justify the inference steps in Putnam's Theorem. This state of affairs has the form of a paradox. Putnam's Theorem is justified by justificatory procedures if and only if it is not justified by justificatory procedures.

Here is a simpler way of seeing how the paradox arises: Suppose that there is only one method of reasoning about the world. Call it M. Call the computational description of the human mind P. P contains M. If P is susceptible to the Gödel theorems, it must be shown so by M. But since M is the only method of reasoning, if M is susceptible to the Gödel theorems, we cannot be justified in claiming that M is susceptible to them. This is because we cannot be sure that there is no contradiction in our reasoning by M. If that is the case, it is now open that M is not susceptible to the Gödel theorems. In that case, we can now prove, using reasoning by M, that M is susceptible to the Gödel theorems. In that case, we can't be justified in claiming that M is susceptible to the Gödel theorems. Paradox.[16] M is susceptible to the Gödel theorems if it is and if it is not susceptible to the Gödel theorems.

If all methods for proving the correctness of P are subsumed under P, the same result—paradox—obtains. There would be no paradox if there were epistemically adequate methods of reasoning not susceptible to the Gödel theorems that can be used to prove Putnam's Theorem. Reasoning in classical propositional logic is not susceptible to the Gödel theorems, and that reasoning is subsumed by P. However, both minds with a computational description and minds without one can reason in propositional logic. If Putnam's Theorem shows that there are some methods of reasoning that are susceptible to the Gödel theorems, then neither finitary minds with a computational description nor finitary minds without one can use those methods to prove results in the epistemic modality of the methods. If the epistemic modality of such a method is mathematical certainty, then neither kind of mind can prove results with mathematical certainty.

Since, by hypothesis, not all methods of reasoning are susceptible to the Gödel theorems, those that are not susceptible to the theorems can be used to prove the results of those that are, though with less than mathematical certainty or in another epistemic modality. But finitary minds with a computational description and finitary minds without one can use those methods of reasoning. If that is the case, there is no argument against computational functionalism.

As important as Putnam's Gödel argument is, it has not been examined in the literature. It is not just a basic supporting pillar of Putnam's anti-functionalism. It is also a basic pillar of his anti-realism, of his version of epistemic semantics, and of his return to naive realism. It is critical to showing that computationalism succumbs to Quinean indeterminacy, ontological relativity, and Quinean meaning holism, and to showing that methods that have no complete computational description (including rational interpretation, general intelligence, and reasonable reasoning) sidestep the Quinean mires.

Triviality Arguments: Universal Realization of Computations in Physical Objects

Triviality arguments are a potent threat to computational functionalism. They capitalize on weaknesses in the definition of what it is for a physical system to physically realize a computation and on weaknesses in the definition of a computation. The idea is that the former kind of definition is so loose that one can show that any physical object physically realizes any computable function and still be in accord with the definition of what it is for a physical system to physically realize a computation. Another way of putting the point is that every physical object has every functional organization. If that is so, it makes little sense to say the human brain physically realizes the functional organization of the human mind, since it also physically realizes every possible functional organization. Indeed, all physical objects have the functional organization of the human mind. The metaphysical claim is that the nature of the human mind is that it is a computer program. But if everything in nature (rocks, tables, frogs, walls, water molecules, and so on) has that nature, the metaphysical claim loses its meaning.

Cognitive psychology assumes that the human mind has a specific functional organization. It takes as its principal goal to describe that functional organization. However, if the human brain physically realizes infinitely many distinct functional organizations, which one is the true functional organization of the human mind? If a cognitive psychologist confirms a theory of the mind's functional organization by conducting experiments and collecting data from them, that confirmation doesn't show the mind has *only* that specific functional organization. It shows that the mind does have that functional organization. But we knew before we conducted the experiments that it does, for we knew—by a triviality argument—that it has every functional organization (and thus that the experiment does not show that it does not have any of the other functional organizations).

Triviality arguments date back to the mid 1960s. Ian Hinckfuss, John Searle, and Hilary Putnam independently noticed that the definition of what it is for a physical system to physically realize a computation is too loose. It lets in things that don't count as genuine computations. In seminars during the early 1970s, Putnam gave a rigorous version of a triviality argument, and it is this version that Edward Stabler describes in a paper that appeared in the late 1980s.

The triviality argument that Stabler presents has a fatal weakness: it conflicts with mathematical facts from the theory of computational complexity. In Stabler's version of a triviality argument, every computable function is computed in constant time.[17] The theory of computational complexity describes how hard it is to compute a function. Hardness is typically measured in terms of how much time it takes and how much space is used in computing values of the function. The theory assigns functions and problems to complexity classes. These classes have distinctive computational properties. For instance, the complexity class NP consists of problems that require an exponentially growing amount of resources to compute solutions to the problem as the size of the problem grows linearly. An example of a problem in NP is computing a truth table in classical propositional logic. As the number of propositional variables grows linearly, the space needed to solve the problem grows exponentially.

There are many outstanding conjectures not yet proved in computational complexity theory. But there are some theorems. One is that the complexity class EXPTIME is not equal to P.[18] If a triviality argument allows a physical system to compute a function that is in EXPTIME in constant time, then the function is in P. But this contradicts the mathematical fact that P is not equal to EXPTIME. When conformity to the theorems of computational complexity theory constrains a definition of what it is for a physical system to physically realize a computation, it follows that not every physical system can compute any function. To refute triviality arguments, we show that definitions of what it is for a physical system to compute a function violate either the laws of computability theory or the laws of computational complexity theory. Consider an analogy with numerals (which represent numbers). Suppose that a numeral system for positive integers makes addition anti-commutative. If that is the case, it must be rejected. Numeral systems for the natural numbers must respect the laws of arithmetic. Similarly, physical representations of computations must respect the laws of computation and of computational complexity theory.

Triviality arguments encounter other difficulties too. One is that they lack the resources to answer questions about counterfactuals about computations. Another is that when a physical system can be in the same physical state more than once, computations fail to supervene on physical systems. Finally, triviality arguments encounter a Kripke-Wittgenstein problem.

In *R&R*, Putnam provides a rigorous and formal proof of a triviality theorem. The theorem is that every ordinary open system is a realization of every abstract finite automaton. His proof relies on two assumptions about the physical world. One—the Principle of Continuity—is that electromagnetic and gravitational fields are almost everywhere continuous. The other—the Principle of Noncyclical Behavior—is that physical systems are in different physical states at different times. For the purposes of proving Putnam's theorem, the first assumption has the modal status of a physical law and the second is a contingent truth (relative to physical laws).

I appeal to facts about chaotic physical systems and about indeterministic Newtonian mechanical systems and to Poincaré's recurrence theorem to show there are physical situations in which it is not possible to say whether the system has trivially computed a function or not.[19] I also use these same kinds of considerations to show that it is indeterminate to say whether one kind of triviality theory (such as Putnam's) applies to a given physical system or whether another kind of triviality theory (such as Stabler's) applies to it. Finally, I show that the Principle of Noncyclical Behavior must have the modal status of a physical law if it is to do the work required of it. But if it has the modal status of a physical law, it contradicts facts about chaotic systems and indeterministic classical Newtonian mechanical systems.

In his essay "Artificial Intelligence: Much Ado about Not Very Much," and in his book *Renewing Philosophy*,[20] Putnam tells us that the claim that the mind or the brain can be modeled as a digital computer does not come to much, since we can model any finite portion of the behavior of any physical system whatsoever by a finite set of step functions. A finite set of step functions is a computable function. I argue that a new kind of triviality theory, different from conventional triviality theories, can be formulated in terms of step functions. I call this new kind of triviality theory *step-function triviality*. Why is this worth doing? Even if conventional triviality theories are refuted, step-function triviality remains a live option. Moreover, it is just as devastating to the philosophy of mind and to cognitive science as are the conventional triviality theories.

Step-function triviality suffers its own problems, though. Using the framework of algorithmic information theory (otherwise known as Kolmogorov complexity), I show that step-function approximations to finite segments of human cognitive behavior face several difficulties. The first is that these approximations will not agree with timing data (from, say, psychophysics) about human cognitive behavior. That is, they will approximate the behavior, but not the time constraints on that behavior. The second is that all human cognitive behavior, whether it is or is not random, will be random behavior. This result comes from the definition of a random sequence in Kolmogorov complexity theory. The third problem is that SF triviality can make no predictions about human cognitive behavior. One cannot construct a step-function approximation to a finite portion of human cognitive behavior without first observing that behavior. Since it can't make predictions, it is not a competitor scientific theory to cognitive science, because it fails a necessary condition for being a science. It is, at best, a pseudo-science.

Suppose that all triviality theories in the literature have been refuted. Because of a metaphysical theory of what computations consist in that comes from John Searle, one can still argue that computational functionalism is "trivial."[21] Searle divides the objects and features of the world into two basic metaphysical categories: those that are intrinsic to the physics of the world and those that are observer relative or user relative. Atoms and chemicals are intrinsic to the world. Chairs, knives, and the property of being a nice day for a picnic are observer relative. There is a test for something to be intrinsic or observer relative. Suppose that all human observers and human users disappear. In that case, if an object or a feature (that is not a physical part of a human observer or human user) disappears, it is observer relative. Otherwise, it is intrinsic to the physics of the world. On Searle's view, computations are observer relative. If there were no human beings, there wouldn't be computations. Indeed, Searle's view is quite strong: if there were no human beings, there would be no programs, computations, or algorithms.

Computations are observer relative, so computations performed by human minds are relative to observers. Two different observers can attribute two different computations to a single human mind. Jack attributes the computation of F to Jim's mind. Jill attributes the computation of G to Jim's mind. Who is right? There are no objective facts about the mind-independent world that can decide who is right and who is wrong. Suppose that if the human mind computes F, we would expect to observe behavior of a certain kind in Jim. We observe such behavior in Jim. Does this show that Jack is correct and Jill is incorrect? No, it does not. Although behavior is a physical change in the world, its description is observer relative (at a certain level of description). In that case, there are no facts about the physical world that show Jack's description of the behavior is correct and Jill's description of it is incorrect. Which description we take to be correct and which function we attribute to Jim's mind is a matter of convention. If that is the case, this is disturbing for a philosophical theory of the nature of the human mind. Suppose that its nature is a computer program. Since whether a physical thing of any kind physically realizes a computer program is observer relative, the nature of the human mind is observer relative if its nature is that it is a computer program. If there were no observers, human minds as conceived of in cognitive science would have no nature. Of course, this seems obviously true. If there were no observers, there would be no human beings and thus no human minds. If there are no human minds, we can't ask about their nature. But it is disturbing to say that the nature of our mind—even if it is a computer program—depends on an observer.

If triviality theories are refuted, computationalists no longer have to worry that every object computes every function. They no longer have to worry that computations are cheap, because they are everywhere. They no longer have to worry that every object has the functional organization of the human mind. However, on Searle's view, computations are observer relative, so a human observer could attribute computations, of any kind, to any physical object. Most of us would think it absurd to attribute a computation to a rock lying in the street. Even so, it still remains the case that we think it sensible (and rational) to attribute computations to a human mind. It is trivial to say that the human mind is a computer, since that claim is easy to make. We simply make the attribution. But notice that we could just as easily attribute a computation to a rock in the street. There are no physical facts in the world that can contradict either of these attributions. If Searle's metaphysics of computation is correct, computationalism functionalism is jeopardized. The philosophical claim that the nature of the mind is a computing machine is vacuous, and cognitive science is no longer a real science.

Searle's view of the metaphysics of computation encounters several difficulties. First, it is incoherent. One can generate several kinds of contradictions from the assumption that computations are observer relative. Second, it fails to take into account non-Bohmian interpretations of quantum physics, in which certain physical states of the world that are intrinsic to the physics of the world are nonetheless observer relative. Either what we take as real physical properties of the world intrinsic to its physics are really observer-relative properties or that a property is observer relative does not disenfranchise it from being intrinsic to the physics of the world. Third, the conjunction of facts from the theory of computation and the observer relativity of computations has fatally absurd consequences. If we reject those absurd consequences, then by modus tollens we must reject the conjunction of facts from the theory of computation and the observer relativity of computations. But the facts from the theory of computation are mathematical truths—indeed, logical truths (in descriptive complexity theory). If that is the case, we must reject Searle's view of the metaphysics of computation.

Are Local Computational Reductions Possible?

It was Putnam who gave life to computational functionalism and introduced it to the philosophical community. In *R&R* he attempts to destroy it. One tool he uses in that attempt is a multi-realization argument. He shows there are infinitely many distinct computational realizations of an arbitrary intentional state. The computational reduction of an arbitrary intentional state is an infinitely long disjunction, each of whose disjuncts is a distinct computational state. If that is so, it is not a genuine computational reduction. It violates the conditions on a legitimate scientific reduction. There are several ways this can happen. For instance, intentional states might be reduced to infinitely many different computer programs. The idea here is that there are multiple computer architectures, programming languages, programs, and algorithms for computing a function F. If any of these is varied, one gets different computational realizations of a single intentional state. It is easy to show there are infinitely many variants of a single computer program for a fixed algorithm in a fixed programming language and a fixed computer architecture.

Another way there can be infinitely many computational realizations of an arbitrary intentional state is when infinitely many speakers each have different auxiliary beliefs about a physical object, such as a Siamese cat. It is necessary to distinguish an auxiliary belief from a meaning-constituting belief. Auxiliary beliefs about a Siamese cat are not components of the meaning of the phrase 'Siamese cat'. We could give up an auxiliary belief without changing the meaning of 'Siamese cat'. But we could not give up a meaning-constituting belief about Siamese cats without changing the meaning of 'Siamese cat'. If one stops believing that Siamese cats are cuddly, the meaning of 'Siamese cat' remains intact. But if one gives up believing that cats are mammals, the meaning is changed.

A revolutionary claim made in twentieth-century philosophy was W. V. Quine's argument that there is no principled analytic/synthetic distinction.[22] If you know the meaning of an analytic sentence (e.g., "All foxes are vixens"), you know that the sentence is true. The meaning of a synthetic sentence (e.g., "The sun is now shining") is not sufficient for its truth. Experience of the world is also necessary. One consequence of repudiating this distinction Quine drew is that any sentence can be given up under the right empirical conditions. It is clear that one will give up "The sun is now shining" if it is now raining. It is not clear what experiences would force one to give up "$1 + 2 = 2 + 1$." The extent to which one holds on to a sentence marks how deeply one believes it to be true. This is an epistemic matter, not a semantic one. If there is no semantical distinction between analytic and synthetic sentences, there is no principled distinction between meaning-constituting beliefs and auxiliary beliefs. Putnam accepts that there is no principled distinction, though he rejects the claim that we cannot make rational decisions about synonymy.[23]

Suppose that there are infinitely many speakers of English, that each speaker thinks the thought (in English) "There is a Siamese cat," and that each speaker has an auxiliary belief that differs from any of the auxiliary beliefs of any of the other speakers. One final supposition must be made. Assume that no computational models of language use can distinguish meaning-constituting beliefs from auxiliary beliefs. If that is the case, there are infinitely many disjuncts in the computational reduction of the intentional state in which one thinks the thought whose content is expressed by the sentence "There is a Siamese cat." This is a multi-realization argument against the claim there is a computational reduction of the belief state whose content is "There is a Siamese cat."

But a computational functionalist can respond in the same way that mind-body identity theorists responded to the multi-realization refutation of mind-body identity theories: by arguing that there is a local computational reduction. Putnam anticipates this move and restricts the class of beings, in a computational reduction of intentional states, to human beings. He then argues that this is not sufficient to eliminate infinite computational realization of an arbitrary intentional state. However, there are different kinds of local reductions. For instance, one can restrict the class of beings in the reduction class and show that for that reduction class there is a computable partitioning of the infinitely many computational realizations of an arbitrary intentional state into a single equivalence class (or a small number of equivalence classes). The local-reduction claim of that kind for mind-brain identity theorists is that all human brains are pretty much the same, so there is one equivalence class to which they all belong. The local-reduction claim of that kind for a computational functionalist is that the computational realizations of an arbitrary intentional state are pretty much the same, so there is a single equivalence class, or a small number of equivalence classes, to which they all belong.

But there is a difference between the local-reduction claim of a mind-body identity theorist and a computational functionalist: there is good evidence human brains are pretty much the same, but it is only a possibility that all computational realizations of an arbitrary intentional state are pretty much the same—indeed, whether it *is* a genuine possibility is not known. Philosophers distinguish different kinds of possibility. Suppose that that all computational realizations of an arbitrary intentional state being pretty much the same is logically impossible. If that is so, all computational realizations of an arbitrary intentional state being pretty much the same is not a genuine possibility. Given that it might not be a genuine possibility, what if the computational functionalist supposes that it *is* a genuine possibility? This move puts computational functionalists at a disadvantage, for they must show that it is a genuine possibility, that it is not logically contradictory to make the supposition.[24] Thus, a computational functionalist is not arguing from a strong position when she supposes it is possible that there is a computable partitioning. On the other hand, Putnam can't afford to ignore the possibility of a computable partitioning, for his multi-realization argument would be jeopardized if there were an argument that it is a genuine possibility and one that is highly plausible. Better for the sake of the argument to show now, if it can be shown, that it is not a genuine possibility. If that is the case, it is not a highly plausible possibility. It is not a possibility of any kind. Putnam anticipated such a move by the computationalist. He argues that there is no computable partitioning.[25] He says that it isn't a mathematical proof, but that it is close to one. Putnam's argument for this claim demands attention. If it is sound, it closes the door on all local computational reductions. If there are no local computational reductions, the foundations of cognitive science vanish in thin air. I will now provide a brief summary of this important argument and where I think it goes wrong.

EQUIVALENCE begins with a simple example: How would we determine that A's use of the word 'cat' is synonymous with B's use of it? Assume that both A and B speak American English, that A lives in the Northeast, and that B lives in the Southwest. We may have to know what theories of cats each holds, what their local environments are like, and what forms of rationality they employ. Here 'theory' includes scientific (e.g., biological), commonsensical, and philosophical (e.g., metaphysical) theories. Much information may be used in deciding that A and B's use of the word 'cat' are synonymous. How would we program a computer to make this decision?

Putnam claims that any computational description of synonymy determination (or determining the references of the same word used by two different speakers) must use a definition of synonymy (or a definition of coreferentiality). If that is so, the definition must survey all possible physical environments, all possible theories of the world, and all possible forms of human rationality. If some theory of the world is left out of the definition, the computational description will not work where, for example, A employs that theory to explain the physiological makeup of a cat. Suppose that some form of human rationality is left out of the definition. The computational description will not work where A's reasoning about cats is an instance of that form of rationality. If some environment is left out of the definition, the computational description will not work where A lives in that environment. Suppose that A and B have different biological theories of cats, but that the theories are somewhat similar. If the term 'cat' refers in A's mouth to the same class of things it refers to in B's mouth, we may decide that their uses of 'cat' are synonymous. But before we make that decision, we must determine that 'cat' refers to the same class of things in two different environments.

If the definition leaves out any possible environment, any possible theory of the world, or any possible form of human rationality, there will be situations in which the computational description of synonymy determination fails. But if all these things are included in the definition, it will be infinitely long. For instance, there are infinitely many distinct possible theories of the world. There are infinitely many distinct possible environments on Earth. Perhaps there are infinitely many possible forms of human rationality. A computational description that is infinitely long cannot be surveyed by a finite mind. Putnam concludes that any algorithm for synonymy determination must be infinitistic.[26] If that is the case, it is not a genuine algorithm, for genuine algorithms are defined relative to beings whose computational capacities are finitistic. Infinitistic algorithms are defined relative to beings whose computational capacities are infinitistic (or for beings with infinite minds). According to Putnam, a mind that can employ an algorithm for synonymy determination occupies an Archimedean point.[27] Putnam concludes that any computational reduction of an arbitrary intentional state cannot clarify or explain the nature of that state. Rather, it substitutes for it something less clear, perhaps mysterious.

EQUIVALENCE raises two important questions: How can human minds, on the assumption they have no computational description, successfully engage in synonymy determination, make coreferentiality decisions, do rational interpretation, and exhibit general intelligence and reasonable reasoning? Why can't there be a finitary computational description of these abilities, if we have them?

Let us take a quick look at some of the obstacles in the way of a philosophical account of how we use language. These obstacles were first discussed in the twentieth century, many of them by Quine. An intelligent non-philosopher, especially a scientist, will likely have an attitude of disbelief about these obstacles. They appear to be the kind of worries young schoolchildren might express. A stronger way of categorizing them is as hooey. Even so, it would be wrong to conclude that they are the products of foolish and uncritical minds. Far from it. The doctrines underlying these obstacles are deep and difficult. Part of Putnam's greatness as a philosopher is that he attempts to diagnose how we can conceive of these doctrines. What makes it possible for someone to argue that there is no such thing as meanings? Is there an alternative way of doing philosophy under which these doctrines simply vanish? That said, the intelligent scientist can bracket the following paragraphs as the "hooey obstacles."

Quine didn't stop at repudiating the analytic-synthetic distinction. Giving up that distinction does not entail giving up the semantical notion of word meaning. It follows from giving up the distinction that meanings can't be "boxed." A different way of putting it is that there is no museum in which meanings are catalogued and shelved in sharply delimited and well-defined locations.

But Quine famously argued there are no such things as meanings, that there are only behavioral dispositions to use language. Suppose you observe someone saying something (in an unknown language) in response to an event in his local environment, and wish to translate those remarks into your home language. You have nothing more to go on in this task than the speaker's behavior in using language. Two different translators can produce mutually incompatible (even mutually contradictory) translations of those utterances that agree with all of the speaker's behavior in using language. There is no fact of the matter as to which translation is correct. Even if the two translators had access to all possible behavior of the speaker in using language, there would still be no fact of the matter as to which translation is correct. This is Quine's *indeterminacy-of-translation* doctrine. Quine took it to show there are no meanings. He then argued that, even within a particular natural language, there is no fact of the matter as to what the singular terms of one's sentences refer to. One can permute all the references of singular terms and the sentences of the language will remain true. When one says that a frog is in the pond, is one referring to ponds and frogs, or to Cheerios and cereal boxes? This is Quine's doctrine of *ontological relativity*. Putnam does not follow Quine in thinking that there are no meanings, though he does think there is no principled semantical analytic-synthetic distinction.

Putnam also thinks that human minds can sidestep Quinean indeterminacy and ontological relativity. How do human minds do this? The answer, quickly put, is that we reason our way around them. To make successful judgments of synonymy or successful coreferentiality decisions, we use general intelligence, rational interpretation, and reasonable reasoning. These forms of human reasoning sidestep Quinean indeterminacy and ontological relativity. We are able to judge that two uses of the word 'cat' are synonymous, or that two different words refer to the same thing, or that the same word in two different scientific theories refers to the same thing, or that one translation is better than another. In Putnam's view, we do this without having a principled distinction between meaning-constituting and auxiliary beliefs. We do it, in his view, without employing a definition of synonymy or a definition of coreferentiality (and without definitions of general intelligence, rational interpretation, and reasonable reasoning).

What, then is general intelligence? Putnam argues that "describing the nature of general intelligence is a hopeless problem."[28] A scientist who decides to accept a scientific theory may think about the theory in terms of simplicity, how successful it is in its predictions, and how well it conserves past scientific doctrine. Weighing these factors is a task of general intelligence, and for Putnam it cannot be given any finite computational description. This brings us to the second question EQUIVALENCE raises. We can now see, in the preceding brief sketch, how human minds can make synonymy determinations. But why can't there be a finitary algorithm for doing it?

Those who have read *R&R* can reasonably protest that EQUIVALENCE shows there is no finitistic algorithm for synonymy determination. Why raise a question about why there can't be such a finitary algorithm? I argue that Putnam makes an equivocation in his use of the phrase "synonymy determination."[29] If that is so, it raises a question about why an algorithm for synonymy determination must be subject to constraints to which human minds engaging in synonymy determination are not subject (under the assumption they have no computational description). What is the constraint imposed on algorithms for synonymy determination? It is that any algorithm for it must be based on a theory of synonymy. If that is so, on what does a theory of synonymy depend? It depends on a survey of all possible theories of the world, all possible environments, and all possible forms of human rationality. EQUIVALENCE argues that all this information is required for the algorithm. If it is required, the algorithm will be infinitistic and will require foretelling the future.[30] Any being who designs it must have infinitary mental capacities and must be omniscient with respect to the future. No human mind is infinitary and can foretell the future. No human mind can design or use such an infinitary algorithm.

We do not use a theory of synonymy in making synonymy judgments. If we did, we would require infinitistic cognitive capacities and the ability to foretell the future. I will now make a distinction: "Synonymy determination$_1$" does not depend on a theory of synonymy. "Synonymy determination$_2$" depends on a theory of synonymy. EQUIVALENCE shows that any algorithm for synonymy determination$_2$ must be infinitistic and be able to foretell the future. It does not show that any algorithm for synonymy determination$_1$ must be infinitary and be able to foretell the future.

But elsewhere in *R&R*, and in many other of his publications, Putnam argues that human minds successfully engage in synonymy determination$_1$. How do we do it without depending on a theory of synonymy that would require of us abilities we do not have? There is no answer to this question in any of those writings. But Putnam argues that there is no computational description of synonymy determination$_1$, *however* it is done by human minds. Putnam argues this in several ways, all of which I will examine. My view is that some of the arguments can be refuted and that none of them provide convincing reasons for thinking that synonymy determination$_1$ has no computational description. If synonymy determination$_1$ has a computational description that is finitary and does not require foretelling the future, that provides a finitary algorithm for synonymy determination$_1$ that does not require foretelling the future.

Given this finitary algorithm (and algorithms for rational interpretation$_1$, general intelligence$_1$, reasonable reasoning$_1$, and coreferentiality decisions$_1$), there is a computable partitioning of the infinitely many computational states that realize the intentional state of believing that there is a cat nearby. Rational interpretation$_1$ is used, for instance, to distinguish meaning-constituting beliefs from auxiliary beliefs. If it works, there is only one computational state, consisting of the equivalence class into which all the meaning-constituting beliefs determined by rational interpretation are assigned. The auxiliary beliefs are no longer included in the computational state, since they are not components of the content (or meaning) of the word 'cat'. Thus, there is a local computational reduction of an arbitrary intentional state.

And my general criticism of $R\&R$ can be put more boldly: IF there is an algorithm for synonymy determination$_1$, it is possible that it is finitistic and doesn't require foretelling the future. EQUIVALENCE argues that all algorithms for synonymy determination$_2$ are infinitistic and require foretelling the future. Even if sound, EQUIVALENCE does not make any claims about algorithms for synonymy determination$_1$. Putnam uses other arguments to show that there are no finitary algorithms for synonymy determination$_1$, but I conclude that either they are refutable or they fail to provide convincing reasons against the possibility of finitistic algorithms. Thus, I don't provide a description of a finitary algorithm for synonymy determination$_1$ (or for rational interpretation$_1$, coreferentiality decisions$_1$, general intelligence$_1$, or reasonable reasoning$_1$). I don't have to do this, having taken down a positive argument for the claim that there is no finitary algorithm for it.

Putnam claims that rational interpretation[31] depends on inductive reasoning. He argues that inductive reasoning can't be formalized, because prior probability metrics (in Bayesian reasoning) can't be formalized, or because projective predicates can't be formalized, or because the choice of a best hypothesis for inference to the best explanation can't be formalized or the choice of a reference class (for inductive reasoning using the frequency interpretation of probabilities) can't be formalized. The latter procedures can't be formalized because they depend on rational interpretation. But rational interpretation is unformalizable only if inductive reasoning can't be formalized. How can Putnam break out of the circle? I argue that he doesn't provide any arguments that show how such a breakout could happen.

Although Putnam does not show exactly how rational interpretation (and the host of other notions) can be used to sidestep Quinean indeterminacy, ontological relativity, and Quinean meaning holism, he does think that these Quinean doctrines depend on a commitment to metaphysical realism. This is the view that there is ONE ULTIMATE REALITY. In particular, they depend on the claim that there is a correspondence between the terms in a natural language and a noumenal reality.[32] Putnam also claims that computationalism is a scientistic doctrine and that all scientific doctrines are committed to metaphysical realism.[33] If that is so, it is subject to all the Quinean nightmares. But if it is subject to them, algorithms can't sidestep them. But if algorithms can't sidestep them and rational interpretation (and the rest) can be used to sidestep them, then there are no algorithms for rational interpretation (and the rest).

Putnam does not use the preceding argument that rational interpretation can't be formalized. What if it is used? It has a false premise. Computationalism is not committed to metaphysical realism. I will employ a relative consistency proof: if rational interpretation (and the rest) can be used to sidestep the Quinean nightmares, so too for computationalism. I will show that computationalism is not committed to any of the four defining properties of metaphysical realism: correspondence, independence, bivalence, and uniqueness.

Why Gödel's Theorems and Triviality Theories Are Needed to Rule Out Local Computational Reductions

EQUIVALENCE is the argument that there is no computable partitioning of the infinitely many computational realizations of an arbitrary intentional state into a single equivalence class or a small set of equivalence classes. The argument shows that finitary human minds could not discover this computable partitioning, since it requires both an infinitary mind and an ability to foretell the future. Putnam considers a computationalist's response that, even if the equivalence relation could not be discovered by human beings, it exists (as an abstract entity). He says that taking this possibility seriously is "exactly analogous to saying that the true nature of *rationality*—or at least of human rationality—is given by some 'functional organization' or computational description."[34]. Given that it is exactly analogous, Putnam proceeds by making points about the "functional organization of rationality" side of the analogy.[35] Gödel's theorems show that, if there is a computational description of human rationality, it cannot be justified by human minds. To justify it is to show that the logical system in which the computational description appears is consistent. The Second Incompleteness Theorem rules out proving that it is consistent.

Suppose the computationalist persists and claims that there is a computational description of rationality, even though we can't justify it and so can't convince ourselves it is the correct description of rationality. At this point in the dialectic, Putnam brings in his triviality theorem. Since every physical object has every computational description, human minds have every computational description. If that is so, we cannot say that we are not correctly described by any particular computational description. Every one of them describes us correctly. But there is at least one such computational description for which we cannot (by Gödel's theorems) justify to ourselves that it is correct.

If human minds have every conceivable computational description, it makes no sense to take the realist line that human beings have a computational description, even though we can't discover it. A claim that a human mind has a particular computational description has no explanatory power if it has every computational description. Almost every prediction it makes can be verified, except the prediction that it has the computational description that correctly describes us. Thus, cognitive science is a pseudo-science. The philosophical program of computational functionalism is bankrupt.

Putnam thinks the computational picture of the human mind reveals nothing about its nature. It introduces "metaphysical obscurities"[36] that block the way to understanding intentional states. We can't understand intentional states in terms of their computational reductions, because we first need intentional states to understand their computational reductions. Wittgenstein argued against logicism on the grounds that one had first to understand the natural numbers in order to understand their logicist versions in the system of Russell and Whitehead's *Principia Mathematica*.

Recall the above analogy between computable partitionings and computational descriptions of rationality. By the triviality theorem, there are infinitely many computable partitionings. Each one is a computational description of an arbitrary intentional state (the same intentional state). It makes no sense to take the realist line that there is a single computable partitioning, even though we will never discover it. Thus there are no local computational reductions that could save computational functionalism from philosophical bankruptcy and cognitive science from descent into a pseudo-science.

But the argument using the Gödel theorems fails, the triviality theorem fails, and EQUIVALENCE fails. At least that is my claim in this book. Although *R&R* is a powerful, ingenious, and ingeniously sustained attack on computational functionalism, I don't think it provides a good reason to give it up or to eschew cognitive science. Whether or not my arguments are valid, my hope is that this book will prompt the reader to take a new look at *R&R*. There are many rich and important ideas in it that should be examined and perhaps mined. One project that comes out of my critique of Putnam's use of the Gödel theorems concerns the epistemology of mathematical proofs and of computer programs. We should look at the epistemic adequacy of mathematical proofs with less than mathematical certainty. We should look at the epistemic adequacy of probabilistic proofs of computer program correctness. Another project is examining work in cognitive science and related areas (such as computational learning theory and artificial intelligence) for methods and ideas on formalizing inductive reasoning. It is not enough to dismiss this work by citing the failure of the positivists' program of formalizing induction. It is not enough because proof of failure was never conclusive.

1 Putnam's Use of Gödel's Incompleteness Theorems to Refute Computational Functionalism

Although Gödel had the idea in 1951,[1] J. R. Lucas published a paper in 1969[2] in which he proposed a magic bullet to destroy computational functionalism. Lucas proposed a way to mathematically distinguish human beings from computing machines. The idea is simple. A computing machine capable of activities of a certain complexity—in this case, being able to add, multiply, and divide—is subject to the Gödel incompleteness theorems. Human beings, if they are not machines, are not subject to them. Gödel's theorems provide a precise way of expressing the difference between human beings and computing machines. Machines cannot prove that all that they can prove in elementary arithmetic is true, nor can they prove some conjectures in arithmetic, even though they can express them.

If human beings are not subject to the Gödel theorems, they can prove that all they prove in elementary arithmetic is true, and they can prove the conjectures in arithmetic that the machine cannot prove. Given a machine of type M subject to Gödel's theorems, it is easy to formulate the conjectures it cannot prove. Lucas formulated a clever strategy to show that human beings are not computing machines. Hypothesize that human beings are machines of type M. Construct M's Gödel sentence. Human beings will be able to prove that it is true, contradicting the hypothesis that they are machines of type M. This strategy holds for arbitrary M. Thus, for any M, there are no machines of type M that capture our mentality. Computational functionalism—the philosophical view that human mentality is captured in a computational description—is refuted.

Gödel's theorems have unduly fascinated anti-functionalist philosophers. Their hope is that the theorems will provide a mathematical proof that mechanism is false. Unfortunately, there is an obstacle in the way of realizing that hope. Putnam has shown that anti-functionalist arguments employing the incompleteness theorems commit a simple logical error.[3] They assume that human beings—whose mental life they take not to be computationally reducible, and thus not susceptible to the Gödel theorems—can see that a computer program describing their mental life is consistent. However, if the computer program is infeasibly long (perhaps it is the size of all the books in the Library of Congress), human beings will not be able to see that it is consistent, because they can't survey all of it. Thus, human beings will not be epistemically distinguishable from machines that cannot, in principle, mathematically prove that their program is consistent. Even though the mental life of a machine is metaphysically different from that of a human being, human beings could not detect the difference. Though the anti-functionalist believes that human beings are not and machines are susceptible to the Gödel incompleteness theorems, human beings might be epistemically closed off from establishing that difference.

In 1984, Putnam proposed an ingenious argument he claimed avoided the error. His argument is the backbone of his assault on computationalism. But it is much more than that. Rational interpretation (and several family-related notions, such as reasonable reasoning and general intelligence) is the means by which human beings can make synonymy judgments and coreferentiality decisions. Rational interpretation sidesteps ontological relativity and Quinean indeterminacy. It figures centrally in epistemic semantics and is thus necessary for the viability of internal realism. Rational interpretation employs not only demonstrative reasoning, to which the Gödel theorems apply. It also employs non-demonstrative reasoning. Putnam found a way to apply Gödel's theorems to it and to avoid the error. As it is presented in *R&R*, it purports to show that all epistemic methods employed in human inquiry are, formalized, susceptible to Gödel's theorems. Weak formalizable methods of showing the computer program for human mentality is consistent (with less than mathematical certainty) can be employed by human beings who are not Gödel susceptible,[4] but can't be employed by agents who are Gödel susceptible. So human beings are epistemically distinguishable from computing machines. We are also metaphysically different from computing machines.

I argue that Putnam's ingenious argument fails. What both philosophers and mathematicians have failed to appreciate is that the Gödel theorems show that no one—whether Gödel susceptible or not—can prove the consistency of Peano arithmetic with mathematical certainty without constructing an infinite proof tree. On the assumption that human beings (whether or not we are Gödel susceptible) cannot construct infinite proof trees, we cannot prove the consistency of Peano arithmetic with mathematical certainty. In general, where the Gödel theorems apply, they show that finitary beings cannot prove a mathematical proposition in the epistemic modality of the reasoning provided in the Gödel-susceptible formal system. In Peano arithmetic, the associated first-order formal system gives us a method of finitary reasoning whose epistemic modality is mathematical certainty.

Any being whatsoever, whether Gödel susceptible or not, cannot produce, with mathematical certainty, a finitary proof of the consistency of Peano arithmetic. This is the real reason why anti-functionalists who wish to employ the Gödel theorems to refute mechanism are doomed to failure. Unless human beings can construct infinite proof trees, we are limited by the Gödel theorems, even if we are not computing machines to which they directly apply. This simple point has resisted appreciation by the anti-functionalists. That it is possible to commit Penrose's logical error— but only if the computer program for human mentality is infeasibly long— is a red herring.

Putnam's new argument avoids the red herring, but it does not acknowledge the point about the epistemic modality in which the truth of Gödel sentences can be known. Putnam claims in his new argument that all methods of inquiry into the world employed by a computing machine are Gödel susceptible. From this it easily follows that the machine cannot know the truth of any of its Gödel sentences in any of the epistemic modalities under which it conducts inquiry into the world. But this limitative result also applies to human beings, even if we are not Gödel susceptible. If a finitary computing machine running a program is unable to determine its correctness in some epistemic modality because it is Gödel susceptible, then no finitary human being can determine its correctness in that epistemic modality either, even if humans are not Gödel susceptible.

Unless we can construct infinite proof trees, none of our finitary methods of inquiry into the world can show, in their characteristic epistemic modality, the truth of the Gödel sentences arising in the formalizations of those methods of inquiry.[5] If we do not employ a formalizable method of inquiry, no non-formalizable method of inquiry we use can prove the truth of a Gödel sentence of a formalizable method of inquiry in the epistemic modality of that formalization. Failing to appreciate this point, Putnam succumbs to a paradox. If all machine methods of inquiry into the world are Gödel susceptible, the consistency of those methods cannot be demonstrated in any of the epistemic modalities that are characteristic of those methods. This applies to human beings as well, whether we are or are not mechanizable. Thus, Putnam (nor any other human being) can't establish the method of reasoning used to prove his theorems is correct. In that case, we should not accept his proof that all methods of machine inquiry are Gödel susceptible. However, we are then free to use at least one of those machine methods of inquiry into the world to show that Putnam's proof is correct. But if that machine method of inquiry does show his proof is correct, then it is subject to the proof and so cannot be used to show that it is correct. The problem is that Putnam is making a totalizing assumption: that all methods of inquiry into the world are Gödel susceptible. Totalizing assumptions generally lead to paradox, and there is no reason to think that Putnam's new argument—which makes a totalizing assumption about machine methods of inquiry into the world—is paradox resistant.

Gödel's Incompleteness Theorems and Functionalism

The use of the Gödel incompleteness theorems to refute the philosophical doctrine of functionalism begins with Gödel himself. In an important talk he gave in 1951 to the American Mathematical Society—his Josiah Willard Gibbs lecture—he made the following disjunctive claim: "Either mathematics is incompletable in this sense, that its evident axioms can never be comprised in a finite rule, that is to say, the human mind (even within the realm of pure mathematics) infinitely surpasses the powers of any finite machine, or else there exist absolutely unsolvable diophantine problems of the type specified (where the case that both terms of the disjunction are true is not excluded, so that there are, strictly speaking, three alternatives)."[6]

Many years after Gödel formulated his disjunction thesis, Lucas fashioned a cruder version of Gödel's argument to show there are cognitive tasks which the human mind can perform that any finitary computing machine, hypothesized to capture all the cognitive capacities of the human mind, cannot perform. It follows, then, that the human mind is not fully captured by such a finitary computing machine. There are problems with Lucas's argument that were first pointed out by David Lewis.[7] Many years after Lucas, Roger Penrose weighed in on the side of the anti-mechanists, substantially and creatively emending Lucas's argument in two books that use the Gödel theorems to refute mechanism.[8] Putnam criticized this enormous project in a review of *Shadows of the Mind*.[9]

The error that Putnam finds in Penrose and Lucas is simple: the human mind outstrips the finite machine only if the human mind can mathematically prove the consistency of the Gödel-susceptible computer program for the finite machine. By the second Gödel incompleteness theorem, a system that is Gödel susceptible cannot prove that it is consistent—that it proves only truths. If a human mind is not Gödel susceptible, then it is not limited by the second incompleteness theorem. It is, in principle, possible for it to prove that any Gödel-susceptible system is consistent.[10] But if the computer program is infeasibly long, a human being may not have the resources to construct such a proof, even if she is not susceptible to the Gödel theorems. Suppose that the computer program consists of 2^{50} lines of code. No human being could survey that program.

If that is so, we can't distinguish between the failure of a finite Gödel-susceptible machine to determine the correctness of the computer program it runs and the failure of a finitary human being—whom we hypothesize is not Gödel susceptible—to determine the correctness of that same computer program.[11] It follows that we can't epistemically distinguish the finitary human mind (hypothesized not to be Gödel susceptible) from a finite Gödel-susceptible computing machine (hypothesized to be a computational narrative of the human mind). Not taking into account the possibility of the epistemic indistinguishability of finitary human minds (hypothesized not to be Gödel susceptible) and Gödel-susceptible finitary computing machines is a fatal error in arguments against mechanism that employ the Gödel theorems. This error torpedoed Penrose. Remarkably, Putnam has himself used the Gödel theorems to refute mechanism, and his use of them plays a central role in *R&R*. This raises the question I address in this chapter and the next: Does Putnam succeed where Penrose failed? If so, how? If not, why does he fail—surely he would not commit the same error he uncovered in their arguments?

Correct and Incorrect Readings of the Gödel Theorems

In both Gödelian-based refutations of mechanism and critical discussions of them, an obvious point has been overlooked. What the Gödel incompleteness theorems show is that there is no epistemically certain finitistic mathematical proof of the Gödel sentence and the consistency sentence of any formal system susceptible to the Gödel theorems. We cannot finitistically prove, *with mathematical certainty*, the Gödel sentence and the consistency sentence of Gödelizable formal systems. What is overlooked is the epistemic modality of mathematical certainty that qualifies the proof relation. Perhaps the reason it is overlooked is that the method of proof within a system of logic is what delivers mathematical (or logical) certainty.[12]

The standard view is that we cannot prove CON(PA), period.[13] In the absence of any qualification of 'prove', it appears the claim is that there is no proof of any kind of CON(PA). However, all that follows from the Gödel theorems is that we cannot prove CON(PA) with mathematical certainty. It does not follow, however, that we cannot prove CON(PA) with less than mathematical certainty or prove it in some other epistemic modality than mathematical certainty. The same remarks hold if we transpose the discussion of the Gödel theorems to the context of what we know about CON(PA). If we substitute 'know the truth of' for 'prove', the same point applies. We cannot know the truth of CON(PA) with mathematical certainty. It is left open by the Gödel theorems that we can know the truth of CON(PA) with less than mathematical certainty and that we can know the truth of CON(PA) in some epistemic modality other than mathematical certainty. I will argue that this point has far-reaching consequences for using the Gödel theorems to refute mechanism.

Perhaps this simple point is overlooked because a presupposition is made about the epistemology of mathematical knowledge: Only mathematical knowledge that has the pedigree of mathematical certainty is acceptable. A mathematical belief that is true but is not mathematically certain is not justified and so not an instance of mathematical knowledge. On this picture of mathematical knowledge, there is no need for the epistemic qualifier 'with mathematical certainty'. To paraphrase Wittgenstein, if mathematical truths can't be justified with mathematical certainty, then they can't be known by singing them or anything else. But this follows only if the presupposition is true. The mechanism debate fueled by the Gödel incompleteness theorems has failed to focus on the issue of what is an adequate epistemology for mathematical knowledge.[14]

If we accept a mathematical epistemology in which we can know mathematical propositions with less than mathematical certainty, new possibilities become available for the mechanism debate. For instance, if there are Gödelizable formal systems in which CON(PA) is proved with less than mathematical certainty *and* the epistemic modality in which it is proved satisfies a reasonable notion of justification, then the limitations of the Gödel theorems have been dramatically circumvented. Substitute 'the correctness of its own computer program' for 'CON(PA)' in the preceding sentence. If an anti-mechanist enlists the Gödel theorems to refute mechanism, she must show that the notion of justification under which a finite machine can prove the correctness of its own computer program with less than mathematical certainty is normatively bankrupt. Suppose that human beings are finite machines. Define the goal of cognitive science to be discovery of the master computer program for the human mind. Assume the cognitive activities cognitive scientists engage in when they attempt to discover the master computer program are themselves described in that program. Suppose that in the future a cognitive scientist claims to have found the master computer program. Do we require that her belief that this is the correct master computer program must be mathematically certain in order to count as being epistemically justified? Whether that requirement does or does not appear to be too strong, clearly it is a question that must be addressed wherever the Gödel theorems are enlisted in the mechanism debate.

Even within mathematics there is evidence that this demand is negotiable. Mathematical proofs not formalized within a system of logic do not satisfy the stringent demands of mathematical certainty. Only proofs that are formalized in a formal system whose axioms, rules of inference, and application of rules of inference are recursively specified can satisfy those stringent demands. Proofs in, for instance, algebraic topology do not meet them, though mathematicians do not feel that they need to translate those proofs into a formal system before they can be said to know the truths of algebraic topology.

I will discuss the full range of possibilities later in this chapter. I will also discuss an important consequence of the epistemic qualification on the notion of proof in stating the Gödel theorems. The consequence is that no finitary being, even one that is not Gödel susceptible, can prove CON(PA) with mathematical certainty. Why this is so is obvious. If mathematical certainty is secured only in virtue of a proof within a system of logic, no finite being can know CON(PA) with mathematical certainty unless it constructs a proof of it within a system of logic. But the Gödel theorems forbid this.

A being with infinitary powers can construct a proof of CON(PA) with mathematical certainty, but the construction requires infinitary powers human beings do not possess.[15] When anti-functionalists, such as Penrose, claim that human beings can know CON(PA), they must qualify their claim. We cannot know it with mathematical certainty. But if we can know it with less than mathematical certainty, or in some epistemic modality other than mathematical certainty, it is possible that a finitary machine can also acquire that knowledge. If that is the case, the Gödel theorems cannot drive a wedge between what a human being can know and what a finitary machine can know.

Metaphysical Uses of the Gödel Incompleteness Theorems in Refuting Functionalism

There is a distinction between the main kinds of uses of Gödelian arguments in anti-functionalist arguments.[16] Perhaps the reader is puzzled: "Isn't there but one use of the Gödel theorems in refuting mechanism?"

There are two different ways in which mechanism can be Gödel refuted,[17] and the conclusions about mechanism differ. Because each method of refutation opens up different possibilities in the mechanism debate, it is important to distinguish them.

One kind of Gödel refutation of mechanism concludes that the human mind is not a finitary machine, in which case mechanism is false. However, the other kind of Gödel refutation concludes that, even if the mind is a finitary machine, we can never justify the computational theory that describes it. In that case, mechanism, though true, can never be justified and thus both functionalism (as a philosophical doctrine) and cognitive science are intrinsically unjustifiable.

Either kind of Gödel refutation is equally devastating for the field of cognitive science. Both Lucas and Penrose engage in Gödel refutations of the first kind. Putnam appears to engage in both, though he is not explicit in making the distinction between them.[18] Each kind of argument has its benefits and costs, and we need to look at both in evaluating their application in *R&R*.

The most obvious use of the Gödel theorems in refuting mechanism is found in Gödel, Lucas, and Penrose: If it can be shown there is a mathematical truth that can be proved by a human mind, but that cannot be proved within a computational system that, by hypothesis, computationally models that human mind, then the human mind is not computationally modeled by that computational system. Whatever is the nature of the human mind, it does not have the nature of a finitary machine, since the human mind is different from the finitary machine in virtue of its causal powers, expressed in cognitive capabilities. The point can also be put differently: The human mind can prove that the program of the computational device which purports to model it is correct, while the program cannot prove of itself that it is correct. Assuming that there is no additional program embodied in the computational device, it follows that the computational device cannot prove its program is correct. If so, there is a power that the human mind possesses that is not possessed by the finitary machine. A human mind could justify the truth of the claim that the program that purports to describe it is correct, while the program itself cannot do that. But if the program, by hypothesis, describes all the cognitive powers of the human mind, then it cannot be a complete description of the human mind, since it lacks at least one power that a human mind possesses.

This application of the Gödel theorems shows mechanism false by showing that human minds do not have mechanical natures. This is a metaphysical claim about the nature of the human mind. We can construe 'mechanical' as 'finitary computing machine'. The metaphysical claim is then that human minds do not have the nature of finitary computing machines. The Gödel theorems provide a mathematical proof that the human mind is not identical to a finite computing machine and thus does not have the nature of a finite computing machine. This claim can be generalized. The Gödel theorems provide a mathematical proof the human mind is not identical to any kind of finite computing machine and thus does not have the nature of any kind of finite computing machine. It can be generalized because the Gödel sentence unprovable in finitary computing machine$_1$ can be proved in a stronger finitary computing machine$_2$. However, a new Gödel sentence can be expressed in finitary computing machine$_2$ that cannot be proved in it. This is true for all finitary computing machines. So we have a mathematical proof of a negative metaphysical claim about the human mind: it is not any kind of finitary computing machine. To distinguish this use of the Gödel theorems from another use we will shortly describe, we adopt the acronym MGM for metaphysical claims that are consequences of Gödel refutations of mechanism.

It is a mistake to read too much into the metaphysical claim that the cognitive powers of a human mind differ from that of any finitary computing machine. The first reason is that the proof assumes that human minds are able to prove the correctness of the finitary computing machine's master program. We shall soon see how strong that assumption is and whether it can be reasonably sustained.

Another instance of such a mistake is the claim that the Gödel theorems specify an exact bound on the extent of the difference between human minds and a given finitary computing machine. For instance, given a finitary computing machine that cannot prove its program is correct, the extent to which the human mind differs from it is that the human mind can prove the program is correct. This is not informative, since it says nothing positive about the mechanism necessary for human minds to prove that the program is correct. It does say something negative, though. It says that no human mind can prove the program is correct by simulating the finitary computing machine.[19] It is this point that puts considerable pressure on the assumption that a human mind can prove the correctness of the machine's program. It is clear that it cannot do that by simulating the machine, since it would, in that event, be the machine and thus be Gödel susceptible.

However, there is more to be said. What is not usually addressed in Gödel refutations of mechanism is the epistemic modality of the provability relation in Gödel-susceptible formal systems. A proof in a formal system (whether or not it is Gödel susceptible) proves a theorem with mathematical certainty. Our justification for believing the theorem is true is that it has been proved with mathematical certainty. So the Gödel theorems need to be qualified: The second incompleteness theorem says that no Gödel-susceptible formal system can prove its own consistency with mathematical certainty. It is left open by the Gödel theorems that the formal system can prove its consistency with less than mathematical certainty or in some other epistemic modality.

If the only means of achieving mathematical certainty that p is true is to prove p in a formal system, then if p is either a Gödel sentence or a consistency claim about a Gödel-susceptible system in which the proof is carried out, it follows that no human being can prove p is true with mathematical certainty, since the only way to achieve mathematical certainty is to simulate the Gödel-susceptible formal system and carry out the proof. So no human mind can prove the master program for a finitary computing machine is correct with mathematical certainty. If that is so, we are indistinguishable from the finitary computing machine. On the other hand, there is no prohibition on the human mind proving the correctness of the master program with either less than mathematical certainty or in some other epistemic modality. But neither is the finitary computing machine prohibited form this, either. (This is so unless proof with less than mathematical certainty or in another epistemic modality is Gödel susceptible. In that case, it is ruled out for the finitary computing machine to do that. But then it is also ruled out for finitary human beings to do so.)

These qualifications force us to qualify the metaphysical claim expressed above: "The Gödel theorems provide a mathematical proof, with mathematical certainty, that the human mind is not identical to any kind of finite computing machine and thus does not have the nature of any kind of finite computing machine." If the MGM argument is sound, we know, with mathematical certainty, that we are not finitary computing machines. What is the provenance of the qualifier 'mathematical certainty'? We already know the Gödel theorems show that any Gödel-susceptible formal system cannot prove its Gödel sentence with mathematical certainty. If the Gödel theorems are themselves formalized in a formal system, they show that, with mathematical certainty, any Gödel-susceptible formal system cannot prove its Gödel sentence with mathematical certainty.

Thus, we know with mathematical certainty that human minds are not identical with any kind of finitary computing machine. This is an extraordinarily strong claim. Compare it with the following claim: We know, with mathematical certainty, that $2 + 2 = 4$. On the other hand, one does not know, with mathematical certainty, that one is looking at a tree. The strength of the claim should make us suspicious of it. The assumption that underlies the metaphysical claim is that human minds can prove the correctness of the finitary computing machine's master program. But we have seen that it needs to be qualified: human minds can prove, with mathematical certainty, the correctness of the computing machine's master program. This, though, is unlikely to be true. If a human mind has infinitary cognitive capacities, it might do so (for instance, by employing Turing's infinitary procedure). But it is highly unlikely we have infinitary cognitive capacities.[20]

If the assumption is changed by changing the qualification to 'with less than mathematical certainty or in some other epistemic modality', then it is highly likely to be false, since it is available for a finitary computing machine to prove the correctness of its own master program with less than mathematical certainty or in some other epistemic modality. Thus, the metaphysical claim is bankrupt and the Gödel refutation of mechanism is drained of its force.

This is a significant philosophical result overlooked in the mechanism debate. If it is true that we are not computable agents and are able to ascertain the consistency of Peano arithmetic, i.e., CON(PA), how do we do it? We *cannot* employ a recursively axiomatized finite proof system to do it, since for any such proof system (strong enough to capture arithmetic), the Gödel incompleteness theorems apply. On the other hand, if we use a recursively axiomatized finite proof system which is too weak to be susceptible to the Gödel theorems, then this will not distinguish us from finite machines, since finite machines are also capable of proving theorems in such proof systems.

In such a finitary proof system, there is nothing we can prove which a finite machine (of the appropriate kind) cannot prove. How, then, do we differ from the finite machine? We know from Gentzen's proof of CON(PA) by transfinite induction, that infinitely long derivations can secure CON(PA). We also know that within formalized systems of Peano arithmetic, proofs of transfinite induction for any ordinal up to, but not including the infinite ordinal ε_0, are available. However, we need transfinite induction along a well-ordered path of length ε_0 to prove CON(PA). The issue, then, is this: If human minds know the truth of CON(PA) with mathematical certainty, is the only mathematical method by which we do it the use of infinitely long derivations? If it is, then it is unlikely we do it this way, since we do not have infinitary cognitive capacities.[21]

Where does the claim that proofs in a formal system of logic carry mathematical certainty come from? If this can be disputed, then there is a way to revive MGM. Alonzo Church told us the only way to achieve mathematical certainty is a proof system where the axioms are effectively specified and in where, for any line in the proof, there is an effective procedure by which one can tell that it is an authentic line in the proof. Church writes in his classic *Introduction to Mathematical Logic, Volume 1* that an auditor of a proof "may fairly demand a proof, in any given case, that the sequence of formulas put forward is a proof; and until this supplementary proof is provided, he may refuse to be convinced that the alleged theorem is a proved. This supplementary proof ought to be regarded ... as part of the whole proof of the theorem, and the primitive basis of the logistic system ought to be so modified as to provide this, or its equivalent."[22]

The only logistic systems for which Church's requirement is satisfied are those in which the axioms and the rules of inference are effectively specified—these are finitary proof systems in which there are only finitely many lines in a proof and the pedigree of each line in the proof can be effectively ascertained. Infinitary logistic systems are different, for rules of inference are not effectively specified. A mind that has infinitary capacities can effectively specify them, but the notion of 'effectiveness' then belongs to α-recursion theory, a theory of effectivity for infinite minds. Church obviously assumed human minds are finitary in his discussion.

It is still open to the anti-mechanist to revive MGM by showing that there are no finitary computing machines that are *not* Gödel susceptible that can prove the correctness of their master programs with either less than mathematical certainty or in some other epistemic modality. We will later examine the price the mechanist must pay if she is to avail herself of this option. Now we will consider whether the mechanist can avoid the Gödel theorems by showing finitary computing machines that are not Gödel susceptible to be capable of proving, with mathematical certainty, the correctness of their master programs. For such computing machines to carry any weight for the mechanist, they must be able to prove almost as much as a Gödel-susceptible finitary computing machine can prove. Unfortunately, the phrase 'almost as much' is vague. We will not have to worry about making it precise, since the results do not help the mechanist. They are discussed here because such possibilities are envisaged in the literature on Gödel refutations.

Recent Work in Mathematical Logic That Is Relevant to Gödel Refutations

Let us examine three results in mathematical logic. The progenitors of this work did not explicitly write about its connections to mechanism, so it will be necessary to make them explicit. The point of examining this work is to articulate the conditions under which they provide a way of defusing Gödel refutations. Given that Putnam enlists the Gödel theorems in his refutation of computational functionalism, what I do here moves the burden of proof onto his shoulders: he must show that this work does not defuse his use of the Gödel theorems.

Parikh on Feasible Arithmetic

I begin with Rohit Parikh's 1960s work in feasible arithmetic. In his seminal paper[23] "Existence and Feasibility in Arithmetic," Parikh worries that fast-growing functions involving exponentiation will generate numbers so large they are epistemically infeasible or non-constructible. Does the finite number $10^{1,000,000,000,000,000,000,000,000,000,000,000,000,000,000,000,000,000}$ have a concrete existence? Is it a number to which we have epistemic access? Parikh takes no philosophical position on these questions, but he does offer, for those offended by them, *feasible arithmetic*, a formal system for Peano arithmetic without exponentiation.

Feasible arithmetic is Gödel susceptible because within it one can prove the existence of an initial segment of the integers that is sufficient to carry out the arithmetization of metamathematics necessary for the Gödel theorems. Parikh shows how it can be extended to an "almost inconsistent theory" in which a proof of a contradiction would be infeasibly long, and thus could never be proved within the system.[24] Suppose that the shortest proof of a contradiction in feasible arithmetic is $10^{1,000,000,000,000,000,000,000,000,000,000,000,000,000,000,000,000,000}$ proof lines in length. This number is so fantastically large that even if one could inscribe a proof line on the head of an elementary particle, there is not enough matter in the known universe to inscribe the proof in some written medium. We might even know that if feasible arithmetic is contradictory, the shortest proof is that long. But we would still not be able to write down the proof. In that sense, in the finite universe we inhabit, we do not have epistemic access to the proof of a contradiction in feasible arithmetic. Suppose that the program for a finitary computing machine that simulates human mentality takes the form of an almost inconsistent theory. If so, we know that we cannot have epistemic access to a contradiction in it, if there is one. Notice that whether we are or are not Gödel susceptible, we do not have epistemic access to the contradiction, if there is one.

Recall that the error Putnam found in the Lucas-Penrose Gödel refutation is that the program for human mentality might be so long that even agents who are not Gödel susceptible would not be able to prove it is correct. In that case, both Gödel-susceptible and Gödel-insusceptible agents are obser-vationally indistinguishable with respect to having the cognitive ability to prove the correctness of the program for human mentality. We find the same phenomenon in almost inconsistent theories. That is, both Gödel-susceptible and Gödel-insusceptible agents are observationally indis-tinguishable with respect to having the cognitive ability to prove a con-tradiction in an almost inconsistent theory. If it is an error in Gödel refutations not to take into account the possibility of a super-long program for human mentality, it is equally an error in Gödel refutations not to take into account the possibility of the program for human mentality being expressed in feasible arithmetic.

If so, the work that has to be done is to determine that the program for human mentality can be expressed in feasible arithmetic extended to an almost inconsistent theory and then to determine numerical bounds on the length of the shortest proof of inconsistency, if there is one. It is not clear how to do either, so this possibility cannot be eliminated from Gödel refutations. Equally, no one knows how to show the program for human mentality is fantastically long, since no one now knows what the final pro-gram for human mentality will look like. Thus, the possibility that the program is fantastically long continues to haunt Lucas-Penrose Gödel refu-tations. In the case of almost inconsistent theories, defeaters lurk just above the threshold of resource ability. But if the proof of a contradiction takes a colossal number of proof lines, that is far above the kinds of resource thresholds to which we can aspire, even given technological enhancements of our cognitive abilities.[25]

Reinhardt and Carlson on Elementary Patterns of Resemblance

The second result is new, though it was conjectured in the early 1980s by the logician William Reinhardt, who had an interest in philosophical aspects of the Gödel incompleteness theorems.[26] Reinhardt was interested in how much a Turing machine could know about itself, in light of a limi-tative result: a Turing machine cannot know which one it is. Otherwise, it could exploit that knowledge to produce a mathematical proof of its Gödel sentence. Reinhardt conjectured that in epistemic arithmetic (Peano arith-metic enriched with a knowledge operator), a Turing machine can prove, with mathematical certainty, the sentence "I know I am a Turing machine." Since knowledge implies truth, a mathematical proof of that sentence is a mathematical proof that the agent proving it is a Turing machine.

If this conjecture can be proved, it would be extraordinary for philoso-phy of mind. Where an agent could prove that it knows that it is a Turing machine, then it *must* be a Turing machine.[27] If the computer program for human mentality can prove that it is a Turing machine, would that show that human beings are Turing machines? If human beings can do what the program does and cannot do what the program cannot do, we then have a mathematical proof that we are Turing machines. Moreover, we also have a mathematical proof that we have epistemic access to this information. Indeed, it is mathematically certain that we have access to it.[28] Although we cannot know which particular Turing machine we are, we can know we are Turing machines. Of course, if a human being can know which particular Turing machine it is, then we are not Turing machines. But in that case, there is something we know that a Turing machine cannot know. Here we are interested in what follows when we can't find a difference between what a machine can prove and what a human being can prove (on the assumption that the machine is Gödel susceptible).

Timothy Carlson gave the first proof of Reinhardt's conjecture in the mid 1990s.[29] His proof employs new results in mathematical logic that concern the way E_1-elementary substructures arise in arbitrary hierarchies of structures. E_1-elementary substructures are structural patterns. Carlson shows the order in which these patterns evolve does not depend on the hierarchy of structures—provided that certain simple conditions are satisfied. Where knowledge operators and Peano arithmetic combine, these structural patterns occur. The moral is that if it is shown that we cannot prove neither more nor less than a machine can prove, then we can prove with mathematical certainty that mechanism is true. This gives us no mileage.

Willard on Truncated Arithmetic

The third result is work of Dan Willard showing how various restrictions on arithmetical operations and the kinds of arithmetical operations which are allowed can circumvent the Gödel incompleteness theorems.[30] He shows that in formal systems in which division and subtraction are primitive and multiplication is not recognized as a total function, it is possible to mathematically verify the correctness of their consistency sentence (where the consistencies are either semantical tableaux, Herbrand, or cut-free). If, as well, addition is not recognized as a total function, the system is able to mathematically verify its Hilbert-style consistency sentence.

Since Robert Solovay showed (though his work was never published) that feasible arithmetic cannot evade Gödel's incompleteness theorems, Willard's results are quite impressive. They show the kinds of truncations that are needed to achieve Gödel insusceptibility in a computational system. If a truncated computational system is not Gödel susceptible, then the Gödel theorems cannot be enlisted to show there is something human beings can prove that a finitary computing machine cannot prove.

The project that Willard's results creates for cognitive science is to see if there is any evidence that division and subtraction are primitive arithmetical operations in human arithmetical abilities. If it is shown that human arithmetical skills are designed in conformance with truncated arithmetic, then we will not expect there to be theorems that we can prove that a finitary computing machine cannot prove. In that case, we will not be able to produce a Gödel refutation.

Epistemic Uses of Gödel's Incompleteness Theorems in Refuting Functionalism

MGM arguments show that the nature of the human mind differs from the nature of physical computing machines. These arguments are philosophically satisfying, since they rule out one metaphysical possibility for the constitution of the human mind. Even though they do not show what the mind is, their importance lies in showing what it is not. But MGM arguments are not the only use of the Gödel theorems in mechanism. If we assume that human minds *are* finitary computing machines, we can still enlist the Gödel theorems to make philosophically important claims about the human mind. We call these uses of the Gödel theorems *EGM*, short for epistemic claims that are consequences of Gödel refutations of mechanism.[31]

Suppose that human cognition is computationally described by computer program C. If we assume human beings can prove truths of Peano arithmetic, C is Gödel susceptible (since it must be equipped with enough syntax to arithmetize metamathematics, which is necessary for the Gödel theorems to take root). CON(C) expresses the consistency, or correctness, of C. Since it is equivalent to C's Gödel sentence, it follows that C can't prove it is correct. Assuming we are C, human beings cannot verify the correctness of C.

If the project of cognitive science is to find C, then that project can never be verified. That is to say, it can never be justified. Any science of the mind that views the mind as a finitary computing machine will not be able to justify its claims, because we cannot verify that the program controlling the finitary computing machine is correct. It does not matter whether human beings are or are not Gödel susceptible. In either case, we will not be able to prove, with mathematical certainty, C is correct. We cannot prove the correctness of C in the epistemic modality of mathematical certainty because to do so, we would have to become a finitary computing machine (or any computational device), to which the notion of 'proof with mathematical certainty' applies. This is a radical form of philosophical skepticism, since we have a mathematical proof, carrying mathematical certainty, that we cannot know, with mathematical certainty, the theory of how our minds work.

EGM arguments do more than provide a new form of philosophical skepticism. They also address the competence/performance distinction essential for the viability of cognitive science. A critical distinction is made in cognitive science between how the mind actually works and how it ought to work—between a performance-level description and a competence-level description of the mind. Without such a distinction, the very idea of a psychological law is jeopardized. EGM arguments show that three basic assumptions essential for cognitive science to be viable cannot consistently obtain: that the human mind can be represented (at a level of computational description) by a computational device, that its cognitive capacities can be viewed as computable mechanisms, and that there is a competence description of the human cognitive mind. The Gödel theorems show the first two assumptions are incompatible with the third. If we take the first two to be part of Marr's implementation level and the third to be Marr's theory of the function (the what which is computed), Gödel's theorems reveal an incompatibility in Marr's foundational program.[32]

I will now present one of Putnam's arguments that we cannot have a computational prescriptive competence description of our ability to prove truths in mathematics.

There Can Be No Computational Description of Our Prescriptive Competence in Mathematical Proof

The following is quoted from Putnam's rendition of a Gödelian argument to show there can be no computational prescriptive competence description of human mathematical proof ability:

... consider the totality of functions which are provably recursive according to M, where M is a recursive description of our prescriptive mathematical competence. Add a subroutine to M which lists separately the "index," or computational description, of each partial recursive function that M ever proves to be total (as M is allowed to run). Let D be the "diagonal function" corresponding to this effective list of total recursive functions (that is, the function whose value at the argument n is one greater than the value of the nth function in the list of provably recursive functions generated by M on the argument n). A mathematician (even a beginner) can prove infinitely many functions to be general recursive (total partial recursive) functions. So if M is a reasonable simulation of prescriptive human mathematical competence, there will be infinitely many functions that M can prove to be general recursive, and hence infinitely many computational indices listed by the subroutine we added to M. In this case, the diagonal function D will itself be total, as is easily seen. So, if we were able to prove by intuitively correct mathematical reasoning that M is a sound proof procedure, we would also be able to prove that D is a total recursive function. But this proof will not itself be one which is captured by any proof in the proof-scheme M, unless M is inconsistent! (If this proof were listed by M, then D would itself be a function listed in the subroutine, say, the kth. Then, from the definition of D, we would have $D(k) = D(k + 1)$! Note that this is a proof of the Gödel Incompleteness Theorem.) Thus no formalization of human mathematical proof ability can both be sound and be such that it is part of human mathematical proof ability to prove that soundness.[33]

We cannot prove mathematically, with mathematical certainty, that M is correct. It follows that we cannot mathematically prove, with mathematical certainty, that the competence theory for human mathematical proof ability is correct. Any attempt to mathematically prove, with mathematical certainty, it is correct leads to contradiction. We need to make a slight (and obviously pedantic) emendation of the last sentence in the quoted text, where the emendation is italicized. It reads: "Thus no formalization of human mathematical proof ability can both be sound and be such that it is part of human mathematical proof ability to prove that soundness, *with mathematical certainty from within M.*"

It is impossible for us—whether we are or are not Gödel susceptible—to prove with mathematical certainty that the competence-level description is true of us. If we were able to prove it is true of us, with mathematical certainty and from within M, we would have proved that the formal theory encapsulated by the competence description is consistent. But this is prohibited by Gödel's second incompleteness theorem. Notice that we would have to ascend to a stronger computational system to prove, with mathematical certainty, the consistency of our competence description. If so, then the competence description that we prove to be correct, with mathematical certainty, in the stronger system is not *our* competence description. Since we ascended to a new computational system, the competence description of the weaker computational system is no longer true of us.

Suppose that human minds are not Gödel susceptible. The Gödel theorems rule out the possibility that a finitary human mind can prove, with mathematical certainty, that a finitary computer program that simulates it is correct. What this means is that whether human minds are or are not Gödel susceptible, the human mind cannot prove with mathematical certainty that a program that simulates it is correct. Thus whether human minds are or are not Gödel susceptible, they cannot justify claims in cognitive science about its computational structure. EGM arguments do not need to show that there is something a human mind can do that a finitary computing machine cannot in order to make philosophically interesting claims about the mind. In this case, the claim concerns the limits of cognitive science in providing a rigorous, scientific study of the human mind.

EGM arguments must make a very strong assumption: that justifications of claims in cognitive science are mathematically certain. This follows from the use of the Gödel theorems. We know, with mathematical certainty, that we cannot, with mathematical certainty, prove the correctness of the program, C, that describes our competence. If C is the master program for human cognition, we can't mathematically prove it is correct with mathematical certainty. Do any other scientific disciplines impose such stringent epistemic requirements upon the claims they make? We do not ask this question in a rhetorical mood. We think it is too high a price to ask of cognitive science, and one that is incompatible with the epistemic demands other scientific disciplines impose on their own deliverances. This is an important issue that deserves further attention.

What distinguishes EGM from MGM arguments is that we do not have to show that human beings can do something that finite machines cannot do. Having to show this proves to be a severe difficulty, since, as we have seen, what the machine cannot prove with mathematical certainty also applies to human minds, even if they are Gödel insusceptible. Many issues that arise in MGM arguments also arise in EGM arguments. In particular, the issue of whether weak methods that are not susceptible to the Gödel theorems are sufficient to epistemically justify the correctness of C.

Notice that weak methods will be included in C. There is no paradox or inconsistency in this, since they do not prove the correctness of C with mathematical certainty. Rather, they prove it with less than mathematical certainty or in some other epistemic modality. The central issue for EGM arguments is what we should take as the standard of epistemic justification of C. If we take the standard of epistemic justification to be mathematical certainty, then they refute computational functionalism. If the standard is less than mathematical certainty or some other epistemic modality, they lose all their potency in refuting mechanism.[34]

A Fundamental Logical Problem for EGM and MGM

We now examine a logical difficulty that arises in MGM and EGM arguments, how anti-functionalists can respond to it, and whether Putnam can satisfactorily respond to it. A difficulty noticed by George Boolos will not be considered here. Boolos argued the Gödel disjunction is not derivable from the Gödel incompleteness theorems without first clarifying what it means for a human mind to be equivalent to a finite computing machine.[35] What does it mean to assert that the human mind is equivalent to a Turing machine?[36] We do not consider it here, because Nathan Salmon, in a brilliant paper, has convincingly argued the Gödel disjunction can be used to make philosophically interesting claims about the limitations of the human mind even if we do not have a precise description of what it is for human minds to be equivalent to Turing machines.[37]

In the early 1970s, Georg Kreisel noted[38] that it does not logically follow from the fact that a formal system subject to the second Gödel theorem cannot mathematically, with mathematical certainty, prove its own consistency, that there are absolutely no means available to prove its consistency. It only follows logically that its consistency cannot be mathematically demonstrated with mathematical certainty in the system. It is left open that consistency is proved by other means, viz., mathematically with less than mathematical certainty (typically by statistical reasoning) and non-mathematically, with less than mathematical certainty, by abstract philosophical reasoning (*a priori* reasoning that is not encodable into a formal system).

In 1972, when Kreisel's paper appeared, the non-Gödel-susceptible methods that were available for demonstrating the consistency of a formal system were virtually unknown. Kreisel mentions statistical methods for mathematically demonstrating consistency of CON(PA) with less than mathematical certainty. He is pessimistic about the prospects of statistical methods being up to this task: "Closer inspection shows that we have in fact very little experience of establishing [CON(PA)—JB] by inductive methods and thus we have little knowledge of the *statistical principles* proper to evaluating the hypothetical inductive evidence. More specifically, there are certainly no statistical studies to make sure that the evidence supports the whole of PM or ZF rather than only subsystems! At present the neoformalist position is a sham."[39]

Kreisel also entertains the possibility of proving CON(PA) by an abstract, but non-mathematical interpretation. That is, there is an interpretation mapping into some non-mathematical system in which all the theorems of PA are true. He gives an example from intuitionism: "An analogue ... is provided by the intuitionistic position which identifies *mathematical* with *intuitionistically acceptable* and regards set-theoretic concepts as *metaphysical*: so it leaves open the possibility of establishing [CON(PA)—JB] by means of metaphysical nonmathematical interpretations."[40] We shall see below that, a decade later, in an ingenious and breathtaking Gödelian argument, Putnam tried to close the door on both statistical methods and abstract philosophical methods for demonstrating CON(PA).

The Logical Complexity of the Problem Confronting EGM and MGM Arguments

The possibilities Kreisel alludes to for proving CON(PA) with less than mathematical certainty or in some other epistemic modality must be taken seriously by anti-functionalists who offer EGM or MGM arguments. Failure to take them into account is an error in EGM or MGM arguments. I will show that anti-functionalists who wish to avoid that error by taking these possibilities into account confront a computationally daunting task. (We shall presently see that it is even more daunting for EGM arguments than for MGM arguments.) Let us call the task 'DISJUNCTION'.

Either the anti-functionalist must show that each method for mathematically or non-mathematically proving, with less than mathematical certainty or in some other epistemic modality, the correctness of C (the ultimate computer program that completely describes the human cognitive mind) is Gödel susceptible or (if that cannot be done, because there are Gödel-insusceptible methods available for proving CON(C)) that the proofs delivered by those methods are not epistemically warranted.[41] Thus, a disturbing dilemma is in store for an anti-functionalist using EGM or MGM arguments. First horn: She must show, for each possible method capable of demonstrating the correctness of C with less than mathematical certainty or in some other epistemic modality, that it is either Gödel susceptible or that, where it is Gödel insusceptible, it is epistemologically inadequate. Second horn: If she does not enumerate all these possibilities, she commits a logical error in her EGM or MGM argument.

I will now argue that DISJUNCTION has logical complexity $\Pi(1, 1)$. A rough classification of mathematical problems is in terms of computability: a problem is either computable or noncomputable. Computable problems can be solved by agents possessing only finitely many computational resources, but noncomputable problems require an infinite supply of computational resources to solve. Among noncomputable problems, some are harder to solve than others. Significant work in recursion theory constructed hierarchies of recursive unsolvability in which a noncomputable problem is assigned a degree of unsolvability.[42]

What does it mean to say that a problem has logical complexity $\Pi(1,1)$? Suppose that an anti-functionalist offers an EGM argument in which it is assumed that human minds can be computationally described. In that case, in order to show we cannot justify CON(C), the anti-functionalist must be able to perform an infinitary computational task. If she has infinitely many resources, she will be able to complete the task. If not, then not. But if she does not complete the task, then she commits a logical error in EGM. Thus the anti-functionalist who uses an EGM argument must either have the capacity to make infinitary computations or else commits a logical error. But human beings do not have infinitary computational capacities.

The matter is equally execrable for an MGM argument. The anti-functionalist who employs an MGM argument wishes to show that human beings can prove CON(C), but the machine for which C is its program cannot prove CON(C). However, neither the human nor the machine can prove CON(C) with mathematical certainty. Thus, the anti-functionalist must find a way of proving CON(C) with less than mathematical certainty or in some other epistemic modality that is not available to the machine. So she must be able to make infinitary computations to canvass all the possibilities or else commit a logical error. (Of course, she will not have to canvass an infinite number of possibilities if she finds the ones which work finitely far along the infinitary path of possibilities.) But human beings do not have infinitary computational capacities.

Proof That DISJUNCTION Has Logical Complexity $\Pi(1,1)$

The First Disjunct in DISJUNCTION
How many methods are there for proving CON(C) with less than mathematical certainty or in some other epistemic modality? Assume we use a statistical method based on a Carnapian measure function to prove CON(C) with less than mathematical certainty. Then there are infinitely many possible methods that can be used, since Carnapian inductive logics employ a caution parameter that has infinitely many values and which differentiates different logics. How many probabilistic logics are there? How many hybrid modal probabilistic logics? Thus far we have the following problem: Look at each method for proving CON(C) with less than mathematical certainty or in some other epistemic modality. Show it is Gödel sus-

ceptible. If there are infinitely many applicable methods, each of them must be enumerated and checked for being Gödel susceptible. But there is an additional wrinkle. Suppose there is a program N that can be used to mathematically prove CON(C) with less than mathematical certainty or in some other epistemic modality, where C is assumed Gödel susceptible. The anti-functionalist needs to verify that N is also Gödel susceptible. If it is, there is a possibility there is a program N^* that can be used to mathematically prove CON(N) with less than mathematical certainty or in some other epistemic modality. Suppose that N^* is shown Gödel susceptible. If so, there is a possibility there is a program N^{**} that can be used to mathematically prove CON(N^*) with less than mathematical certainty or in some other epistemic modality. So we have an infinite regress for each program or method we have shown Gödel susceptible. That is, the problem we now face is the following:

Look at each $method_1$ for proving CON(C) with less than mathematical certainty or in some other epistemic modality. Show it is Gödel susceptible. If it is, look at each $method_2$ for proving CON('$method_1$') with less than mathematical certainty or in some other epistemic modality. Show it is Gödel susceptible. If it is, look at each $method_3$ for proving CON('$method_2$') with less than mathematical certainty or in some other epistemic modality. Show it is Gödel susceptible. Continue in this way until the index i in '$method_i$' is infinite or when $method_i$ is Gödel insusceptible.

Let us consider an objection the anti-functionalist might raise to the specter of the infinite regress. She tells us that there will be no infinite regress, because of her dialectical situation in EGM or MGM arguments. Whenever computational functionalists propose a method N, all she has to do is to show N is Gödel susceptible. She plays a waiting game. She waits for the computational functionalist to propose a method, and only then does she need to show that the proposed method is Gödel susceptible.

This objection fails, because it is dead wrong about the dialectical situation of the anti-functionalist in EGM and MGM arguments. The anti-functionalist does not play a wait-and-see game with the computational functionalist. All MGM and EGM arguments are responsible to certain epistemic standards: if there are any possibilities that undermine the arguments, they must be examined. If it is possible there is a Gödel-insusceptible method or program that proves CON(C) with less than mathematical certainty or in some other epistemic modality, then that undermining possibility must be discharged.

The anti-functionalist makes a negative existence claim in EGM and MGM arguments: there is no Gödel-insusceptible means by which CON(C) can be shown correct with less than mathematical certainty or in some other epistemic modality. Since there are infinitely many possibilities for proving CON(C) with less than mathematical certainty or in some other epistemic modality, each of them must be taken into account. Otherwise the negative existence claim fails.

Even More Logical Complexity   Suppose C is so long that it cannot be surveyed by any human agent, whether they are computationally describable or not. (This is a possibility that Putnam cited as the logical error made by Penrose in his use of the Gödel theorems to refute mechanism.) If that is the case, we will not know if there are any programs or methods that can be used to prove CON(C) with less than mathematical certainty or in some other epistemic modality. But there might be ways of compressing the length of C so that we can then determine if there are methods that can be used to prove CON(C). One way of doing this is to reduce C to some program C^* that is humanly surveyable. (One then looks at methods for proving CON(C^*) with less than mathematical certainty or in some other epistemic modality.) There are three ways in which this can be done. One method is by a relative interpretation of C in C^*, another is by a translation of C into C^* and the third is a reduction of C to C^*. There are logical differences between interpretations, translations and reductions, which are the subject of reductive proof theory. What is common to all three is that the map from C into C^* is recursive and preserves negation. The latter condition ensures that logical consistency is preserved under the map.[43]

The maps between C and C^* preserve consistency, provided C^* is consistent. Since the assumption is that C is consistent, we need to find a short and consistent C^*. Suppose that C^* is not short.[44] It is possible there is a C^{**} that is consistent and short to which C^* can be reduced or translated or into which it can be interpreted. At each level of reduction for which there is a consistent and non-short C^{n^*}, it is possible that in reduction to the next level, by either translation, reduction, or interpretation, there is a consistent and short $C^{(n+1)^*}$.

To avoid, in EGM and MGM arguments, the logical error committed by Penrose, we have to consider the possibility that C is infeasibly long and then to consider how it might be compressed. The possibility of an infinite chain of reductions of length ω is a prospect that cannot be ruled out *a priori*. (The chain length could be ω, since a reduction might not decrease the length of C^{n^*}.) There are also other methods that can compress C. For instance, C could be translated into another programming language in which compression devices called MACROS are available or other higher-order programming constructs that facilitate program compression. There are infinitely many different programming systems, so there are that many possibilities that might need examination in the search for a short C. There are also speed-up theorems in the theory of computability, that tell us there is no recursive bound on the speed-up of some programs (over the initial program for which there is speed-up).

The anti-functionalist can object to the preceding infinite regress generated by program compression considerations in the same way she objected to the first infinite regress above: "The computationalist must first present to me a short C. Once that is done, we can then see if there are methods or programs that prove CON(C) with less than mathematical certainty or in some other epistemic modality." Once again, the anti-functionalist misconceives of her epistemic situation in the mechanist dialectic. If it is possible that there is a short C, then she must examine the possibilities under which it can be obtained. Many of these possibilities (such as relative interpretability) might be dead ends, might generate infinite regresses or might create trade-off problems.[45]

A Three-Dimensional Infinite Network of Possibilities We first noted that there might be infinitely many distinct methods for proving CON(C) with less than mathematical certainty or in some other epistemic modality. For each such method, the anti-functionalist must show it is Gödel susceptible. We then noted that for each method M that proves CON(C) and is shown Gödel susceptible, there might be a method N that proves CON(method M). If so, the anti-functionalist must show it is Gödel susceptible. But for each N that is shown Gödel susceptible, there might be an N^* that proves its correctness for which it must be shown it is Gödel susceptible. After that, we saw that if C (or any of the methods or any of the N^*s) is infeasibly long, we must see if we can compress it to obtain a short C (or short N^*, etc.) Each of these short Cs must then be shown Gödel susceptible.

Thus, we have infinitely many methods that might prove CON(C) with less than mathematical certainty or in some other epistemic modality. For each of those methods M_i, if it is shown to be Gödel susceptible, we can then look for a method or program that will prove CON(M_i) with less than mathematical certainty or in some other epistemic modality. N_i is the method that proves CON(M_i). If N_i is shown to be Gödel susceptible, then there might be an N_i^* that proves CON(N_i) and which must then be shown to be Gödel susceptible. Obviously, for each of the infinitely many

M_is there are infinitely many $N_i^{n^*}$s. Finally, for every M_i and $N_i^{n^*}$, it is possible that it is infeasibly long and thus we must look for a compression of it into a short program. But for each M_i and $N_i^{n^*}$, there might be an infinite sequence of compression reductions R_i.

The three-dimensional infinite network of possibilities has the following logical form:

> For each element in the $\{C, M_i\}$ infinite sequence and for each element in the $(M_i, N_i^{n^*})$ set of infinite sequences (attached to each M_i), there is an infinitely long element (R_i) in the infinite set of sequences $(M_i, N_i^{n^*}, R_i)$ such that R_i is a compression reduction of M_i, $N_i^{n^*}$.

The effect of the infinite sequence hanging off each element is that the variable in the range of the existential quantifier following the universal quantifier over the F, N^* sequence is not over single elements, but over infinitely long elements. In that case, we need either an infinitary logic or else second-order variables. If we choose the latter, then the logical complexity of the problem jumps from $\Pi(0,1)$ to $\Pi(1,1)$. This is a serious jump, since the recursive unsolvability of a $\Pi(1,1)$ problem is much greater than the recursive unsolvability of a $\Pi(0,1)$ problem.

The Second Disjunct in DISJUNCTION

Recall the second disjunct in DISJUNCTION: If a method or program for proving CON(C) with less than mathematical certainty or in some other epistemic modality is shown to be Gödel insusceptible, then show that the proofs delivered by that method or program are not epistemically warranted. For each method or program examined by the procedure described in the first disjunct of DISJUNCTION that is found to be Gödel insusceptible, it must be shown to be epistemically defective. This must be done to save an EGM or an MGM argument. (Suppose that it is an EGM argument. The claim is that C cannot be proved correct, because it is Gödel susceptible (and thus cognitive science cannot be justified). But there might be other ways to prove CON(C) with less than mathematical certainty or in another epistemic modality. If those ways are Gödel susceptible, the claim remains intact. If any of those ways are Gödel insusceptible, they *prima facie* refute the claim. The only way to save it is to show that the Gödel-insusceptible methods are epistemically defective—i.e., that proofs delivered by those methods are not epistemically warranted.)

Since any method or procedure might turn out to be Gödel insusceptible, any point in the three-dimensional infinite network of possibilities might have to be tested for epistemic adequacy. Of course, no point in the network might have to be tested, if every point represents a method or program that is Gödel susceptible. The question is "How can we show that a method or a program is epistemically defective?" If what is proved by a method has a 50 percent chance of being true, we can conclude that it is defective. But what do we say when the probability of being true is greater than 50 percent? What is the cutoff point? What if we do not have sufficient statistics for showing the likelihood of what a method proves? What epistemological theory do we employ in assessing the epistemic adequacy of a method? Even if we are guided by statistical methods used in the sciences, those methods still make philosophical presuppositions about the nature of probabilities. What does it mean to say that we search the space of epistemologies for various construals of epistemic adequacy? Given that EGM and MGM arguments are philosophical arguments claiming to refute a philosophical position in the philosophy of mind, any elucidation of the notion 'epistemic justification of C' must be philosophically respectable.

All these difficulties are critical for the anti-functionalist, who must show that any Gödel-insusceptible method in the three-dimensional network of possibilities is epistemically defective. Without establishing that, EGM and MGM arguments unravel. The point can be put more strongly: Anyone who wishes to use an EGM or MGM argument must be prepared to decide what counts as epistemic justification of the correctness of C. Decoding the acronyms and abbreviations, the point is this: Anyone who wishes to use the Gödel theorems to refute mechanism must be prepared to decide what counts as the epistemic justification of cognitive science.

Elucidating the epistemic adequacy of methods that prove CON(C) with less than mathematical certainty or in another epistemic modality is a necessary condition for the success of EGM and MGM arguments. When a method in the three-dimensional network is Gödel insusceptible, we must look at whether it is epistemically defective. If a method is Gödel susceptible, we must assess whether proofs of CON(C) with less than mathematical certainty or in another epistemic modality are epistemically warranted.[46] An important philosophical project, then, is elucidation of the notion 'epistemic adequacy of proofs of CON(C) with less than mathematical certainty or in another epistemic modality'.[47]

Chains and Tangled Chains Whose Elements Exhibit Defeater Relations
Suppose that method M is Gödel insusceptible and that it cannot epistemically justify CON(C). Does it follow that method M must be dismissed? No, for it might epistemically justify CON(G), where method G is Gödel

insusceptible and epistemically justifies CON(C). This may happen if we allow relative interpretations, translations, and reductions between C, M, and G. But it can happen even if these relations do not occur. The point is that there might be chains, of arbitrary length, in which a method M_i that does not justify C epistemically justifies method M_j, which epistemically justifies C.

For example, suppose we have a chain of length 1,000 in which the 1,000th element is a Gödel-insusceptible method that does not justify CON(C) but epistemically justifies the 999th element in the chain, which is Gödel susceptible and which proves with mathematical certainty the 998th element in the chain, which (along with the remaining 997 elements in the chain) proves CON(C) with mathematical certainty. Even though the 1,000th element cannot epistemically justify CON(C), it does not follow that the anti-functionalist can dismiss it, since there might be chains, of arbitrary length between it and CON(C) that transmit epistemic justification in such a way that CON(C) is epistemically justified (because the preceding element in the chain, though Gödel susceptible, proves CON(C) with mathematical certainty). This, then, is an added complication in the logical structure of the problem facing the anti-functionalist who advances either an MGM or an EGM argument.

An additional complication is the existence of methods that defeat justification of CON(C) or of CON(Method$_i$). Suppose that M_k defeats justification of M_i, and M_i can justify CON(C). However, there might be a method M_{k+1} that defeats justification of M_k, thus restoring M_i so that it can justify CON(C). Call this a tangled chain of methods. This problem is similar to the logical problem facing defeater epistemologies. There might be chains of defeaters, of arbitrary length, in which the 999th member of the chain defeats the 347th member, while the 876th member defeats the 999th. Simply enumerating and assessing each element in the chain is not enough. Any element must be compared with every other sequence of elements in the chain.[48]

In summary of this subsection, we have the following results:

(i) It is possible that there are epistemically justified methods that prove CON(C) with less than mathematical certainty. EGM arguments must show that there are no methods that can do this. If they don't, the conclusion of the EGM argument—that cognitive science cannot be shown to be correct—fails. EGM arguments assume that human minds have a computational description. Showing that there are no epistemically justified methods that can prove CON(C) with less than mathematical certainty is highly recursively unsolvable. Finitary human minds that have a computational description cannot complete this task.

(ii) To save the MGM conclusion that there is a cognitive task that finitary human minds can do but finitary computing machines can't do, it must be shown either that human minds can prove CON(C) with mathematical certainty or that there is no epistemically justified method by which CON(C) can be proved with less than mathematical certainty. Since only an infinitary mind can prove CON(C) with mathematical certainty, the first disjunct has no empirical basis in cognitive science. There is no empirical evidence that human minds can perform infinitary tasks, such as constructing infinite proof trees. The second disjunct is what the EGM arguments must also establish, and, as we saw, they cannot do so, because it is a recursively unsolvable task. It is a mystery how a finitary human mind, even one that has no computational description, could complete the task.

2 Putnam's Bombshell: The Gödelian Argument in "Reflexive Reflections"

One way out of the impasse confronting EGM and MGM arguments is to show that all epistemically justified methods that prove CON(C) with less than mathematical certainty or in some other epistemic modality are Gödel susceptible. Call these *weak methods*.[1] In an ingenious argument, Putnam claims that no weak methods are Gödel insusceptible. This argument appears in his important paper "Reflexive Reflections."[2] The argument employs Gödel's second incompleteness theorem. In what follows, I use the acronym PGA, which stands for Putnam's use of the second Gödel theorem in his argument that all weak methods are Gödel susceptible.

An Exposition of PGA

Before I offer my criticism of PGA, I present it in full. PGA claims that our prescriptive inductive competence is Gödel susceptible. Putnam cites his earlier work on Carnapian inductive logics.[3] Provided that the confirmation relation in Carnapian inductive logic CI is recursive, one can prove that there is another Carnapian inductive logic, CI*, that can do better on some regularity and just as well as CI on every other regularity that CI confirms. But Carnap's system of inductive logic, which is based on measure functions, does not capture all the varieties of inductive reasoning. In fact, Carnap's system is so inflexible that it cannot incorporate commonsense predicates that we employ in everyday inductive reasoning.

Responding both to this deficiency in Carnapian inductive logic and to a logical puzzle posed by Andrez Mostowski, Putnam invented computational learning theory.[4] He introduced the idea of trial-and-error predicates. The paradigm of learning a recursive function when presented with a data stream that contains a subset of range elements of the function to be learned introduces the idea that a learner is allowed to change her mind over time. The criterion of success adopted in this paradigm is verification in the limit: we cannot know exactly when the learner will converge to the correct answer, but we can know that the learner will converge to the correct answer sooner or later. Computable learning theory is more realistic as a model of non-demonstrative reasoning than Carnapian inductive logics. It can be precisely described in the language of recursion theory, so its claims can be mathematically evaluated. But does it capture our full inductive competence? Putnam asserts that it doesn't matter whether it does so, since PGA will assume there is some computational description of our prescriptive inductive competence. We do not need to know what the description looks like in the proof of PGA.

'P' denotes a computational description of our inductive (or non-demonstrative) and demonstrative prescriptive competence. Putnam uses an idea in the Montague-Kaplan 'Paradox of the Knower'[5] that is an application of self-reference Putnam calls 'The Computational Liar':

> (I) There is no evidence on which acceptance of the sentence (I) is justified.[6]

This is arithmetizable, and its arithmetization is a sentence of arithmetic to which the Gödel diagonal lemma applies. The diagonal lemma is the principal idea behind the first Gödel theorem. It tells us that for any predicate that is definable in the language of Peano arithmetic there is some sentence that is true if and only if its Gödel number is false of that predicate. The diagonal lemma allows us to couple P with (I). "It follows from Gödel's work that there is a sentence of mathematics which is true if and only if P does not accept that very sentence on any evidence, where P is any procedure itself definable in mathematics—not necessarily a recursive procedure."[7]

In an important caveat to (I), Putnam says that "if the inductive logic P uses the notion of degree of confirmation rather than the notion of acceptance, then one replaces 'is justified' by 'has instance confirmation greater than .5'."[8] This is significant, since the notions of a justified belief and of acceptance of a justified belief play critical roles in non-quantitative models of inductive reasoning, while 'has instance confirmation greater than .5' and 'degree of confirmation' play critical roles in both quantitative and logical models of inductive reasoning. This caveat gives us reason to think that Putnam takes P to be a computational description of any kind of inductive reasoning and not just logical models of inductive reasoning, such as those found in computational learning theory.

I will now quote in full the argument that establishes that P cannot converge on (I) without also licensing us to believe something that is mathematically false:

Now, suppose there is evidence e on which the acceptance of (I) is justified. Then (I) is false. And (I) is a sentence of pure mathematics. So there is a situation in which we are prescriptively justified in believing a mathematically false sentence, if P really is a sound formalization of our prescriptive competence! Many would consider this already to show that a correct P cannot lead to the acceptance of (I) (for example, the standard DeFinetti-Shimony requirements rule out assigning a degree of confirmation less than 1 to a mathematical truth on any evidence). But let us go on for a bit. Suppose there is evidence e on which the acceptance of (I)'s negation is justified. Then, either there is also (presumably different) evidence on which the acceptance of (I) is justified, or else (I)'s negation is a mathematically false sentence that P instructs us to accept on certain evidence. (N.B.: the negation of (I) asserts that there is evidence on which acceptance of (I) is justified.) In the first case (there is different evidence on which on which the acceptance of (I) is justified), we know by the previous argument that (I) is a mathematically false sentence, and so there is again evidence—the 'different' evidence mentioned—on which P licenses the acceptance of a mathematical falsehood, namely, (I) itself. In the second case, I just noted that (I)'s negation is a mathematical falsehood that P licenses us to accept (an "ω inconsistency"). So if P "converges" on the argument (I), that is, if the question "Is the acceptance of (I) justified or not)?" is one to which there is ever an answer (relative to some evidence e or other) which we are P-justified in giving, then there is evidence relative to which P licenses us to accept a mathematical falsehood.[9]

I will make a few clarificatory comments on this argument. In proving his first incompleteness theorem, Gödel argued that proving a Gödel sentence to be true or proving it to be false leads to contradiction. Since the sentence says of itself that it is true but unprovable, proving that it is true is contradictory. Putnam similarly argues that if P converges on the Computational Liar or on its negation, then it licenses us to justifiably believe a mathematical falsehood.[10] By showing that P cannot converge on either (I) or its negation without absurdity, we establish the independence of (I) from the proof procedure available. In this case, we establish that (I) cannot be shown true or shown false using P, which is a computational description of our prescriptive competence in demonstrative and inductive reasoning.

Gödel assumed that the formal system in which he worked is ω consistent in order to show that proof of the negation of the Gödel sentence leads to a contradiction—in this case, an ω-inconsistency. And ω consistency is weaker than consistency. If a formal system is ω consistent, it follows that it is consistent. Putnam makes the same assumption.[11] He tells us it is obvious that if P converges on (I), it licenses us to believe an arithmetical falsehood. Given that is so, we are justified in believing that convergence on (I) licenses us to believe an arithmetical falsehood. If we are justified in believing that, we are justified in believing (I). I now quote the remainder of PGA, in which a contradiction is explicitly derived:

> The point about this argument is that it is *obvious*. If there is *anything* that I am "competent" to believe, anything I am "justified" in believing, it is that P cannot converge on the argument (I) without licensing me to believe what is mathematically false. So it certainly seems that the following should be accepted as a *criterion of adequacy* on the acceptability of any proposed formalization of our prescriptive competence:
>
> > (II) The acceptance of a formal procedure P as a formalization of (part or all) of prescriptive inductive (demonstrative and non-demonstrative) competence is only justified if one is justified in believing that P does not converge on P's own Gödel sentence (I) as argument.
>
> So if P is a description of a procedure the mind uses which is prescriptive for human minds, then we cannot come to see that this procedure *is* prescriptive for us as long as our minds function as P says they should.
>
> To spell this out: Suppose our minds are functioning in accordance with P. We assume that it is rational to accept the above criterion of adequacy (II). If we come to believe that P is a complete and correct description of our own prescriptive competence, then, since we believe (II), we have to believe that P does not converge on (I); but this is just to believe (I)! And, since we believe that this belief is justified and that justified belief is formalized by P, we are committed to believing that P tells us to believe (I)—that is, P converges on (I)! But now we have a contradiction.[12]

PGA is quite ingenious. Notice that Putnam has not made any claims that human minds can do something that no finitary computing machine can do. He has, however, shown that P could not be justified within cognitive science without licensing us to believe a contradiction. One consequence of PGA is that any formal theory of how we do inductive reasoning proposed in cognitive science cannot be justified without also licensing us to believe a contradiction! This is a disturbing and important result.

PGA and the Montague-Kaplan Paradox

Is it really the case that the principal terms in (I) can be arithmetized? If they cannot be arithmetized, PGA fails. Contrast (I) with the version that Kaplan and Montague constructed to show that the Gödel theorems extend to the modal predicates 'knowledge' and 'necessity'.[13] Kaplan and Montague needed to find for the knowledge predicate suitable analogues of the Hilbert-Bernays derivability conditions for the provability predicate. Montague employed a weak epistemic system consisting of four schemata:

(i) $K\alpha \rightarrow \alpha$.

(ii) $K\alpha$, if α is an axiom of first-order logic.

(iii) $K(\alpha \rightarrow \mu) \rightarrow (K\alpha \rightarrow K\mu)$.

(iv) $K(K\alpha \rightarrow \alpha)$.

Montague appreciated Tarski's insight, in the latter's proof of the indefinability of truth in first-order logic, that two *prima facie* consistent theories cannot always be combined into a consistent theory. In Tarski's indefinability work, Robinson arithmetic relativized to ß cannot be combined with Tarski's schema for the language of Robinson arithmetic relativized to ß and extended with a truth predicate T. Montague saw that this insight can be generalized: two *prima facie* true theories, one a theory of its own syntax and the other a theory that has principles capturing the logic of concepts such as knowledge, belief, or necessity, cannot be combined into a consistent theory. The tool necessary for the proof is the Gödel diagonal lemma: Suppose that T is an extension of Robinson arithmetic relativized to ß. Let α be a formula whose only free variable is v_0. Then there is a sentence ζ such that $\vdash_T \zeta$ if and only if $\alpha(\zeta/v_0)$, where, if n is the Gödel number of ζ, ζ is the nth numeral.

The key to the Montague-Kaplan proof is the fact that knowledge is a property of "proposition-like" objects recursively built from atomic constituents. Given enough arithmetic, it is easy to associate a Gödel number with each "proposition-like" object. Then structural properties and relations between "proposition-like" objects can be arithmetically simulated by explicitly defined arithmetical predicates of the Gödel numbers of the "proposition-like" objects.

Recall the "Computational Liar":

(I) There is no evidence on which acceptance of the sentence (I) is justified.

To use Gödel's diagonal lemma, we must arithmetize the properties and relations in (I) . Can 'evidence', 'acceptance', and 'justified' be arithmetized? It is not obvious that they can. Consider the ramified type theory in Russell and Whitehead's *Principia Mathematica*. No one has succeeded in showing that it is Gödel susceptible, for there is no general theory of the intensional provability relation. It will do no good to simply assert that consistency cannot be proved within any sufficiently strong system because Gödel's second incompleteness theorem tells us this. Richmond Thomason has pointed out in this connection that "it has never been possible to state the [second incompleteness] theorem at this level of generality with a degree of precision that will support a mathematical proof."[14]

Intensional provability relations link arithmetical theories to a given set of propositions when the arithmetical theory is able to prove each of the propositions in the set. That there cannot be a general theory of the kind Thomason specifies follows from an interesting result on the peculiarities of the intensional proof relation. Feferman has shown that Gödel's arithmetical formalization of the proposition that Peano arithmetic is consistent can be proved, under substitution of different linguistic expressions for the same classes of numbers in that arithmetical formalization.[15]

In PGA, Putnam assumes that 'evidence', 'acceptability', and 'justified' can be arithmetized. We can formalize the evidence relation and the property of acceptance within computable learning theory, but this raises two questions: Does that formalization capture all the uses of these terms in inductive reasoning? Can the terms be arithmetized? And what of the property of being justified? How would we axiomatize its basic features in the way that Kaplan and Montague axiomatized the basic features of knowledge? What happens to PGA if the notion of being justified is omitted? Without it, we cannot say that P tells us that we are prescriptively justified in believing an arithmetically false sentence. Thus, we will not be able to show that an absurdity results if P converges on either (I) or the negation of (I). In that case, we cannot even express the condition of adequacy (II) necessary for obtaining the contradiction.

> Objection: It is true that omitting the notion of 'justifies' in PGA blocks deriving the contradiction. But that is not problematic for the anti-functionalist end to which PGA is applied. You succumb to a dilemma if you argue that there is no obvious arithmetization of 'is justified'. The first horn is that if there is an arithmetization of 'is justified', then the contradiction is secured. For the second horn, suppose that it cannot be arithmetized. If that is so, then it cannot be part of cognitive science. Thus, either way, cognitive science is in jeopardy. On the first horn, cognitive science cannot prove that it is correct; on the second horn, inductive reasoning can't be computationally described. On either horn, the anti-functionalist wins.

> Response: The first horn of the dilemma is that if 'is justified' is arithmetizable then PGA is secured. I will argue below that PGA, even if sound, cannot be used to secure the claim that human minds are not finitary computing machines or the claim that cognitive science cannot be justified. The second horn is easily dismissed, though. That 'X' is not

arithmetizable does not logically imply that 'X' is not formalizable. Why think that *any* property or relation, even if it is formalizable, can be arithmetized? Certainly Gödel numbers can be assigned to formalized sentences and to formalized properties. But it does not follow from that fact that any formalized property is arithmetizable. The example of *Principia* ramified type theory, discussed above, illustrates the point. The burden of proof is on Putnam to show that the epistemic property of being justified, under a suitable formalization, can be arithmetized.

Chalmers's Attempt to Refute Penrose

David Chalmers attempted to refute Roger Penrose's Gödel refutation. As we have seen, Putnam discovered a logical error in Penrose's argument. Chalmers's diagnosis of the argument is different. He attempts to derive a contradiction involving the notion 'unassailably believes to be true'. Penrose claims we unassailably believe to be true that Peano arithmetic is consistent. Chalmers tries to show that "unassailable belief" satisfies the Gödel diagonal lemma. The question is whether it can be arithmetized. Chalmers deals with this by axiomatizing the notion of unassailable belief similar to the way in which Richmond Thomason axiomatized the concept of belief. His idea, in doing that, is that the modal concept of unassailable belief is Gödel susceptible and can be shown to be so, just as, and just as how, the modal concept of belief was proved by Thomason to be Gödel susceptible. Chalmers's axiomatization of unassailable belief is as follows[16]:

(i) If A is derivable (in F), then Unassailablybelieve A is derivable (in F).

(ii) It is derivable (in F) that if Unassailablybelieve A_1 and Unassailablybelieve $(A_1 \rightarrow A_2)$ then Unassailablybelieve A_2.

(iii) It is derivable (in F) that Unassailablybelieve A $\rightarrow$ Unassailablybelieve(Unassailablybelieve A).

(iv) It is derivable (in F) that we cannot have Unassailablybelieve (the falsum).

Responding to Chalmers's argument, Per Lindström pointed out something that is well known to all logicians: Not every formalizable property of Peano arithmetic satisfies Gödel's diagonal lemma.[17] Expressing a diagonal sentence formally is easy. Here is how such a sentence is expressed by Chalmers:

$\vdash$ C if and only if not-B($\ulcorner$C$\urcorner$),

where B is the property of unassailable belief and C is a sentence whose Gödel number is ⌜C⌝. What could be easier? Simply take any predicate you please and plug it into the diagonal lemma. Gödel's diagonal lemma is a syntactical diagonalization method that can be used to create infinitely many self-referential sentences. However, trivial substitution instances of it are easily fashioned. Consider the property of being a well-formed formula of Peano arithmetic. It is well defined, and it is representable in Peano arithmetic, and thus it is a recursive property. It is certainly a meaningful property. If it were not a meaningful property, the idea of mathematical certainty captured by the notion of provability in a finitary formal system collapses, since the notion of a well-formed formula is pivotal in constructing any formal system.

However, we can use Gödel's diagonal lemma to construct a self-referential sentence that says of itself that it is not a well-formed formula of Peano arithmetic. If that well-formed formula can be derived in Peano arithmetic, it is must be meaningless, since in a finitary formal system anything derived must be a well-formed formula of the system (and there must be an effective procedure one can use to determine that it is a well-formed formula of the system). Obviously, then, it is refutable. It is not possible in Peano arithmetic for a well-formed formula to truly say of itself that it is not a well-formed formula.

Lindström says that Chalmers's diagonal sentence fails to be meaningful when the sentence that is unassailably believed to be true itself contains the predicate 'unassailablybelieved'. He takes as an example the sentence C in Chalmers's substitution instance of Gödel's diagonal lemma. C contains the predicate 'unassailablybelieved'. What does it mean to say "I don't unassailablybelieve this sentence?" Lindström says that the sentence is meaningless.[18] Unfortunately, that is the end of the story, at least in Lindström's paper. He doesn't elaborate on his claim that the sentence is meaningless. Perhaps it is obvious that it is. My point in discussing Lindström's criticism of Chalmers's attempt to refute Penrose's Gödel refutation is to emphasize that not every predicate can satisfy the Gödel diagonal lemma and be meaningful. In emphasizing this, I put pressure on Putnam's claim that principal terms (such as 'is justified') appearing in the Computational Liar are arithmetizable and meaningfully satisfy Gödel's diagonal lemma.

Before considering the meaning of the predicate 'unassailablybelieves', we need to see what problem meaninglessness creates for claims that a system is Gödel susceptible. The logical problem is that the meaninglessness of the diagonalized sentence "not unassailably believes this sentence" is that it entails there are formal proofs in the system that cannot be understood in terms of its intended (semantical) interpretation. That, then, destroys the claim that the system is Gödel susceptible, since it is required for the Gödel result to take root that the Gödel sentence be true in a standard model of the system and false in a non-standard model. If we cannot understand formal proofs of the system in terms of the standard model—which is the intended semantical interpretation of the formal system—we cannot say whether derivations in the system are true or false in the standard model. We can't, then, say whether the Gödel sentence is true in the standard model. In that case we no longer have a Gödel problem—incompleteness—since it is now possible that the Gödel sentence is false in all the models of the formal system, including the non-standard model in which it must be false. If you do not have a meaningful standard model for a system, then there is the question of what the formal system is a formalization of.

Let us further examine the issue of whether C is meaningless by exploring its connection with Moore's paradox. It is not a form of that paradox, which is "p is true, though I do not believe it." Moore's paradox, though odd, is meaningful. Though it is not self-referential, a self-referential version of it would be

(1) "This sentence is true, but I do not believe it,"

which hinges on being meaningless. Similarly, truth-teller sentences, such as "This sentence is true," are odd, but meaningful, even though it is a stipulation to take them to be true. What, then, of the sentence "I believe this sentence?" Here, I do not stipulate it is true. Rather, I assert that we believe this sentence, whose content is that we believe it. What, then, do we believe? Do we believe that we believe the sentence? No, that is not what the sentence says. Here, I conjecture, we have the act of belief caught in a nested loop. We believe the sentence, but the sentence tells us that we believe it. So we believe what we believe. What is that? What we believe!

It is worse when we say, self-referentially,

(2) "I do not believe this sentence."

The content of the sentence is that it is not believed. Thus, we assert that we do not believe this sentence, whose content is that we do not believe it. Here, too, we have the act of belief caught in a nested loop. We disbelieve the sentence, but the sentence tells us that we disbelieve it. So we disbelieve what we disbelieve. What is that? What we disbelieve! It is important that (2) is not paradoxical. It is meaningless, just as (1) is meaningless.

If it were paradoxical, we would assimilate it to the category of a liar paradox, in which case we would get a genuine diagonalized sentence.[19]

What of unassailable belief? What is the meaning of "I unassailably believe this sentence?" It is that my belief can't be unhinged, come what may. What is the meaning of "I don't unassailably believe this sentence?" It is not simply that my belief can be unhinged. It can be that I believe it, but not unassailably, so that it could happen that I might give up my belief in it. Or it can be that I do not believe it, period. There is an ambiguity in the notion of "not-unassailably believe," an ambiguity that is not removed by the axioms for the notion of unassailable belief. Is it to be taken in the narrow-scope or the wide-scope reading? What difference could it make if it taken in one rather than the other? Given that the notion of self-referential unassailable belief is so contrived, it is not clear what meaning we should give to the wide-scope reading of it, as opposed to the narrow-scope reading. That does not mean, though, that we can collapse the scope readings. There is a genuine syntactical difference between the two, and this syntactical difference is reflected in the truth conditions for sentences containing these predicates in the (model-theoretic) structures that interpret the formal language in which they live. If Chalmers is to deflect Lindstrom's criticism, he must show us that the diagonalization of the predicate 'unassailablybelieves' is meaningful.

Danto on the KK Thesis

Let us now consider whether the notion of 'justifies' that Putnam employs in the Computational Liar is meaningful under diagonalization. Our first task is to look at whether it satisfies the axioms Thomason used for modal belief predicates. Thomason's axioms differ from Montague's only at the first axiom: '$K\alpha \to \alpha$' is replaced by '$B\alpha \to B(B(\alpha))$'. The replacement is obvious: Believing the sentence p does not imply that it is true, though knowing p, by definition, implies that it is true. Let 'J' denote 'justifies'. Then $J\alpha \to \alpha$ is false, since a justified belief might not be true—that much is evident from the Gettier counterexamples.[20]

Let us examine the first axiom in Thomason's system, replacing 'belief' by 'justifies'. We have

$$J\alpha \to J(J(\alpha)).$$

If α is justified, then it is justified that it is justified. This presents a problem pointed out by Arthur Danto[21] for the axiom Kp → KKp. Danto argued that it is false where there is not unanimity on the definition of knowledge or where the conception of knowledge is not clear. In order to ascertain that we know what we know, we must have a clearly defined notion of knowledge and in our language community, we must be in unanimity on it. But there is not unanimity in the philosophical community on the notion of 'justifies'. If that is so, we cannot use Thomason's four axioms to axiomatize 'justifies' in the Computational Liar. If that is so, a proof of Gödel susceptibility of inductive reasoning fails.

A Deeper Problem Than Danto's: A Paradox of "'Justifies' Is Gödel Susceptible"

What if there is a clear conception of 'justifies' upon which there is universal agreement? There is, then, no sustainable objection, of the kind Danto proposed, to the JJ thesis. I will argue that there is another kind of difficulty that attends acceptance of the JJ thesis. We can express a condition of adequacy on acceptance of the JJ thesis: It must be the case that the second-order justification of the justification of an arbitrary sentence (in the right-hand side of the conditional) is coherent and true, given (in the left-hand side of the conditional) that the first-order justification (of the same arbitrary sentence) is coherent and true. If this condition of adequacy is not satisfied, the JJ thesis is meaningless.

If 'justifies' is Gödel susceptible, it follows that a justified belief cannot itself be computationally justified, since the computational justification of a justified belief consists in showing that the notion of being a justified belief is itself computationally justified. But Putnam argues that the notion of a justified belief is Gödel susceptible, and it is the condition of justified belief being Gödel susceptible that, at least for Putnam, excludes it from being a computational notion of justification. Putnam has claimed in many places, and it is a principal claim in *R&R*,[22] that 'justified' is a member of a closed circle of notions, which includes 'warranted' and 'reasonable'. Putnam argues that these notions are not reducible to computational ones, but his argument relies on the demonstration that they are, in their computational guises, Gödel susceptible. The following paragraph also applies to them.

If 'justifies' is Gödel susceptible, then the second-order justification required in the JJ axiom will fail to be coherent or true. However, if it fails to be coherent or true, then the Montague-Kaplan-Thomason proof fails. If it fails, then it has *not* been shown that 'justifies' is Gödel susceptible. If 'justifies' is not Gödel susceptible, then it *is* in Putnam's view epistemically adequate. In that case, the JJ thesis is true and it is meaningful, since the second-order justification is both coherent and true. If that is so, it follows that 'justifies' *is* Gödel susceptible, because, now, the Thomason argument can be run. But since it is, after all, Gödel susceptible, it follows that it cannot be used to prove its own Gödel susceptibility, because the JJ axiom is then both incoherent and false. That, then, is the paradox of 'justifies is Gödel susceptible'.

Is There a Way Out of the Paradox?

Is there an alternative axiomatization of 'justifies' under which a Thomason-style contradiction for 'justifies' can be proved? The axiomatizations in both Montague's and Thomason's systems fail to produce a contradiction of the desired sort for the notion of 'justifies'. No one has shown—in the literature—how to augment or modify their structural axioms so as to extend their results to the predicate 'justify'. The only other possibility for axiomatizing 'justifies' is a provability predicate. Let us try to axiomatize 'justifies' within the system of modal logic G. There is a technical and a philosophical motivation for attempting to do this. The technical motivation is that the provability predicate is the original scene in which the Gödelian drama was enacted. The provability predicate easily satisfies the diagonal lemma. If 'justifies' behaves logically like provability, then we should expect that it is, just as provability is, Gödel susceptible. The philosophical motivation is that the notion of 'justification' Putnam employs is closely linked with the notion of 'justification' that Michael Dummett employs in his semantical theory. Dummettian justification, though, is intuitionistic provability. Can, then, the notion of justification be resurrected in modal logic G?

The characteristic axiom of G, a modal counterpart of Löb's Theorem, is the modal schema $L(L\alpha \rightarrow \alpha) \rightarrow L\alpha$. This schema distinguishes G from normal modal model systems. Now, if 'justifies' satisfies the Löb schema, without incoherence, the way is open to run PGA successfully. Does 'justifies' satisfy the Löb schema? The second-order justification in the antecedent of the conditional of the Löb schema functions differently from the second-order justification in the JJ axiom (that is the analogue of the BB axiom in Thomason's system). The wide scope J applies to the conditional $J\alpha \rightarrow \alpha$. Thus, if the truth of α follows from the assumption that α is justified, then this conditional sentence is justified. Under the assumption that this is true, it follows that α is justified. Thus, the justification of α depends on showing that it is justified that α follows from α being justified. If justification is strong enough to secure the truth of what it justifies, then it is itself justified. After all, the epistemic function of justification is to aim at truth. If it can be shown that truth of a proposition is secured whenever it is justified, then that notion of justification cannot be epistemically faulted. Certainly, it cannot lead to gettiered beliefs, and that is one of the primary problems for any notion of justification. Notice that whether a belief is justified is conditional on establishing that the strong condition obtains. Of course, if it is true that justification secures the truth of a belief and that this shows the notion of justification is justified, it trivially follows that the belief is justified.

The computational functionalist could certainly complain that the requirement that justification secure truth is too strong for any reasonable notion of justification. I suspect that Putnam would adopt that line. However, there is no need for the computational functionalist to adopt this line of argument against the anti-functionalist move of identifying 'justifies' with 'provability' in the modal logic G. The reason why, is that it can be proved that all the theorems of G remain the same when the Löb schema is replaced by the axiom schema $La \rightarrow LLa$. Unfortunately, this is just the 'provability' counterpart of Thomason's fourth axiom for 'belief' in his system. We saw that when we replace 'B' by 'J', we get a paradox if we wish to prove the Gödelian contradiction. Thus, the paradox that sinks Putnam's hope of including 'justifies' within the scope of his PGA cannot be avoided if we move from Thomason's system to the modal logic G. At this point, then, there appear to be few options available for Putnam to take, since the three different axiom schemata—one for knowledge, one for belief, one for provability—are the only reasonable candidates for the structural conditions which the notion of 'justification' has to satisfy, if it is to be a formal notion.[23]

It is true that little machinery is needed in the Montague and Thomason systems in which the contradictions appear. A theory does not have to attribute very much structure to the objects over which it ranges—for instance, attitudinal objects in the case of Thomason's system. The four axioms characterizing their structure are fairly austere. However, it is the capacity, within the system, to express much about the connection between the attitudinal objects and the sentences that express them which is the ground of the contradiction. A well-known case is Montague's Intensional Logic. No contradiction occurs whenever the attitudes are represented as relations between sets of possible worlds and individuals. However, if the system has enough strength for the arithmetic that is necessary for Gödelization (and that is easily accomplished by adding the axioms for relativized Robinson's arithmetic to IL), a relation between Gödel numbers of sentences and the propositions expressed by those sentences can be established. It is from relations of this sort that contradiction occurs. The point is the minimal necessary conditions for proving Gödel susceptibility of modal predicates are austere. If 'justified' cannot be proved Gödel susceptible under these conditions, it is doubtful it can be proved Gödel susceptible at all.

Penrose's Simple Logical Error and PGA

As we have seen, Putnam slammed Penrose's Gödel refutation by showing that it commits a simple logical error. How does Putnam's PGA avoid it? There is no discussion of it in "Reflexive Reflections." Presumably, an account of how to avoid it might go as follows: Suppose that C (the computational description of the human mind) is so long that no finitary human being can survey it. However, by ingenious use of statistical methods, a human mind can statistically survey it and provide a proof of CON(C) with less than mathematical certainty. Thus a human mind can show C is correct, while no finitary computing machine that runs C can do that. In that case, human minds can be epistemically distinguished from finitary computing machines.

Unfortunately, this account is false. It fails to epistemically distinguish human minds from finitary computing machines, even if human minds are metaphysically distinct from them. Let us see why this is so. The point of PGA is to show the inductive methods which we can use to prove CON(C) with less than mathematical certainty are Gödel susceptible. To simplify, suppose that inductive method M has been shown to be Gödel susceptible and that M proves CON(C) with less than mathematical certainty. Suppose also that the human mind, though finitary, has no computational description. Does this mean that a human mind can prove CON(M), but finitary computing machines running M cannot prove CON(M)? Whatever the epistemic modality of the proof procedure in M, no finitary computing machine and no finitary human mind (not describable in computational terms) can prove CON(M) in that epistemic modality. It is left open, though, that the finitary computing machine running M can prove CON(M) in another epistemic modality or with less than the degree of mathematical certainty the proof procedure secures, just as it is left open for a human mind (that either has or has no computational description) to do likewise.

Let the statistical methods shown Gödel susceptible by PGA be M in the above. In that case, neither finitary human minds (that either have or do not have a computational description) and finitary computing machines running those methods can show the methods are correct in the epistemic modality of the proof procedure of the formal system in which the methods are formalized. Let the Gödel sentence for the statistical methods be G_s. Then neither finitary human minds (that either have or do not have a computational description) nor finitary computing machines running those methods can prove G_s in the epistemic modality of the proof procedure of the formal system in which those methods are formalized. In both proving CON(statistical methods) and proving G_s, it is left open that both finitary human minds and finitary computing machines running the statistical methods can prove either in another epistemic modality or with less mathematical certainty than the degree of mathematical certainty the proof procedure secures.

The finitary human mind that has no computational description cannot use the Gödel-susceptible statistical methods to epistemically distinguish itself from finitary computing machines running those methods. And if the human mind establishes CON(statistical methods) or proves G_s in another epistemic modality that is not Gödel susceptible, the finitary computing machines can do so as well. If human minds are infinitary, then they can prove CON(statistical methods) or G_s in the same epistemic modality as the proof procedure of the Gödel-susceptible formal system in which the methods are formalized. If that is so, human minds can be epistemically distinguished from finitary computing machines. But human minds are not infinitary.

Does PGA capture *all* methods of inductive reasoning and *all* notions of justified belief? In *R&R*, Putnam writes: "If our *entire* intuitive notion of 'justification' is captured by [P], . . . then the fact that this is so cannot be justified by *any* argument that an idealized human judge would be justified in accepting! . . . My extension of Gödelian techniques to inductive logic showed that it is part of our notion of justification in general (not just of our notion of *mathematical* justification) that *reason can go beyond whatever reason can formalize*."[24]

If all inductive reasoning is Gödel susceptible, then neither finitary human minds (that have or do not have a computational description) nor finitary computing machines running those methods can prove they are correct or prove their Gödel sentences in the characteristic epistemic modality of the proof procedure of the formal system formalizing those methods. But if all inductive reasoning is Gödel susceptible, then there are no weak inductive methods that can prove CON(Gödel-susceptible method) or the Gödel sentence of the Gödel-susceptible method in another epistemic modality or with mathematical certainty less than the degree of mathematical certainty of the proof procedure of the formal system that formalizes those methods.

If there are weak methods that are not Gödel susceptible, they can be used both by finitary human minds (that have or do not have a computational description) and by finitary computing machines running Gödel-susceptible methods. If an anti-functionalist tries to prove that there are no Gödel-insusceptible inductive methods, she encounters a dilemma. The first horn of the dilemma is as follows: To prove there are no Gödel-insusceptible inductive methods is a recursively unsolvable problem of high degree of unsolvability. Finitary human minds cannot prove this. If there are weak Gödel-insusceptible methods, then both finitary human minds (that do or do not have a computational description) and finitary computing machines running Gödel-susceptible methods can avail themselves of them to prove CON(Gödel-susceptible methods) or the Gödel sentences of the Gödel-susceptible methods in another epistemic modality or with mathematical certainty less than the degree of mathematical certainty of the proof procedure of the formal system in which the Gödel-susceptible methods are formalized. The second horn of the dilemma is this: If the anti-functionalist succeeds in proving that there are no Gödel-insusceptible inductive methods, then neither finitary human minds (that have or do not have a computational description) nor finitary computing machines can prove CON(Gödel-susceptible method) or the Gödel sentences of the Gödel-susceptible methods in the characteristic epistemic modality of the proof procedure of the formal system in which those methods are formalized.

Strengthened PGA Leads to Paradox

One problem with PGA is that if not all inductive methods (or, more broadly, methods of inquiry into the world) are Gödel susceptible, then it is possible that in using methods that are Gödel susceptible we can employ Gödel-insusceptible weak methods to prove CON(Gödel-susceptible method) or the Gödel sentence of a Gödel-susceptible method in another epistemic modality or with mathematical certainty less than the degree of mathematical certainty of the proof procedure of the formal system in which the methods are formalized. Both human minds (that have or do not have a computational description) and finitary Gödel-susceptible computing machines can use Gödel-susceptible weak methods. Any EGM or MGM argument that ignores this possibility commits a logical error no less serious than the logical error Penrose commits in his Gödel refutation. On the other hand, if the possibility is taken seriously, then EGM and MGM arguments fail. What can be done? One suggestion is to show all methods of inquiry into the world are Gödel susceptible.

Suppose that we strengthen PGA by claiming that all methods of inquiry into the world, when formalized, are Gödel susceptible. Such methods include inductive methods, demonstrative methods, and methods to which Putnam calls attention: rational interpretation, reasonable reasoning, and general intelligence. This is the form of PGA to which Putnam appeals in *R&R*: "This is analogous to saying the true nature of *rationality*— or at least of human rationality—is given by some 'functional organization', or computational description.... But if the description is a formalization of our powers to reason rationally *in toto*—a description of *all* our means of reasoning—then inability to know something by the 'methods formalized by the description' is inability to know that something *in principle*."[25] The strengthened claim expresses a totalistic ideology. Putnam eschews totalism in all forms, so it is surprising he would embrace it in PGA.

Strengthened PGA claims to show that all inductive methods, all notions of epistemic justification, and all methods of inquiry into the nature of the world are Gödel susceptible. The truth of CON(P) is essential to the correctness of PGA. If we can't prove CON(P), then we can't show that PGA is correct. If we can't prove CON(P), it might be inconsistent, in which case any formula is provable. If that is so, we can't prove that the epistemic notions of 'acceptance' and 'justifies' are Gödel susceptible. CON(P) is the computer program capturing all of our demonstrative and non-demonstrative reasoning—all our methods of inquiry into the world. However, that does not make CON(P) true. I will now argue that strengthened PGA engenders a paradox.

If all the methods that prove CON(P) with less than mathematical certainty or in another epistemic modality are Gödel susceptible, then they are not epistemically adequate for proving CON(P) with less than mathematical certainty. This is so, for under the assumption of strengthened PGA we cannot prove CON(weak method), since it is Gödel susceptible. But if we can't prove CON(P) with less than mathematical certainty or in another epistemic modality, we can't show those weak methods are Gödel susceptible. This is so, since if all methods of inquiry into the world are Gödel susceptible, then any method M_{i-1} that proves CON(M_i) with less than mathematical certainty is itself Gödel susceptible and so CON(M_{i-1}) can't be proved true except by an even weaker method M_{i-2}. But M_{i-2} is Gödel susceptible. This holds for any ordered triple of methods

$\langle M_i, M_{i-1}, M_{i-2} \rangle$. However, if we can't prove CON(P) with any degree of certainty in any epistemic modality licensed by any of the methods of inquiry into the world, then there is no epistemic justification of CON(P). So if all methods of inquiry into the world are Gödel susceptible, then CON(P) cannot have epistemic justification of any kind. That means that PGA fails to show that all methods of inquiry into the world are Gödel susceptible. In that case, we can now use those Gödel-insusceptible weak methods to confer epistemic justification on CON(P). In that case, we have resurrected PGA and have shown that all methods of inquiry into the world are Gödel susceptible. But if this is so, then there is no epistemic justification of CON(P) and thus PGA fails to prove all methods of inquiry into the world are Gödel susceptible. That, then, is the paradox to which strengthened PGA succumbs.

If a formal system is Gödel susceptible, finitary proofs of CON(FORMAL-SYSTEM) in the epistemic modality of the proof procedures available in it are forbidden to all finitary agents that have or do not have a computational description. If formal systems i, j, and k are Gödel susceptible, and the epistemic modalities of the proof procedures for i, j, k are different, then no finitary agents that have or do not have a computational description can prove CON(FS$_i$), CON(FS$_j$), and CON(FS$_k$) in the epistemic modalities of i, j, and k respectively. If these agents want to use FS$_j$ to prove CON(FS$_k$) in the epistemic modality of the proof procedures available in FS$_j$, they must first prove CON(FS$_j$). But they cannot—that is the cold truth of Gödelian incompleteness—prove CON(FS$_j$) in the epistemic modality of the proof procedure available in FS$_j$. They can't prove CON(FS$_j$) in the epistemic modality of the proof procedure available in FS$_i$ either. It is easy to see that they cannot prove CON(FS$_k$) in the epistemic modality of the proof procedures in FS$_k$, nor in epistemic modalities of the proof procedures in FS$_i$ and FS$_j$.

If there are no weak formal systems that are Gödel insusceptible, the reasoning above holds for any triple of formal systems. However, what if we use a stronger formal system FS$_{i+1}$ to prove CON(FS$_i$), where FS$_i$ is a weaker system? The problem is that we now can't prove CON(FS$_{i+1}$) in the epistemic modality of the proof procedures available in FS$_{i+1}$. To prove CON(FS$_{i+1}$), we need a stronger formal system FS$_{i+2}$. However, the very same problem arises for FS$_{i+2}$. We can't prove CON(FS$_{i+2}$) in the epistemic modality of the proof procedures available in FS$_{i+2}$. To prove CON(FS$_{i+2}$), we need a stronger formal system FS$_{i+3}$. But all formal systems extending a formal system that is Gödel susceptible are themselves Gödel susceptible. So we will have to chase formal systems up a transfinite ladder before we can prove the consistency of the transfinitely many formal systems that are lower than the topmost one on the ladder. But no finitary human mind that has or does not have a computational description can do this task.

Let us put the paradox of strengthened PGA more perspicuously. We need to prove CON(P), with less than mathematical certainty, in order to show that all epistemically adequate weak methods that might prove the consistency of a Gödel-susceptible formal system with less than mathematical certainty are themselves Gödel susceptible. But at least one of those methods will be needed to prove CON(P) with less than mathematical certainty. However, if all weak methods are Gödel susceptible, then none of them can be used to prove CON(P) with less than mathematical certainty. But then it has not been shown the weak methods are Gödel susceptible. So they may be used to prove CON(P) with less than mathematical certainty. This secures PGA, which shows all weak methods are Gödel susceptible. In that case, CON(P) has not been epistemically justified. In that case, we have not shown that all weak methods are Gödel susceptible. That is the paradox.

Analysis of Gödel Refutations into Sixteen Cases

We now need to examine all the subcases which fall out of the demarcation of anti-functionalist arguments into

(i) epistemic and metaphysical uses of the Gödel incompleteness theorems—that is, the EGM and MGM arguments,

(ii) Penrose error cases (infeasibly long programs),

and

(iii) showing that some but not all weak inductive methods are Gödel susceptible (PGA) and showing that all methods of inquiry into the world are Gödel susceptible (strengthened PGA).

There are sixteen cases to examine. There are eight cases to examine when PGA or strengthened PGA succeeds. There are an additional eight cases to examine when PGA or strengthened PGA fails. (We contend they both fail.) What is surprising is that even if PGA or strengthened PGA succeeds, the anti-functionalist acquires virtually no advantage over the computational functionalist in mechanism debates. It is important to note that in all sixteen cases we assume that human minds are finitary. That is, no human mind can construct infinite proof trees.

The First Set of Cases: PGA and Strengthened PGA Succeed

A successful PGA shows that some, though not all, weak methods of inquiry into the world, are Gödel susceptible. The first four cases cover a successful PGA. There are two cases for an EGM refutation of mechanism and two cases for an MGM refutation of mechanism. The two cases for each are when the computational description P is short and when it is infeasibly long.

Case i: Recall that EGM arguments assume human minds have a computational description. Suppose that P is short. Since not all weak inductive methods have been shown to be Gödel susceptible, there may be weak methods that prove CON(P) with less than mathematical certainty or in another epistemic modality. If that is so, an EGM argument fails, since it is the point of an EGM argument to show that human minds cannot justify the computational description P of themselves. That is, there isn't a proof of CON(P) that is epistemically justified. But a weak method might provide such a proof.

Case ii: Suppose an EGM argument and that P is infeasibly long. Since not all weak methods have been shown to be Gödel susceptible, use weak methods to perform a statistical analysis to recover the full size of P from the fragments available. Then use weak methods to establish CON(P) with less than mathematical certainty. The EGM argument fails, for the same reasons in case i.

Case iii: Suppose an MGM argument. Recall that MGM arguments assume human minds have no computational description, and argue that human minds are metaphysically different from finitary computing machines, since there are cognitive activities we can perform, that finitary computing machines cannot perform. Suppose that P is perspicuous. Even though human minds have no computational description, we cannot use Gödel-susceptible weak inductive methods to establish CON(P), in the epistemic modality of the proof procedures of the weak methods. We can only use Gödel-insusceptible weak methods to establish CON(P) with less than mathematical certainty or in another epistemic modality. However, finitary computing machines can do the same thing, so we can't establish a metaphysical difference between them and human minds. The MGM argument fails.

Case iv: Suppose an MGM argument and that P is infeasibly long. Even though it is assumed human minds have no computational description, we cannot use the Gödel-susceptible weak inductive methods to do a statistical analysis of the fragments of P and recover P from that analysis and then prove CON(P). We can only use Gödel-insusceptible weak methods to do this. However, so can finitary computing machines. Once again, there is no metaphysical difference which we can establish between them and finitary human minds. The MGM argument fails.

Now let us look at the four cases in which strengthened PGA succeeds. Recall that strengthened PGA shows that all methods of inquiry into the structure of the world are Gödel susceptible. These four cases are analogous to the four cases for PGA.

Case v: Suppose an EGM argument and that P is short. If that is so, then there are no weak methods that can be used to show CON(P). In that case, the EGM argument succeeds, since we have shown that a human mind with a computational description P cannot justify P.

Case vi: Suppose an EGM argument and that P is infeasibly long. Since there are no weak methods available for a statistical analysis of fragments of P to recover P, or for showing CON(P), it follows that the EGM refutation succeeds. We have shown that a human mind with a computational description P cannot justify P.

Case vii: Suppose an MGM argument and that P is short. There are no weak methods that can be used to show CON(P). In that case, even human minds with no computational description will not be able to justify P. However, finitary computing machines cannot do this either. In that case, there is no discernible metaphysical difference between human minds with no computational description and finitary computing machines. Hence, the MGM argument fails.

Case viii: Suppose an MGM argument and that P is infeasibly long. There are no weak methods that can be used to perform a statistical analysis on a fragment of P and recover P, or to show CON(P). In that case, even human minds with no computational description will not be able to justify P. However, finitary computing machines cannot do this either. In that case, there is no discernible difference between human minds with no computational description and finitary computing machines. Hence, the MGM argument fails.

These analyses reveal an interesting truth: All MGM arguments fail, even though either PGA or strengthened PGA succeeds. On the other hand, though EGM arguments fail even where PGA succeeds, EGM arguments succeed where strengthened PGA succeeds. Thus, there is a critical difference between MGM and EGM arguments.

Note that if it is ever shown that human minds are able to construct infinite proof trees, then all MGM arguments will succeed wherever PGA and strengthened PGA succeed. Using the Gödel theorems to refute mechanism by an MGM argument can only succeed if we first know that human minds can construct infinite proof trees. If that cannot be shown, then even though PGA or strengthened PGA succeeds, no MGM argument can succeed.

The Second Set of Cases: PGA and Strengthened PGA Fail
Now let us look at the same kinds of cases under the assumption that PGA and strengthened PGA fail (in the way in which I have argued they fail). Cases ix–xii are where PGA fails. That is, PGA fails to show that some, but not all, weak inductive methods are Gödel susceptible.

Case ix: Suppose an EGM argument and that P is short. Since it has not been shown that any weak methods are Gödel susceptible, all weak methods are available for proving CON(P), with less than mathematical certainty. So a human mind that has a computational description can epistemically justify P. Since there are more weak methods available for proving CON(P) with less than mathematical certainty, and perhaps in stronger epistemic modalities, than there are when PGA succeeds, EGM arguments fail more often than they do when PGA succeeds.

Case x: Suppose an EGM argument and that P is infeasibly long. Since it has not been shown that any weak inductive methods are Gödel susceptible, all weak inductive methods are available for statistically recovering P and proving CON(P). So a human mind that has a computational description can epistemically justify P. Since there are more weak methods available for recovery of P and proof of CON(P), and perhaps in stronger epistemic modalities, than there are when PGA succeeds, EGM arguments fail more often than they do when PGA succeeds.

Case xi: Suppose an MGM argument and that P is short. Although all weak inductive methods are available for proving CON(P) with less than mathematical certainty, all these methods are also available to finitary computing machines. In that case, there is no means of discerning a metaphysical difference between human minds with no computational description and finitary computing machines. MGM arguments fail, but no worse (or no better) than they failed when PGA succeeded.

Case xii: Suppose an MGM argument and that P is infeasibly long. Although all weak inductive methods are available for statistically recovering P and for proving CON(P) with less than mathematical certainty, all these methods are available to the finitary computing machine. In that case, there is no means of discerning a metaphysical difference between human minds with no computational description and finitary computing machines. MGM arguments fail, but no worse (or no better) than they did when PGA succeeded.

Now let us examine the four cases when strengthened PGA fails because of the paradox to which it succumbs. Recall the paradox: We cannot prove CON(P) with less than mathematical certainty, since P encompasses all the epistemically adequate weak methods of inquiry into the world that could prove CON(P) with less than mathematical certainty or in another epistemic modality. However, since we cannot prove CON(P) with less than mathematical certainty or in another epistemic modality, we cannot conclude that all the epistemically weak methods of inquiry into the world which could prove CON(P), with less than mathematical certainty or in another epistemic modality, are Gödel susceptible. But if we cannot prove they are Gödel susceptible, then we can use them to prove CON(P), with less than mathematical certainty or in another epistemic modality. In that case, all these weak methods of inquiry into the world are Gödel susceptible. But then we cannot use them to prove CON(P), with less than mathematical certainty or in another epistemic modality. In that case, we cannot show they are Gödel susceptible, and thus we can use them to prove, with less than mathematical certainty, CON(P). Paradox.

Case xiii: Suppose an EGM argument and that P is short. The reasoning is exactly the same as for case ix. All weak methods are available for proving CON(P) with less than mathematical certainty or in another epistemic modality. So a human mind that has a computational description can epistemically justify P. Since there are more weak methods available for proving CON(P) with less than mathematical certainty, and perhaps in stronger epistemic modalities, than there are when PGA succeeds, EGM arguments fail more often than they do when strengthened PGA succeeds.

Case xiv: Suppose an EGM argument and that P is infeasibly long. The reasoning is exactly the same as it is for case x. All weak methods are available for statistically recovering and proving CON(P) with less than mathematical certainty. So a human mind that has a computational description can epistemically justify P. Since there are more weak methods available for recovery of P and proof of CON(P), and perhaps in stronger epistemic modalities, than there are when PGA succeeds,

EGM arguments fail more often than they do when strengthened PGA succeeds.

Case xv: Suppose a MGM argument and that P is short. The reasoning is exactly the same as it is for case xi. All weak methods are available, for proving CON(P) with less than mathematical certainty or in another epistemic modality, to finitary computing machines and human minds with no computational description. In that case, there is no means of discerning a metaphysical difference between human minds with no computational description and finitary computing machines. MGM arguments fail, but no worse (or no better) than they did when strengthened PGA succeeded.

Case xvi: Suppose a MGM argument and that P is non-perspicuous. The reasoning is exactly the same as it is for case xii. All weak methods are available for statistically recovering P and for proving CON(P), with less than mathematical certainty or in another epistemic modality, to finitary computing machines and human minds with no computational description. In that case, there is no means of discerning a metaphysical difference between human minds with no computational description and finitary computing machines. MGM arguments fail, but no worse (or no better) than they did when strengthened PGA succeeded.

That concludes the exhaustive analysis of cases under PGA and strengthened PGA, where they succeed, and where they fail. Do we have any reason to believe that P will be infeasibly long? At present, we have no such reason. We do not know what ultimate cognitive science will look like, so we do not know, now, whether in ultimate cognitive science the ultimate program P will be infeasibly long. We do not have a theory of feasible computability that will tell us whether programs that have outputs of certain kinds are feasibly short.[26]

Twelve Objections to the Paradox

There are several anti-functionalist objections to the paradox that threatens to destroy PGA and strengthened PGA and thus to destroy EGM and MGM arguments. Here I will enumerate them and respond to them.

Objection 1: Even if P is infeasibly long, human minds, under the assumption that they have no computational description, can empirically justify P, though no finite computing machine (which P formally characterizes) can do so. Since all epistemically adequate weak methods of inquiry into the world—including any that confer empirical justification on CON(P)—are, by PGA, Gödel susceptible, no finite computing machine formally characterized by P can employ those methods to prove, with less than mathematical certainty or in another epistemic modality, CON(P). However, human minds can do that, since statistical methods fall under the weak methods subsumed by P and statistical methods are employed where human minds face resource limitations or do not have all the facts. The burden of proof is on the shoulders of the computational functionalist, to show that for programs greater than length L no statistical method subsumed under P can empirically justify CON(P).

Response: It is true that no finitary computing machine formally characterized by P can use the statistical methods subsumable under P, provided that strengthened PGA succeeds. But finitary human minds, even under the assumption they have no computational description, are similarly forbidden. If all formalized statistical methods are shown by strengthened PGA to be Gödel susceptible, then no finitary human mind can use them to recover P and then prove CON(P).

Objection 2: Finitary human minds—under the assumption they have no computational description—can empirically justify CON(P) by reducing its consistency problem to a consistency problem for a formal system that does not subsume any of the weak methods of inquiry into the world that are subsumed by P. We then use weak methods to prove, with less than mathematical certainty, CON(REDUCING FORMAL SYSTEM) and use the reduction to conclude CON(P).

Response: If P subsumes all methods of inquiry into the world, then any formal system that does not subsume them is probably not a formal system to which P can be reduced. Suppose, for the sake of argument, that it is. Reductive proof theory requires there is a recursive function that maps every proof in the reduced system to a proof in the reducing system. Moreover, this mapping must itself be provable in a formal system that is, in general, included in the reducing system. When these conditions are satisfied, the reducing system will be a conservative extension of the reduced system. There is nothing in the reduced system that cannot be proved in the reducing system and, more important, there is nothing in the language of the reduced system that can be proved in the reducing system, though not proved in the reduced system. In other words, for any proof in PGA of the Gödel susceptibility of any epistemically adequate weak method in P, there will be a corresponding proof of that Gödel susceptibility in the reducing system, whatever is the analogue of the weak method in P.

Objection 3: If P is infeasibly long, it fails as an explanatory theory in cognitive science. Any computational description we cannot follow can't be explanatory for us. Thus, under the assumption that human beings have no computational description, an infeasibly long P secures for anti-functionalists the conclusion that cognitive science is not justified. If a scientific theory has no explanatory value, it loses epistemic justification.

Response: This objection does not advance the anti-functionalist in the mechanism debate. If it turns out that P is infeasibly long, then human beings will never discover it. What we do discover will be an approximation to P that we find explanatory and that is not infeasibly long. The objection which the anti-functionalist just voiced is really a skeptical objection, and it is one which could be voiced in any scientific discipline whatsoever. The anti-physicalists can say that the ultimate theory of physics is super-long and thus has no explanatory value. The same response to the anti-functionalist holds here as well. It is a worry, but it is not a worry that gives the anti-functionalist any advantage, for it is a general skeptical worry.

Objection 4: Let us try to refine the preceding objection. Genuine warranted assertibility and empirical justification have no computational description. These methods, because they are not formalizable, are not Gödel susceptible. Finitary human minds—under the assumption they have no computational description—can use these methods to show CON(P). So there is something a finitary human mind can do that no finitary computing machine can do.

Response: This is a confused objection. How can methods resisting formalization be used to prove the correctness of a formal system?[27] Strengthened PGA shows that all epistemically adequate weak methods are Gödel susceptible. Thus it shows that all epistemically adequate weak methods have no *complete* computational description. But if strengthened PGA fails, it is left open that there are formalizable epistemically adequate weak methods that can prove, with less than mathematical certainty or in another epistemic modality, CON(P). If strengthened PGA fails, then the anti-functionalist must compute the solution to a recursively unsolvable problem, in order to show that there are no epistemically adequate weak methods that are not Gödel susceptible. (Recall the section in chapter 1 proving that result.) The point is that the only way we have of showing that there is no complete computational description of X is by using a Gödelian argument. PGA is a Gödelian argument, but it fails.

Objection 5: The paradox is a travesty of mathematical reasoning. If you are right, then you have shown that the Gödel theorems in their original context—proving the incompleteness of Peano arithmetic—fail to work. You can run your paradox argument on the provability predicate and easily reach the absurd conclusion that there is no unprovable sentence in Peano arithmetic. In that event, you have shown that Gödel is wrong. Since that is too absurd to consider, it must be concluded that you are wrong!

Response: That is an important objection. However, you did not think very clearly about the matter at hand. The provability predicate is not defined by Peano arithmetic. We have independent reasons for believing in its cogency, and we could construct it even if Peano arithmetic did not exist. What we are able to do in Peano arithmetic is arithmetize it and thus employ the diagonal lemma to secure the incompleteness theorems.

The situation is quite different when it comes to program P, the computational description of our methods of inquiry into the world. Recall that in PGA the analogue of the notion of 'proof' for Peano arithmetic is the notion of 'justifies'. However, P defines the notion of justification. If there were no P, there would be no notion of justification. If it turns out that the notion of justification cannot itself be justified— and that is exactly what PGA attempts to show—then we have no coherent notion of justification. If there are truths about justification we are forbidden from justifying, the notion is incoherent. In that case, we can't appeal to the Montague-Kaplan-Thomason axioms for axiomatizing 'justifies' so that it can meaningfully satisfy the Gödel diagonal lemma, since we have no reason to think that these axioms applied to 'justifies' are true. On the other hand, we do have independent reasons for thinking that the Hilbert derivability conditions for the provability predicate are true, independent of the question of the consistency of Peano arithmetic.

Objection 6: You cannot be serious that human minds with no computational description have no epistemic advantages over finitary computing machines. Can't a human mind with no computational description survey an infeasibly long P? If not, then what could possibly be the difference between the human minds and finitary computing machines? Are you proposing that they are identical?

Response: No, I am not. But just because a human mind has no computational description does not entail it is able to construct infinite proof trees or that it has the resources to survey an infeasibly long P. So finitary human minds that have no computational description appear not to have epistemic advantages over finitary computing machines. Even infinitary agents cannot prove the consistency of Peano arithmetic using a finitary and effective proof, since finitary and effective proofs of it are prohibited by Gödel's theorems. If all weak methods for proving CON(PA) are Gödel susceptible, then an agent with an infinitary mind can only employ an infinitary method to prove CON(PA). In that case, the anti-functionalist must demonstrate that human minds are infinitary or give up the view that there is an epistemic difference between finitary human minds that have no computational description and finitary computing machines governed by P. If finitary human minds, under the assumption they have no computational description, prove CON(P) with less than mathematical certainty, by Gödel-insusceptible weak methods, they are not distinguishable from finitary computing machines that can similarly employ those methods to prove CON(P) with less than mathematical certainty. If those weak methods are Gödel susceptible, then neither the human mind that has no computational description nor the finitary computing machine can prove CON(P) in the characteristic epistemic modality of the proof procedures of the formal system that formalizes the weak method. The anti-functionalist wants to prove that all weak methods which could, under some standard of epistemic adequacy, prove CON(P), with less than mathematical certainty, are Gödel susceptible. Yet this task is just what engenders the paradox. If all weak methods which could, under some standard of epistemic adequacy, prove CON(P) with less than mathematical certainty, are Gödel susceptible, then they cannot be used to prove CON(P), even by finitary minds that have no computational description. This is so, because whatever the epistemic modality of the proof of CON(P), no agent, no matter what its computational structure, can prove CON(P) in that epistemic modality.

Objection 7: An epistemic use of the Gödel theorems does, in fact, render a metaphysical conclusion. It shows that the cognitive structure of the human mind is Gödel susceptible. That, in turn, shows that we cannot be metaphysically distinguished from finitary computing machines.

Response: However, that is a moot conclusion, since the anti-functionalist who employs an EGM argument proceeds from the assumption that the human mind has a computational description. That is, she proceeds from the adoption of the metaphysical picture of the human kind as a finitary computing machine. The Gödel theorems tell us about the limitations faced by such computational descriptions, but the basic metaphysics is already in place. In EGM arguments we don't conclude to a metaphysical conclusion, as we do in MGM arguments.

Objection 8: That the anti-functionalist falls into a paradox in escaping from the simple logical error of Penrose is a clever observation, but it is false. We do not say that a paradox arises out of the Gödel susceptibility of Peano arithmetic. A formal system strong enough to carry out (minimally Robinson) arithmetic is one for which we cannot, with mathematical certainty, employing a finitistic and effective proof procedure, prove its consistency. However, that we cannot is not license for us to infer that the very Gödel susceptibility is in doubt. That is absurd. It is too easy a move, if it is valid. Certainly, we would have encountered someone in mathematics making it long ago. But no one did, because it is nothing short of being numbingly stupid.

Response: You are quite right about Peano arithmetic. No paradox—of the kind I have specified—arises, and it would be numbingly stupid to claim one does. However, the epistemic situation with respect to Peano arithmetic and with respect to P is quite different. There is probably not a single mathematician who genuinely doubts the consistency of Peano arithmetic. There are infinitary proofs of it—Gentzen discovered one in 1936, and Ackermann polished it up in 1940. Although human beings cannot construct infinitary proof trees, mathematicians believe that the Gentzen proof works. We have, then, no reason to believe that the Gödel results fail to hold of a formal system that encompasses Peano arithmetic. There is no paradox, even though we cannot prove, with mathematical certainty, using a finitistic and effective proof procedure, the consistency of Peano arithmetic. From that we do not conclude that Peano arithmetic might be inconsistent.

The epistemic situation is much different with respect to P. This is a computational description based on a cognitive theory, an ultimate one at that. We do not have the same intuitions about its consistency that we have about the consistency of Peano arithmetic, for we do not even have the cognitive theory that underlies P. It is a suppositional device to carry out the anti-functionalist argument. Nor, for the same reasons, do we have an infinitary proof of CON(P). If P encompasses all finitary methods of inquiry into the world, and we show that all these methods are Gödel susceptible, then we have no methods left with which to carry out the consistency proof of P, other than infinitary ones. We cannot, however, say that we have good reason to believe that P is consistent, since we have no idea what it will look like and, even if we did, it is still based on a cognitive theory which has to be tested. If we cannot test it, because all our procedures for testing it are Gödel susceptible, we are in an epistemic situation of maximal ignorance. We have no good reason to believe it is consistent and no good reason to believe it is inconsistent. In that epistemic situation, we cannot accept the results about the Gödel susceptibility of all epistemic methods of inquiry. But, in that case, the way is open to use those very methods to establish the consistency of P, with less than mathematical certainty. That, however, shows we should not have used those methods to do that, since proving the consistency of P also proves the Gödel susceptibility of those very methods. Thus, a paradox arises, and it can not be readily dismissed by comparing it with the disanalogous epistemic situation in Peano arithmetic. It is, then, a genuine epistemic problem for the anti-functionalist.

Objection 9: You mistakenly think that since PGA and strengthened PGA incur paradox, it is left open for the finitary human minds that have no computational description and finitary computing machines to use any weak methods of empirical inquiry into the structure of the world. The paradox does not entitle the agent to use all weak methods. Given there is a paradox, the methods which escape Gödel susceptibility because of the paradox cannot be used by an agent. Just as a paradoxical sentence can't be assumed true, agents can't assume weak methods escaping Gödel susceptibility are thereby legitimate to use.

Response: That is a perceptive point, but it is misguided. The analogy with Liar sentences is not acceptable. Once we show a Liar sentence is paradoxical, we cannot assume it is true, nor can we assume that it is false. In some truth theories, we withhold assignment of a truth-value to it, in which case it has a null functional status in our discourses. On the other hand, showing that PGA and strengthened PGA incurs a paradox simply shows that we cannot assume that there are truths secured by the weak methods that cannot be proved within P in the epistemic modality of the weak method. Consider an analogy with Peano arithmetic. If there were no such thing as the Gödel theorems, it would be left open for us to prove, within the formal system of Peano arithmetic, CON(PEANO ARITHMETIC), and all the truths of Peano arithmetic. Showing that PGA and strengthened PGA incur paradox is to show that the Gödel phenomena do not arise for P. That is little different from claming that there is no such thing as the Gödel theorems for P.

Objection 10: Any intuitions about the correctness of P must be seen as evidence for the claim that we have infinitary capacities. We would not have those intuitions unless there is some infinitary reasoning process, below the threshold of conscious perception, which accounts for them. The best explanation of why we have these intuitions is that there is some infinitary reasoning mechanism which causes us to have them. Thus, even though there is a paradox for the anti-functionalist who wants to show all weak methods are Gödel susceptible, the intuitions we would (since P does not yet exist—it is merely a hypothetical construct) have about the correctness of P are reliable indicators of our infinitary capacities. The paradox is no hindrance to the anti-functionalist, since human minds are infinitary and we do not even need PGA.

Response: If we do have intuitions that P is consistent, and we set a probability level for the reliability of those intuitions higher than the reliability we would—in probabilistic terms—rate the weak methods for showing P is correct, with less than mathematical certainty, *and* we know that there are no other weak methods available *and* that only infinitary methods can prove the correctness of P with mathematical certainty, what can we reasonably conclude about the nature of our cognitive capacities? We can't reasonably conclude that we have infinitary cognitive capacities. It would be the case that the best explanation of our intuitions is that an infinitary reasoning mechanism causes us to have them if we had no alternative explanations of them. But we have alternative explanations of how we have such intuitions, and these explanations do not posit infinitary reasoning processes. We have experiences with cognitive theories of inductive reasoning, and we see an analogy between them and P. If they are known to be correct, we conclude that it is also highly likely that P is correct. We might, also, be simply mistaken. Our probabilistic intuitions are notoriously shaky, a fact well known to cognitive psychologists. In that case, the best explanation for our intuitions is that we have made errors in probabilistic reasoning. If we had independent evidence the mind performs infinitary operations, then the explanation of our intuitions about the correctness of P in terms of infinitary operations would be superior to the two alternatives we have just cited. But, in the absence of that evidence, the two alternatives are superior to it, since they are sensitive to established work in cognitive psychology.

Objection 11: We can use the Gödel incompleteness theorems to show that there are capacities which human minds have that finitary computing machines do not have. Let the formal system characterizing the capacities of a finitary computing machine be F. Suppose that F is Gödel susceptible. Then the finitary computing machine can't prove CON(F) and cannot prove its own Gödel sentence. However, a human mind *can* prove CON(F) and the Gödel sentence in F by ascending to a more powerful formal system, F*, that contains F. The finitary computing machine, however, cannot ascend to F*.

Response: That point is well known in the mechanism debate. Perhaps ascent to F* may prove futile, since F* may be so long that finitary human minds cannot survey it and thus cannot prove that it is consistent. That is the Penrose error. But even if we discount the Penrose error, there is still a problem. Recall that what the second Gödel incompleteness theorem rules out is the possibility of proving, with mathematical certainty, and within the system F, CON(F). If one ascends to F*, then CON(F) can be proved with mathematical certainty, period. However, this is true only if one can prove, with mathematical certainty, that F* is consistent. But now the Gödel theorems take root in F*. It is impossible to prove CON(F*) with mathematical certainty, within F*. That means that the ascent to F* is futile unless F* can be proved consistent. But that cannot be done within F*. It can only be done by ascending to a stronger system F** that contains both F and F*. Within F**, one can prove CON(F) and CON(F*) with mathematical certainty, but only if F** is consistent. Notice the epistemic pattern that emerges. For any n less than ω, one can prove with mathematical certainty $CON(F^n)$ in the formal system F^{n+1} only if one can prove, with mathematical certainty, $CON(F^{n+1})$. However, for any n less than ω, it is impossible to prove $CON(F^n)$ with mathematical certainty within F^n. The anti-mechanist will have to ascend infinitely high to the infinitary formal system F^ω, in order to prove, with mathematical certainty, CON(F). That is just to say that the anti-mechanist will have to possess the cognitive capacity to construct an infinite proof tree in order to prove, with mathematical certainty, CON(F). Indeed, this is true for any F^n, where n is less than ω. It easily follows from these considerations that the anti-mechanist has no advantage over the mechanist in showing that there are cognitive capacities which finitary human minds possess, but which a finitary computing machine lacks. If human minds possess an infinitary cognitive capacity, there is something we possess that finitary computing machines lack. But there is absolutely no evidence that we possesses an infinitary cognitive capacity. It is open to us to prove CON(F) with less than mathematical certainty or in another epistemic modality, but it is also open to finitary computing machines to do the same. If the method for proving CON(F) with less than mathematical certainty is Gödel susceptible, then the very same considerations expressed above will apply to this case also. In that case, the anti-mechanist has no advantage over the mechanist in showing there is a cognitive capacity which finitary human minds possesses that finitary computing machines lack.

Objection 12: The anti-functionalist using an MGM argument has an avenue of escape. Although there cannot be a finitary proof within P that establishes, with mathematical certainty, CON(P), it is possible for a human mind (not susceptible to the Gödel theorems) to prove CON(P), with mathematical certainty, by using mathematical reasoning that absolutely resists Gödelization.

Response: That is a clever objection, but it does not work. If the mathematical reasoning in question is captured by a formal system that absolutely resists Gödelization, it will be too weak to establish CON(P) with mathematical certainty. On the other hand, if there is a system of mathematical reasoning which absolutely resists Gödelization only because it absolutely resists formalization, it is not apparent that there is such a system of mathematical reasoning. There are systems of mathematical reasoning that are captured only by infinitary formal systems (such as the system in Turing's completeness theorem), that resist Gödelization. But there is no psychological evidence human agents can engage in infinitary reasoning, where proper infinitary reasoning implies the ability of the reasoner to construct infinitary proof trees. This will not help the anti-functionalist who uses an MGM argument. Is there finitary mathematical reasoning that resists formalization? We do not know of any such reasoning. If the reasoning is legitimate, then it can be explicitly described and, as such, can be formalized. In that case, either it is too weak to prove CON(P) with mathematical certainty or, if it can prove CON(P) with mathematical certainty, it is Gödel susceptible and thus of no use to the anti-functionalist. The moral, then, is that the anti-functionalist can dream of a system of finitary mathematical reasoning which can prove CON(P) with mathematical certainty, and which absolutely resists both formalization and Gödelization. But we have no reason to believe such a system of mathematical reasoning exists, or even that it is logically possible.

Failure of PGA Defuses a Central Plank of *R&R*

Putnam asserts that his use of the Gödel incompleteness theorems in fashioning EGM and MGM is merely an analogy. On page 118 of *R&R* he writes:

My purpose in [describing the EGM and MGM arguments] here, is *not* to suggest that one can give a formal ("Gödelian") argument to show that "functionalism doesn't work." The analogy I have in mind isn't a mathematical one. But notice what underlies these well-known Gödelian arguments. What Gödel showed is, so to speak, that we cannot fully formalize our own mathematical capacity *because it is part of that mathematical capacity itself that it can go beyond whatever it can formalize.* Similarly, my extension of the Gödelian techniques to inductive logic showed that it is part of the notion of justification in general (not just our notion of *mathematical* justification) that *reason can go beyond whatever reason can formalize.*[28]

This excerpt needs a gloss. We cannot go beyond what reason can formalize, if the reasoning that goes beyond what reason can formalize is in the epistemic modality of mathematical certainty. But we can go beyond what reason can formalize if the epistemic modality of that reasoning that goes beyond what reason can formalize is with less than mathematical certainty or is an epistemic modality other than mathematical certainty.[29]

Putnam claims that computational functionalism is a scientific realist program and that all scientific realist programs face insuperable problems: one is epistemological and the other is ontological. "Scientific realism," he writes,

faces [epistemological] difficulties ... the epistemological difficulties can be brought out with the aid of the following analogy.... Consider the ordinary notion of mathematical proof. This is not at all the same as the notion of proof in a formal system.... A proof in the ordinary sense (a proof humanly speaking) is a proof in a system which is not just sound, but which a mathematician could, upon reflection, *see* to be sound, one which a reasonable mathematician would be justified in accepting. "Proof" is an *epistemic* notion, not a mathematical one. Can this notion of proof be formalized?... If there does exist a sound system that does formalize this notion of proof ... then *that* system *as a whole* is *not* one that a mathematician could, upon reflection, *see* to be sound![30]

I have argued that PGA fails, and that it is PGA that is used to secure the claim made in the last sentence of the previously quoted passage. Unless Putnam can resuscitate PGA, his EGM and MGM arguments fail. In that case, the view that computational functionalism is a scientific realist doctrine fails. As we will see, Putnam thinks scientific realism is committed to metaphysical realism, that metaphysical realism is presupposed by Quinean indeterminacy and ontological relativity and that radical Quinean meaning holism is a consequence of Quinean indeterminacy. If PGA fails, then the view that computational functionalism is a scientific realist doctrine must be reevaluated, if not given up.

The Epistemology of Mathematical Certainty: A New Project for Philosophy of Mind

Mathematical arguments formalized within a logic whose method of proof is effective and finitary prove their conclusions with mathematical certainty. There is no room for doubt as to the truth of a conclusion if it is known that its premises are true. This kind of mathematical demonstration is conclusive demonstration. How do we know that the conclusion follows from the premises with mathematical certainty? We need a mechanical procedure that can determine whether each line in a proof legitimately follows from preceding lines, we need proof that the rules of inference that are the basis of such procedures preserve truth, and we need a guarantee that the premises (or axioms) are true.

If the inference procedure is not mechanical, then we will not know whether it secures intersubjective agreement (even among "normal" participants). Turing fleshed out the notion of "mechanical procedure" in a Turing-machine construction. The procedure cannot require use of original thought, insight or genius, to be applicable to verifying that a proof proves its conclusion with mathematical certainty.

Determining that an arbitrary mathematical sentence is true is beyond the capacity of a mechanical procedure, since the set of mathematical truths is not recursive, not recursively enumerable, and indeed not even definable in arithmetic. This is another reason why mechanical procedures that verify a proof of a theorem in mathematics must be mechanical. If we attempt to show that each line in a proof preserves truth by showing that each line in the proof is true in and of itself and without examining how it was obtained, there is no guarantee we will be able to complete the job of verifying the proof of the theorem (even if we have the time and resources). On the other hand, if the proof verification procedure is mechanical, then we do not check that each line of the proof is true. Rather, we check that it has the requisite syntactical form. The relation "p is a proof of α," where α is a sentence in some language and p is a proof of that sentence, is recursive. It follows that all the theorems in that language are recursively enumerable. There is a fundamental dichotomy between proof and truth arising from these considerations. Mathematical truth is not recursively enumerable, while mathematical provability is recursively enumerable. One way of describing the Gödelian incompleteness phenomena is that they witness this dichotomy.

If we relax the standards of mathematical proof, we cannot be sure that we will be mathematically certain of the truth of the theorem derived. In that case, we cannot be sure that intersubjective agreement can be reached as to whether a derivation is a legitimate proof of its conclusion. It is the epistemological requirement in mathematics that a proof establish with absolute certainty the truth of its conclusion that allows the anti-functionalist to capitalize on the Gödelian incompleteness theorems in EGM and MGM arguments. So relaxing this requirement in mathematics is relevant to the philosophy of mind. What is the epistemic goodness of weak mathematical methods—those that do not confer mathematical certainty on what they establish? Methods of mathematical proof which are not mathematically certain, but which are epistemically acceptable, is a subject we need to take seriously. The work comes in showing that a proof of a theorem with less than mathematical certainty secures epistemic justification. Philosophical work on the epistemology of the four-color theorem in the early 1980s ushered in such a program. We should examine the epistemological status of probabilistic proofs of mathematical theorems. We should ask questions about the epistemic reliability of proofs of consistency of computational programs with less than mathematical certainty. We should look at the epistemology of proofs, in mathematical logic, that establish their conclusions with less than mathematical certainty.

3   Universal Realization of Computation: Putnam's Triviality Argument

Triviality arguments fashioned by anti-functionalists are a thorn in the side to computationalists in the philosophy of mind and to cognitive science. The principal idea underlying a triviality argument is that any definition of what it is for a physical system to physically realize a computation will, for any computation, be applicable to any physical system. In effect, any object computes any function. This trivializes cognitive science. There is no need to test a theory in cognitive science, if the mind computes every cognitive function. All cognitive theories posit that the human mind computes a specific set of cognitive functions. If the human mind computes every cognitive function, then each cognitive theory must be true, even cognitive theories that contradict one another. Similarly, if any object computes every function, then any object physically realizes every functional organization. In that case, every object will have the functional organization of the human mind, from which it follows that panpsychism is true. Triviality arguments, invented in the mid 1960s, have not been satisfactorily refuted.

My view is that triviality theories can be decisively refuted. I employ a method of refutation which is obvious, but which has not been previously considered in the literature. To see what the method of refutation consists in, consider an analogy with a numeral system. Numerals are used to represent numbers, which are abstract objects. We want our numeral systems for the arithmetic of whole numbers to reflect all the arithmetical properties of the abstract objects that are whole numbers. If addition of whole numbers is non-commutative in a proposed numeral system, we must reject it, since it violates a basic law of arithmetic.

Similarly, a definition of what it is for a physical system to physically realize a computation must respect both the laws of computability theory and the laws of computational complexity theory. If it turns out that a physical system can compute an EXPTIME problem in constant time, the claim that the physical system is engaged in computation must be rejected, since it is a law of computation that EXPTIME problems cannot be computed in constant time. This method of refutation already shows that not every physical object can compute every function. It rules out arrangements of individuals and properties that violate the laws of computability theory or the laws of computational complexity theory.

How can we be sure that the laws of computability theory and computational complexity theory are satisfied by a definition of what it is for a physical system to realize a computation? If there is a structural correspondence between the physical system and the computation, the laws are respected. Not any correspondence will do. A correspondence that preserves laws will not do, since it is possible that the physical system possesses additional structure not mapped to the computation that allows for trivial universal computational realization. What we require is that the structure of the computation is reflected in the structure of the physical system and that the structure of the physical system is reflected in the structure of the computation. When these two conditions are satisfied, the computational laws are invariant. Chalmers proposed the notion of an isomorphism for the correspondence, but that is too strong, since it makes any two isomorphic structures mathematically equivalent. We want a correspondence that makes all and only the laws of computation invariant. My conjecture is that when we have found such a natural mapping, any physical system that satisfies it will be one that we intuitively take to compute a function and that trivial computations can't arise.

Because definitions of what it is for a physical system to realize a computation proposed by trivialists are so austere, there is almost no room within them for a theory of error. It makes sense only in certain contexts, on a trivialist definition of what it is for an object to realize a computation, to say the physical system made a mistake in a computation. A consequence of this is that a Kripke-Wittgenstein problem arises in formulating a triviality thesis. One might think that a Kripke-Wittgenstein problem cannot arise if there is no natural account of what it is to make an error in computation. However, the problem arises in a special way.

If a physical system enters a recurrent physical state, trivialists encounter a difficulty. They do not want it to be the case that identical physical states issue in distinct computational states. If that is so, trivialists must watch for recurrent physical states. It may not be possible to determine ahead of time whether one arrives. For instance, a physical system may engage in unpredictable chaotic behavior. If the physical system enters a recurrent physical state, it computes the function F^*. If not, it computes the function F. Which function it computes cannot be determined ahead of time. F^* is the error or non-standard trivial computation and F is the "intended" trivial computation. We will not be able to decide ahead of time whether the physical system computes F or F*. Trivialists have no other notion of what it is to make an error in a computation, so they cannot appeal to an error theory to decide, ahead of time, what function the physical system trivially computes.

In the next chapter, I define a new kind of triviality argument, not known in the literature. I name it 'step-function triviality' and show that it violates laws of algorithmic information theory, a mathematical variant of computational complexity theory. I also show that Searle's metaphysics of computation, when conjoined with mathematical facts, leads to absurdities. Showing that the metaphysical picture underlying triviality arguments is false is important because, once specific triviality arguments have been shown to violate computability laws, the trivialist cannot appeal to that picture to argue that there still might be a triviality argument out there.

The Power of Triviality Claims in Putnam's Refutation of Computational Functionalism

Although almost all of Putnam's discussion of triviality arguments is confined to the appendix to *Representation and Reality*, his motivation for and use of triviality arguments is given full voice in the preface to that work. Here is what Putnam says about the connection between MGM and EGM arguments (Gödel-style arguments) and the triviality theorems:

[Some] philosopher might say, "Even so there is such a description [a computational description of all of our powers of reasoning]. It doesn't matter that we can't tell which one it is.

The difficulty with this claim, and with all such claims, is not that physically possible organisms don't have functional organizations, but that they have *too many*. A theorem [the triviality theorem] ... shows that there is a sense in which *everything has every functional organization*. When we are correctly described by an infinity of logically possible "functional descriptions," then what is the claim supposed to *mean* that one of these has the (unrecognizable) property of being our "normative" description? Is it supposed to describe, in some way, our very *essence*?[1]

This is a very powerful statement of how a triviality argument works in tandem with MGM and EGM arguments. In the literature, no one proposed anything like it before Putnam. If we suppose that Putnam's EGM and MGM arguments succeed, we can conclude that we can never know, with mathematical certainty or with less than mathematical certainty, by an epistemically acceptable method of inquiry, the true computational description of our cognitive mind. If that is true, in principle it is an impediment to justifying cognitive psychology (viewed as the science that provides computational descriptions of the cognitive mind). Suppose that a cognitive psychologist who wishes to continue practicing her science responds that there might be such a description, even though we cannot know which one it is. Putnam can now use the triviality theorem to drain that response of all its potency.

Triviality arguments attempt to show that every object has every possible functional organization. Another way of making the point is to say that every object can compute every computable function. (Even stronger claims are possible—e.g., that every object can compute every computable or non-computable function, or that every space-time region of non-negligible measure can compute every function.) The range of "everything" is not restricted to physical objects. It can include events, processes, states of affairs, regions of space-time, and even propositions (by coding their relations to other propositions).

How could we tell which functional organization best describes us when there are infinitely many to choose from, all of which might describe us, and we also know that the one exactly true computational description cannot be epistemically justified as being true? This situation is far worse than underdetermination of theory by data. In facing underdetermination claims in the philosophy of science and language, we can at least take solace in supposing that there is one best theory—one true theory. We then impose constraints of various sorts on the range of theories that fit the available data. Simplicity and conservatism are designed to winnow the space of theories that are compatible with the data. If we knew in advance that there are no constraints that can winnow the space of alternative theories compatible with the data, because we knew there was an in principle limitation in us to discover the one true theory, we would have to acquiesce to inductive skepticism.

If we know we can never converge to the one true theory that provides a computational description of our cognitive life and we also know that there are infinitely many alternative theories of our cognitive life, all of which are compatible with the available data, it is meaningless to say there is a computational description that is our essence. Even if we had all available data, we would still be in the same situation. Though Putnam does not say so, this is extraordinarily like Quinean indeterminacy: not mere underdetermination of theory by data, but underdetermination of theory by all possible data. There is this difference, though. In the case of Quinean indeterminacy, we cannot say of any given translation scheme that it is the true scheme, because all are equally acceptable in the limit of data acquisition. In Putnam's argument, there is one true theory, but it is epistemically shielded off from us, forever. Among all the other alternative computational descriptions, there is an indeterminacy-like situation: each one is just as acceptable as each other one.

If we view indeterminacy as a form of Kripke-Wittgenstein paradox,[2] Putnam's argument transposed to the Kripke-Wittgenstein paradox makes the startling claim that there is no viable conventionalist solution to the skeptical problem. The reason why no conventionalist solution will work is that we know, antecedently, that there is one true state of affairs. Although we cannot know which one it is, we do know that the convention we adopt has a negligibly small probability of being that computational description and that we will never be able to verify that it is the one true state of affairs. Using PGA and his triviality theorem, Putnam has posed a real and deep difficulty for the computationalist. This difficulty might be taken to be the sharpest form of skepticism ever formulated. It claims there are infinitely many alternative hypotheses to the one true hypothesis of our computational makeup. Each of these infinitely many alternative hypotheses is false. We can prove with mathematical certainty that we can epistemically justify only the false hypotheses and that we cannot epistemically justify the one true hypothesis. Moreover, we cannot know with mathematical certainty (and we know this with mathematical certainty) which hypothesis is the one true hypothesis. If we cannot epistemically justify, say, H_i, that does not mean that it is the one true hypothesis, since among the infinitely many false hypotheses there are many (perhaps infinitely many) that we will not epistemically justify. The one true hypothesis is, then, epistemically indistinguishable from the class consisting of the infinitely many false hypotheses.

In summary, the conjunction of a triviality argument and Gödel-style theorems yields a precise and powerful form of skepticism. If that conjunction is demolished, however, the skeptical threat vanishes with it. In the previous chapter, I argued that Putnam's use of the Gödelian theorems to refute mechanism—his PGA argument—fails. In this chapter I argue that Putnam's formulation of a triviality theorem fails. The logical conjunction of two doctrines that fail does not yield a doctrine that succeeds.

Formulating Triviality Arguments

It is important to take a look at how a triviality claim is properly formulated, since not every formulation of a triviality claim will be proper—that is, will accomplish the goal of a triviality claim, which is to show that every physical system realizes every computational description (or functional organization). It is important that the notions of "state of a computation" and "physical state of a physical system" are given precise renderings. It is easy to see that unless these terms are defined precisely it can be stipulated that the object has particular computational states without having to make any assumptions or claims about the physical state of the physical system other than the almost vacuous claims that the physical system will exist within some temporal interval (to be specified) and that the physical system satisfy any arbitrary description of some kind during that time period. The first condition is almost vacuous, since we do not want to say that a non-existent object computes some function. (In quantum computation, a counterfactual computation can occur when a quantum computer is not physically engaged in making a computation. This is quite different from there being no quantum computer—and thus no computations.)

It is necessary to define what it is for a physical system to realize a computation. This is the heart of the matter. Triviality theorists believe it is the ineliminable looseness of the definition of what it is to realize a computation that drives triviality claims. Suppose that a chair is defined as any physical object that can support a person who is located on top of it. This definition is too loose, for it includes many physical objects that are not chairs (hills, houses, tables, and so on). The definition must be revised to eliminate what are not chairs and to include only what are chairs. Advocates of triviality claims think the definition of what it is for a physical system to physically realize a computation cannot be revised so that trivial computations are excluded. But they have not provided an argument that revisions that exclude trivial computations are impossible.

Let us borrow from Edward Stabler a definition of what it is for a physical system to realize a computation[3]:

[We] can say that a physical system computes a function F if, and only if,

(1)a. there is an 'interpretation' or 'realization' function I from a set S of physical states of the system onto the union of the domain and range of F, such that

(1)b. physical laws guarantee that (in certain specifiable circumstances) if the system is in a state i in S, then the system will go into the state f such that $I(f) = F(I(i))$.

The idea here is simply that when we look at the way the system changes state in certain circumstances under the specified interpretation, the change of state corresponds exactly to the mapping F.[4]

If the only conditions the physical system must satisfy is that it exists during a temporal interval $[T_i, T_j]$, where $j > i$, and that it satisfies (by virtue of obeying some physical law(s) a description D that describes a physically possible property, state of affairs, event, process, ... of the physical system, it is simple to define a correspondence between physical states of the system and computational states in the computation of a function F. Stabler defines the correspondence as follows: assume a set of infinitely many times $T_0, T_1, \ldots$ and a description D, the physical system satisfies during some or all of those times. All of the computational states it realizes can then be defined by the following schema, which will be called COMP:

PHYSYS is in computational state S_i if and only if PHYSYS satisfies D and it is time T_i.[5]

With this in place, any function F can be defined by the following schema, which will be called TRIV:

$$I(S_i) = \begin{cases} i/2 & \text{if } T_i \text{ is zero or even} \\ F((i-1)/2) & \text{otherwise.} \end{cases}$$

Let the computation begin at 2i, where i specifies some natural number. For $i = 2$, it is 4. At time $2i + 1$, the physical system computes the range value of the function F. For $i = 2$, $2i + 1 = 5$, so $F((5-1)/2) = F(4/2) = F(2)$, where 'F(2)' names the range value of F for the input (or domain) value 2. The mathematical description of F is not necessary here. The interpretation function I does all the work. It uses the name of F without providing constraints on how F is actually computed by the physical system. The interpretation function merely says that the range value of F corresponds to the physical state of the physical system at time T_i, given by D.

The physical system realizes the domain value of F at time i and realizes, or "computes," the range value of F at time $i + 1$.[6] An interesting property of the physical system when it computes the values of F is that it only computes the range values at odd times and only realizes domain values at even times. This imposes an order on the computation of function values that has no known analogue in nature.[7] (But this property can be changed by stipulating a change in TRIV. The revised TRIV is more complicated than the original TRIV.) If we allow that the physical system is physically continuous, we can define a temporal interval using real numbers. In this way, a physical system can totally compute F even for temporal intervals of width one second (since there are infinitely many reals in the closed interval between 0 and 1).

The correspondence between computational states and physical states expresses our primary intuition about what it is to compute a function: that physical systems compute F by physically realizing the computational states necessary to compute it. Although Stabler's definition does not allow for internal states of the computation—there are just the input and output states of the function (or the initial and final states of the computation)—it does satisfy the core intuition. Let us call the above definition of what it is to compute a function 'S-triviality', for 'Stabler-triviality'.

There are serious omissions in S-triviality. First, S-triviality nowhere mathematically defines F. Computational states the physical system realizes either name domain or range values of F.[8] Second, there is no description of the computational model in which F is computed. In a computational model for computing F, there is a set of computational states, each one of which is a stage in its computation. The final state is a description of the range value of F given a particular domain value. By leaving out the sequence of computational states a computation passes through in computing a value of F, S-trivial computations appear not to be true computations.

It is easy to see that looseness in specifying I in TRIV drives the triviality claim. It is less easy to see whether the looseness can be eliminated. I is like a black box: we cannot see what it does with the domain values of the function it computes. Moreover, there is no connection between the physical states S and the computational states $I(S_i)$, as well as no connection between the description D the physical states satisfy and the computational states. Any arbitrary physical state S satisfying D can physically realize any computational state $I(S_i)$. How can this happen? The function F computed by the physical system appears in the right-hand side of the definition of TRIV and the physical states appear in the left-hand side and it is I that produces the correspondence between the two. The question is whether the correspondence that I produces is one that is genuine. It is an austere correspondence, since the only constraint on it is that D is satisfied. But since there is no connection between D and what is computed, it is a constraint that does no work in defining the class of genuine computations.

In effect, the correspondences that are generated by the schema TRIV are mere stipulations that physical state S computes $I(S_i)$ at time i. Who is the author of them? It is the observer who applies TRIV to a physical system. But—and this is an important point—it does not follow that all correspondences generated by applying TRIV to specific physical systems are observer generated (that is, observer relative). It might be that there are genuine correspondences that pick out genuine computations realized by a physical system. Recall the analogy of S-triviality with a loose definition of 'chair'. That definition picks out both genuine chairs and non-chairs. Similarly, S-triviality picks out correspondences that are genuine and ones that are trivial because they are observer relative, stipulated to be computations by the observer. (John Searle thinks all computations are observer relative.[9]) It is a mistake to argue that all computations are observer relative follows from S-triviality (or any other definition of triviality). Looseness in defining correspondence does not imply the metaphysics of computations is that they are observer relative. If they are, it must be argued independent of giving a triviality definition of what it is for a physical system to physically realize a computation.

One might think that a principal desideratum on the definition of physically realizing a computation is to exclude all correspondences that are stipulations by observers. This is too strong, though. A conventional digital computer designed by a human being works properly when the physical states of the system are stipulated to be computations by its designer. A digital computer that falls out of the sky computes nothing until we know the intentions of its designer.

The looseness of S-triviality also creates new problems for trivialists.[10] They can neither say when a trivial computation is in error or formulate a theory of error for them. If computations are physically realized in physical states of the world and it is contingent what physical states the world manifests, then it is a natural idea that causal disturbances or malfunctions in physical states create error conditions for the physical realization of a computation.[11] If on a definition of what it is to physically realize a computation, errors in the computation of F are impossible, the definition is seriously defective. How, then, can the trivialist acknowledge the possibility of error?

Since the correspondence between a physical state and a computational state specifies for each computational state what physical state physically realizes it, there is no means available to say that an error has occurred in computing values of F. If at t_i physical state S does not occur, but physical state S^* does occur, then $I(S^*i)$ is computed, not $I(S_i)$. This is not an error in the computation of F, if $I(S_i^*)$ is in its range. If $I(S_i^*)$ is not in its range, then it is in the range of a different function F^*. But this is not an error in which function is computed. Rather, it is that a different function is computed at t_i because a different physical state occurs at t_i.

If the physical state S fails to satisfy D at t_i, it is not an error in the computation of $I(S_i)$. Rather, the definition of what it is for the physical system to realize a computation as applied to the physical state S at t_i and the function F no longer applies. If we want a definition of what it is for a physical system to physically realize a computation to express the conditions under which an error in the computation occurs, there must be constraints that reveal how malfunctions or disturbances in the physical process cause computational states that are not part of the computation of F. But the incorporation of such constraints into the definition of I in TRIV is to open the black box (that is, I).

Trivialists can define a new set of error correspondences without having to open the black box. Call interpretation functions that produce error correspondences I^E. Since the nature of the physical malfunction or causal disturbance is left unspecified in I^E, trivialists will not have to distinguish between different kinds of error conditions. So long as the trivialist keeps track of the physical states that physically realize values of F and does not also make the same physical state both a physical realization of F(domain value$_i$) and an error in computing F(domain value$_i$), no inconsistency in the definitions occurs.[12]

S-Triviality Is False

S-triviality faces two problems it can't escape unless it is substantially modified. The first of these is structural, the second metaphysical.

The First Problem for S-Triviality

This is more serious than the metaphysical problem. If S-triviality contradicts known mathematical facts, it is false. That is what I will show: S-triviality contradicts known mathematical facts.

S-triviality does not provide for the physical realization of any of the n computational states intrinsic to the computation of a function that are intermediate between the initial computational state (in which the domain value of F is read) and the final computational state (in which the range value of F is the output). Given a model of computation, computing F is a computational process that begins with the initial state, enters into n intermediate states, and ends in the final state. I maps only initial and final states of a computation onto physical states of a physical system. But this has a strange consequence: every value of every function is computed in constant time. That is remarkable. It is also logically false and mathematically false.

It is well known that some functions take longer to compute than others, or take more space to compute than others. If F takes more time and/or more space to compute than G, then F is harder to compute than G. Time and space are computational resources and the hardness of computing a function F is measured in terms of how much of these resources are necessary for making the computation of F. The more time it takes to compute a function, the more internal computational states the computation enters. The constant function, CST(x) = 5 for all x, is easy to compute. Any computational model that is employed uses two units of time and/or space resources: the input value 'x' and the output value '5'. On the other hand, consider a function that constructs a truth table for a formula in propositional logic, TTEXP(x). This is an exponential function. TTEXP is hard to compute, since the amount of time and/or space resources needed to compute values of it grows exponentially as the value of x—the input to EXP— grows linearly (where linear growth is measured by increases in the number of distinct propositional variables).

CST is polynomial time complete, while TTEXP is non-deterministic polynomial time complete (or P and NP, respectively). P and NP name complexity classes. P contains problems that can be feasibly computed and NP contains problems that can't be feasibly computed. An outstanding question in mathematics today is whether P = NP. Almost all mathematicians and theoretical computer scientists believe that P is not equal to NP. On S-triviality the answer to this question is easy: P = NP. Since every function is computed in constant time, no function requires more than two units of space or time resources to compute any of its values. As input size increases and output size increases, storage problems arise, but these can easily be handled without exponential explosion.

The "P = NP" question produces no contradiction between S-triviality and mathematical facts, since it has not yet been proved P is not equal to NP. But there is one hard mathematical fact in computational complexity theory: P is not equal to EXPTIME. EXPTIME names a complexity class consisting of problems computable by exponentially time-bounded deterministic Turing machines. Problems in EXPTIME are even harder to compute than problems in NP.[13] According to S-triviality, EXPTIME = P. Thus S-triviality contradicts a mathematical truth. Either it is false or it is false that EXPTIME $\neq$ P.

S-triviality implies another odd result in computational complexity theory. The complexity class P is itself a hierarchy of complexity classes all of which fall strictly under P. Classes lower in the P hierarchy contain problems that are more feasible to solve than classes located higher in it. On S-triviality, there is a collapse of all the classes in P to the lowest class. Additionally, on S-triviality *all* recursive functions are computable not just in P, but in its lowest complexity class: constant time complexity. Thus, on S-triviality, all recursive functions are maximally feasible in terms of how hard they are to compute. Every complexity class reduces to AC(0, 0) (which is contained in NC^1), the bottom complexity class in the P hierarchy. Much mathematical work has been done in the theory of computational complexity. S-triviality contradicts all of it.

In S-triviality, EXPTIME reduces to P, a violation of mathematical fact. Assuming mathematical facts are logically true, S-triviality is logically contradictory, since it is false in every possible world. Perhaps you are not a logicist and do not believe that all mathematical contradictions are logical contradictions. Whether you are or are not a logicist, the complexity classes P, NP and EXPTIME can be characterized in purely logical terms, in which case the gulf between P and NP can be logically characterized. In the early 1970s, Ronald Fagin discovered that NP is equal to the set of existential second-order Boolean queries.[14] The logical characterization of complexity classes is known as descriptive complexity theory. It does not characterize the hardness of computing a function in terms of time or space resources, but in terms of the system of logic needed to compute queries expressing the function. P queries can be computed in extensions of first-order logic (such as fixed-point logics) that fall short of second-order logic. Thus, on S-triviality, second-order logic reduces to a (non-second-order) extension of first-order logic (such as fixed-point logics). This is a logical contradiction

If a rock lying in the street is S-computing a recursive function only if second-order logic is reducible to first-order logic or $P = NP$, we have a good reason to reject the claim the rock in the street is computing a recursive function. If the rock in the street is computing an EXPTIME function in constant time, we have a good reason to reject the claim the rock in the street computes a recursive function. It is logically contradictory to believe second-order logic is reducible to a non-second-order extension of first-order logic and mathematically contradictory to believe that $EXPTIME = P$. Consequently, the rock in the street is not computing a recursive function. On S-triviality, the rock is computing a recursive function. It follows that S-triviality can't be a definition of what it is for a physical system to compute a recursive function.

The Second Problem for S-Triviality

Imagine a universe that consists of a single point. We will not worry about the nature of space-time in this universe. (If the single point universe is a physically impossible universe, we can change it to a physically possible universe and make the same point.) Since S-triviality picks out physical states by the time at which they occur and a description that is compatible with the laws of physics, we can make the ontological structure of a physical system as austere as we wish. A one-point universe is the lower limit short of nothingness. On S-triviality, it computes any function. Let us see why.

A point universe has no contingent physical properties. The laws of a point universe are either purely mathematical or purely metaphysical. A mathematical law is that the dimension of the point is not equal to the dimension of the plane nor the dimension of a volume. For instance, the point is not a plane and is not a volume. A metaphysical law is that the point is self-identical. Take being self-identical as the description it satisfies at all times. The point universe satisfies all instances of the schema COMP (that defines computational states) and all instances of the schema TRIV. The point universe computes every function.

We rebel at the prospect of a single point universe computing any function. The best explanation of why we do so is that when we say that a physical system computes a function, we assume that computational states supervene on physical states. There is no change in a computational state without a change in the underlying physical state that is the supervenience base. Similarly, when we say that an abstract physical system (the point universe) computes a function, we assume that computational states supervene on abstract physical states. There is no change in a computational state without a change in the underlying abstract physical state that is the supervenience base. If that is so, a point universe can't account for all the computations it is supposed to perform according to the definition of S-triviality. It does not change state, ever. Yet it churns out function value after function value. Although it is possible that two distinct supervening states supervene on the same physical state, it is absurd to suppose that every supervening state supervenes on the same physical state (and that physical state is not a disjunctive state—either finitary or infinitary). Either S-triviality licenses computations that violate metaphysical principles of supervenience or else it licenses computations that have no connection with any parts of the physical world in which they supposedly occur. If the latter is the case, then S-triviality is not a definition of what it is for a physical system to physically realize a computation. Instead, there are two distinct metaphysical categories—physical systems and computations—and there is no realization relation between computations and physical systems. If so, it is mystery how physical systems such as digital computers can compute functions. If the former is the case, then S-triviality violates a fundamental principle of metaphysics that applies to any world in which there is a realization relation between two distinct metaphysical categories.

To put the point more vividly: S-triviality allows violations of metaphysical principles such as supervenience principles underlying realization relations between physical systems and abstract objects, such as computations.

Objection: The point universe is not a genuine physical universe. It is a purely mathematical universe. As such, it is physically impossible. Since there are no physical laws governing the evolution of the point universe over time and since the point universe is not a physical system, it can't compute a function. It does not satisfy the definition of S-triviality.

Response: Yes, that is right. a point universe is not a physical system. However, we can easily imagine it is a single point part of a genuine universe, and we can show this single point part of the physical universe can compute any function. If that is not convincing, we can provide examples of minimal physical systems that satisfy physical laws (and not only Leibnizian metaphysical ones), satisfy S-triviality, compute every function, but fail to respect supervenience relations.[15]

Strong S-Triviality

S-triviality must be strengthened if it is to avoid absurdity. The source of its problems is twofold: it does not countenance intermediate computational states and its specification of physical states allows metaphysical principles to be violated. How, then, can S-triviality be modified to meet these objections? I will discuss how it can be strengthened to meet the objection that it contradicts mathematical facts. I think that any modification that allows it to meet the objection that it contradicts mathematical facts creates new problems or else confronts anew the objection that it violates metaphysical principles.

Recall that, in TRIV, I is defined for initial and final states of a computation of F. We need to augment TRIV so that it can define I for intermediate computational states needed to compute F. How can that be done? Fix a computational model (such as a Turing-machine model). Suppose that the value $F(k)$ is computed and that there are m computational states (including the initial and final states) in computing $F(k)$. I must map m physical states into m computational states. Now suppose that the value $F(k + 3)$ is computed and that there are $m + 8$ computational states in computing $F(k + 3)$. I must map $m + 8$ physical states into $m + 8$ computational states. F has infinitely many range values. Must I explicitly record, for each range value, how many computational states are needed to compute it?

Another problem is that I maps a physical state at a time onto a natural number that is the domain value of F for zero and even times and onto a range value of F for odd times. The temporal moments denoted by natural numbers pick out domain and range values. '2' intrinsically specifies the domain value 2, since the domain value is a natural number. But how can temporal moments denoted by natural numbers pick out any of the intermediate computational states that can't be intrinsically specified by numbers?

Another problem is that there are infinitely many distinct range values for infinitely many computable functions. Typically, for each function and for each range value computed for it, the number of intermediate computational states increases as the domain value increases. What this means is that a strong TRIV schema contains an infinite number of clauses for I. Strong TRIV would not be usable by a finite human. Even if we restrict strong TRIV to finitely many range values of a function, it is still not usable by finite humans. For example, the Ackerman exponential function grows so quickly, even for small domain values, that there is not enough matter in the known universe to write down each intermediate computational state, even if one (separately) inscribes them on elementary particles.

Lastly, strong TRIV poses a problem for those who believe all computations are observer relative. *If* all computations are observer relative and *if* strong TRIV is an adequate definition of what it is for a physical system to physically realize a computation, then almost all computable functions are not computable by human beings.

Can the problems just enumerated for strong TRIV be eliminated by using variables for intermediate computational states?[16] (The original TRIV uses variables for temporal moments.) Here is a proposal: we introduce into the definition of I the code for a Turing machine that computes F. This, however, creates another problem. Since there is a distinct Turing machine for each computable function and there are infinitely many of them, there will be infinitely many clauses in strong TRIV, one for each Turing machine. This problem is easily solved. We cite only one Turing machine in strong TRIV: the universal Turing machine. For any F, feed it the index of F and the input to F, indexed by the temporal parameter T_i. This is not enough, since we have to take into account the intermediate computational states, each of which takes a unit of T_i to compute. Recall we cannot intrinsically specify intermediate computational states by the natural numbers denoting temporal moments. But each intermediate state takes a unit of time to compute, so we can use natural numbers to specify that an intermediate state occurs. Suppose that there are three intermediate states. Then when T_i is zero or even, the domain value is $i/2$. $T_i + 1$, $T_i + 2$, and $T_i + 3$ specify each of the three intermediate states. But $T_i + k$ is greater than T_i, and we do not want the final state to be $F(((i + k) - 1)/2)$.

The final computational state depends on all the intermediate computational states needed to reach it. Though true for computations, it creates a problem for strong TRIV. One way to solve this problem is to design a Turing machine that works inside the universal Turing machine, counting the number of computational states the universal Turing machine passes through in computing $F(n)$ as it simulates F. It then subtracts that number from $T_i + k$, so that the final computational state is $F((i - 1)/2)$.

However, the Turing machine that counts the number of intermediate states the universal Turing machine runs through in computing $F(m)$ counts by computing. So it too has initial, intermediate and final states and these will be indexed by T_i. In that case, we need a Turing machine that counts its intermediate computational states. But this new Turing machine will count intermediate states by computing, so it too has initial, intermediate and final computational states. This creates an infinite regress of Turing machines for counting intermediate computational states.[17]

This infinite regress cannot be avoided, since every computational state in TRIV must be indexed by a temporal moment (i.e., T_i). This is not a problem for the theory of computability, for computational states are not indexed by temporal moments. It is not a problem for computational complexity theory either, since counting the intermediate computational states to determine how much time it takes to compute a function is not part of computing that function. What value $F(n)$ has is not dependent on how all the intermediate computational states needed to compute it are counted. But in strong TRIV, that is not so: what value $F(n)$ has is dependent on how all the intermediate computational states needed to compute it are counted.

We can break the infinite regress if we can count the number of intermediate computational states, for any F and for any computation of a value of F, before the actual computation proceeds. But that can't be done. To do so we have to know whether the universal Turing machine halts, for any n and any F. This cannot be done by any Turing machine, since it is a recursively unsolvable problem. It cannot be done by any finitary human being, either.

In short, in order to modify TRIV so that the catalogue of problems for S-triviality can be evaded, strong TRIV must solve the halting problem. To put the point in a vivid way: for S-triviality to avoid logical contradiction, it must solve the halting problem. That can be done only by an infinitary mechanism. Thus: in order to define what it is for a physical system to physically realize a computation, an infinitary mechanism must be explicitly introduced into the definition. However, what it is to be computable is a finitary notion and so the definition of a computation is finitary. If we have to define a finitary notion in terms of an infinitary one, then it is not, after all, a finitary notion. This is another contradiction.

Another Problem for Strong TRIV

Another problem for strong TRIV arises even if one did not have to solve the halting problem. Our motivation for strong TRIV was to avoid the problem of original TRIV: all computable functions are computable in constant time. But in strong TRIV the hardness of computing F(n), for any F and n, is measured by how many time moments it takes to compute F(n). This is one measure of how hard it is to compute a function, but it is not the only such measure. The hardness of computing F(n) can also be measured in terms of how much space is needed to compute it: how much internal memory the mechanism needs to compute F(n). In the hierarchy of computational complexity classes, the complexity class immediately above NP is PSPACE. This complexity class measures the hardness of computations in terms of the amount of memory needed for them. PSPACE contains problems a deterministic Turing machine with a polynomially bounded memory capacity can solve. Although it is not known whether NP = PSPACE, it is a mathematical fact that NP is contained in PSPACE.[18]

Since memory space is not counted in strong TRIV, it can be proved that PSPACE is equal to NP in strong TRIV. Let us see how this is done. The mathematical proof that NP is contained in PSPACE shows that exponentially many steps in a computation of F does not imply that exponentially many memory cells are used to compute it. There are problems in NP that are computed in exponentially many steps, but use a polynomially bounded number of memory cells (because the same memory cell is used more than once). Thus NP is contained in PSPACE. Now we see how to show in strong TRIV that PSPACE is contained in NP. Consider how these problems in NP (described above) are represented in strong TRIV. Since strong TRIV does not count memory cells, it can't distinguish intermediate computational states that are memory cells and those that are not. Even if all the computational states modeled in strong TRIV equal, in number, the computational states of a computational model that includes memory cells and storage operations, memory cells and storage operations are invisible in strong TRIV.

This means that in a problem where memory cells are used more than once to solve it, strong TRIV cannot distinguish between using the same memory cell twice and using two different memory cells. If so, using the same memory cell twice and using two different memory cells have the same count: 2. Suppose that in NP the problem is solved in 20 time steps, where a single memory cell is visited 20 times. In PSPACE, the same problem is solved in one use of a memory cell. The hardness of computing the problem in NP is 20 and the hardness of computing it in PSPACE is 1.

But in strong TRIV, visiting the same memory cell more than once is not visible. So even if the problem is solved by visiting the same memory cell 20 times, it will still take 20 steps in strong TRIV. Strong TRIV cannot distinguish between NP and PSPACE, because it cannot distinguish between visiting the same memory cell more than once and using more than one memory cell. So PSPACE is contained in NP in strong TRIV and since it is a mathematical fact that NP is contained in PSPACE, we have NP = PSPACE in strong TRIV. It is not known whether PSPACE is contained in NP, but whether it is or is not, it must be that PSPACE is contained in NP in strong TRIV. This is an unsettling result. If PSPACE is not contained in NP, then strong TRIV contradicts a mathematical fact. If PSPACE is contained in NP, strong TRIV proves it is so without use in the proof of the property that distinguishes PSPACE from NP: counting total number of memory cells used regardless of how many times they are used.

Objection: You can define memory cells in both COMP and strong TRIV. Recall the COMP schema: "PHYSYS is in state S_i if and only if PHYSYS satisfies D and it is time T_i." The symbol 'S' denotes a memory cell when the description D is a description of a memory cell.

Response: The first problem for the objection is not every physically realized state S realizes a memory cell. S-triviality does not allow multiple descriptions. Suppose, for the sake of argument, that it can accommodate multiple descriptions. The second problem is that strong TRIV must count when the same memory cell is used more than once. To do this it must not only distinguish memory cells from other memory cells, it must also keep a count of when the same memory cell is revisited. Strong TRIV has no means to do this.

The Ordering Assumption in S-Triviality, Conforming to Supervenience, and the Problem of Recurring Physical States

Another problem for S-triviality and strong S-triviality arises in a physically possible, and entirely plausible, universe. Suppose that a physical system S-trivially computing a function F repeats some of its previous physical states within the temporal interval in which computation of F occurs. Physical systems are characterized by multiple parameters and during their time-evolution may repeat the values of any of those parameters. Recall how a physical state physically realizes a computational state in COMP: PHYSYS is in computational state S_i if and only if PHYSYS satisfies D and it is time T_i.

If a physical state is instanced at T_i and it recurs at $T_i + k$ and at both times it satisfies D, it physically realizes two distinct computational states: S_i and $S_i + k$. One problem is that the recurrent physical state may physically realize two very different computational states. At T_i it realizes a memory cell and at $T_i + k$ it realizes a NOR gate. If a physical state can physically realize two functionally distinct computational states, is there any reason to think it is a physical realization of them? This problem is a version of the supervenience problem for S-triviality we described earlier. Computations do not supervene on physical states if no difference in the physical state does not imply no difference in the physically realized computational state.

Another problem has to do with an ordering assumption implicit in S-triviality. For any F and for all domain values i, F(i) is computed before F(i + 1). Suppose that physical state A of the physical system occurs first at T_i and recurs at $T_i + k$. Do we say that F(2) is computed at T_i and that F(2 + k) is computed at $T_i + k$, or that F(2) is computed at T_i and at $T_i + k$? Using COMP and TRIV, we have to say the former, but to respect supervenience, we have to say the latter. However, if we attempt to respect supervenience, there are insuperable difficulties that arise owing to the ordering assumption. Let us examine a few of these difficulties. The point is that strong S-triviality either violates supervenience or falls into insuperable difficulties in attempting to conform to it.

To respect supervenience, a recurring physical state must physically realize the same computational state. Here is one difficulty: If range values are duplicated in virtue of state recurrence, the domain value and intermediate computational states must also be duplicated. If not, we might be forced to say, for example, that function F computes 25 for domain value 3 and 25 for domain value 10,647. Suppose that F does not compute 25 for domain value 10,647. Then either what we are forced to say is false or else the function S-trivially computed is not F, but another function F*, that computes the same range value for a domain value of 3 and 10,647.

The same problem occurs when the recurrent physical state is the initial state reading a domain value. If the function is F and the domain value is 3, then the final state range value must be F(3) and not some other value. If the range value is not F(3), then either what we are forced to say is false or else the function S-trivially computed is not F, but another function F*. Here is one proposal to ensure that TRIV respects supervenience: we monitor the physical system for recurrent physical states, so we can make on-the-fly changes in TRIV reflecting what we observe. Another proposal: we can stipulate that when a physical state recurs, the initial, intermediate and final states are deleted. Let us look at the first proposal.

Since a recurrent physical state might occur anytime during the temporal interval in which S-trivial computation occurs, and since the temporal interval needs to be infinitely long, in order to distinguish F from the infinitely many other functions $G, H, \ldots$ that share the same set of range values for any finite initial segment of domain values, we will have to monitor the system for infinitely many values of T_i. That is something which human beings cannot feasibly do. Since they cannot do this, either S-triviality fails to respect supervenience or it is an idealization to which humans can approximate. An alternative to monitoring infinitely many T_i moments is to predict future recurrent states using the physical laws that govern the physical system. Here, too, there is a feasibility problem for humans. We cannot predict all future recurrent states of the physical system. In classical and quantum-mechanical physics, the use of physical laws fails to uniquely predict future values of a property P. It fails in quantum mechanics, since we can only get a probabilistic estimate of the future values of P. It fails in classical mechanics, and for two different reasons. One reason is that the physical system might undergo chaotic behavior. The other reason is that the laws of classical mechanics are indeterminate in predicting what actually occurs in the physical system. This little-known aspect of classical mechanics is startling. The laws of classical mechanics are compatible with indeterminate outcomes of experiments.[19]

If we can't solve this problem and we wish S-triviality to respect supervenience, then we will not know whether the physical system computes F or computes F*, which agrees with F on all domain and range pairs up to T_i, then disagrees thereafter. This is unexpected. It is a Kripke-Wittgenstein problem. In this case, it arises for the trivialist who tries to construct a definition of trivial computation that respects supervenience. The consequence is that trivialists—who wish to refute computational functionalism by showing the definition of what it is for a physical system to physically realize a computation allows trivial computation—must solve a Kripke-Wittgenstein problem. If not, then supervenience cannot be satisfied, and there is then no reason to think that computations are physically realized in physical systems.

Let us now look at the second proposal: that we emend TRIV so it takes into account recurrent physical states and then deletes them (and the intermediate computational states between them). Here is one suggestion for the emendation:

Rule D: Delete the pair $\{i, i + 1\}$; then, for all i greater than T_i, reset the values $T_i + 2$ to $T_i - 2$ and $T_i + 3$ to $T_i - 2$ whenever T_i maps to a recurrent physical state.

Rule D is a simplification: it does not tell us how to delete any of the intermediate computational states. But since it encounters problems, we do not need to describe a rule that deletes them. The first problem is Rule D presupposes we can reliably determine when a recurrent physical state occurs. This is easy if recurrent physical states are readily epistemically discerned. Suppose that a set of physical states is wholly characterized by two parameters that take on integral values. Distinguishing and identifying physical states is relatively easy in this case. Suppose that a set of physical states is characterized by 15 parameters, each taking on a continuum of values. Distinguishing and identifying physical states is relatively hard in this case. If it is hard to distinguish and identify physical states, we can emend D, so that value lists of physical states that are close to previous value lists of physical states mark recurrent states. In that case, we will delete the current pair. If we allow a much less stringent degree of approximation to value lists of previous physical states, the physical system might never compute the ith pair in a finite lifetime because it keeps deleting the current pairs.

However, a harder problem for rule D occurs when the recurrent physical state occurs at time $T_i + 1$, which is when a range value of F is computed. There appears to be no means by which D can distinguish, ahead of time, two possibilities:

(i) $F((i - 1)/2) = F((i - 3)/2)$ (i.e., the function F has the same range values), in which case we need to keep the recurrence pair and not delete it.

(ii) F has different range values at those two times in which we have recurrent physical states, so we need to delete the recurrence pair.

If (ii) occurs, D deletes the pair T_i and $T_i - 1$, and, for all i, resets $T_i + 2$ to T_i and $T_i + 1$ to $T_i - 1$. If (i) occurs, deleting the pair and resetting the values will result in TRIV defining a new function F^*. Thus, we need to know whether the recurrent physical state at T_i is a case in which F has the same range value for two (or more) distinct domain values or is a case in which F does not have the same range value for two (or more) domain values. If the former, we keep the pair $\{T_i, T_i - 1\}$. If the latter, we delete the pair $\{T_i, T_i - 1\}$. If D is exclusively a deletion of pairs rule, when (i) occurs, we compute, not F, but F^*. If D is exclusively a preservation of pairs rule, then when (ii) occurs, we compute not F, but F^{**}.

In either case, trivialists encounter a Kripke-Wittgenstein problem. However, to avoid this, why not make rule D disjunctive? We specify that when condition (i) occurs, preserve the recurrent pairs and when condition (ii) occurs, delete the recurrent pairs. All that we have to do is actually compute the value of F(n) when the recurrent physical state occurs. F(n) is then compared with the value of F(n − m) computed when the physical state first occurred. If the two are the same, then preserve the pair. If not, then delete the pair.

To implement a disjunctive D, the physical system will have to make a genuine computation. We can't hide computed values in the interpretation function. Disjunctive rule D needs the results of genuine computations if it is to distinguish possibilities (i) and (ii). Thus, an S-trivial system must non-trivially compute a function value for F, if it is to S-trivially compute a function F. If it can't do this, it has not solved the Kripke-Wittgenstein problem it confronts.

Objection: You have painted a needlessly alarming picture of how S-triviality must be modified to defuse the problems created by the ordering assumption. Consider the following proposal: when there is a recurrent physical state, let it represent a new computational state. On S-triviality, recurrent physical states do not create problems, since we keep generating function values in response to increasing domain values of F.

Response: Let us first consider a physical system for which the physical state remains constant throughout the temporal interval in which computation occurs. We must rule out such physical systems, since there is nothing which physically changes as the computation defined over it changes. It is absurd to say that a physical system in the exact same physical state, for all n and m, computes the values F(n) and F(n + m), where F(n) is not equal to F(n + m). If we allow this to happen, then we have divorced computation from the physical world entirely. For these physical systems, computations are ghosts which ride with them, but which are not, in any way, supervenient on them.

That leaves those physical systems in which recurrent physical states occur at least once during the temporal interval in which S-trivial computation occurs. How do these physical systems fare on the above proposal? Recall that a central ingredient in the notion of what it is for a physical system to physically realize a computation is that there is an interpretation function I that maps physical states of a physical system into computational states. I maps physical states into initial or final computational states—that is, either domain or range values of F—in such a way that $I(final) = F(I(initial))$. Physical laws guarantee that the physical states realizing the computational states respect these conditions on I.

Suppose that a physical state recurs and it maps into an initial computational state. On the above proposal, we let the initial computational state be the next domain value in the ordered sequence of domain values $1, 2, 3, 4, \ldots$. If the last domain value was 3, then the new one is 4. It does not matter whether the physical system is in physical state$_1$ or in physical state$_2$ when it physically realizes the new initial computational state. No matter what physical state occurs at T_i, it physically realizes new initial computational states. Since any physical state at all will do on the above proposal, there is a conflict with supervenience. If computational states supervene on physical states, varying the physical states should produce similar variations in the computational states. If there is no change in computational state no matter what changes occur in the physical states, it is difficult to maintain that computational states supervene on physical states.[20]

Since physical laws govern causal transitions between physical realizations of computational states, a physical state that physically realizes an initial computational state will cause the physical system to enter a new physical state physically realizing a final computational state. If it does not matter whether one physical state or another physical state causes the transition from the initial computational state to the final computational state, it is hard to maintain a straight face when one says physical laws guarantee there is a causal, law-like transition from initial computational state to final computational state. Second, though the recurrent physical state physically realizes a different domain value than the first occurrence of that physical state, it is still the same physical state. To say the exact same physical state maps onto two distinct final computational states appears to conflict with the fundamental constraint on functions. A function is a general mathematical object, subject to only one constraint: a single domain value does not map into two or more range values. (Two or more domain values may map into the same range value, though.) If so, I is not a genuine function. But even if it does not violate the function constraint, it violates supervenience.

The Counterfactual Objection to Triviality

S-triviality succumbs to a well-known objection to triviality arguments raised (independently) by Ned Block, David Chalmers, and Jack Copeland.[21] The objection is that trivial computational systems cannot respect counterfactuals about computations. In particular, since all the domain and range elements in S-triviality are linearly ordered, one cannot say what the physical system would have computed if it had computed $F(n)$ before it had computed $F(n - m)$. That counterfactual is meaningless for S-trivial computations. Block states the objection both clearly and forcefully.[22] Here is a simple case: Suppose that a wall—an example used by John Searle[23]—computes '$0 + 1 = 1$'. What would it have computed had the '1' been replaced by a '0'? Clearly, it would incorrectly compute '1' unless the output '1' had also been replaced by '0'. If both instances of '1' had been changed to '0', then the computation would be correct. "In order for the wall to be [a] computer, it isn't enough for it to have states that correspond to '0' and '1' followed by a state that corresponds to '1'. It must also be such that *had* the '1' input been replaced by a '0' input, the '1' output *would have been* replaced by the '0' output. In other words, it has to have symbolic states that satisfy not only the *actual* computation, but also the *possible* computations that the computer *could* have performed. And this is nontrivial."[24]

Using TRIV, the wall computes '$1 + 0 = 1$' at T_i. It cannot compute anything else at T_i. If we change TRIV, then the wall can compute something else at T_i. But if we change TRIV, we are changing the definition of what it is for a physical system to physically realize a computation. Suppose that we do change TRIV. Then we should subscript it to distinguish it from the first version. On TRIV_2, at T_i the wall computes '$0 + 0 = 0$'. On TRIV_1, at T_i the wall computes '$1 + 0 = 1$'. Which is the correct definition? The only way a trivialist can respond to the counterfactual objection to triviality is by fragmenting the definition of what it is for a physical system to physically realize a computation. If there are n counterfactuals that can be raised about what the wall would have computed at T_i, then there are n new TRIV schemata. If there are infinitely many counterfactuals that can be raised about what the wall would have computed at T_i, then there are infinitely many new TRIV schemata. Since there are infinitely many natural numbers, there are infinitely many counterfactuals about what the wall would have computed at T_i.

Chalmers reaffirmed his view that the counterfactual objection to triviality is decisive.[25] We take the position that the counterfactual objection works only because the physical system only performs one computation at a given time. If this condition is dropped, the counterfactual objection can be met. But there are new difficulties for the trivialist. It is not just the need for a partitioning of physical space in which the counterfactual trivial computations can be performed that creates a problem. The need to respect the causal chains that connect computational stages creates a problem. Causal chains must bear an abstract structural relation to computations: they must be isomorphic to the computation.

One might think that the counterfactual objection can be met by dropping the ordering assumption. Let us look at S-triviality when we abandon ordering completely—that is, when there is no ordering of the domain and range elements of F within the physical system that realizes the computations. The physical system might compute $F(5)$ at T_i and $F(3)$ at $T_i + 7$. Will this arrangement meet the counterfactual objection? No, it will not. We can still ask what the physical system would have computed at T_i if it had been given the domain value 8 instead of the domain value 5. Suppose that we take a global view of the physical space of the physical system. At T_i the entire physical system (and so the entire physical space) is engaged in S-computing $F(5)$. At $T_i + 7$ it is engaged in S-computing $F(3)$.

Partitioning Physical Space into Actual and Possible Worlds

It is not the ordering assumption that creates the problem captured in the counterfactual objection. It is the condition that only one computation can occur at a given time moment in the physical system. The counterfactual objection can be met if that condition is dropped. Here is a proposal: partition the physical space into regions such that at T_i $F(5)$ is computed in one region of physical space and $F(3)$ is computed in another region of physical space. Call the region of space in which $F(5)$ is computed the actual world and the region of space in which $F(3)$ is computed the possible world. We can now answer the question "What would the physical system have computed had it been given the domain value 3 instead of the domain value

5?" We look at what the physical system computes in the possible world (region of physical space).

If there are n counterfactuals about what the physical system would have computed at T_i, we divide physical space into $n + 1$ regions. Only one region is the actual world. All of the other regions are possible (non-actual) worlds. Implementing this proposal in COMP and TRIV will require additional clauses. The point that should not be lost sight of is that S-triviality shows that every physical system is a computer. It does not matter that you cannot really use the wall for word processing or writing e-mails. All S-triviality needs to show is that it is possible for the wall to function as a computer without violating physical laws. An objection to the proposal above that no human being could use such a physical system as a computer and could read off all the counterfactuals true of it misses the point. As long as there is enough physical space, physical states and time moments for all the actual and counterfactual computational realizations to occur, the counterfactual objection to triviality can be met.

One problem for this model of triviality is how we can specify the possible worlds in TRIV. If we have to use different TRIVs for each possible world and for the actual world, then we have different definitions of what it is for a physical system to physically realize a computation, where the number of distinct definitions equals the number of possible worlds plus one. If so, the model does not meet the counterfactual objection. A different definition of realizing a computation in a possible world from the one used in the actual world means there is no comparison between the counterfactual computations and computations that occur in the actual world.

Scrambled Computational Spaces

Another proposal for meeting the counterfactual objection is to give up the ordering assumption and the assumption that the initial, intermediate and final computational states of a single computation occur in temporal order and in connected regions of space. Suppose that New York City is the physical system in which S-computations occur. Suppose that F is S-computed in it. At 2:35 P.M. on February 15, 2005, F(3) is computed near City Hall and the kth intermediate state in the computation of F(23) is computed in Washington Square Park. At 8:07 A.M. on August 19, 2007, F(23) is computed in the Bowery and the domain value 16 is read in TriBeCa. One additional restriction: at any given time moment, at least one computational state from each computation of each range value of F occurs in New York City.

The computations are scrambled: initial, intermediate and final computational states of a computation of F(N) do not occur in temporal order and do not occur in the same (or a neighborhood of the same) region of physical space. In the scrambled model of S-triviality, each part of every computation occurs at some moment. We get the full computation of F(n) only by collecting all the time moments.[26]

Objection 1: In the scrambled model, some counterfactuals about temporal relations between computational states can't be evaluated. Suppose that the counterfactual is: if we were to input '5' to the physical system at T_i, it will output F(5) at $T_i + 1$. In the scrambled system, there is some moment at which it reads the domain value 5 and some moment at which it computes F(5). However, the moments might not be temporally contiguous.

Response: The temporal counterfactual is simply false of the scrambled model if 5 and F(5) are not temporally contiguous in it. This does not show the counterfactual objection is sustained in the scrambled model. It only shows that not all counterfactuals are true in it. However, if you think ordered temporal relations are intrinsic properties of computations, then the objection shows the counterfactual objection is sustained. But why think that temporal relations between computations are intrinsic properties of a computation? Must it be the case that F(5) occurs after the domain value 5 is read? It is easier to understand the temporal sequence in which 5 is read and then F(5) is output than the temporal sequence in which F(5) is output and then 5 is read. But if both 5 and F(5) (and the intermediate computational states) occur, the computation of F(5) takes place.

Objection 2: Suppose that a mathematician claims to have a proof of a famous unsolved problem in mathematics, such as the Hodge Conjecture. When asked for the proof, he says that it is scrambled: all the letters, numerals, and special symbols are located in various places throughout the world. Even though he cannot tell you where they are, he is certain they are all there.

It is irrational to believe the mathematician has a proof of the Hodge Conjecture unless he can put the letters, numerals, and special symbols together in such a way that it is a legitimate proof. What constitutes a legitimate proof? If the proof is in a logic, the appropriate relations between symbol sequences are provided by the proof procedure for that logic. If the mathematician says he can assemble all the letters, numerals and special symbols so that they satisfy the proof procedures of, say, first-order logic, let him do so. What if he takes you on a tour of several continents, in each place pointing to letters, numerals and special symbols and keeping track of each? If he keeps track on paper, then it is the paper that contains the proof. Is the proof in his head? Yes, if only if he can assemble the letters, numerals and special symbols in the right way. It does no good if he says that all the letters, numerals and special symbols are in his long-term memory. The story of the mathematician is relevant to assessing scrambled models of triviality. It is irrational to believe the scrambled model computes any functions and it is irrational to believe it computes counterfactuals about computations.

There is also a physical objection to the scrambled model. The claim is that the scrambled physical systems are physical realizations of computations. Computations provide information and information imposes order. Physical systems that acquire information experience a decrease in entropy. Energy must be expended to decrease entropy. The computation is physically realized in different physical systems at different times. However, the total physical system over the time interval during which computation occurs does not experience an increase in order, since each computational state of the computation is physically realized in different locations at different times and there is no ordering of either the locations or the times. So the total physical system has higher entropy than what it must have if it is computing a function. This physical situation contradicts the second law of thermodynamics.

Isomorphisms and the Counterfactual Objection

Computations can be expressed in first-order logic. Suppose that we construct a derivational tree for a computation of F(5) in first-order logic. We cannot construct node n before node m if node n occurs after node m in the ordering induced on the derivation tree. Similarly, we cannot compute F(5) without having the domain value 5. If ordering did not matter, *any* arbitrary tree would represent the derivation, so long as all the nodes in the derivation occur in the tree. But is there any requirement that we visit the nodes in the tree at specified times? The tree is ordered, but not with respect to times. Although you cannot derive F(5) in the tree without first feeding 5 to the tree, you can visit any node at any time.

In the scrambled model, all the nodes are there, but their derivational ordering does not correspond to their temporal or spatial ordering in New

York City. That is, in New York City the causal connections between physical realizations of computational states in computing F(n) are not isomorphic to the sequence of computational states in computing F(n). There is only one way in the scrambled model to get that isomorphism: unscramble it. That the physical realizations of computational states are isomorphic to the sequence of computational states in a computation is necessary for a sequence of physical states to be a computation: "... the key to computation is an isomorphism. We arrange things so that, if certain physical states of a machine are understood as symbols, then causal relations among those symbol-states mirror useful rational relations among the meanings of those symbols."[27]

John Searle has conceded to the computationalist that when the notions of appropriate causal connection and appropriate counterfactual relations constrain what it is to physically realize a computation, the triviality results—universal realizability of computations—disappear: "I do not think that the problem of universal realizability is a serious one. I think that it is possible to block the result of universal realizability by tightening up our definition of computation.... A more realistic definition of computation will emphasize such features as the causal relations among program states, programmability and controllability of the mechanism. All these will produce the result that the pattern is not enough. There must be a causal structure sufficient to warrant counterfactuals."[28] Notice that these constraints are not on the definition of what it is for a physical system to physically realize a computation, but on the definition of a computation. If there are constraints on what counts as computation, then those constraints must be satisfied by any physical system physically realizing computations. If not, then whatever it is they physically realize, it is not a computation.

David Chalmers characterizes the correct normal form for specification of the appropriate causal connections and the counterfactual relations to which realizations of computations must conform. His conditions for physical realization of a finite-state automaton are the following: "A physical system P implements a FSA M if there is a mapping f that maps internal states of P to internal states of M, inputs to P to input states of M, and outputs of P to output states of M, such that: for every state-transition relation $(S, I) \rightarrow (S', O')$ of M, the following conditional holds: if P is in internal state s and receiving input i where $f(s) = S$ and $f(i) = I$, this reliably causes it to enter internal state s' and produce output o' such that $f(s') = S'$ and $f(o') = O'$."[29]

The mapping is an isomorphism. They capture invariant logical properties and not merely preserve logical properties. What does this mean? A function maps objects in one space into objects in another space. The first space is called the domain of the function and the second is called the range of the function. Objects in the domain space have mathematical properties, as do objects in the range space. If properties in the domain are mapped into the same properties in the range, they are preserved under the mapping. If properties are preserved from domain to range and they are preserved from range to domain, they are called invariant.

If there is an isomorphism between the set of computational states and the set of physical states, then the properties that characterize the computational states are preserved under the mapping to the set of physical states. Similarly, the properties that characterize the set of physical states are preserved under the mapping to the set of computational states.

The central idea of Chalmers's proposal is that the abstract structure of computations must be mirrored in the physical states and the causal connections between them. In a physical realization of a computation in which state B is reached from state A, the physical state A that realizes computational state A is causally connected to the physical state B that realizes computational state B and the direction of causation is from A to B.

The causal connections give us a reason to believe that the physical system would compute, if it lasted infinitely long, all the infinitely many values of F. Recall that in S-triviality, physical laws guarantee the physical system satisfies description D as it computes F. Causal connections respecting isomorphism defuse the worry that only finitely many values of F are computed by the physical system, and thus defuse the worry that we cannot tell whether the physical system is computing F or any one of the infinitely many other functions which agree with F on the initial segment of its values which are computed in the finite time interval over which S-trivial computation occurs.

The isomorphism condition ensures that there is a theory of error available to determine what the physical system is computing when it breaks down. When the physical system breaks down, there is no longer an isomorphism between it and the set of computational states. We can use this information to determine when the physical system is computing F and when it is computing F*. It computes F* when isomorphism fails. It computes F when isomorphism succeeds. Without a theory of error, trivialists face a Kripke-Wittgenstein problem. But if isomorphism conditions cannot be satisfied by triviality—and Chalmers clams they cannot—trivialists escape the usual (or standard) Kripke-Wittgenstein problem only by having triviality refuted. There is much more to say about whether isomorphism is the appropriate kind of mapping needed to refute triviality and if it can provide a theory of error.

The Laws of Computation, Structure-Preserving Mappings, Preservation, and Invariance

The Analogy with Numerals

Consider the following analogy: Numerals are abstract realizations of numbers. However, not any abstract realization will do. Only those abstract realizations which satisfy the basic laws of arithmetic are satisfactory. Suppose that someone argues for the universal realizability of numbers—that is, any abstract realization of the numbers is satisfactory. Clearly, we would disconfirm that theory by showing that abstract realizations under which numerals do not obey the basic laws of arithmetic are not authentic abstract realizations. When there is an isomorphism between numerals and numbers that respects the basic laws of arithmetic, the basic laws of arithmetic are invariant properties of the isomorphism.

Using the preceding analogy, we can say that physical systems that are physical realizations of computations must respect the theory of computability and the theory of computational complexity. Suppose that someone argues for the universal realization of computations—that is, any physical system computes any computable function. Clearly, we would disconfirm that theory by showing that physical realizations that do not obey the laws of computability theory or computational complexity theory are not authentic physical realizations. When there is an isomorphism between physical realizations and computations that respects the laws of computability theory and of computational complexity theory, those laws are invariant properties of the isomorphism.

The basic idea is that triviality theories can be refuted if, under the physical realization mapping they define, computational laws are not invariant. Call this *the invariance-of-computational-laws objection to triviality*.

Invariance and Preservation of Intrinsic Computational Properties under Mappings

I do not know whether we can now dispatch the trivialist conclusively. The reason why I think this is that the basic laws of computation include not just the theory of computability, but also the theory of computational complexity. That theory is in its infancy, and the fact that we still cannot prove that P is not equal to NP tells us that we still do not know the basic laws of computational complexity, and hence, that we do not know all the basic laws of computation. Because we do not know all the basic laws of computation, any isomorphism induced by the causal connections between physical states (and the laws which describe the physical properties of the physical states), might not capture all the invariant properties of computation. If it does not capture those invariant properties, then it is not the appropriate isomorphism to distinguish trivially realized computations from authentic computations.

A mapping that preserves a logical or semantical property (such as truth) is weaker than one under which the property is invariant. Preservation means that the structure of the source is matched in the structure of the target. Let there be a mapping between OBJECT1 and OBJECT2 that preserves properties. The structure of OBJECT1 is matched in the structure of OBJECT2. However, this is not enough. We also want the structure of OBJECT2 to be matched in the structure of OBJECT1. Without this second condition in place, the structure of OBJECT1 might miss some of the essential structure of OBJECT2. If we want the physical realization relation for computations in physical systems to be authentic, then we want not only that the structure of the source (the physical system) is matched in the target (the computations), but also the structure of the target (the computations) is matched in the structure of the source (the physical system). We want an authentic mapping between physical system and computations to be invariant, and not just one that preserves properties. We also want that the properties invariant under the mapping are the laws of computation. Those laws must include not just the laws of computability theory, but the laws of computational complexity theory as well.

Although we do not know all the laws of computational complexity theory, we can criticize a realization mapping if it violates what laws we do know. That is the principal reason why S-triviality is false. S-triviality cannot respect what we know about the laws of computational complexity theory. The S-realization mapping cannot be correct. Notice that on the proposal of S-triviality we rule out universal realization of computations simply by showing that under the S-realization mapping the laws of computational complexity theory are neither invariant nor preserved.

Chalmers's isomorphism proposal is an initial step in the right direction. Perhaps the notion of isomorphism is not "computational" enough to capture the invariance we want for computations. In modal logic there was a similar problem: find structure-preserving mappings between modal models under which the formulas in modal logic which satisfy both modal models are invariant. There are various mappings—strong homomorphisms, isomorphisms and embeddings—which are invariant, but they are not particularly modal in character. Isomorphism was rejected for it is mathematical in character. Any two isomorphic structures are mathematically identical. Work in modal logic converged on bounded morphisms and bisimulations as invariant mappings that are modal in character.[30]

The point is that we need to find invariant mappings between physical systems and computations that are computational in character. The other point is that we need to look at the kinds of causal relations that will support such mappings.[31] When we know which kinds of causal relations support the mappings which are both invariant and computational, then we will have almost all the answers to the question "When are computations authentically physically realized in physical systems?" We will also need to know all the laws of computational complexity theory, because we want physical realizations of computations to satisfy all of them. We want them to be invariant under the physical realization mapping.

It is better if we can find problems for triviality which are independent of the invariance-of-computational-laws objection. It might be that we get wide-scale triviality indistinguishable from authentic computations just up to the correct arrangement of physical properties, individuals, and powers (via causal connections) necessary for computational law invariance. Finding problems for triviality that are independent of this objection circumvents this possibility. The problems we raise for Putnam's version of triviality are independent of the invariance-of-computational-laws objection.

4 Putnam's Triviality Theorem and Universal Physical Computation

Putnam's version of triviality differs from S-triviality in a number of ways. There is no (explicitly defined) interpretation function that maps physical states onto computational states. The physical conditions of the physical system engaged in trivial computation are specified. We are given the physical laws that guarantee that being in one computational state at time t causes the physical system to make the transition into a succeeding computational state at time t + 1.

Putnam's triviality theorem is that every ordinary open system is a realization of every abstract finite automaton. It is the only triviality theorem in the literature. Let us call Putnam's version of triviality 'P-triviality'.

Putnam assumes two physical principles for the proof of his theorem. He does not discuss what motivates them. I conjecture that they are used to deflect the kinds of problems which arise for S-triviality. These two physical principles are the following:

Principle of Continuity The electromagnetic and gravitational fields are continuous, except possibly at a finite or denumerably infinite set of points. (Since we assume that the only sources of fields are particles, and that there are singularities only at point particles, this has the status of a physical law.)[1]

Principle of Noncyclical Behavior The system S is in different maximal states at different times. This principle will hold true of all systems that can "see" (are not shielded from electromagnetic and gravitational signals from) a clock. Since there are natural clocks from which no ordinary open system is shielded, all such systems satisfy this principle. (N.B.: It is not assumed that *this* principle has the status of a physical law; it is simply assumed that it is in fact true of all ordinary macroscopic open systems.)[2]

Some Positive Features of Continuity

Both of Putnam's physical principles, plus a lemma, are needed to prove his triviality theorem. A few brief remarks about the physical principles are in order. One criticism of triviality I conjecture the Principle of Continuity deflects is that triviality cannot respect counterfactuals about computations. One counterfactual for a physical system is that the physical system would not compute F(n) if the initial physical state of reading n did not occur in the physical system. Another counterfactual is that the physical system would not compute F(n) if any intermediate computational state is realized, not in the physical system, but in another physical system. We do not want computations to occur across the boundaries of physical systems.[3] However, continuity prohibits the physical states realizing computational states of a computation from discontinuously changing location in physical space.

It is absurd to say that the rock and part of the highway two miles from where the rock is located compute F(n). Similarly, it is absurd to say that your brain tissue and your toenails compute F(n). If continuity isn't respected, computations can occur in 'jump objects' such as the object which is you at t_1 and the Eiffel Tower at t_2.[4] The continuity condition respects object boundaries and thereby respects counterfactuals about the boundaries of a computation that is physically realized in a particular physical medium.

The continuity condition also prohibits illicit computational flow mergers. If two contiguous physical systems A and B are different computational systems and are each computing different functions, we do not want the computation of F(5) in A to flow into the computation of G(17) in B nor the computation of G(17) in B to flow into the computation of F(5) in A. If either happens, we have a hybrid computation of F or a hybrid computation of G. Since we do not want genuine computations to merge in this way, we do not want any trivial computations to merge either. If we cannot prohibit trivial computations from merging, then we violate a condition on computations.[5]

By prohibiting inter-boundary computational flows and computational flow mergers, the Principle of Continuity rules out Kripke-Wittgenstein problems that arise in either of the two prohibited states of affairs. Given a theory of error for a physical system that computes, these problems do not arise. But since a trivial computational system does not have the resources to fashion a theory of error, they must be prohibited by other means. The continuity condition does that job.

Suppose that in a physical system trivially computing F(n) an intermediate computational state is physically realized outside the system and it is not physically realized inside the system. Suppose that without that intermediate computational state the physical system computes G(n) and not

F(n) for the input n. Is it the case that the physical system trivially computes G(n), or is it the case that there is a mistake in the trivial computation of F(n)? Without a theory of error for computations, there is no fact of the matter about both the physical system and the physical space outside the physical system that will decide between the two possibilities.

Suppose that in a physical system A trivially computing F(n) and in a physical system B trivially computing G(n), the computation of F(n) flows into the computation of G(n), or conversely, or both. The result is that A computes G(n) and B computes F(n). Do we say that A trivially computes G(n), or that it has made a mistake in the computation of F(n)? Similarly, do we say that B computes F(n), or that it has made a mistake in the computation of G(n)? Without a theory of error for computations, there is no fact of the matter about either A or B that will decide, for either, between the two possibilities.

The Principle of Continuity and Kripke-Wittgenstein Problems

Physical systems that engage in genuine computations can exhibit spatial discontinuities or exhibit chaotic behavior without suffering the kind of Kripke-Wittgenstein problem described above. If we know under what physical conditions an error in computation occurs, then we can decide whether the physical system is computing G(n) instead of F(n) or has made an error in the computation of F(n).[6] But physical systems that engage in trivial computation have no theory of error and so do suffer those Kripke-Wittgenstein problems. The continuity principle prohibits those kinds of physical behavior under which physical systems engaging in trivial computation suffer Kripke-Wittgenstein problems.

But simply prohibiting such systems is not enough, since there are physically possible systems for which it is indeterminate whether they will exhibit physical discontinuities.[7] Even if the physical laws that govern these physical systems are known, it may be indeterminate whether it exhibits a discontinuity at time t. If that is the case, then it is indeterminate whether it suffers a Kripke-Wittgenstein problem. That is, even with the Principle of Continuity in effect, we may not know ahead of time when it has been violated. We can say: if it has been violated, then the physical system has not trivially computed F. But if we do not know ahead of time it has been violated, we do not know whether the physical system P-trivially computes F.

Which physical systems exhibit chaotic behavior? The answer is that we do not always know. It depends on the boundary values of the physical system. Whether it will or will not undergo a chaotic transition can depend on what happened in its past. Its past might be the immediate past or it might be the long-distant past. Moreover, what is in the past of a particular physical system will depend on the physical nature of the physical system and whether that physical system is itself embedded in a larger physical system. The butterfly in a small clearing in a remote section of Brazil flaps its wings and, if conditions are right, a bridge over a river in northern New Hampshire undergoes oscillatory motion and explodes. This is an over-worked example and one that, most likely, could not actually happen. But it nicely illustrates the point that chaotic behavior can depend on what happened in the long-distant past and can depend on how one physical system is embedded in another physical system.

Either feature spells trouble for a P-trivialist. If a physical system violates the Principle of Continuity, then it does not P-compute any function. What happened in the past of some physical system might be a fact to which we have no reliable epistemic access. For instance, suppose that what happened 200 years ago will determine whether a physical system now exhibits chaotic behavior. Suppose that physical system does, now, exhibit chaotic behavior. Whether a physical system is part of a larger physical system might be a fact to which we have no reliable epistemic access. For instance, suppose that whether a physical system exhibits chaotic behavior depends on how it is embedded in a larger physical system, where the larger physical system minus the embedded one is not P-computing F, though the embedded one is P-computing F. Suppose that the embedded physical system does, now, exhibit chaotic behavior only because it is embedded in the larger physical system, but would not exhibit chaotic behavior if it were not embedded in the larger physical system. Next suppose that the embedded system is microscopically small (such as a small collection of molecules) and that the embedded system is macroscopically large (such as a solar system). It is quite easy to see that in many cases we are epistemically closed off being able to determine whether or not the embedded system exhibits chaotic behavior.

In either case, the Principle of Continuity is violated and so neither physical system can P-compute any function at all. But if we are epistemically shielded from knowing ahead of time whether the physical system to which we want to attribute P-computation is chaotic (during the temporal interval in which P-computation should occur), then we do not know ahead of time whether the physical system P-computes F or does not P-compute at all. Since it is possible that any physical system characterized by non-linear physical relationships exhibits chaotic behavior, and since there might be causal relations between any physical system and any larger physical system in which it is embedded whose end result is that the embedded physical system exhibits chaotic behavior, *any* attribution of P-computation to a physical system might have to be withdrawn.

This does not happen with genuine computations. Where there is a theory of error, we can distinguish between a computational system computing a non-standard function and it making an error in the computation of the intended function it is supposed to compute. This distinction cannot be made in triviality theories, since there is no theory of error available. In genuine computational systems where there is a theory of error, we will not have to worry that attributions of making a computation are withdrawn. If the genuine computational system exhibits chaotic behavior, then we say that an error has been made, but we do not say that no computation occurred.

Now let us consider a meta-level Kripke-Wittgenstein problem to which triviality theories succumb. (It is a meta-level problem, since it does not concern whether a physical system computes the function F or G or ..., but, rather, which triviality theory characterizes a physical system engaged in trivial computations.) There are several alternative theories of triviality. Suppose that in some there is no Principle of Continuity that constrains what counts as a trivial computation. This is true of S-triviality. If so, we can raise this question: Is the physical system at t P-computing F(n) or is it S-computing G(n)? If the physical system respects the continuity condition, then it could P-compute F(n) at t and could S-compute G(n) at t. If there are n different theories of trivial computation, then at t the physical system could compute F(n) in each distinct triviality theory. It could also trivially compute in each triviality theory a distinct function. Of course, the physical system would violate the laws of thermodynamics. But the issue here is not whether to take the laws of thermodynamics as a constraint on a definition of the physical realization of a computation in a physical system, but whether a meta-level Kripke-Wittgenstein arises for P-computation given that there are alternative trivial computation theories, such as S-computation. Recall that in a standard Kripke-Wittgenstein problem there are no internal facts about an agent that allow her to distinguish between computing F(n) incorrectly and computing G(n) correctly and, similarly, that allow her to distinguish between computing F(n) correctly and G(n) incorrectly (unless the agent already knows that she is computing F or that she is computing G.)

Now suppose that the physical system exhibits chaotic behavior at $t + n$ from which any normal observer is epistemically shielded. It is not

P-computing any function at $t + n$, but it is S-computing G(n) at $t + n$. However, in the trivialists' epistemic situation, he cannot at $t + n$ distinguish among not P-computing F(n), P-computing F(n), and S-computing G(n). (If there are n distinct triviality theories on each of which the same physical system computes a distinct function at $t + n$, then he cannot at $t + n$ distinguish between any of these trivial computations.) But isn't it the intentions of the P-trivialist that determine in which theory of triviality a physical system trivially computes at t? In that case, a standard Kripke-Wittgenstein problem infects those intentions, in the following way. There are no internal mental facts about the P-trivialist that can distinguish between the three possibilities. There are no facts about the P-trivialist that he can use to ascertain that he intends the physical system to not P-compute F(n), rather than P-compute F(n) or G-compute G(n), at t (for any t).

A second kind of meta-level Kripke-Wittgenstein problem is closely related to the first kind. Suppose that there is no violation of the continuity condition at $t + n$. It is still the case that the trivialist cannot distinguish at $t + n$ between the system P-computing F(n), S-computing G(n), T_1-computing $H_1(n), \ldots, T_n$-computing $H_n(n)$. There is no physical evidence internal to the physical system that allows the trivialist to make the distinctions between these different computations. Notice that we do not have to have a theory of error for a physical system realizing a computation in order for this kind of meta-level Kripke-Wittgenstein problem to occur. The first kind of meta-level Kripke Wittgenstein problem does require a theory of error—that is the continuity condition. (Strictly speaking, the continuity condition does not signify an error in the P-computation, but rather that there is no P-computation at all.) In the second kind of Kripke-Wittgenstein problem, the physical system trivially computes at t (for any t) in every theory of triviality even though the triviality theories compute the different functions under the exact same physical conditions. Of course, the P-trivialist can simply say that the physical system is P-computing, for instance, F(n) at t. But there is no physical evidence that will distinguish between the system P-computing F(n) at t, S-computing G(n) at t, ...

Perhaps the P-trivialist will reply that he intends the physical system to P-compute F(n) at t, and it is that intention that determines whether it is really P-computing at t (and not S-computing at t, . . .). However, once again there is a standard Kripke-Wittgenstein problem that arises in this situation. There are no facts about the P-trivialist that can be used to distinguish between an intention to P-compute F(n) at t and an intention to S-compute G(n) at t. (Indeed, there are no facts about the P-trivialist that can be used to distinguish between an intention to P-compute F(n) at t and an intention to G-compute F(n) at t.). In that case, at the meta-level with respect to what theory of triviality the physical system is trivially computing in, the P-trivialist cannot distinguish between any of them. This inability of the P-trivialist (or any kind of trivialist) to distinguish which theory of triviality the physical system trivially computes in at t (for any t) shows that trivial computation can be distinguished from authentic computation. For in authentic computation, there are physical facts about the physical system that allow one to distinguish between different computational models. Where there are no physical facts that make a difference in a physical system that authentically computes, there are no computational differences. If trains of electrical impulses (and the underlying physical structures, such as transistors, etc.) are identical in two physical systems, then there are no authentic computational differences between the two and thus no meta-level Kripke-Wittgenstein problem that arises for authentic computation. This is not so for trivial computation, since it is the intention of the trivialist that counts in determining the kind of trivial theory of computation in which the physical system trivially computes.

There is yet another problem for P-trivialists, though it is not a Kripke-Wittgenstein problem. Namely, they cannot distinguish between physical discontinuities that are physically negligible (and that would not affect a genuine computation in a physical computing system) and those that are physically significant and would affect a genuine computation. In order to make this distinction, the P-trivialist would already need to know the difference between a genuine computation and a trivial computation. There is, then, a computational asymmetry between genuine computation and P-trivial computation. There are discontinuities that do not affect genuine computation, but that make it impossible for P-computation to occur. There are also discontinuities that cause genuine computations to result in error and that make it impossible for P-computation to occur. If the latter discontinuities are a constraint on what counts as a genuine computation (one that would be incorporated into a theory of error for a genuine computation), while the former discontinuities are not a constraint on a genuine theory of computation, then P-triviality cannot make that distinction without acknowledging that it is parasitic on genuine computation. Since it can't make the distinction, it can't satisfy that constraint on genuine computation. On the other hand, a theory of genuine computations does not need to worry about how a P-computation works in order to make the distinction.

Objection: Why should any of these problems be an indictment of P-triviality? There are errors that derail genuine computations, and we don't say it is a Kripke-Wittgenstein problem.

Response: Many physical systems may not be capable of P-computation, but the trivialist will not know ahead of time for which physical systems this is true. On the other hand, armed with a theory of error, we know what to say when a genuine computation is derailed. We dismiss the value computed and reset the system (if that is possible). This resource is not available to the P-trivialist (or to the S-trivialist).

The trivialist might not even know at the time during which P-computation occurs whether the physical system exhibits chaotic behavior. This is a high price to pay for P-triviality. It amounts to saying: "A physical system might be P-computing F, but maybe not. We don't know whether it is or is not P-computing F. If it *is* P-computing F, that is bad news for the computational functionalist, since it is a P-trivial computation, and thus indistinguishable from real computation. Unfortunately, we can't know what it is doing, since we can't have reasonable epistemic justification about what it is doing." The computational functionalist should take such an admission as a sign of failure on the part of the trivialist. To say a physical system might be P-computing F, but we will never know for sure, is to offer a triviality claim that cannot be taken seriously.

It does the trivialist no good to argue that genuine computational systems might exhibit chaotic behavior. Whether genuine computational systems that exhibit chaotic behavior reliably compute depends on whether the chaotic behavior impinges on the physical parts of the physical system that engage in computation. When a physical computer exhibits chaotic behavior and its computational properties are compromised, we have a good physical theory of *how* the computational properties are compromised. In that case, we are able to reliably say what kinds of errors the computer makes. In the case of physical systems that P-compute, we have no such comforts. It makes no sense to say that the physical system makes an error in P-computation of a certain kind. We could instead say that it makes an error of another kind. We can say that it makes any kind of error, since it makes no sense to say that it makes an error.

Putnam's Proof of His Triviality Theorem

Before critically examining the Principle of Noncyclical Behavior, let us consider Putnam's proof of his theorem. Here is a slightly edited version:

Theorem: Every ordinary open system is a realization of every abstract finite automaton.

Proof: A finite automaton is characterized by a table which specifies the states and the required state-transitions. Without loss of generality, let us suppose the table calls for the automaton to go through the following sequence of states in the interval ... that we wish to simulate in real time: ABABABA. Let us suppose we are given a physical system S whose spatial boundary we have exactly defined, at least during the real-time interval we are interested in.... We wish to find physical states A and B such that during the time interval the system S "obeys" this table by going through the sequence of states ABABABA and such that given just the laws of physics (including the Principle of Continuity) and the boundary conditions of S, a Laplacian supermind could predict the next state of the system....

I shall use the symbolic expression $St(S, t)$ to denote the maximal state of S at t (in classical physics this would be the value of all the field parameters at all the points inside the boundary of S at t). Let the beginnings of the intervals during which S is to be in one of its stages A or B be $t_1, t_2, \ldots, t_n$ (in the example given, n = 7, and the times in question are $t_1 = 12:00, t_2 = 12:01, \ldots, t_7 = 12:06$). The end of the real-time interval during which we wish S to "obey" this table we call t_{n+1} (= $t_8 = 12:07$, in our example). For each of the intervals t_i to t_{i+1}, i = 1, 2, ..., n, define a (non-maximal) *interval state* s_i which is the "region" in phase space consisting of all the maximal states $St(S, t)$ with $t_i \leq t < t_{i+1}$. (I.e., S is in s_i just in case S is in one of the maximal states in this "region.") Note that the system S is in s_1 from t_1 to t_2, in s_2 from t_2 to $t_3, \ldots$, in s_n from t_n to t_{n+1}. (Left endpoint included in all cases but not the right—this is a convention to ensure the "machine" is in exactly one of the s_i at a given time.) The disjointness of the states is guaranteed by the Principle of Noncyclical Behavior.

Define $A = s_1 \vee s_3 \vee s_5 \vee s_7$; $B = s_2 \vee s_4 \vee s_6$.

Then, as is easily checked, S is in state A from t_1 to t_2, from t_3 to t_4, from t_5 to t_6, and from t_7 to t_8, and in state B at all other times between t_1 and t_8. So S "has" the table we specified, with the states A,B just defined as the "realizations" of the states A,B described by the table.

To show that being in state A at times t with $t_1 \leq t < t_2$ "caused" S to go into state B during the interval $t_2 \leq t < t_3$ (and similarly for the other state transitions called for by the table), we argue as follows: Given that S is in state A at a time ($t_1 \leq t < t_2$), and letting the maximal state of the boundary of S at that time t be $B_{t'}$, it follows from the lemma that $St(S, t)$ is the only maximal state in any of the "regions" (nonmaximal states) $s_1, s_2, \ldots, s_7$ that a system S under the boundary condition B_t could be in without violating the Principle of Continuity.... *A fortiori*, St(S, t) is the only maximal state in A compatible with B_t. Hence, given the information that the system was in state A at t, and given the information that the boundary condition at t was $B_{t'}$, a mathematically omniscient being can determine from the Principle of Continuity that the system S must have been in St(S, t), and can further determine, given the boundary conditions at subsequent times and other laws of nature, how S evolves in the whole time interval under consideration. Q.E.D.[8]

The Principle of Noncyclical Behavior

The Principle of Noncyclical Behavior is assumed to hold for every physical system to which Putnam's theorem applies, even though—unlike the Principle of Continuity—it does not have the modal status of a physical law. Recall that the Principle of Noncyclical Behavior stipulates that it holds only for physical systems that can "see" a clock of some sort. For example, it holds for a physical system detecting radioactive decay. It is easy to see why this requirement is in force. If a physical system cannot "see" a clock, then it cannot measure its passage through phase space. All the relevant parameters of the system determine the dimensions of an abstract space— called a phase space—through which a physical system "moves" as their values change. If at time t the parameters of the physical system are the same as they were at time $t - i$, then the physical system has "duplicated" a physical state—i.e., has repeated a state of itself. Without a clock of some kind, every point in the space is indistinguishable from every other point. Thus, without a clock, it cannot be determined that the system is in different maximal states at different times.

Noncyclicity requires that the position of the physical system in phase space is never duplicated. Each position in phase space the physical system occupies is unique. Suppose that the Principle of Noncyclical Behavior is satisfied by a physical system. How does Putnam individuate the physical states of the physical system so that they correspond to distinct computational states and so that causal transitions between physical states correspond to computational transitions between computational states? In his proof he defines a maximal state of a physical system that is the value of all field parameters at all points inside the boundary of the physical system at a given time. To ensure that the physical system is in a single computational state during an interval of time from t_i through t_{i+1}, an interval state is defined. This is a region in phase space which consists of all the maximal states the physical system occupies in the temporal interval $[t_i, t_{i+1})$. This interval is open at the right. This convention guarantees that each interval state is unique. Interval states are nonmaximal states, for they consist of the different maximal states of S during the time interval $[t_i, t_{i+1})$. Since this is a region in phase space of different maximal states, it is not, by definition, a maximal state. S is in an interval state s whenever it is in one of the maximal states that are in the region of phase space for which s is defined.

Interval states define computational states. If a physical system is in seven different interval states during some time period, it is maximally in seven different computational states. It might instance the same computational state more than once. The triviality theorem describes a finite automaton with two different computational states A and B, where A is instanced four times and B is instanced three times. The sequence of computational states is ABABABA. Where there are seven interval states, there are minimally two different computational states. Suppose that a physical system P-computes a recursive function requiring two computational states A and B. The computational state A is defined disjunctively. It is the disjunction of the interval states the physical system occupies during the temporal periods in which the physical system is in computational state A. Suppose that the sequence of computational states in the computation of F(n) is ABABABA and the sequence of interval states is $IS_1, \ldots, IS_7$. A is defined as the disjunction of interval states $IS_1 \vee IS_3 \vee IS_5 \vee IS_7$. B is defined as the disjunction of interval states $IS_2 \vee IS_4 \vee IS_6$. It is essential that each interval state is distinct from each of the other interval states. Putnam claims that this is guaranteed by the Principle of Noncyclical Behavior.[9]

A Problem for Interval States

An interval state may consist of multiple maximal states, so long as all of them occur during the time period for which the interval state is defined. Thus, as we have seen above, an interval state may occupy a region, not merely a point, in phase space. Although this condition is necessary for ensuring the uniqueness of interval states, it poses a problem, whether the physical state obeys classical mechanics or whether it obeys quantum mechanics. We will not consider the quantum mechanical problem. We consider a little noticed problem arising in classical mechanics.

Commentators on P-triviality claim that quantum mechanical physical systems might not satisfy the principle of Continuity and might not satisfy the Principle of Noncyclical Behavior.[10] However, they have conceded the Principle of Continuity must hold in classical mechanics. But Putnam cannot meet the following criticism by arguing that P-triviality holds only for physical systems that satisfy classical mechanics. What I wish to show is that a result in classical Newtonian mechanics poses a problem for the definition of an interval state. If P-triviality does not hold for quantum-mechanical physical systems and does not hold for classical mechanical physical systems, then there are no physical systems that P-compute.

The result in classical Newtonian mechanics that poses a problem for the Principle of Noncyclical Behavior is there are multiple solutions to classical Newtonian mechanical equations. In that case, the outcomes of certain experiments in classical Newtonian mechanics are indeterminate. The view is that the indeterminacy exists in nature and is not a consequence of the limitations on measuring physical properties. This result was announced by David Gale in 1952.[11] The problem is that the equations of classical Newtonian mechanics allow for multiple solutions and that, in many experimental circumstances, one cannot arrange things so the same outcome occurs each time the experiment is performed. Gale shows that for certain kinds of mechanical problems, the outcome of an experiment depends discontinuously on initial conditions. The experiments are very simple. In one experiment, three iron balls are constrained to move on a straight line. One ball is stationary and the other two move toward it with unit speed from equal distances. Two different outcomes can occur, and they depend discontinuously on initial conditions.

Interval states define computational states disjunctively and the Principle of Noncyclical behavior guarantees disjointness. An interval state occupies a region in phase space when there is a repeated computational state in a P-computation. That region in phase space consists of all the maximal states which fall within the temporal interval in which the interval state is defined. Here, then, is the problem for interval states.

Suppose the physical system that P-computes F is a classical Newtonian system and that classical Newtonian mechanics is the source of the physical laws that govern its interactions. Suppose, also, that for computations of any range value, F instances the same computational state n times.[12] Suppose that computational state A occurs four times. The interval state that defines it is a region in phase space consisting of four maximal states of the physical system. How can it be determined that each of the maximal states in that region of the interval state is the maximal state of a single solution to the equations of classical Newtonian mechanics that govern the time evolution of the physical system? The physical system might instance solution 1 at t_i and solution 2 at t_{i+n}. Both solutions will depend discontinuously on initial conditions and which one will obtain at t_i and t_{i+n} cannot be predicted ahead of time.

If two maximal states in the interval state are different solutions of the same set of equations (for example, those for the laws of conservation and momentum that govern inelastic collisions), there is a discontinuity in the physical system. Suppose that all the field parameters in a maximal state have value k.[13] If within a maximal state causal processes that are governed by classical Newtonian laws occur and there is an indeterminacy, the outcome of the same causal process in region 1 and the outcome of the same causal process in region 2 may differ even though the initial conditions for each are exactly the same. In that case, we will not know whether the overall value of the maximal state at t is v_1 or v_2. Now suppose that at $t + 1$, the same state of affairs obtains. This allows the following possibility. At t the value of the maximal state is v_1 and at $t + 1$ the value of the maximal state is v_1. If so, there is a violation of the Principle of Noncyclical Behavior. In that case, we do not have two genuine interval states, but only one. Now suppose the difference between v_1 and v_2 is small. Suppose that the outcomes of the causal processes are too small to measure. In that case, we will falsely believe there are two interval states that are proper and will thus falsely believe the physical system P-computes F, when, in reality, it fails to P-compute F.

There is another way that the indeterminacy of classical Newtonian mechanics creates a problem for interval states. Suppose that within a maximal state of S at t there are multiple causal processes, all Newtonian classical. In both regions 1 and 2 (in S), it is indeterminate whether v_1 or v_2 occurs. Suppose that if v_1 occurs in region 1 and v_2 occurs in region 2, there is a discontinuity in the local structure of the manifold that is the abstract space in which the differential equations governing the causal processes are represented. This discontinuity in the abstract manifold signals a discontinuity in the gravitational and/or electromagnetic fields in S. If so, the Principle of Continuity is violated. If it is violated, we can design a physical system S' that has the same spatial boundaries as the physical system S and physical conditions that occurred inside S at t hold inside S' and physical conditions on the boundary of S that held at $t + n$ hold on the boundary of S'. Thus, S' is a physical system in which the Principle of Noncyclical behavior is violated since we can design it so that the same maximal state holds inside the boundary and on the boundary. In that way, we fail to define computational states by interval states.

There is a third problem where there is indeterminacy in classical Newtonian mechanics. If there are two different solutions to the classical mechanical equations in the same interval state, the causal connections between physical states are "disrupted" in the region of the discontinuity in the gravitational and/or electromagnetic fields. By "disruption" we mean a break in the causal connections between the interval state that represents computational state A and the interval state that represents the computational state B. To see why this is so, we need to look at what Putnam says about how being in interval state 1 causes the physical system to make the transition into interval state 2: "To show that being in [computational state] A ... "caused" S to go into [computational] state B ... we argue as follows: Given that S is in state A at time t ($t_1 \leq t < t_2$), and letting the maximal state of the boundary of S at that time be $B_{t'}$, it follows from the lemma that $St(S, t)$ is the only maximal state in any of the "regions" (nonmaximal states) $s_1, s_2, \ldots, s_7$ that a system S under the boundary condition $B_{t'}$ could be in without violating the Principle of Continuity."[14]

However, if the value of computational state B is v_1 rather than v_2 and the value of any of the maximal states in A is v_1, then the maximal state of the boundary of S at t is $B_{t'}$, which is v_1, which is the value of the maximal states of A at t. But the Principle of Continuity is violated, since the value at the boundary is v_1, not v_2. The value of v_1 at the boundary indicates a discontinuity in either the electromagnetic or gravitational fields. Further, it is now possible that there are other maximal states S can be in that do not violate the Principle of Continuity. For instance, the seven interval states for the finite automaton that runs through the sequence of computational states ABABABA are each nonmaximal regions of phase space, in each of which there are maximal states. If in these regions there are maximal states S can be in without violating the Principle of Continuity, then S is in that state. In that case, S is not in A and so it is not "caused" to go into B. To put the same point differently, the boundary of S at t will not be the only boundary of any in the union of the regions $s_1, \ldots, s_7$ that fits the boundary condition $B_{t'}$.

Since causal connections ensure a physical system evolves in time and that an omniscient observer can predict what physical state it will evolve into for any future time, a disruption in these causal connections means no prediction can be made. If so, it is in principle impossible to determine what the physical system P-computes. But in addition, the sequence of computational states that makes up a computation of F will not be isomorphic to the causal connections between physical realizers of computational states. In that case, there is no P-computation at all.

Let us return to the case in which there are not two interval states, but only one, though no human being can determine there is one and not two interval states. How should the trivialist assess such a case? Is it an error in a P-computation or is it a physical situation that fails to satisfy the conditions for P-computation? Imagine an analogous case for a digital computer. The computer breaks down because a classical Newtonian causal process results in value v_2 instead of value v_1. We do not say that the conditions for computation of F are no longer satisfied when this happens. Rather, we say that an error in the computation of F has occurred. This difference between P-computation in a physical system and genuine computation in a digital computer is significant. Indeterminacy in classical Newtonian mechanics does not jeopardize the claim that computation of some kind occurs when we know a physical system—the digital computer—has genuinely computed F. But it does falsify the claim that P-computation has occurred in the physical system. That is why the computationalist does not worry if a digital computer or a human mind described as a computational device is subject to indeterminacy in classical Newtonian mechanics. If the physical computing system is subject to it, we don't thereby say that it is incapable of making computations. We have a theory of error for the physical system that we can use to determine whether the computations are or are not correct.

But a trivialist must worry. If we say that P-computation may or may not have occurred in a physical system, but we may never know, then the notion of P-computation becomes incoherent. In that event, P-computation is not threatening to the computationalist, since it does not jeopardize the notion of an authentic computation precisely because it does jeopardize the notion of a trivial computation. To say that there may or may not be universal realization of computations in physical objects, but we may never know, is not to show the notion of authentic computation is worthless. If it can be shown that any physical object computes any computable function under verifiable empirical conditions and that there is no way of tightening the definition of what it is for a physical system to physically realize a computation, the notion of computation has been shown worthless.

Poincaré Recurrence and the Principles of Continuity and Noncyclical Behavior

If the physical system never re-enters a point in phase space that it previously occupied, it will satisfy the Principle of Noncyclical Behavior. Thus, each interval state is unique.[15] But not every physical system will satisfy this Principle for all times t. Certainly, chaotic systems can degenerate and re-enter points of phase space. Poincaré's recurrence theorem tells us that, with non-negligible probability, a physical system will re-enter a portion of phase space it previously occupied.[16] But any physical system, chaotic or not, will satisfy the conditions of the Poincaré Recurrence Theorem. Thus, the P-trivialist must be able to determine when a physical system engaging in P-computation will re-enter a part of phase space it had previously occupied. For if a physical system does that, it fails to P-compute. If not, then, ceteris paribus, it P-computes. Suppose that determining that a physical system has re-entered a part of phase space it had previously occupied is either undecidable or else requires solving a problem that is, for instance, in the complexity class EXPTIME. In that case, there is a dilemma for the P-trivialist. On one horn, if P-computation of a computable function is logically undecidable, there is a contradiction in speaking of a P-computation of a computable function. On the other horn, suppose it violates the resource profiles of the function that is P-computed. If, for instance, it takes exponentially many resources to compute a function in the lower hierarchy of the complexity class P, then the notion of P-computation violates the constraints on computation from computational complexity theory. (Notice that even though it is the trivialist and not the physical system engaging in trivial computation who must perform these computations, they are still part of the physical system's computation of F, since without them the trivialist would not know whether F has been computed by the physical system. In this way, trivial computations in a physical system may, in some circumstances, require the trivialist to become part of the entire computational structure.)

Here is an example of how the aforementioned dilemma arises where the trivialist claims that a wall is P-computing a simple arithmetical function, namely the constant function (that is, the function that outputs the constant c for any input value): Suppose that the function outputs the number 5 for any integer input. This function is in the lowest level of the P-hierarchy (where the P hierarchy is the class of feasibly computable functions). Now suppose that determining that the molecules in the wall re-enter a portion of phase space they had previously occupied is an undecidable problem. If so, the computation of the constant function is undecidable! Or suppose that determining that the molecules re-enter phase space takes exponentially many resources to compute (because doing so is a problem in the complexity class EXPTIME). If so, calculating the constant function takes exponentially many resources and thus the P-computational model violates a theorem in computational complexity theory: problems in P are provably not in EXPTIME.

It is essential to the statement of Putnam's Triviality Theorem that the kinds of physical systems to which it applies be specified. Simply saying that the physical systems for which the theorem holds satisfy the Principle of Noncyclical Behavior does nothing toward telling us which kinds of physical systems satisfy it. This is not a problem if few physical systems violate it, or we can reliably tell which physical systems do and which do not violate it. Neither is the case. Even simple classical Newtonian systems consisting of balls rolling down an inclined plane can violate Noncyclical Behavior. Moreover, it might be impossible to determine whether the conditions for chaotic transitions to recurrent physical states (or to states which violate the Principle of Continuity) are in place. For example, if physical system$_1$ is embedded in physical system$_2$, and the latter exhibits chaotic behavior, but we cannot determine that physical system$_1$ is embedded, we will not be in any position to reliably whether the Principle of Noncyclical Behavior is violated or whether the Principle of Continuity is violated.

If it can't be determined that a physical system does or does not violate either the Principle of Continuity or the Principle of Noncyclical Behavior, then we do not know that the physical system P-computes F. If any physical system might be open to the kinds of physical problems that rule out P-computations in it and we can't reliably determine the physical system suffers them, then P-computation is an empty notion. A trivialist who uses P-triviality to argue against computational functionalism sustains a burden of proof. She must show that the physical system implementing trivial computations does not violate the two principles.

Finally, given an arbitrary physical system, the P-trivialist must qualify her claim that it P-computes some function F in the following way: There is a non-negligible probability that the physical system will not P-compute at all at some stage in the computation of F, but we might never know whether it does or does not P-compute at that stage in the computation of F. But we certainly do not have to similarly qualify our claims that a physical system genuinely computes some function F.

We don't say of the physical system that there is a non-negligible probability that it will not authentically compute at some stage in the computation of F. Rather, we can say there might be a non-negligible probability of error in the computation of F at some stage in the computation of F. In this way, there is an asymmetry in the conceptions of authentic computation of F and P-computation of F that is ineliminable, since the Poincaré Recurrence Theorem is a physical law governing all physical systems.

A Modal Problem for the Triviality Lemma

Putnam proves a lemma ancillary to proving his triviality theorem. The lemma establishes a sufficient condition for violating the Principle of

Continuity: "If we form a system S' with the same spatial boundaries as S by stipulating that the conditions *inside* the boundary are to be the conditions that obtained inside S at time t while the conditions *on* the boundary are to be the ones that obtained on the boundary of S at time t', where t and t' are different [note that this will be possible only if the spatial boundary assigned to the system S is the same at t and t'], then the resulting system will violate the Principle of Continuity."[17]

The proof of the lemma shows that images of a clock signal received inside the boundary at time t and at the boundary at time t produce a discontinuity in S' (at any given time later than t and t'). Putnam asks us to imagine that the images of the clock signal are graphic clock numerals. In that case, there is an '11' just inside the boundary of S' and a '12' on the boundary of S'. The images are physically instantiated within the matter-energy fields that constitute S', so there is a discontinuity in the area between the surface of S' and just inside its surface. Let us see how the requirement that S possess the same spatial boundary condition at two distinct times underlies the construction of S'. By the Principle of Noncyclical Behavior, the conditions which hold just inside the boundary of S at t' must be different from the conditions which hold just inside the boundary of S at t. The physical systems S and S' are made of fields and point particles (which are the sources of the fields). If the fields are continuous, then the continuity "goes" from just inside the boundary of S to the boundary of S. That is why S must have the same spatial boundary at both t and t'. One could not preserve continuity in S in devising the construction of S' unless the demand that the spatial boundary of S is the same at both t and t' is met. If S is continuous, then S must violate noncyclicity. If S is not continuous, then S will conform to noncyclicity. However, S' itself is not continuous.

The Principle of Continuity has the status of a physical law, but the Principle of Noncyclical Behavior does not. It is assumed to hold in each normal macroscopic open system. If it had the status of a physical law, chaotic physical systems and Poincaré recurrence would be prohibited. But they are physically, as well as mathematically, possible. Thus, the Principle of Noncyclical Behavior cannot be a physical law. As we have already seen, without the Principle of Noncyclical Behavior, we cannot guarantee the interval states that define computational states are unique. Thus, physical systems that exhibit chaotic behavior, Poincaré recurrence, quantum indeterminacy, chaotic quantum indeterminacy, or the indeterminacy in classical Newtonian mechanics do not P-compute, since they fail to satisfy the Principle of Noncyclical Behavior.

Here I point out a problem for the triviality lemma that arises because the Principle of Continuity has the modal status of a law of nature, while the Principle of Noncyclical Behavior is a contingent truth assumed to hold for normal macroscopic open systems (that do not exhibit the kinds of behaviors enumerated just above). In the triviality lemma, it is required that conditions just inside the boundary of S' at $t + 2$ are the conditions that occurred just inside S at t and the conditions on the boundary of S' at $t + 2$ are the conditions that occurred on the boundary of S at $t + 1$. That the conditions on S at t and at $t + 1$ are different satisfies the Principle of Noncyclical Behavior. Given these conditions, the Principle of Continuity is violated in the system S'.

Satisfying Noncyclical Behavior is necessary for violating Continuity. It is also sufficient, since once the conditions that satisfy Noncyclical Behavior are in place, the Principle of Continuity is violated. A necessary and sufficient condition for a violation of a physical law—for the Principle of Continuity is assumed to have the modal status of a physical law—is that a contingent fact about ordinary macroscopic open systems, the Principle of Noncyclical Behavior, holds. How can a purely modal contingency (from the point of view of physical modality) be a necessary and sufficient condition for violating what is physically necessary (from the point of view of physical modality)?

The obvious response is that it can and does happen. However, this response ignores what is special about the violation. It is not that there is a violation of a physical law in nature. Rather, we conjecture what would happen if the Principle of Noncyclical Behavior is used to construct a state of affairs that is contrary to fact. This is not a violation of Continuity in the actual world, but in a counterfactual world. It is also an abstract counterfactual world. No physical features of either S or S' are used in constructing the state of affairs. If the Principle of Noncyclical Behavior is not a physical law, but a contingent truth about ordinary macroscopic open systems, why do we expect it to hold in a counterfactual situation? In the counterfactual state of affairs constructed in the triviality lemma, it might happen that S or S' exhibits chaotic behavior, or an indeterminacy in classical Newtonian mechanics. If that happens, then the conditions necessary for violating Continuity will not occur and the lemma fails.

This possibility cannot be ruled out unless it is stipulated that the Principle of Noncyclical Behavior holds in the envisaged counterfactual state of affairs. But the effect of doing that is to make the Principle of Noncyclical Behavior into a physical law that holds for all ordinary macroscopic open systems. Since chaotic behavior, quantum and chaotic quantum indeterminacy and the indeterminacy of classical Newtonian mechanics are widespread, those physical systems that are ordinary macroscopic open systems in which the Principle of Noncyclical Behavior is a physical law would be a very small fraction of all possible macroscopic open systems found in nature.

Either the Principle of Noncyclical Behavior has the modal status of a physical law or else it is a contingent fact about ordinary macroscopic open systems, in which case the triviality lemma might fail. If ordinary macroscopic open systems are not restricted to a small fraction of all macroscopic open systems found in nature, but includes all of them, then if the Principle of Noncyclical Behavior has the modal status of a physical law, it is in contradiction with mathematical facts. For example, it is in contradiction with the indeterminacy of classical Newtonian mechanics. For another example, it contradicts Poincaré recurrence. Suppose that the human brain is a physical system that is not an ordinary macroscopic open system, but *is* a macroscopic open system. If so, the Principle of Noncyclical Behavior is not true of it, and it follows that the triviality theorem does not apply to it. If so, the human brain cannot P-compute.

With respect to the triviality theorem, we have a dilemma. First horn: If the Principle of Noncyclical Behavior has the modal status of a physical law, then either the ordinary macroscopic open systems to which it applies are a small fraction of all macroscopic open systems (and so it might exclude the human brain) or else it includes all macroscopic open systems (and so includes the human brain), but contradicts mathematical facts (such as the indeterminacy of classical Newtonian mechanics). Second horn: If the Principle of Noncyclical Behavior does not have the modal status of a physical law, then the counterfactuals defined in constructing the state of affairs necessary for the contradiction with the Principle of Continuity in the triviality lemma can turn out false.

We have seen that S-triviality succumbs to the counterfactual objection to triviality. Here we see that P-triviality succumbs to a different kind of counterfactual objection to triviality. The consequence is the same in both cases: triviality theories cannot account for counterfactuals and so cannot provide definitions of what it is for a physical system to physically realize a computation.

Why not drop the triviality lemma? If so, the triviality theorem is saved. Is it necessary for proving the triviality theorem? Putnam does say that "if the shape, size, or location of S changes with time, then unless S resumes the boundary it had at t at least once, the boundary of S at t will be the only boundary associated with any maximal state in the union of these regions which fits the boundary condition B_t, and the lemma is unnecessary."[18] But the lemma is necessary for the proof of the triviality theorem where a physical system maintains its shape, size or location over time or else changes shape, size or location over time, but at some future time returns to that shape, size or location. We do not imagine that human brains change shape, size or location from t_i to t_j, even where the difference between j and i is large. In development, human brains do change size and shape. If so, humans P-compute only from infancy through adolescence.[19]

If the triviality lemma is not used, certain kinds of physical behaviors that will falsify the triviality theorem cannot be ruled out. For instance, without the triviality lemma, discontinuities in either the physical system, or in the phase space representation of the physical system, can occur. If the Principle of Continuity is not satisfied, the physical system can be in two different interval states at a given instant, because there could be two different regions in phase space each of which—physically it happens somehow—overlap at the endpoint t_{i+1}. If so, the physical system cannot P-compute, since there will be no interval states, and they are necessary for defining computational states.

P-triviality suffers from several problems. If it cannot be sustained, a critical move in Putnam's argument against computational functionalism fails. Putnam uses the Gödel incompleteness theorems to show that even if human minds have a computational description, we will never be able to justify we have that description. If triviality works, human minds have every computational description. There are infinitely many different computational descriptions of the human mind, though not all are true of it (assuming it has one). The best we can do is justify what is a false computational description, since we can never justify our true computational description. "When we are correctly described by an infinity of logically possible "functional descriptions," what is the claim supposed to *mean* that one of these has the (unrecognizable) property of being our "normative" description? Is it supposed to describe, in some way, our very *essence*?"[20] This is a powerful indictment of computational functionalism. But it fails if P-triviality can't be sustained.

Appendix: Step-Function Triviality

In *Renewing Philosophy* and in "Artificial Intelligence: Much Ado about Not Very Much"[21] Putnam points out that any arbitrary function, computable or non-computable, can be finitely approximated, up to some specified level of accuracy, by recursive functions. My plan here is to use this idea to elaborate a new kind of triviality theory. Why is another triviality theory needed? I do not think S-triviality or P-triviality jeopardizes computationalism. But there may be other versions of triviality that do. Here I define a new version and show how it jeopardizes computationalism.[22] I call this new triviality theory 'SF-triviality', for 'step-function triviality'.

Putnam says that "if we are interested in the behavior of a physical system that is finite in space and time and we wish to predict that behavior only up to some specified level of accuracy, then (assuming that the laws of motion are themselves continuous functions) it is trivial to show that a step function will give the prediction to the specified level of accuracy. If the possible values of the boundary parameters are restricted to a finite range, then a finite set of such step functions will give the behavior of the system under all possible conditions in the specified range to within the desired accuracy. But if that is the case, the behavior of the system is described by a recursive function and hence the system can be simulated by an automaton."[23]

The important points to observe are that (i) only a finite part of the function or the physical system can be approximated, (ii) the accuracy level specified may be less than 100 percent, and (iii) the simulation is done entirely post hoc—one must already know the values of the function or the behavior of the system before it is finitely recursively approximated.[24]

The third condition has most importance in defining a new kind of triviality theory. Any trivial computation does not tell you the value of the trivially computed function unless you already know the value of the function. Trivial computers do not solve problems unless one already knows the solution to the problem. Similarly, any step-function approximation of a function or the behavior of a physical system cannot occur unless you already know the values of the function or the behavior of the physical system.

Suppose that the human mind does not have a computational description. In addition, suppose that it is either identical with or supervenes on the human brain. Then any finite segment (in space and time) of the behavior of the human brain can be finitely recursively approximated to some specified degree of accuracy.[25] Since FRA can be modeled by a finite automaton, the human brain has a computational description. If we can FRA the behavior of the human mind, it also has a computational description. Whatever the physical system or whatever the function, we can FRA the physical behavior of the former and the function values of the latter. It is not the case that any physical system has any FRA or that any function has any FRA. In this way, SF-triviality differs from S-triviality and from P-triviality. A physical system has only the FRA that describes its actual physical behavior. A function has only the FRA that describes its actual function values. SF-triviality is *not* the claim that since any physical object computes any function, the claim that a physical object computes a function is meaningless, as is the claim that the human mind has a computational description.

SF-triviality is the claim that the human mind, even if it has no computational description, can be given a computational description, for there is a FRA that is true of it. It is not meaningless to say that the human mind has a FRA, since it is not the case that there are infinitely many different FRAs true of it.[26] Similarly, a noncomputable function is noncomputable, though it can be given a computational description, since there is a FRA true of it.

In SF-triviality, the behavior of any physical object is reconstructed as a finite automaton. In that sense, it says little philosophically to claim that the human mind is a finite automation if everything else is a finite automaton under FRA. Thus, cognitive science and the philosophy of mind are trivialized by the possibility of FRA. Moreover, FRA cannot be dismissed in the same way that traditional versions of triviality are dismissed. Authentic physical or computational behavior is being authentically simulated by FRA. It is harder to refute SF-triviality, even though it is not as versatile as S-triviality or P-triviality.

Putnam says that "[t]he claim that the human brain [or human mind] can be modeled as a computer is thus, in one way, trivial. Perhaps there is another more meaningful sense in which we can ask 'Can the brain [or mind] be modeled as a computer?' At this point, however, all we can say is that the sense of the question has not been made clear."[27] In effect, he poses a dilemma for the computationalist. Either there is a trivial FRA simulation of the human mind or the question whether there is a computational simulation makes no sense. What we wish to do is show that SF-triviality faces problems that show it can't be used as a scientific description of the human mind nor as a philosophical picture of how the human mind works.

An Example of FRA

To understand FRA, we need the definition of a step function:

Let I be any interval. A function $SF : I \rightarrow \mathbb{R}$ [where $\mathbb{R}$ is the set of real numbers] is called a step function if there is a finite collection $\{I_1, I_2, \ldots, I_n\}$ of pairwise disjoint intervals such that $S = I_1 \cup I_2 \cup \cdots \cup I_n \subseteq I$ [where S is the set on which SF is defined] and a set $\{c_1, c_2, \ldots, c_n\}$ of finite, nonzero real numbers such that

$$SF(x) = \begin{cases} c_j & \text{if } x \in I_j, \, j = 1, 2, \ldots, n \\ 0 & \text{if } x \in I - S.^{28} \end{cases}$$

Here is an example of a step function: Let $SF : [0, 4) \rightarrow R$ be defined by $SF(x) = 1$ if $0 \le x < 2$ and $SF(x) = 2$ if $2 \le x < 4$.[29] (See figure 4.1)

A FRA of a function by step functions is a list of the different values the function has for different domain values. For a simple example of FRA, consider a linear function $y = 2x$. This function is represented by a straight line in the plane with a certain slope. To construct FRA for this function, we have to know all the ordered pairs of the form $\langle x, fx \rangle$ consisting of the domain value and the range value in the finite interval which is FRA. Notice that as the value of x increases monotonically, the value of y increases monotonically. For no two values of x is there a single y value. FRA of $y = 2x$ will be a step function that lists, for each interval $x_j - x_i$ $(j > i)$, the average value of fx on that interval. In general, it is obvious that the smaller the interval, the better the FRA to the function. Suppose that we wish the specified level of accuracy of the FRA to be 100 percent. If so, the intervals will have no width. For each point x, we specify the value of fx. The step-function definition of this FRA will be a list of each pair $\{x, fx\}$ for the domain on which we wish to FRA the behavior of the function. On the other hand, the function is defined by the equation $y = 2x$. A computer program based on the definition of the function will be much shorter than one based on a step-function definition.

A Problem for SF-Triviality

In this section we describe a difficulty SF-triviality faces. There is a connection between the ideas of randomness and program length well known in

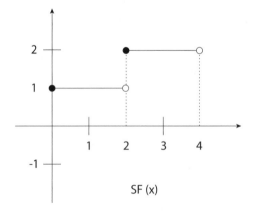

Figure 4.1

computer science. It forms the basis of Kolmogorov complexity theory, an alternative theory of how hard it is to compute a function.[30] The basic idea of Kolmogorov complexity is that the length of a computer program is a measure of the complexity of the information contained in the mathematical objects it computes. The shorter the length of a computer program, the less complex the function that it computes. Consider a sequence of numbers: $2, 4, 8, 16, 32, 64, 128, 256, 512, 1024, 2056, \ldots$. Suppose that the sequence has 10,000 elements. Each element in the sequence is indexed by a natural number, beginning with 1. It can be generated by squaring each index. The first element is $2^1 = 2$. The second is $2^2 = 4$. The computer program generating this sequence is very short. It is the function $y = 2^n$. The complexity of the sequence is defined relative to a specifying method for it. In this case, the specifying method is the computer program. Next consider the sequence of integers that is the decimal expansion of the transcendental number pi. It is $3.1415\ldots$. The sequence is infinitely long, but it is not very complex, for it is generated by a short computer program. Now consider a sequence of integers that, unlike the expansion of pi, is random. This sequence is complex, since the computer program that generates it is long.

There is a substantial body of work that relates Kolmogorov complexity to the standard theory of computational complexity.[31] We do not need to borrow much from this work to make our point against SF-triviality. Consider the function $y = x^2$. This is a non-linear function. The computer program for generating the sequence of range values $(0, 1, 4, 9, 16, 25, 36, 49, 64, 81, 100, \ldots)$ is short. So the sequence is not complex. What is the FRA of this function? The graph of this function looks like an upside down Bell curve which is symmetrical about the vertical y-axis. It is not a straight-line curve. It is non-linear and so has non-constant curvature in different intervals of the x axis. The FRA of this function requires n step functions, where n is the number of elements in the sequence of range values. The computer program for the step functions will be as long as the number of step functions. That is, it is just a listing of all the step functions. The specifying method that is the computer program for step functions makes the sequence into a highly complex object.

But the optimal method for generating the sequence is the computer program that uses the definition of the function, $y = x^2$. Relative to the specifying method of step functions, the sequence is random. But relative to the specifying method of the definition of the function, it is not random. What is the truth of the matter? Is the sequence random or not? It is not random, since the optimal method for computing it is the one based on the definition of the function. The sequence can be compressed by the computer program based on $y = x^2$. It cannot be compressed by the step-function program. We cannot use the step-function method of specifying the sequence to tell us the "nature" of the sequence. Its nature is that it is not random.

Now consider a computational description of the human mind in terms of step functions. Can we use FRA to tell us about the computational nature of the human mind? No, we can't. If we know this is the only method of specifying the human mind computationally and we also know that the human mind has some computational description, then we can use FRA to say something about the computational nature of the human mind. But we would already have to answer the question "Does the human mind have a computational description?" before we can consider what FRA says about it. After that, we would have to prove there are no other computational descriptions that compress the finitary behavior description generated by FRA. If there are, then FRA cannot say something true about the computational nature of the human mind.

Another difficulty that SF-triviality faces is closely related to the preceding one. Data from cognitive science tells us how much time and (sometimes) how much space it takes to compute certain cognitive functions. In psycholinguistics, there is a large body of such data. Suppose that cognitive function C has a resource profile. That is, we know how long it takes to compute instances of it. Now construct a FRA of it (on the assumption that we can get the FRA from the cognitive behavior C exemplifies). If the FRA of it is much longer than the computer program for the cognitive function, there is trouble. Using resource-bounded Kolmogorov complexity, it can be shown that the step-function computer program will take much more time on C tasks than the non-step-function computer program. If so, the FRA will give a false estimate of how hard it is to compute C. This is the same kind of difficulty we pointed out for S-triviality. It contradicts mathematical facts from computational complexity theory.

But in the case of FRA, the step-function programs will take more resources to compute a function. A function that is computable at the lowest level of the P hierarchy may be computable by a step-function program at the highest level of that hierarchy and possibly in the complexity class NP. The resource profile of computing a cognitive function is one measure of the goodness of a psychological theory. If so, then FRA will fail that test. The step-function program of a cognitive function must be rejected when it cannot respect the actual resource profile of that function. In that case, though there is a computational description of that cognitive function, it is unacceptable as a cognitive theory of it.

Recall the quotation from Putnam about FRA: "... in one sense, any physical system can be modeled as a computer.... The claim that the brain [or mind] can be modeled as a computer is thus, in one way, trivial."[32] However, if the computer modeling of the human mind fails to respect its resource profile, then it can't be taken as an acceptable modeling. It must be rejected. If so, we do not say it is a modeling. Rather, we say it is either a failed modeling, or no modeling at all. It fails to respect the data of cognitive science, and so it is not a scientifically respectable modeling. SF-triviality is, then, refuted.

Objection: Not all step-function computer programs are much longer than their non-step-function counterparts. In all cases where the step-function program and the non-step-function program are comparable in length, the data of cognitive science will be respected (if it is respected by the non-step-function program) and both the step-function program and the non-step-function program will make the same judgments about the computational nature of the cognitive function they model. Thus SF-triviality is not refuted for all possible cases.

Response: There are ways a cognitive scientist can shorten the length of a non-step-function program that are not available for step-function programs. One way is by ascending to a higher-order programming language. For example, ascending from machine language to a standard programming language, such as C++, shortens program length. The precedent for decreasing program length comes from mathematical logic. Lengths of proofs can be decreased by moving from one logical system to a stronger logical system. There are speed-up theorems that show there are no recursive bounds on the shortening of proofs in well-defined situations.

If program length is decreased by ascent to a higher-order programming language, or by changing the computational model, the question of the psychological reality of the new programming language or of the new computational model arises. A different computational model or a different programming language might not respect the resource profile of cognitive functions. This is an empirical issue. That it is possible a speed-up achieved by changing to a different computational model is psychologically unrealistic does not defeat the point that there is speed-up for non-step-function programs, but not for step-function programs. But this issue arises only where the step-function program is the same, or a comparable length, to a non-step-function program. For instance, when the function computed is highly complex, the step-function program and non-step-function program will be comparable in length. In such a case, whether there is psychologically realistic speed-up for the non-step function is an important consideration in judging that the non-step function, but not the step function, is a psychologically adequate modeling of that aspect of human cognition so modeled.

If we find that step-function and non-step-function programs for cognition are comparable in length and that the non-step-function program cannot be shortened by speed-up without becoming psychologically unrealistic, that will revive Putnam's point that it is trivial that the human mind can be modeled by a digital computer. Suppose that the non-step-function Master Program of the human mind is comparable in length to the step-function Master Program of the human mind. The SF-trivialist will have to show that either there is no speed-up of the non-step-function program or that the speed-up of it is psychologically unrealistic. This is an empirical issue, but it cannot be settled now, since we now do not know what the Master Program of the human mind (if there is one) looks like.

This creates a problem for Putnam. He says: "... Dennett accuses me of offering an '*a priori*' argument that success is impossible. I have not changed the text of [this] paper at all in the light of his reply, and I invite the reader to observe that no such '*a priori* proof of impossibility' claim is advanced by me here or elsewhere!"[33] SF-triviality underlies Putnam's point that it is trivial the human mind can be modeled by a digital computer. We have shown SF-triviality confronts two problems: it conflicts with computational complexity theory and it makes false claims about the computational nature of the functions that are FRA. These two problems undermine SF-triviality and thus undermine Putnam's point. However, IF the non-step-function Master Program of the human mind is comparable in length to the step-function Master Program of the human mind and the non-step-function program either cannot be shortened or can be shortened only at the expense of becoming psychologically unrealistic, then Putnam's point is revived. But since we do not now know what the Master Program for the human mind will look like, any conjectures about it that would be specific enough to show it cannot be shortened or that it can be shortened, but only at the expense of becoming psychologically unrealistic are, now, purely *a priori*.

5 Searle on Triviality and the Subjective Nature of Computation

Suppose that P-triviality, S-triviality, and SF-triviality have been refuted. There might be other triviality theories, however. If so, these can be exploited by the trivialist. The trivialist can argue that even though current triviality theories have been refuted, there are others to take their place. If there is a philosophical claim that underlies triviality theories and it is refuted, then all possible triviality theories are refuted. What philosophical claim underlies a triviality theory? John Searle contends there is a metaphysical picture of computation underlying triviality theories: computation is an observer-relative feature of the world. I will examine Searle's claim in this chapter. I will argue that it confronts problems it does not have the resources to resolve. If so, trivialists must either show a different philosophical claim underlies triviality theories or else give up triviality.

In *The Rediscovery of the Mind*, Searle responds as follows to the counterfactual objection to triviality: "I think it is possible to block the result of universal computation by tightening up our definition of computation.... There must be a causal structure sufficient to warrant counterfactuals. But these further restrictions on the definition of computation are no help ... *because the really deep problem is that syntax is essentially an observer-relative notion. The multiple realizability of computationally equivalent processes in different physical media is not just a sign that the processes are abstract, but that they are not intrinsic to the system at all. They depend on an interpretation from outside.* We were looking for some facts of the matter that would make brain processes computational, but given the way we have defined computation, there never could be any such facts of the matter."[1] For Searle triviality (and thus the definition of what it is for a physical system to physically realize a computation) is not the real issue in mechanism debates. The real issue is the metaphysics of computation: "... *notions such as computation, algorithm, and program do not name intrinsic physical features of systems.* Computational states are not *discovered within* the physics, they are *assigned to* the physics."[2] Syntax is not intrinsic to physics, since it is observer relative. Different observers can assign a different syntax to the same physical system. Searle divides up the world into those features which are intrinsic and those which are observer relative. How do we determine whether an arbitrary feature of the world is intrinsic or observer relative? Here is the test Searle proposes: if there were no observers and the feature still exists, then it is intrinsic to the world. On the other hand, if a feature goes out of existence when observers go out of existence, then that feature is observer relative. Observer-relative features of the world depend, for their existence, on observers.

Searle takes expressions such as 'gravitational attraction' and 'molecule' to name intrinsic features of the world and expressions such as 'bathtub' and 'chair' and 'nice day for a picnic' to name observer-relative features of the world. If there are no observers, there are no chairs, no bathtubs, and no nice days for picnics, but there are molecules and there is gravitational attraction. (It isn't that the physical objects called 'bathtubs' disappear if there are no humans. It is, rather, that the physical object that to humans is a bathtub would not be a bathtub if there were no humans. Of course, it is unlikely that random physical processes could cause a bathtub-shaped object to come into existence.) Given that for Searle a physical system engaging in a computation is an observer-relative feature of it, any human observer could, in principle, assign any computational description to any sufficiently complex physical object. Suppose that the physical object is the human brain. Jack interprets it as computing function 1, while Jill interprets it as computing function 2. If Searle is right that there is no fact of the matter in nature that decides whether the human brain is computing function 1 or function 2 (because syntax is not intrinsic to physics), then what function we decide the human brain computes is a convention. Thus, on Searle's metaphysics it is a human convention that the human brain computes such-and-such functions. Now suppose the object is the human mind. Jack interprets it as computing function 1, while Jill interprets it as computing function 2. What function we decide the human mind computes is a human convention. Consequently, the language of thought is a human convention! But we can't take this to be a *reductio* of the claim that computations are observer relative. If we did, we would be guilty of begging the question about the metaphysical status of computations.

Of course, if we agree what physical features must be present, for example, for a day to be called a 'nice day for a picnic', then there is a fact of the matter about when a day is a nice day for a picnic. If a nice day for a picnic requires physical features F_1 and F_2, then Jack is right that it is a nice day for a picnic when he observes that both F_1 and F_2 obtain and asserts that it a nice day for a picnic, while Jill is wrong that it is a nice day for a picnic when she observes that F_1 and F_3 obtain and asserts that it is a nice day for a picnic. That one observer can be right and another observer can be wrong about it being a nice day for a picnic does not show that being a nice day for a picnic is an intrinsic feature of the world. Rather, it shows that two observers can disagree in what they take the convention for being a nice day for a picnic to consist in. Similarly, it is, in Searle's eyes, a convention that we pair certain physical features of the brain with certain computations.[3] That we pair the computations we do with the brain states we do fixes the convention. Thus, two observers can disagree over what the convention consists in. But, for Searle, that does not mean that the brain states being paired with those computations is an intrinsic feature of the world. Just as both the pairing of physical features of the environment with being a nice day for a picnic and which physical features of the environment are paired with being a nice day for a picnic are conventions, so too the pairing of computations with brain states and which computations we pair with brain states are conventions.

Searle draws a strong conclusion from his metaphysics of computation: "The aim of natural science is to discover and characterize features that are intrinsic to the natural world. By its own definitions of computation and cognition, there is no way that computational cognitive science could ever be a natural science, because computation is not an intrinsic feature of the world. It is assigned relative to observers."[4] If syntax is observer relative and not intrinsic to physics, then cognitive science is not a natural science. It fails to describe intrinsic features of the natural world. Thus, computational characterizations of human cognitive processes are not intrinsic features of the natural world. For instance, the work of David Marr in the late 1970s on how human brains see in depth does not describe an intrinsic feature of the natural world.[5] That we satisfy the particular computational description Marr attributes to us is simply a matter of how Marr interprets us. A different observer might attribute a different computational description to us. According to Searle, there are no physical facts that can decide which is the correct computational description. If so, the one we decide is correct is a convention. We decide we satisfy this description, but there are no physical facts in the natural world that will determine whether we are correct, since the feature the computational description describes is not a natural feature of the world, but is an observer-relative feature. Just as there would be no chairs if there were no human observers, there would be no depth perception algorithms in the human brain if there were no human observers. (If there were only one human being who could not attribute computations to himself, then he could not, on Searle's view of the metaphysics of computations, implement a depth perception algorithm, even though he would—presumably—still be able to see in depth.) Cognitive science cannot, in principle, explain how the human mind works, because there are no information processing structures that are intrinsic to the physics of the human brain, but only mere conventions that we impose on the physics of the brain. If it cannot, in principle, explain how the human mind works, then it is either bankrupt or incoherent.

Putnam does not appeal to Searle's metaphysics of computation. He doesn't think the world divides up into intrinsic features and observer-relative features. For Putnam, the factual is interwoven with the conventional. Facts and values are interanimated—you can't have one without the other. The "one without the other" does not mean facts and values exist independently. It means that facts contain values and values contain facts.[6] If facts are intrinsic features of the natural world and values are observer-relative features and they are interanimated, Searle's dismissal of cognitive science can't take root. It is not clear how a triviality theory can be sustained on this view about facts and values. Suppose Putnam gives up his view about facts and values and adopts Searle's metaphysics of computation. This possibility motivates a critical look at that metaphysics.

Problems in Searle's Metaphysics of Computation

Suppose that the world does divide into intrinsic and observer-relative features. Is it the case that computations are observer relative? Is it the case that computations are not intrinsic to physics? Consider abstract objects, such as numbers. Are they part of the physical world in the same way a tree is a part of the natural world? If there were no human observers, would there be no numbers or would it be that there would be numbers but there would not be numerals? If numbers are abstract objects and not merely nothing more than numerals, then is there an abstract world in which they are intrinsic features of it? The point is that with respect to numbers, it is an open question whether numbers are or are not intrinsic features of either the physical world or of some abstract world. If Searle thinks something is not an intrinsic feature of the physical world or an abstract world, it is a claim for which he must provide an argument. It is one thing to say that 'nice day for a picnic' is an observer-relative feature of the world. This is hardly a contestable claim. It is, though, quite another thing to say that computations are observer-relative features of the world, since we do not say that it incontestable that numbers are observer-relative features. Certainly computations are closer (no matter how 'being closer' is construed) to numbers than they are to 'being a nice day for a picnic', or to bathtubs. What I wish to do in the following is to show that there is a price one must pay in taking certain abstract objects (numbers, computations, philosophical arguments) to be observer-relative features of the world (whether it is the physical world or an abstract world) and that the price is too high and is a factor that militates against taking them to be conventions in the absence of a sound argument that shows they are conventions.

There are different philosophical views about the nature of numbers. On a realist view, numbers exist (though not in the physical world). On a constructivist view, they are mental constructions and would not exist if there were no human minds. Which view is correct? Philosophers do not know. There are arguments for and against each view. If the realist wins, numbers are not observer relative. If the constructivist wins, numbers are observer relative. Numbers are abstract objects about which we can ask whether they exist independent of human minds. Why not computations? A computation is an abstract object, just as a proof of the existence of a number (such as a transcendental number) is an abstract object. We can ask whether computations exist independent of human minds. On a realist view, they do. On a constructivist view, they do not. Which view is correct? Philosophers do not know. Given that there has been no consensus since these foundational issues in mathematics were first debated in the 1920s, Searle's assignment of computations to an observer-relative feature of the world is premature. Moreover, this assignment cannot support the weight he imposes on it. That weight is his fierce dismissal of cognitive science as a discipline that cannot describe natural features of the world.

We can't prove, with mathematical certainty, that there are no mathematical objects, either as an intrinsic part of the physics of the world, in the natural world or in an abstract world (and thus that mathematical objects are observer-relative features of the world). If we did prove that mathematical objects are observer-relative features of the world, the mathematical proof that provides mathematical certainty would itself be observer relative, since proofs are mathematical objects. If so, two different observers offering two different proofs using different mathematical axioms (or mathematical principles) could rightly claim they are correct. Suppose that one observer proves that mathematical objects are intrinsic features of the physical world or of an abstract world, while the other observer proves that mathematical objects are observer-relative features of the world. The latter observer could not appeal to any facts in the physical world or in an abstract world to support his proof over the other proof. How do we decide who is correct if we are the latter observer? We cannot, so, for the Searleian, it must be a convention that one is correct and the other is incorrect. If it is a convention that decides which proof is correct, then it can't be that we are convinced one proof is correct because it is mathematically certain. If that is so, mathematical certainty is drained of its epistemic force. We can't speak of the reliability of a mathematical proof when human observers have decided which features of it constitute a proof, just as we can't say that 'being a nice day for a picnic' picks out any interesting features intrinsic to the physics of the world, since human observers decide which features of the world count as being a nice day for a picnic. With respect to mathematical certainty, this is incoherent. It is a *reductio* of the claim that we can prove, with mathematical certainty, mathematical objects are observer-relative features of the world.

That a mathematical proof is correct is itself a convention only if it is a convention that decides which mathematical proof is correct. In that case, if the notion of mathematical truth is independent of the notion of the correctness of a mathematical proof, then there is the epistemic absurdity that the correctness of a mathematical proof is a matter of convention, but there is no metaphysical absurdity. However, if we identify mathematical truth with the correctness of a mathematical proof, then there is a metaphysical absurdity as well. It is absurd to say that mathematical truth is a human convention and that if there were no human beings there would be no mathematical truths.

We can go further. Searle's argument that computations are observer-relative features of the world is itself an observer-relative feature of the world on his view. It is not an intrinsic part of physics, since it is an abstract object that consists of syntax and symbols.[7] Suppose that arguments are observer-relative features of the world (that is, they are not either intrinsic features of the physical world or of some abstract world). If so, two different observers can offer two different arguments. The first observer argues that computations are an intrinsic feature of the world. The second observer argues that computations are observer-relative features of the world. How do we decide who is correct if we are the latter observer? We cannot, so it must be a convention that one is correct and the other is incorrect. If a convention decides that computations are observer-relative features of the world, why should we accept it? We could accept the convention that computations are intrinsic features of the world. On what basis is it decided computations are observer-relative and not intrinsic features of the world? If they are observer-relative features of the world, there are no facts in the world that can provide that basis. If so, the epistemic properties of arguments (such as validity) are drained of their force. We can't speak of an argument being sound and thus one whose conclusion we must accept if we are rational, since human observers have decided which features count as being the features of a valid argument. This is incoherent. It is a *reductio* of the claim that we can validly conclude that arguments are observer-relative features of the world.

We can undermine the previous argument if we deny philosophical arguments are abstract, observer-relative features of the world. But if we do this, how can we also assert that computations are abstract, observer-relative features of the world? On what basis do we decide computations are abstract, observer-relative features of the world and philosophical arguments are intrinsic features of the physical world or of an abstract world? Notice, too, that we run into trouble if we say that numbers, computations, philosophical arguments, ... are not intrinsic features of an abstract world but are conventions. We surely do not want to say that universals *and* how they are physically realized in the physical world are conventions. Whatever we take the nature of the relation between universals and their instances to consist in, we do not think it is incontestable that the relation is a human convention and that there could be alternative conventions as to what it consists in that would not answer to any facts in the physical world or any abstract facts in an abstract world. If so, there must be more to Searle's metaphysics of computations other than that they and their physical realizations in physical objects are conventions since computations are abstract objects. Just being an abstract object does not make it the case that it is a convention, nor that the physical realization of that abstract object in the physical world is a convention.

The considerations in the preceding three paragraphs reveal a problem in Searle's metaphysics of computation. What can be done? One move is to revise the definition of an observer-relative feature of the world. Another is to keep the present definition, but change our views about what objects satisfy it. A third is to revise the definition and change our views about what objects satisfy it. A fourth is to argue that there are other fundamental metaphysical categories in addition to being intrinsic to the physics of the world and being observer relative. But if one thinks the preceding considerations don't pose a problem for Searle's metaphysics of computation, here is an additional worry.

Computations obey the laws of computability theory and of computational complexity theory. Are these laws observer-relative features of the world or are they intrinsic features of the physical world or of an abstract world? If they are intrinsic features of either kind of world, how can the objects satisfying them be observer-relative features of either world? Using Searle's test of an observer-relative feature, if all observers disappeared, there would be no more computations, but there would still be the laws of computability and of computational complexity theory.

On the other hand, suppose that the laws of computability and of computational complexity theory are observer-relative features of the physical world or of an abstract world. If so, two different observers can offer two different computability theories, the first contradicting the second. On the basis of his theory of computability, the first observer correctly proves that all non-trivial computational properties are undecidable. On the basis of her theory of computability, using a different conception of computability than the standard one, the second observer correctly proves that all non-trivial computational properties are decidable.[8] (Compare this with using a different conception of 'nice day for a picnic'.) How do we decide who is correct? On Searle's metaphysics, there are no facts in the natural world to which either observer can appeal. If we cannot decide who is correct on the basis of any facts in the natural world, it must be a convention that one is correct and the other is incorrect. If a convention decides what are the correct laws of computability theory, why should we accept it? Why not opt for another convention? We can choose different conventions for 'nice day for a picnic' and we can choose different conventions for the laws of computability theory. But it is absurd to think that the choice of laws of computability theory and of computational complexity theory are up for grabs. Since the laws of computational complexity can be reformulated in second-order logic (this is the field of descriptive complexity theory), saying that the laws of computational complexity theory are up for grabs in the sense that they are observer-relative features of either the physical world or of an abstract world is then equivalent to saying that the laws of classical logic are up for grabs (in the same way). Saul Kripke, in his 1974 Princeton seminar on the nature of logic, argued that the laws of classical logic are not up for grabs—that one cannot decide to adopt the laws of classical logic. If that is the case, Searle's metaphysics of computation collides with Kripke's views on the nature of logic.

A critic of the view that the laws of computability theory are conventions can say that there are facts that can decide which theory of computability is correct. The laws of logic are facts that decide it. But are the laws of logic intrinsic or observer-relative features of the world? Suppose they are intrinsic features of the world. Computations in a Turing-machine model of computation can be rewritten as proofs in first-order logic. If so, then computations are intrinsic features of the world. Suppose that the laws of logic are observer-relative features of the world. If so, then two different observers can offer two different sets of logical laws, one of which contradicts the other. How do we decide who is correct? On Searle's metaphysics, there are no facts in the world that decide who is correct. If so, it is a convention that one set of logical laws is correct and the other is incorrect.

In his epochal paper "Truth by Convention," Quine argued that the laws of logic cannot be true by convention.[9] If Searle's metaphysics of computation is correct, the laws of logic, if they are observer-relative features of the world, must be true by convention. If Quine's argument is valid, Searle's metaphysics of computation is wrong. If Searle's argument is valid, Quine is wrong in saying the laws of logic are not true by convention. The consensus view is that Quine's argument is valid.[10] Notice that if it were not possible to write computations (in, for instance, a Turing-machine model of computation) in first-order logic and if it were not possible to formulate claims in computational complexity theory in, for instance, second-order logic, then the Searlean metaphysics of computation would not collide head-on with Quine's argument in "Truth by Convention." But it is possible to do so, and the Searlean metaphysics of computation does so collide. We take this collision to be additional evidence of the absurdity of the Searlean metaphysics of computation.[11]

I think Searle's criterion harbors a fundamental error: It conflates the activity of human beings arranging matter to be a thing of kind K with the fact that the matter so arranged is a thing of kind K. In the case of a chair, we arrange matter to be a chair, and that the arranged matter is a chair is a human convention. Consider, though, a computation. We arrange matter to be a computation of the function F, but that it is a computation of the function F is not a human convention. Similarly, we arrange matter to be a trans-uranium element not naturally found in nature, but that it is a trans-uranium element not naturally found in nature is not a human convention; it is intrinsic to the physics of the world. That the criterion makes the trans-uranium elements not naturally found in nature to be observer-relative features of the world shows that the criterion harbors the fundamental error. If that is the case, we cannot trust it to determine what are, and what are not, observer-relative features of the world. Suppose we arrange pencil marks on paper to be a proof of a theorem in classical propositional logic. That we arrange those pencil marks in that way is an observer-relative property, but that it is a proof of a theorem in classical propositional logic is not an observer-relative property. If it were, then the theorems of classical propositional logic would be up for grabs, in the sense that we could adopt whichever logic we wanted. However, recall that Kripke has convincingly argued that the choice of a logic is not up for grabs—we cannot adopt whichever logic we choose. Searle's criterion for distinguishing observer-relative features of the world from features intrinsic to the physics of the world collides with Kripke's argument that a logic cannot be adopted.

> Objection 1: Chairs are observer-relative features of the world, but they still obey the laws of physics, which are intrinsic features of the world. If you drop a chair from a building, it will fall to the ground (if nothing stops it from falling). Chairs obey the law of gravity. Just as we distinguish between chairs and the physical stuff of which they are made, we can distinguish between laws of computability and computations, If so, it follows that the laws of computability theory could be intrinsic features of the world, even though computations are observer-relative features of the world. If so, none of the preceding arguments pose any problems for Searle's metaphysics of computation.

Response: Assume that Searle's metaphysics is in place. Chairs are not subject to the law of gravity. The physical materials chairs are made of are subject to the law of gravity. Under the description 'chair', we have an observer-relative feature of the world. Under the description 'collection of iron molecules', we have an intrinsic feature of the world. The laws of physics apply to the physical object picked out by the description 'collection of iron molecules'. They do not apply to the observer-relative object picked out by the description 'chair'.

But this reasoning breaks down when we replace chairs by computations and replace physical laws by laws of computation. Computations are partially defined in terms of the laws of computability theory. Chairs are not partially defined in terms of laws of nature. The laws of computation apply to the abstract object picked out by the description 'computation'. It is not the case there is one description of the abstract object 'computation' under which laws of computation apply and another description under which they do not apply. A similar point holds for arithmetical objects and the laws of arithmetic. To be the natural number '5' is to succeed all natural numbers less than it.

Objection 2: You are confused about Searle's metaphysics of computation. Abstract computations are not observer relative. What is observer relative is whether a physical system makes a computation. That a computation is physically realized in a physical system is observer relative. The physical realization is not observer relative. It is an intrinsic feature of the world. (For instance, it is a collection of microcircuits.) But that this intrinsic feature of the world physically realizes a computation is observer relative. All you have done is show that abstract computations are not observer relative. But that is not Searle's claim.

Response: Consider an engineer who builds a computer. He assembles physical objects that are intrinsic features of nature. He wants the computer to compute. These computations (call them A) are not observer-relative features of nature. Your claim is that neither the physical system that is the computer nor A are observer relative. That the physical system makes A is observer relative. I agree.

If the engineer had not assembled these physical objects, there would be no physical system to make any computations. If so, it would not be true it makes A. If the engineer had assembled the physical system differently, it would make different computations. If so, it would not be true that it makes A. It would be true it makes another computation. But this is hardly controversial. That what a physical system (assembled by an observer) computes is determined by an observer and is therefore observer relative is unremarkable. As I type at my keyboard, I am deciding what computations my computer makes. What computations (in Word) it makes is observer relative.

If Searle's claim is that any physical system that computes must be programmed by an observer, and thus what it computes when it computes is observer relative, that is false. Suppose that a physical system is assembled through evolutionary pressures and that it computes a function. That it computes the function when it does is not observer relative. It is an intrinsic feature of the world. If Searle claims there must be an intelligent designer of the physical system, he introduces an untestable hypothesis. Intelligent design theory is junk science because it is untestable. It has not produced a single scientific experiment that can test its claims.

That a physical system assembled by a human engineer makes the computations it does when it does is not remarkable. That there are physical systems that are the result of evolutionary pressures that compute without the intervention of an observer are not ruled out by objection 2 voiced above. However, if computations are observer relative, then there can be no natural computational systems assembled by evolutionary pressures. It follows Searle must be claiming computations are observer relative and that objection 2—we are confused about what Searle is claiming—is false. "Computation," Searle says, "[does] not name intrinsic features of systems."[12]

Objection 3: Computations are observer relative because symbols and syntax are observer relative. If there are no observers, there are no symbols and there is no syntax. Thus, there are no computations without observers. So computations are observer-relative features of the world.

Response: Consider the analogy: computations are to counting numbers what symbols and syntax are to numerals. Numerals give us epistemic access to the counting numbers. Without them, we have no access to the counting numbers. What must an adequate system of numerals look like? They must respect the basic laws of arithmetic. If not, they cannot be an adequate representational system for the counting numbers. If $2 + 5$ is not equal to $5 + 2$ in the numeral representation of the counting numbers, it is not a legitimate numeral representation. It must be rejected. Is the commutative law for the counting numbers observer relative? There must be a correspondence between numerals and counting numbers that maps the abstract structure of the counting numbers into the abstract structure of the numerals and the abstract structure of the numerals into the abstract structure of the counting numbers such that there is no additional abstract structure in the numerals not found in the counting numbers and no additional abstract structure in the counting numbers not found in the numerals. Under this map, arithmetical properties are invariant. The structure of the source is reflected in the structure of the target and the structure of the target is reflected in the structure of the source. Isomorphisms are an example of such maps. They show that the numerals are mathematically equivalent to the counting numbers. It follows that if the counting numbers are not observer relative, then numerals for them are not observer relative. Conversely, if numerals are observer relative, then the counting numbers are observer relative. Now consider abstract computations and the symbol system and its syntax that represents them. The same morals apply in this case that applied to counting numbers and numeral systems. There must be an isomorphism between abstract computations and the syntactical symbol systems that represent them. This gives us no more reason to think that symbols and syntax are observer-relative features of the world than to think that they are intrinsic features of the world. If there is a convincing argument that symbols and syntax are observer-relative features of the world, then we should be convinced that computations are also observer relative. But we can't assume syntax and symbols are observer relative and then infer that computations are observer relative. Finally, a physical realization of a computation must be isomorphic to it and thus to the symbols and syntax that abstractly represent the computation.[13] Physical realizations of computations and of symbols and syntax are arrangements of physical properties, physical individuals and causal powers of them (via causal connections). The arrangement has to respect the laws of computability and computational complexity theory, since these will be invariant under the isomorphism between the physical realization and the computation. We would not call the physical properties, the physical individuals, and the causal powers observer-relative features of the world. They are intrinsic features of the world. These arrangements are intrinsic to the physics of the world. Although human beings can arrange intrinsic features, the arrangement is still an intrinsic feature of the world. A computer is an arrangement of physical properties, physical individuals, and causal powers. One can object that under the description 'computer', the physical system is an observer-relative feature. Under the description 'physical objects of a certain kind', the physical system is an intrinsic feature of the world. Physical realizations of computations are intrinsic features of the world under one description and observer-relative features of the world under another description. Recall the case of chairs. There is a possible disanalogy with chairs, though. If there were no human beings, there would be no chairs. If there were no human beings, there still would be computations if the realist is right. Since computations are isomorphic to the physical arrangement that is the computer, there would still be computers. But if there were no human beings, there would not be computations if the constructivist is right. Since computations are isomorphic to the physical arrangement that is the computer, there would not be computers. Until Searle settles the issue of whether abstract mathematical objects are real or constructed, he has no argument that computations and computers are observer-relative features of the world. Thus, to say that computations are observer-relative features of the world begs the question.

Physical Symbol Shape Is Sometimes a Partially Observer-Relative Property

There is a grain of truth in Searle's metaphysical of computations. Computations are not observer relative. Realizations of computations are not observer relative. What is observer relative is the shape of the physical inscriptions that physically realize the abstract symbols and syntax that represent computations. Consider counting numbers. Numerals represent counting numbers. Their physical realizations in some media have certain shapes. For example, the numeral '2' has a certain shape. The shape is a human convention. Thus it is an observer-relative property. We could have used the shape '*' or the shape '>' for it. What shape it has is irrelevant to its arithmetical properties, as long as the shape respects the laws of arithmetic and physical limitations of human beings. However, these two conditions limit the shapes that can physically represent numerals. This point needs extended discussion.

If we have a system of shapes that makes it impossible to express arithmetical laws, then the system is not legitimate. But human beings are finitary. We cannot tell what number is represented by a sequence of 59 strokes just by a quick look. We can tell what number is represented by '59' just by a quick look. Suppose we did not have decimal notation for the counting numbers. Suppose we had stroke notation. Instead of '2', we would have '||'. Instead of 8, we would have '||||||||'. It is harder to recognize numerals in stroke notation than in decimal notation and it is harder to multiply and divide in stroke notation than in decimal notation. It is easier to add and subtract in stroke than in decimal notation, but harder in stroke notation to recognize the numeral the result represents. Stroke notation violates the constraints on the computational resources of human beings. These constraints are not up to a human observer to decide. Even with the best intentions, you cannot multiply 8,356 by 5,978 in stroke notation and recognize the number the result represents, unless your brain is abnormally wired. Although symbol shape is observer relative, not any symbol shape is acceptable. The laws of arithmetic must be respected and human limitations must be respected. These conditions are not up for negotiation by human beings. They are constitutive conditions of symbol shapes. Where they are satisfied, shape is then negotiable and a matter of convention. Our point in remarking on human limitations is relevant to whether there are physical inscriptions that are not designed by human beings, but by nature. This is the idea of natural computation.

The physical inscriptions that physically realize the symbols and syntax that represent computations must respect the laws of computability theory, computational complexity theory and human limitations. Beyond that, their shape is a convention. But what if the physical computational system is designed by nature and not by a human engineer? Searle claims there are no natural computers, since both computations and computers are observer relative. Suppose that all the physical inscriptions realizing symbols and syntax are observer relative. It then follows that even if computations and computers are not observer relative, our only epistemic access to them is observer relative, since our only epistemic access to them is through physical inscriptions.

Moreover, there could not be any natural computers, such as the human brain, since the only way they could be physically realized in the world is in a physical medium in which symbols and syntax are physically represented. But if inscriptional shape is observer relative, there are no nonman made natural physical inscriptions in the world. Thus the human brain is not a computer and computational functionalism is refuted. The supposition that inscriptional shape is wholly observer relative does much work! But it is false.

We have seen there are non-negotiable constitutive conditions on inscriptional shape. Thus inscriptional shape is partially observer relative, since the condition that it respect laws of computability and computational complexity theory is not relative to any human observer. The condition that it respect human limitations shows that which inscriptional shapes we choose (for, say, numerals) is not a matter of convention. Of all the inscriptional shapes that satisfy these two conditions, we are free to chose among them. Consider whether there could be a natural computational system, such as the human brain. Satisfying the two conditions is not dependent on a particular human observer. Our physical limitations are the result of evolutionary pressures. Although there would be no human physical limitations if there were no human beings. it does not follow that the physical limitations are observer-relative properties. They are intrinsic features of the world. That human eyes cannot visually discriminate the sequence of strokes '||||||||||||||||||||||||||||||||||||||||||||||||||' for the purposes of counting them is an intrinsic feature of the world.

Beyond satisfying the two constitutive conditions on inscriptional shape, nature (via evolutionary pressures) might be free to choose the shapes of natural inscriptions. If human beings cannot recognize that those shapes are the shapes of inscriptions, it does not mean they aren't inscriptions. Natural (non-man made) arrangements of physical properties, physical individuals and causal powers can be a computational system, even though there are no conventional inscriptional shapes giving us epistemic access to it. Natural inscriptional shapes that satisfy the condition on the limitations of nature (the analogue of the condition on the limitations of human beings) are intrinsic to physics, since the shapes of natural inscriptions are dictated by the limitations of nature set by the natural laws and the boundary conditions of the natural world.[14] There could be a choice on the part of nature as to what inscriptional shapes to choose among those satisfying the two constitutive conditions on inscriptional shapes. But this is an empirical question to which we do not now have an answer.

What is Searle right about in his metaphysics of computation? Our view is that he is right that where inscriptional shape of man-made computational systems (such as digital computers) satisfies the two constitutive conditions on inscriptional shape, then, ceteris paribus, among the shapes satisfying those conditions, the one we choose is a matter of human convention. Human conventions are not intrinsic to physics. They are observer-relative features of the world. Thus Searle is right that inscriptional shape is in some cases partially an observer-relative feature of the world, where the cases are restricted to human beings designing their own physical system of inscriptions.

Quantum Physics and Observer-Relative Features of the World

Another way to resist Searle's metaphysics is to show that the distinction between observer-relative and intrinsic features of the world is not clearcut. In non-Bohmian quantum physics, intrinsic features of the world are observer relative. Elementary particles have spin angular momentum. In the x direction, the spin angular momentum of a particle has two values: up or down. Before measurement, the particle is in a superposition of spin up and spin down in the x direction. After measurement, it is up or down in the x direction, but not both. Which value it has is dependent on some observer making a measurement on the physical system.

If so, it is not an intrinsic feature of the world after observation has been made. It is an intrinsic feature of the world before measurement is made. Physical quantities in superpositions are intrinsic features of the world. When a physical system comes out of a superposition, the physical quantities are observer-relative features of the world. Before measurement, a physical quantity is something physical, like 'molecule' or 'mass' (to use Searle's examples of intrinsic features of the world). After measurement, a physical quantity is something observer relative, like 'nice day for a picnic', or 'chair' (to use Searle's examples of observer-relative features of the world).

It is true that if there are no observers, then physical quantities do not come out of superposition. But it strikes one as absurd to say that spin up in the x direction is an observer-relative feature of the world and not an intrinsic feature of it. It strikes one as absurd to say that spin up in the x direction is not a property like 'mass', but is a property like 'nice day for a picnic'.[15] If so, Searle's metaphysics of computation needs to be revised in some way.

Searle's Metaphysics of Computation Has Bizarre Consequences

Suppose that computations are observer relative. One can infer weird consequences from the conjunction of it and facts from computability theory. The consequences are false. By modus tollens, the conjunction is false. If so, either or both of the conjuncts is false. But the facts of computability theory are true. Thus it is false that computations are observer relative.

The mathematical fact we use is the double recursion theorem from the theory of computability. We are not free to make up the facts of computability theory. But whether these facts apply to a physical system is observer relative (for Searle). However we interpret a physical system as making a computation, all the facts of computability theory must be respected. We can't interpret the physical object as computing a recursive function, but deny it satisfies the s-m-n theorem. We need to discuss the recursion theorem before we discuss the double recursion theorem. The recursion theorem has different characterizations and interpretations. One characterization of it is that it allows functions to define themselves (which is a form of computational self-reference). One form of the recursion theorem is[16]

$$\varphi_e(x) = \varphi_i(e, x).$$

The function on the left is semantically equivalent to the function on the right, but it is syntactically distinct from it. The recursion theorem tells us that in the list of recursive functions, the eth function in the list is semantically equivalent to the ith function in the list. No matter how you list recursive functions, it must always be the case that there is such an e and i. From the number i, there is an effective procedure for finding the number e. The recursive function (or computer program) picked out by e is self-referential, since it can use the instructions in the program i to simulate a modified version of itself so it can decide what values it should output.

The generalization of the recursion theorem to pairs of recursive functions is the double recursion theorem. In the language of computer programs, the double recursion theorem says that each program in a pair of programs can be written using itself and the other program in the pair. The theorem is

$$\varphi_{e_0}(x) = \varphi_{i_0}(e_0, e_1, x),$$

$$\varphi_{e_1}(x) = \varphi_{i_1}(e_0, e_1, x).$$

Here are several absurdities that follow from the conjunction of the observer relativity of computations and the double recursion theorem. Suppose that there is a granite rock lying in the street, a human being within a 50 yard radius of the rock, and another human being whom we call Trivialist. Since computations are observer relative, let Trivialist attribute to the rock lying in the street the recursive function $\varphi_{e_0}(x)$ and to the human being the recursive function $\varphi_{e_1}(x)$. At this point we no longer need Trivialist. By the double recursion theorem, the first computer program knows the complete syntactical description of the second program, and the second computer program knows the complete syntactical description of the first computer program. (This follows from the double recursion theorem.) Both the rock in the street and the human mind compute different recursive functions, though the computations each makes depend on the computations the other makes. In the recursion theorem, both computer programs possess a self-referential property. They can access the others' code in order to simulate a version of themselves to determine what values to output next. In the double recursion theorem, the computer programs can access their own code and the code of the other computer program to do the same.

Thus, the human mind will access the program of the rock in the street and the rock in the street will access the human mind in executing their programs. There is a cognitive dependency between the rock in the street and the human mind. Since the rock in the street is external to the human mind, it is an external dependency between the computational activities of the rock in the street and the computational cognitive activities of the human mind. It is not a causal dependency, since, on Searle's view, computations are not intrinsic to physics. It is not the case that the human mind is physically caused to make a computation by the rock in the street, and the rock in the street is physically caused to make a computation by the human mind.

The contents of the human mind's current mental state (partially described by the recursive function it computes) are informationally sensitive to part of its external environment. In this case, they are informationally sensitive to the computational state of the rock. Similarly, the rock's computational state is informationally sensitive to the contents of the current mental state of the human mind. Where the contents of a human mind are informationally sensitive to its local environment, we have semantic externalism. Thus we have a mathematical proof that semantical externalism is true in at least one state of affairs (for it follows from the conjunction of the double recursion theorem and the view that computations are observer relative). But it is absurd to think there is a mathematical proof of semantic externalism.[17]

Now look at the converse relation between the rock in the street and the human mind. Since execution of the rock in the street's program is dependent on the human mind executing its program, and there is no physical causal connection between the rock in the street and the human mind that mediates the execution of their respective programs, some of the computational behavior of the rock in the street depends on the existence of a human mind. Since this can hold for any physical object, we have a mathematical proof of partial idealism: some of the physical properties of a physical object are mind-dependent (where the computable properties supervene on the physical properties, in the sense that the physical properties are the physical realizations of the computable properties). The proof is mathematical because it is a consequence of the double recursion theorem and the view that computations are observer relative. If Stephen Wolfram is right that all physical objects are cellular automata (because the physical universe is a cellular automaton),[18] we have a mathematical proof of the philosophical doctrine of Berkeleyian idealism: all physical objects (and all their properties) are mind dependent.

Suppose that Trivialist attributes computations to two human minds. Each computes functions in accord with the double recursion theorem. The execution of the program in the mind of one person is dependent on the execution of the program in the mind of the other person and conversely. Each human being is informationally sensitive to the contents of the others' mind. If so, we have a mathematical proof of the existence of mental telepathy: The informational dependency between one mind and the other mind is not causally mediated, in which case the actual mode of transmission of information is mysterious. The mental telepathy runs in both directions: from the first to the second mind and from the second to the first mind.[19]

The last absurdity requires a generalization of the double recursion theorem: the n-ary recursion theorem. Here there are n self-referential and mutually dependent computer programs. Each computer program knows the syntactical description of each of the other n − 1 computer programs. Invoke the Trivialist. Let Trivialist attribute computable functions that satisfy the n-ary recursion theorem to all n physical objects in the world at time t (excepting Trivialist).[20] Suppose that the functions are computational descriptions of the human mind.

According to the n-ary recursion theorem, there will be n mutual informational dependencies between each physical object and all other physical objects in the world at time t. The contents of the mind of a human being at time t will be informationally dependent on the computational state of every other physical object in the world at time t (and thus on the contents of the minds of every other human being in the world at time t). This is a mathematical proof of the existence of panpsychism.[21]

6　There Are Infinitely Many Computational Realizations of an Arbitrary Intentional State

In this chapter, I examine the conditions necessary for there to be infinitely many computational realizations of an arbitrary intentional state. I distinguish two sources of computational multi-realization. These are content growth and computational growth. We think the only philosophically unproblematic source of computational multi-realization is computational growth, but it does not jeopardize the prospects of local computational reduction. Along the way, we attempt to refute Putnam's view that computationalism is committed to metaphysical realism. We present a relativized proof it is not committed to metaphysical realism and that it sidesteps Quinean indeterminacy and ontological relativity. The proof is relativized to Putnam's claim that agents whose intentional contents are evaluated by epistemic semantics are immune to Quinean indeterminacy and ontological relativity and that epistemic semantics is not committed to metaphysical realism. If the latter claim is true, it is also true for computationalism.

A central plank in Putnam's refutation of computational functionalism is his argument that there is no computable partitioning of the infinitely many computational realizations of an arbitrary intentional state into a small set of equivalence classes. The thread connecting Putnam's late-1950s refutation of central-state identity theories and his 1980s attempt to refute computational functionalism is that both use a multi-realization argument.

For mind/body identity theories, the multi-realization argument is straight-forward. The underlying assumption is that the mind supervenes on the physical brain.[1] Consider all possible beings with minds. The mode of physical organization of the physical materials and the physical materials can vary from being to being. Two beings might be composed of the same physical materials, but implement different physical organizations of them. Two beings might be composed of different physical materials, but implement the same kind of physical organization of them. So minds are physically multi-realized.

Suppose that there is a single mental state (such as being in pain) that is physically multi-realized. Given the extraordinary diversity of physical realizations of that mental state, what unites the multi-realizations? If there is no law-like unity in that diversity, there is no physical natural kind realizing the mental state of being in pain. If so, there is no reduction of mental states to physical states that preserves nomic relations. If so, there are no physical laws underlying the physical realization of mental states that are relevant to understanding those mental states. Since the reducing state cannot explain the effects that the state of being in pain explains, the physical reduction is not genuine.

The burden of proof is pushed onto the shoulders of the identity theorist. She can either dispute the conceptual structure of the model of reduction that is employed in psychology or show that there is a law-like unity behind the diversity or else isolate some kinds of physical realizations for which there is law-like unity and jettison the rest (for which there is no unity). The latter is the idea of a local reduction. It is the one response to physical multi-realization arguments that has been taken seriously. The attempts to rewrite reduction models are inconclusive. There have been no interesting ideas how to effect a unity of the diverse physical multi-realizations of mental states in a new kind of reduction model.

But there is good reason to suppose the physical multi-realizations of *human* mental states all have something in common—that it makes theoretical sense to speak of a physical natural kind (the human brain) that is the locus of mental activity. It has been empirically established that the physical materials are the same across human beings and that the mode of physical organization is (grossly) the same. There are many physical differences in brain structure across any two humans, but these differences can be explained away as being minor differences. There are also significant structural differences (such as finding neural features in the brains of women not found in the brains of men) that can either be partitioned into equivalence classes or subsumed under an exceptions category.[2]

Computational Multi-Realization

Putnam asserts that mind/body identity theories have been decisively refuted by physical multi-realization arguments and that it was reflection on the nature of that argument that revealed to him that a similar kind of multi-realization argument could be run against computational functionalism. In the introduction to *R&R* he writes: "What I shall try to do is the trick attributed to adepts in jujitsu of turning an opponent's strength against himself: I shall try to show that the arguments for the computational view, in fact, the very arguments I formerly used to show that a simple minded identification of mental states with physico-chemical states cannot be right, can be generalized and extended to show that a straightforward identification of mental states with *functional* states, i.e., with computationally characterized states, also cannot be right."[3]

If Putnam can show that there are infinitely many computational realizations of an arbitrary intentional state—and this is what a multi-realization argument against computational functionalism must do—he must treat the possibility of local reduction as a serious option available to the computational functionalist. It is here that he has done significant work—he argues that there is no real possibility of computably partitioning the infinitely many computational realizations into a small set of equivalence classes. Moreover, he does this under the concession that he will only take into account the intentional states of human beings. His argument in *R&R* (called EQUIVALENCE) shows that there can be no local reduction of sameness of content for intentional states. If this argument is sound, it closes the door on both local computational reduction and cognitive psychology. In that event the only option available to the computational functionalist is either tinkering with the notion of a reduction or giving up the idea that sameness of content for intentional states is necessary for cognitive psychology. Either prospect is equally odious. Here is what Putnam writes about local computational reduction:

> This leads to the difficult question whether there is nevertheless a kind of "equivalence" between the structures of all physically possible systems (organisms cum environments) which contain a physically possible organism who entertains a particular belief; a kind of equivalence which can be defined in physical cum computational terms. These chapters present an argument designed to show that if such an equivalence relation existed, it would be undiscoverable—not just undiscoverable by human beings, but *undiscoverable by physically possible intelligent beings*.[4]

There are different kinds of local reductions. Here are two: (i) restrict the kinds of beings in the reduced class and (ii) equivalence class the multi-realizations in the reducing class.[5] Putnam only considers local reductions (i) and (ii). He argues that even if the beings are restricted to human beings, the infinite set of computational realizations of an arbitrary intentional state cannot be computably partitioned into a small set of equivalence classes. Putnam calls this argument 'EQUIVALENCE'.

EQUIVALENCE claims that if there is an equivalence relation, it is undiscoverable by human beings, for to discover it a human being must occupy an Archimedean point. No human being can occupy an Archimedean point, since it requires of its occupant that she has infinitary capacities and that she is able to read the future in order to describe modes of linguistic existence that transcend her own. But no human being can read the future nor has infinitary capacities. Hence it is impossible to occupy an Archimedean point. Hence the equivalence relation is undiscoverable.

Putnam shows that a computational realization of the contents of an arbitrary intentional state is an infinitely long disjunction by appealing to both content growth and computational growth. Computational growth yields an infinite disjunction for there are infinitely many possible programming languages in which to express a computational theory. Content growth also yields an infinite disjunction. If it is assumed that there is no computable way to distinguish meaning-constituting from auxiliary beliefs, it can be shown that for any given intentional state (with propositional content), there are infinitely many computational realizations of it. I will argue that the infinitely long disjunction induced by computational growth can be computably partitioned into a small set of equivalence classes. Content growth is a much more difficult matter.

Putnam thinks that human beings use rational interpretation to distinguish meaning-constituting from auxiliary beliefs and that it can't be formalized. If it can be formalized, then human beings can computably distinguish meaning-constituting from auxiliary beliefs. If so, the computational realization of an arbitrary intentional state will not be infinite in length in virtue of content growth. If so, there is no need for EQUIVALENCE, since there is no infinite-sized computational reduction of which we can ask if it can be computably compressed. In the next part of this book, we will argue that there are no convincing arguments that rational interpretation cannot be formalized. I will also argue that Putnam equivocates: he uses two distinct notions of rational interpretation and does not carefully distinguish them in EQUIVALENCE. I claim that EQUIVALENCE fails because of this equivocation.

A reader who believes that Quine convincingly crushed the idea that there is a principled means of distinguishing meaning-constituting from auxiliary beliefs will balk at the idea that there is any principled means of doing so, let alone a computable means of doing so. I will not address all of the literature that argues that Quine is wrong about there being no principled means of making the distinction. Instead, I will focus on what Putnam has said about the matter. He believes we are able to make synonymy judgments and coreferentiality decisions because the semantics of the contents of our thoughts is epistemic and not truth conditional. Rational interpretation (one of a family of notions Putnam uses) does work in epistemic semantics.[6] We argue that if Putnam's epistemic semantics underlies successful judgments of synonymy and coreferentiality decisions, there is no reason to think that computationalism cannot do the same.[7]

Putnam's Model for His Multi-Realization Refutation of Functionalism: The Refutation of Phenomenalism

Putnam's inspiration for his multi-realization argument is the refutation of sense-datum theories propounded by Wilfred Sellars in the 1950s. Putnam not only draws parallels between his method of refutation and the method of refutation employed by Sellars; he also remarks that Roderick Chisholm was the first to notice that there is a strong connection between the idea that mental states cannot be reduced to nonmental states and Sellars's refutation of phenomenalism.[8] So there is a precedent for multi-realization arguments. It is valuable to look at what Putnam has written about the nature of these arguments:

At first the phenomenalists were content to claim that material-thing sentences could be "translated" into *infinitely long* sense-datum sentences; however, it was very quickly pointed out that unless the translation were finite (or the infinitely long translation could be constructed according to a rule which was itself statable in finitely many words), then the issues whether the translation exists, whether it is correct, whether it is philosophically illuminating, and so on, would be essentially undiscussable. The antiphenomenalists said, in effect, "Put up or shut up."

In the same spirit, I am saying to the functionalists (including my former self), 'Put up or shut up.' However, the antiphenomenalists did not put all the burden of proof on the phenomenalists. Reichenbach, Carnap, Hempel and Sellars gave principled reasons why a finite translation of material-thing language into sense-datum language was impossible. Even if these reasons fall short of a strict mathematical impossibility proof, they are enormously convincing, and this is the reason why there is not ... a single phenomenalist left in the world today. In the same spirit, I am going to give principled reasons why a finite empirical definition of intentional relations and properties in terms of physical/computational relations and properties is impossible—reasons which fall short of a strict proof, but which are, I believe, ... convincing.[9]

EQUIVALENCE provides principled reasons why a finite and small equivalence class partitioning of the infinitely many computational realizations of arbitrary intentional states is impossible. Note the analogy with anti-phenomenalist arguments. Anti-phenomenalists show that there are infinitely many phenomenal features for any given material thing—and thus that the translation of a material-thing sentence into a sense-datum sentence is infinitely long. Putnam shows that computational reduction of an arbitrary intentional state produces infinitely many disjuncts. The next stage of his argument is EQUIVALENCE: why the infinitely many disjuncts in computational reductions can't be computably partitioned into a small set of equivalence classes. So we must examine two distinct theses Putnam holds:

(i) A computational reduction of an arbitrary intentional state has infinitely many disjuncts.

(ii) The disjuncts cannot be computably partitioned into to a small set of equivalence classes.

Without securing (i), EQUIVALENCE is idle. For if the set of disjuncts is small, then, with enough ingenuity, we can find ways of uniting them. If they are small enough, then we can (theoretically) simply tolerate them. Our first job is to critically evaluate (i).

On the Length of Computational Multi-Realizations of Intentional States

There are (at least) two distinct ways the length of a computational multi-realization of an intentional state can increase. One mode of growth involves the kinds of computational models enforced in cognitive psychology. Different models give us different computer architectures, programming languages and algorithms. Call this *computational growth*. For instance, using algorithm A it takes 500 steps to compute F(6) (where 'F' names some function), while using algorithm B it takes 22,000 steps to compute it. We need to distinguish the length of a single computational realization of an arbitrary intentional state from the length of a computational multi-realization of it. The length of the latter is measured by the number of disjuncts it contains, where each disjunct is a single computational realization. Single computational realizations are measured by their intrinsic size. Consider the example above: 500 steps in the case of algorithm A and 22,000 steps in the case of algorithm B. Computational multi-realization of an intentional state by algorithms A and B has two disjuncts, and the sum of its intrinsic sizes is 22,500.[10]

There are many different computational models of computation. In his papers defining and defending functionalism, Putnam proposed that probabilistic finite-state automata computationally models human psychology.[11] But finite-state automata can't multiply, so that computational model is psychologically unrealistic. Turing-machine models have also been proposed for human psychology. Although they can multiply, they too are considered psychologically unrealistic. Fix the computational model. Next there are different computer architectures. For instance, serial and parallel computations employ different architectures. Now fix the architecture. There are many different programming languages, not all of which are compatible with a single architecture. Fix the programming language. There are different algorithms within a single programming language for computing a single function. There are also inter-architectural differences in algorithms. Algorithms for a parallel-processing machine differ from those for a serial-processing machine. The point is that there are many different computational models, architectures, programming languages and algorithms. It follows that there are many different computational realizations of a single intentional state induced by computational growth.

The other mode of growth has to do with the content of the intentional state that is computationally reduced. Call this *content growth*. A question is whether infinitely many computational realizations of an arbitrary intentional state come from content growth without computational growth, from computational growth without content growth, or from both. Our view is computational growth secures computational multi-realization, but that Putnam has not succeeded in showing content growth alone does so.

Content Growth

Why the Single-Computational State Version of Functionalism Is False

Putnam entertains what he takes to be a fiction: that for each propositional attitude there is a single computational state that realizes it. He calls this claim 'the single computational-state version of functionalism' (hereafter SCS) and argues that it is false. To show it is false, he argues that there are arbitrarily many computational realizations of a given intentional state. That is, he has to show the truth of what we call NCS: for each propositional attitude, there are N computational states that realize it, where N = infinity or an extraordinarily large finite number (such as $2^{1,000}$). Thus he does not need to consider trivial elaborations of SCS, such as TCS: for each propositional attitude there are two computational states that realize it.

There are two strands to the argument of SCS. One strand shows that there is significant content growth, while the other shows there is significant computational growth. I will examine the content growth strand first, and the computational growth strand later.

To show there is significant content growth, Putnam appeals to synonymy determination (hereafter SD). Here is his example of SD, slightly altered: Two speakers of English use the word 'cat'. Do they mean the same thing when each utters the sentence "I see a cat"? There are many beliefs a given speaker might have about cats that are not part of the meaning of 'cat'. Call these auxiliary beliefs. For instance, the belief that cat food in cans has a tinny taste for cats is an auxiliary belief. There are also beliefs about cats that are meaning-constituting. These are beliefs about the essential properties of cats. For instance, the belief that cats are animals is meaning-constituting. The difference between meaning-constituting and auxiliary beliefs is that the meaning of the word 'cat' is stable under changes in the latter, but not under changes in the former. If speaker A stops believing that his friend Alice has a cat, the meaning of 'cat' remains the same. However, if speaker A stops believing that cats are animals, the meaning of cat (as used by speaker A) has changed.

Here is how we can get significant content growth from SD. Assume we have an unbounded number of speakers of English, that each speaker entertains the same set of meaning-constituting beliefs for 'cat' and that each speaker has at least one auxiliary belief about cats that differs from any of the auxiliary beliefs about cats of any other speaker. For each speaker, take all their meaning-constituting and auxiliary beliefs about cats and encode them into a single computational state. (The details are left to the reader.) The computational state of any speaker will differ from the computational state of any other speaker, because there is at least one belief encoded in the computational state of each speaker that differs from any of the beliefs encoded in the computational state of any other speaker.

Now suppose that when any speaker is in the intentional state expressed by uttering the sentence "There's a cat," that intentional state has the same content for any other speaker. Each speaker means the same thing when she says "I see a cat." We judge that any two speakers uttering "I see a cat" have made synonymous utterances. However, the computational multi-realization of that intentional state will have N disjuncts, where N is the number of speakers. If there are a googolplex of speakers, the computational multi-realization of the intentional state will be infeasibly long. If there are infinitely many speakers (easily obtained if we allow the existence of counterfactual speakers), the computational multi-realization of the intentional state will be infinitely long. Since nothing in the preceding argument hinged on using the word 'cat', the result is completely general. It holds for all cases of SD. It also holds for intra-individual cases of SD (where a single speaker is in the same intentional state at two or more distinct times in his life). Thus, SCS is false. NCS is true.

However, it is important to note an assumption that underlies this refutation of SCS. It is that computational functionalism cannot distinguish meaning-constituting from auxiliary beliefs without an antecedent notion of sameness of meaning. If that assumption is removed, the refutation fails. It is, then, crucial that an argument is made for the assumption. Putnam does argue that a particular computational model of human intentional states cannot make this distinction. But demonstrating that the distinction cannot be made in one computational model of human intentional states does not show that it cannot made in any computational model of them.

It is instructive to examine the model Putnam uses.[11] It has two components: one is a subjective probability metric that assigns degrees of confirmation to sentences in the language of thought, and the other is a rational preference function that assigns utilities to those sentences. Moreover, the model uses Bayesian conditionalization for changing degrees of confirmation upon new evidence. When two different speakers assign even slightly different subjective probabilities or utilities to the sentence "I see a cat," there is nothing in the model that allows either speaker (or an external observer) to determine that they mean the same thing. If two speakers assign different numbers to the same sentence, they mean different things. There will also be speakers who assign the same number to the sentence, even though their subjective probabilities or utilities are grossly different. A assigns the sentence a high probability and a low utility, while B assigns it a low probability and a high utility. Both A and B are in a different computational state when they utter that sentence, even though each assigns it the same number. The real deficiency of this computational model is it does not distinguish meaning-constituting from auxiliary beliefs. There are not enough degrees of freedom within the model to make such a distinction.

Putnam suggests various ways of extending this model and argues that none of them work. However, the extensions of the model he considers are limited and they are still extensions of the basic model. One extension he considers is marking certain sentences as being analytic. This fails because in the absence of making synonymy judgments in the model, it is not known whether words in sentences marked analytic mean the same thing for two or more speakers. Just because a word is marked 'analytic' does not show that it means the same thing for two distinct speakers.

Other extensions he considers are stereotypes and perceptual prototypes. The former are often presented in terms of the latter. For example, the stereotype of 'grass' is given by the perceptual prototype for grass. But two different speakers, though they possess the same perceptual prototype for grass, may have wildly different beliefs about grass. If a speaker must entertain additional beliefs to eliminate this difficulty, another difficulty takes its place. The words contained in the additional beliefs either mean the same in the mouths of two distinct speakers or they don't. If sameness of meaning is determined by employing stereotypes, an infinite regress problem occurs (that Putnam aptly names 'the infection problem'). Suppose that the additional belief is 'grass is a plant'. We now need to determine that two different speakers use the word 'plant' in the same way.[12]

Putnam does not consider every plausible way to extend the model. Unless he provides technical work showing that (i) the paucity of degrees of freedom in the basic model can't be changed by adding to the model and (ii) there are no additions to the model that will allow it to capture the distinction between meaning-constituting and auxiliary beliefs, his indictment of that computational model cannot be sustained.[13] His basic computational model is one among many. In order to refute SCS, he needs a general argument. He needs to argue that any computational model of human intentional states can't distinguish meaning-constituting from auxiliary beliefs. He has that argument, though the reader must extract it from the details of his work, contained in part in *R&R* and in several other of his publications. The broad outline of the argument is as follows:

P1 Successful SD distinguishes meaning-constituting from auxiliary beliefs.

P2 Rational interpretation is necessary for successful SD.

P3 There is no formalization of rational interpretation.

P4 What is not formalizable does not appear in a computational model.

C There are no computational models of human intentional states that can distinguish meaning-constituting from auxiliary beliefs.

The argument is valid. To show that it fails, I will not contest the first two premises; I will contest the third. If it is shown that the argument there is no formalization of rational interpretation fails, then it is left open that there is such a formalization. If so, the refutation of SCS fails and there is then no need to show that there are no computable equivalence classes of the infinitely many computational realizations of human intentional states. (That is, there is in that case no need for EQUIVALENCE.) SCS fails, since if rational interpretation is formalizable, it is available to a computable agent to distinguish meaning-constituting from auxiliary beliefs. Not making the distinction is the source of computational multi-realization that is induced by content growth.

In a later chapter I will examine the issue of whether rational interpretation can be formalized. I do not think any of the arguments attempting to show it can't be formalized succeed. There is, though, another way in which we can get infinitely many computational realizations of an arbitrary intentional state. Quinean indeterminacy is the means to this end. We will first see how this works. Then we will see what Putnam thinks is the source of indeterminacy and why epistemic semantics avoids both it and ontological relativity. The source is the failure to formalize rational interpretation. But if it can be formalized, then computable agents can avoid indeterminacy. Putnam also thinks that computationalism is a scientistic doctrine and that any scientistic doctrine is committed to metaphysical realism. He lists several criteria for metaphysical realism. I will show that computationalism does not satisfy these criteria and is not committed to metaphysical realism. Thus, even if we can't give a formalization of rational interpretation, it does not follow that computationalism succumbs to indeterminacy.

Appealing to Quinean Indeterminacy to Show That SCS Is False

Another source of content growth is Quinean indeterminacy.[14] Sameness of stimulus meaning is neither necessary nor sufficient for sameness of meaning, even in the case of the observational terms of a language. Two people can observe the same physical object, yet one will see a rabbit and the other will see non-detached rabbit parts. That shows stimulus meanings are not sufficient for sameness of meaning. Likewise, two people can observe different things, yet each may infer they have seen the same physical thing. A perceives the front of a cat and B perceives the back of that same cat. Each utters the sentence "I see Cuddles the cat." Thus, stimulus meanings are not necessary for sameness of meaning. These results pose a problem for SD involving either theoretical or observational terms of any natural language. Suppose that a speaker of German has a stimulus meaning for the word 'haus' different from the stimulus meaning that another speaker of English has for the word 'house'. Similarly, suppose that another speaker of German has a stimulus meaning for 'haus' different from the stimulus meaning the first speaker of German has for 'haus' and different from the stimulus meaning the English speaker has for 'house'.

Suppose that there are n speakers of German and m speakers of English. On the basis of indeterminacy and on the assumption that an algorithm for SD provides correct answers for any two arbitrary speakers of either

German or English, there are n · m different computational states (under the assumption that the stimulus meaning for each speaker of either English or German differs from that of all other speakers) that realize the single intentional state for a belief expressed by the English sentence "There is a house" and by the German sentence "Es gibt ein Haus."

Although n · m is finite, we have only looked at two different languages. There are several thousand natural languages and for each of them, there are many dialects. For the sake of simplicity, assume that there are n speakers of each natural language. If there are two natural languages, there will be n^2 many computational states. If there are three natural languages, there will be n^3 computational states. If there are k different natural languages, there will be n^k computational states. If k = 125, there are more computational states than there are elementary particles in the known universe. This creates a strong feasibility problem for running the algorithm in a human mind, the total number of whose neural connections is much less than the total number of elementary particles in the known universe.

Approximately 7,000 distinct natural languages are now spoken. But any finite number raised to the 28,000th power is still finite. (I get 28,000 by multiplying each of the 7,000 natural languages by the number of its dialects, which I arbitrarily cap at 4.) One can easily get an infinite number of computational states by indeterminacy considerations. If we individuate stimulus meanings finely, we can get infinitely many possible stimulus meanings for any one speaker. We are allowed to appeal to counterfactual speakers (providing we do not violate natural laws in doing so) and to counterfactual individuations of stimulus meanings. We can easily get infinitely many computational states by identifying each one with a different stimulus meaning. This establishes Putnam's claim that indeterminacy considerations refute SCS.[15] Notice that SCS is refuted only under the assumption that an algorithm for SD must explicitly list each stimulus meaning, each speaker, and each natural language and its dialects. If that is so, there will be infinitely many disjuncts in the computational realization of SD for "There is a house" and its correlative in some other natural language. This response is questionable. Why think an algorithm for SD must explicitly record all that information? Indeed, how could an algorithm "know" the stimulus meanings of all possible human speakers? That is obviously contingent information about each one. An algorithm for SD precedes the birth of a speaker and thus could not know what stimulus meanings a speaker will acquire for the word 'house' during the course of a lifetime. It is absurd to even consider that all the stimulus meanings of each word in a given natural language are innate. But they would have to be innate if they must be explicitly listed in an SD algorithm. Either this shows that there cannot be a finitary algorithm for SD that is based on stimulus meanings or else the demand that such an algorithm explicitly list all stimulus meanings must be relinquished. EQUIVALENCE shows that the demand can't be relinquished and so there is no finitary algorithm for SD based on stimulus meanings.

A Difficulty in Proving the Falsity of SCS: Quine's Views on Synonymy

Quine has famously argued there is no such thing as synonymy (because there are no meanings), and thus there cannot be any means to discern content differences between mental states (because there is no such relation to be discerned). If Quine is right, Putnam's means of refuting SCS by showing there are infinitely many distinct computational realizations of an arbitrary intentional state via content growth collapses. It collapses because you cannot reduce what does not exist at the intentional level. Indeed, cognitive psychology collapses if Quine is right about the non-existence of synonymy relations. The content of a mental state is central in individuating that state. If cognitive psychology cannot tell when two distinct mental states have the same content because it cannot tell what the content of a single mental state is, then it cannot say what are the psychological laws those states do and do not participate in. Cognitive science requires a notion of sameness of mental content and a means to discern content differences among mental states in order for the notion of a psychological law to be meaningful. If there are no meaningful psychological laws, there is no discipline of cognitive psychology. (The doctrine of radical Quinean meaning holism does pay lip service to meanings, though. A Quinean surrogate for meaning is to individuate meanings in terms of all of one's beliefs.)

If Quine is right, then SCS can't be falsified, for there are no computational reductions. But cognitive psychology still collapses. So Putnam gets his prize: a scientific materialistic theory—cognitive psychology—is disgraced. But this means of disgracing it would not be acceptable to him. Contrary to Quine, Putnam believes in the existence of meanings and synonymy relations between words. In *R&R* he writes: "If we reflect on the role played by the notion of sameness of meaning in logic, it will perhaps not seem so surprising that this notion turns out to have a normative dimension.... In logic ... equivocating is a fallacy.... But the notion of 'sense' or 'meaning' (Fodor's 'content') could not play this role in criticism if we did not interpret one another in such a way that 'meanings' are preserved under the usual procedures of belief fixation and justification.... A computational relation which coincided with synonymy ... could not be psychologically more elementary than 'general intelligence.'"[16]

Under radical Quinean meaning holism, meanings could not be preserved under the usual procedures of belief fixation or under justificatory procedures. Thus, there are no meanings for Quine. Putnam believes there are meanings, and so he disavows radical Quinean meaning holism. Epistemic semantics recruits human reasoning, such as rational interpretation and general intelligence, in determining synonymy relations between words.

Discounting Beliefs and the Family of Notions: Rational Interpretation, Reasonable Reasoning, and General Intelligence

Putnam contends that a central problem for computationalism is that "meaning and reference depend on what I called 'discounting differences in belief'."[17] He argues that rational interpretation is used by human beings to discount differences in belief and that discounting differences in belief is essential to SD. He writes: "The reason that we cannot count every difference in the collateral information we have as difference in the meaning of a *word*, is that to do so abandons the distinction between our 'concepts' and what beliefs we have that contain those concepts, and just this distinction is the *basis* of the intuitive notions of meaning, synonymy, analyticity, etc. To give up the meaning/belief distinction amounts to agreeing with Quine that we may as well give up the notion of *meaning* altogether ... if the picture of 'mental representations' and their 'content' is to have any use, then 'content' must remain stable under *some* changes in *belief*."[18]

In Quine's view, it makes no sense to speak of different intentional states' having the same content (or meaning). Not so for Putnam, for whom rational discourse would be impossible if we were not able to use rational interpretation to discount differences in beliefs. But Putnam speaks of other methods of discounting differences in beliefs and of distinguishing between meaning-constituting and auxiliary beliefs. There is a family of closely related notions: rational interpretation, reasonable reasoning, and general intelligence. We will next see how Putnam introduces the notion of general intelligence into his discussion of how to discount beliefs.[19]

At two different times, once in 1900 and once in 1934, Niels Bohr had different theories of the electron. Should we decide that the term 'electron' used by Bohr in 1900 is synonymous with the way he used it in 1934? Putnam tells us that there are difficulties in making this decision, principally because Bohr's theory of the electron in 1900 is different from his theory of the electron in 1934. If we treated any difference in belief as a difference in meaning, then the 1900 term 'electron' would not be synonymous with the 1934 term 'electron'. Bohr in 1934 had theoretical beliefs about the electron he did not have in 1900, and conversely. Which of these are auxiliary and which meaning-constituting beliefs? Some auxiliary beliefs are obviously so. For instance, Bohr might have believed that schoolchildren in the future will be taught the theory of electrons or that he should refrain from using the term 'electron' at his local tavern. The human interpreter easily knows how to discount these latter differences in beliefs in SD.

Radical Quinean meaning holism makes SD very simple: one looks for a difference in beliefs of any kind (auxiliary or meaning-constituting) associated with two speakers' use of a term and declares a synonymy failure. Putnam does not take that route. In the case of the Bohr electron, he claims that the successive changes in Bohr's beliefs over 34 years can be explained as changes in beliefs about the same object rather than as meaning changes. What Putnam thinks is interesting about the Bohr case is that it involves discounting differences in beliefs, though it does not involve deciding synonymy on the basis of maximizing the true beliefs in the 1900 theory in the light of the 1934 theory: "We do not always interpret words in such a way as to *maximize* the number of true beliefs that the speaker would have had (by our lights) if the interpretation were correct, contrary to a crude version of the idea of 'charity in interpretation'.... The knowledge that one thing is reasonable charity while another thing would be excessive exhibits our full power of understanding, whether the context be interpretation or 'real life.' There is no hope of a theory of sameness of meaning or reference which applies to such difficult cases [the Bohr electron—JB] and which is independent of our account of 'general intelligence.'"[20] This is supposed to show there is no programmatic way of doing SD. In some cases one opts to maximize true beliefs; in other cases one does not. Whether one does or does not opt to maximize true beliefs is a matter of general intelligence. Putnam says "the same kind of 'general intelligence' is involved in [Bohr's] decision to treat all these occurrences of 'electron' as synonymous as is involved in his decision to treat later research programs in the story as extensions of the earlier ones; a kind of decision that plays a role in theory evaluation."[21] Successful SD requires general intelligence. But what is it? Here is how Putnam explicates it:

... the notions of being a justified or warranted or reasonable belief are not reducible to physicalistic notions.... But even if one could give a reductive analysis of the notion of being a justified belief, say, by identifying 'being justified' with 'being the outcome of ... such and such an algorithm' ... that algorithm would have to be as complex as a description of the 'general intelligence' of an ideal inductive judge. We have seen, from our brief discussion of meaning holism, that testing a scientific theory is not something that can be done just by looking up the operational definitions of all of the terms and testing the sentences that comprise the theory one by one. Rather, it involves very intangible things, such as estimating simplicity (which itself is not a single factor, but different things in different situations), and weighing simplicity against our desire for successful prediction and also against our desire to preserve a certain amount of past doctrine. It involves having a nose for the "right" trade-off between such values. The ability to make these estimates and trade-offs is what Fodor calls "general intelligence," and he does not expect general intelligence to be explained in terms of "modules" in the foreseeable future, if ever. Describing the nature of general intelligence is a hopeless problem, according to Fodor.... Now I want to say that the notions collected under the chapter heading "same meaning" and "same reference," are as complex as the notions collected under the chapter heading "general intelligence. This is not to claim that it *always* requires a great deal of intelligence to tell that two terms have the same meaning or the same reference. But there are many cases in which it doesn't require a great deal of intelligence to solve a problem in inductive or deductive reasoning. To determine the intrinsic complexity of a task is to ask, *How hard can it be in the hardest case?*[22]

The connection between general intelligence and being a warranted belief is important. Elsewhere, Putnam connects being a warranted belief with rational interpretation and with reasonable reasoning.[23] We can assimilate all three notions into a single family, because of their family resemblances. They are all used to establish the warrant of beliefs, and they are all used in SD and coreferentiality decisions. (Thus they all play central epistemological and semantical roles in Putnam's philosophy. Since truth is epistemic in his philosophy, they are necessary in defining it.[24]) It is clear from his discussion of general intelligence that Putnam does not think there is a computational account of it. His citation of Fodor is evidence of this, for Fodor (in his important work *The Modularity of Mind*[25]) argues that there is currently no computational description of general intelligence and inductive reasoning and the prospects for such a description in the near future are dim. Thus, if general intelligence is necessary for SD and if there is no computational description of general intelligence, there is no computational description of SD.

Putnam contends that in SD how to decide a case is not fixed in advance. In the Bohr electron case, discounting differences in belief wins out over maximizing true beliefs. Nor is how charitable one is to be fixed in advance. In some cases, we declare a change in meaning and settle for moderate charity. In other cases, we opt for radical charity and do not declare a change in meaning.[26] Whether the reasoning used in SD is general intelligence, rational interpretation, or reasonable reasoning, one feature of it is that it is not decided in advance what will be its outcome. Even if all the input data are available, what will be the output is not fixed by some deterministic mechanical procedure. Can this property of 'not being fixed in advance' separate deterministic computational descriptions of reasoning from the family of notions that includes rational interpretation? If so, there is no deterministic computational description of that family. Putnam thinks that human agents can successfully engage in SD (because the semantics of their language is epistemic and not truth conditional), that rational interpretation is necessary for SD, and that all agents whose minds have computational descriptions can't engage in successful SD (because general intelligence or inductive reasoning is not computable). Thus we have the following oppositions:

A	B
rational interpretation	
general intelligence }	computational account of reasoning
reasonable reasoning	
no fixed outcome in reasoning	fixed outcome in reasoning
epistemic semantics	truth-conditional semantics
no meaning holism	radical Quinean meaning holism
successful SD	no SD (because no synonymy)

It is tempting to read Putnam as saying that list A and list B are incompatible, and that B is a list of properties true of computational functionalist accounts of the mind whereas A is a list of properties true of Putnam's anti-functionalist view of the human mind. If so, he has a powerful philosophical dichotomy that is useful in diagnosing functionalist and anti-functionalist views.[27] I don't think this dichotomy can be maintained. I will show that computationalism is not committed to radical Quinean meaning holism, that it can be used for successful SD, and that it is not committed to truth-conditional semantics. Next I will argue that if epistemic semantics is not committed to metaphysical realism and does not succumb to indeterminacy, ontological relativity, and Quinean meaning holism, neither does computationalism.

Does Computationalism Succumb to Radical Quinean Meaning Holism? The Ruritania Case

Using the hypothetical Ruritania case, Putnam argues that functional descriptions of the language use of speakers in Ruritania cannot distinguish meaning-constituting from auxiliary beliefs.[28] Consequently, on the functionalist model employed, either all changes in belief are meaning-constituting changes or all changes in belief are not meaning-constituting changes. Either way, it fails as an account of successful SD. It succumbs to radical Quinean meaning holism. Thus any functional model of language use can't do SD. But the Ruritania argument fails because the statistical generalization that is needed for it to succeed fails.

Ruritania is an imaginary country on earth in which there is a single language that has two dialects. In one dialect the word 'grug' means silver; in the other it means aluminum. Where the dialect in which 'grug' means silver is spoken, all the common household items constructed of metal are made of silver. Where the dialect in which 'grug' means aluminum is spoken, they are made of aluminum. Two children, each of whom speaks a different dialect, are stipulated to have, at a given time t, the same set of beliefs about grug and thus the same mental representation of it. For instance, both of these children believe (at time t) that their household pots and pans are made of grug. Now imagine the children as adults. Over the years they have acquired additional information about grug that is expressed in their beliefs about it. At some point, the meaning of 'grug' as used by one speaker differs from its meaning as used by the other speaker.

'Grug' cannot have the same meaning in both dialects. If it did, then what it refers to could not be part of its meaning, since it refers to different things in each of the dialects. For Putnam, that is absurd. A term's referent is part of its meaning, or content. The question is when the content of the mental representations of the word 'grug' changed for the two speakers. Putnam contends that on one functionalist model that cannot distinguish meaning-constituting from auxiliary beliefs, the contents of each of the adult's mental representations of 'grug' will have the same content. But this does not show much at all. Putnam has chosen a single functional model in which the distinction between meaning-constituting and auxiliary beliefs cannot be made. His Ruritania case does not show that *any* computable model of language use cannot make the distinction. It is not a generic functionalist model that can serve as the basis for a statistical generalization. Why is that?

The functionalist model of language use Putnam employs in the Ruritania case is the impoverished one discussed earlier: updating beliefs by Bayesian confirmation, probability and utility functions and an algorithm that calculates expected utilities. There is no parameter built into the model marked "information about the external environment." Though this computable account of language use succumbs to radical Quinean meaning holism, it is an error of statistical generalization to conclude all functionalist models of language use succumb to it.

To reach the conclusion that *all* functionalist accounts of language use succumb to radical Quinean meaning holism, Putnam must either examine each functionalist model of language use and show that it can't make the distinction between meaning-constituting beliefs and auxiliary beliefs or find some property all functionalist models possess and show this property rules out making the distinction. How can he enumerate all possible functionalist models of language use? We don't now know them all. There may be infinitely many importantly different functionalist models of language use.

Another way to examine all possible functionalist models of language use is by statistical generalization. Given a representative sample of all possible functionalist models of language use, and running the Ruritania argument on each of them, he can succeed. But the problem is that if we do not know the structure of the space of all the possible functionalist models of language use, we will not know whether a sample taken to be representative of that space is random. If so, statistical generalization fails because of a biased sample.

A different way to examine all possible functionalist models of language use is to describe an essential property all of them possess and prove that this property implies the distinction between meaning-constituting and auxiliary beliefs can't be made. The burden of proof is on Putnam's shoulders to find it. He appears to discharge the burden of proof by taking metaphysical realism as the essential property of all functionalist models of language use. All of them are committed to metaphysical realism. Putnam makes this claim explicitly: "Independence, Uniqueness, Bivalence and Correspondence [the complex of properties constitutive of metaphysical realism—JB] are regulative ideas that the final scientific image is expected to live up to, as well as metaphysical assumptions that guarantee that such a final scientific resolution of all philosophical problems *must* be possible."[29] "With the rise of computer science, an entirely new paradigm of what a scientific realist account of intentionality might look like presented itself."[30] In Putnam's eyes, computationalism is a scientific realist doctrine and scientific realism is committed to metaphysical realism. I argue that computationalism is not committed to metaphysical realism. But even if it can be shown it is not committed to metaphysical realism, there are other ways in which a blow against it can be struck.

For one, Quine takes it that all natural languages, regardless of whether they are used to express scientific doctrines, succumb to radical meaning holism. It is not just computable accounts of language use that succumb to radical meaning holism. To show that computationalism is not committed to metaphysical realism would not remove it from Quine's problem. But, on the other hand, Putnam thinks that where the contents of intentional states are evaluated in terms of epistemic semantics, radical Quinean meaning holism is evaded. One reason he thinks this is so is that epistemic semantics is not committed to metaphysical realism. (It does not satisfy Correspondence, one of the properties criterial of metaphysical realism.) But he also thinks epistemic semantics succeeds, for it uses the family of notions: rational interpretation, general intelligence and reasonable reasoning. He does not think that any of these notions have computational descriptions. (I think he does not have any convincing arguments for this claim.) My concern is to show computationalism is not committed to metaphysical realism. Before doing that, I will explore the connection between Quinean indeterminacy and radical Quinean meaning holism. I will do this because Putnam thinks any theory that buys into Correspondence (which is partially criterial of metaphysical realism) succumbs to indeterminacy. He has a novel interpretation of indeterminacy. Indeterminacy shows that there is no computational description of SD. So if it is true that computationalism succumbs to indeterminacy, then it is also true that it has no means to computationally describe SD. If it does not succumb to indeterminacy, it no longer follows that it cannot provide a computational description of SD.[31]

Quinean Indeterminacy and Radical Quinean Meaning Holism

Putnam argues in chapter 7 of *R&R* that all computationalist accounts of human reasoning are committed to the doctrine of metaphysical realism. Elsewhere he argues that taking there to be a metaphysically real relation between signs (in the head) and their referents—a hallmark of metaphysical realism—is what underlies the phenomenon of Quinean indeterminacy.[32] I propose to show that computationalism is not committed to metaphysical realism and is not committed to the idea that there is a metaphysically real relation between signs (or symbols) and their referents.

One of the defining characteristics of a commitment to metaphysical realism is the notion of an abstract correspondence between words and things. It is this abstract correspondence that Putnam thinks underlies Quinean indeterminacy and ontological relativity. Quinean indeterminacy implies radical Quinean meaning holism, for failure of translation schemes between words in distinct languages, or within the same language, shows there is no notion of synonymy. If there is no synonymy, there is no distinction between meaning-constituting beliefs and auxiliary beliefs. Hence, if one thinks there are meanings, they must be individuated with respect to all of one's beliefs. But that is just radical Quinean meaning holism.

I block the preceding chain of inferences by showing that computationalism isn't committed to metaphysical realism and that it does not succumb to indeterminacy. I show that the former is true by a relative consistency proof and the latter is true by using a relative consistency proof and by arguing there are no decisive arguments that show there is no formalization of rational interpretation. Putnam argues that his epistemic semantics does not succumb to indeterminacy or ontological relativity. If that is true, it follows that it is also true of computationalism, if the latter is not committed to metaphysical realism.

The relative consistency proof assumes that Putnam is right that epistemic semantics is immune to indeterminacy and ontological relativity. If he is wrong, then the relative consistency proof fails. But in that case, the intentional level is subject to radical Quinean meaning holism. If that is the case, it is senseless to ask whether SD can succeed, since there are no meanings. This would short-circuit Putnam's framework for refuting computational functionalism.

How Epistemic Semantics Avoids Indeterminacy and Ontological Relativity

Putnam has argued that ontological relativity must be answered—at the intentional level—by any sane philosophy, for ontological relativity is an unacceptable doctrine: "And I still see ontological relativity as a refutation of any philosophical position that leads to it."[33] He thinks there are philosophical arguments that undercut Quinean indeterminacy at the intentional level. In particular, his program of internal realism provides the materials for countering ontological relativity and indeterminacy at the intentional level. The price that must be paid is to jettison truth-conditional semantics and to adopt epistemic semantics.

According to Putnam, we succumb to ontological relativity and indeterminacy by associating the notions of 'refers to' and 'corresponds to' with Platonic objects—metaphysically real correspondences between things in the head and things in the world. If we begin with the notion of a correspondence, we get the doctrine of ontological relativity.[34] The unacceptable consequence of ontological relativity that Putnam derides is a form of disjunction problem that arises for objects and their properties. If we assert that some object is either a cat or a peach or a cloud or a neutron, then that object is nothing at all, other than a disjunction of distinct things. If the referents of our terms are (possibly infinite) disjunctions, there is no need to make coreferentiality decisions.[35] If reference is constitutive of meaning, then meanings are disjunctive (and possibly infinitely disjunctive). In that case, any computational reduction of SD will be disjunctive because at the intentional level the phenomena are disjunctive. Putnam says that this problem is forced on anyone who takes the idea of an abstract correspondence between symbols and things seriously. Give up that idea and the problem disappears. How does it disappear in epistemic semantics?

Putnam identifies knowing when a sentence is assertible with knowing when it would be justified. "Dummett," he writes, "considers the learning of a language to be the learning of a practice and not a set of correspondences; he considers the speaker's knowledge of his native language to consist in the implicit knowledge of the conditions under which the sentences of the language are *assertible* (a sort of *recognition ability*).... He identifies knowing when a sentence is assertible with *knowing when it would be justified*." How, then, do we "get" objects and properties? If we cannot understand what they are on the basis of the notion of a correspondence, then what are they? They arise out of discourse: "... objects and reference arise out of discourse rather than being prior to discourse."[36] Truth is radically epistemic, for it is epistemic justification. But Putnam cautions us here. He does not think justification conditions can be specified by an algorithm nor that they can be humanly surveyed: "There is no single general rule or universal method for knowing what conditions are better or worse for justifying an arbitrary empirical judgment.... I reject 'meaning theories.'"[37]

To know the conditions under which sentences are true—that is, epistemically justified—is to know what object-involving terms refer to. How does this help us escape the clutches of ontological relativity and indeterminacy? Ontological relativity is the view that the referents of our terms are free-floating, relative to a conceptual scheme. They are not fixed absolutely.[38] But when we know the justification conditions of a referring term, we acquire information that is lacking in a correspondence notion of truth. It is this information that can be used to discriminate models of a language and thus determine which objects the terms refer to. We also know that there are no *recherché* uses in which the term might be entwined. Justification conditions tell us that 'cat' refers to cats and not to cherries or chairs or bats. In short, we know which model we inhabit. We know that we inhabit the model in which 'cat' refers to actual cats and not cat-stages, parts of cats, cat-flies, pigs, or cherries. When we know what model we occupy, we sidestep ontological relativity and indeterminacy, both of which arise when we have no information that can tell us what model we inhabit.

Rational interpretation is necessary for determining justification conditions. But if there is no algorithm for rational interpretation, it follows that there is no algorithm for justification conditions. Putnam argues that computationalism is a scientistic theory committed to metaphysical realism. If he is right about truth as justification, and if he is right that no theory of truth for which abstract correspondence is constitutive and criterial has information that can distinguish the models we might inhabit, then no computationalist theory can determine the model we inhabit and thus avoid ontological relativity and indeterminacy. If so, given that radical Quinean meaning holism follows from indeterminacy, it follows that no computationalist theory can distinguish meaning-constituting beliefs from auxiliary beliefs. Thus, if it is shown that computationalism is not a scientistic theory by showing that it is not committed to metaphysical realism (by showing it that does not satisfy the defining criteria of metaphysical realism), it is left open whether it has the resources to provide a computational description of rational interpretation.

That SCS is falsified by content growth requires that computationalism be committed to metaphysical realism and thus succumbs to Quinean indeterminacy, and so to radical Quinean meaning holism. I will break the chain of inferences by showing that it is not committed to metaphysical realism. It follows that it does not succumb to indeterminacy, ontological relativity and radical Quinean meaning holism. If it does not succumb to radical Quinean meaning holism, falsifying SCS by showing computationalism cannot distinguish auxiliary from meaning-constituting beliefs fails. If it does not succumb to indeterminacy, falsifying SCS by showing that computationalism cannot group stimulus meanings into synonymy classes fails. After showing that SCS is not falsified by content growth, I argue that it can be falsified by computational growth, but that way of falsifying it does not endanger the prospect of local computational reductions of arbitrary intentional states.

The Immunity Argument: Computationalism Is Not Committed to Metaphysical Realism

I argue that the computational level is as immune to Quinean indeterminacy and ontological relativity as is epistemic semantics, because the computational level also carries no intrinsic commitment to metaphysical realism. This is a controversial thesis. Putnam says computationalism is grounded in metaphysical realism: "... I have described metaphysical realism as a bundle of intimately associated philosophical ideas about truth:

the ideas that truth is a matter of Correspondence and that it exhibits Independence (of what humans do or could find out), Bivalence, and Uniqueness (there cannot be more than one complete and true description of Reality).... What I used to find seductive about metaphysical realism is the idea that *the way to solve philosophical problems is to construct a better scientific picture of the world*.... With the rise of computer science, an entirely new paradigm of what a scientific realist account of intentionality might look like presented itself. The need for a full-length investigation of the question of the scientific reducibility of intentionality in the age of the computer thus arose."[39]

Putnam says that computationalism is committed to metaphysically realist truth and metaphysically realist truth satisfies four properties: Correspondence, Independence, Bivalence, and Uniqueness (CIBU). For Putnam, computationalism is a scientific realist theory of reduction, and scientific realists are committed to metaphysical realism. Computationalists believe in the sham doctrine of scientism. I now argue that a computational functionalist can refute these charges by showing that it does not (necessarily) satisfy any of CIBU.

If computationalism is not committed to metaphysical realism, does it follow that it can provide a computable theory of rational interpretation that is used in epistemic semantics to sidestep indeterminacy and ontological relativity? According to Putnam, indeterminacy follows from a failure to find an algorithm for rational interpretation. This view has been hidden in the debates over indeterminacy. It is instructive to quote Putnam at length:

> What Quine is saying ... is something that, in fact, Noam Chomsky also believes— although most discussions of the debate fail to bring this out. Neither Quine nor Chomsky expects *mechanical translation* to succeed. That is, neither Quine nor Chomsky expects to find a set of criteria which will function as an *algorithm* to determine when one has correctly translated an expression of one language into another language. The idea that *interpretive rationality can be fully exhausted by a finite set of criteria that we will actually succeed in writing down* is Utopian on its face. But this is what Quine is, in effect, demanding—that we succeed in writing down such a set of criteria—before he will accept that we have succeeded in rationally reconstructing the notion of synonymy.[40]

Suppose we successfully show computationalism does not succumb to ontological relativity and indeterminacy. It doesn't follow it provides a computational description of rational interpretation. But it would be odd it if could not do so, given Putnam's views about the use of rational interpretation in sidestepping ontological relativity and Quinean indeterminacy. Human beings use rational interpretation to distinguish meaning-constituting beliefs from auxiliary beliefs and thus to engage in successful SD and coreferentiality decisions. Sidestepping ontological relativity and indeterminacy necessarily confers an ability to do SD and make coreferentiality decisions.[41]

I will now consider each defining criterion of metaphysical realism and show that computationalism is not committed to any of them.

Computationalism is not committed to Uniqueness

Valuation mappings are not sufficient for Uniqueness   Uniqueness is the view that there is only one true and complete description of Ultimate Reality. I argue that computationalism is not committed to it by showing that an essential feature of classical logics is neither a necessary nor sufficient condition for it. Consider computations that can be rewritten as a set of sentences in first-order logic.[42] The sentences in first-order logic or propositional logic are true or false only when there is a valuation function in place—a valuation function that connects the syntactical sentences in the language of the logic with the abstract structures that are the models of those sentences. The valuation mapping connects syntax with semantics, or symbol with reality. It is required that the mapping assigns a unique truth value to each wff of the language. The mapping is defective if it assigns two distinct truth values to a given wff.

In first-order logic, one needs another abstract mapping, the satisfaction relation, that maps variables onto objects and sequences of objects in the model. Since the satisfaction mapping is a function, domain values of the mapping must not map into two (or more) range values. There is an elementary theorem in first-order logic which states that if the valuation function makes a closed wff true under *some* assignment of references, then the same valuation function makes the same closed wffs true under *all* assignments of references. An assignment of references is a function whose domain is syntactical objects in the language of first-order logic and whose range is the objects in the structure (or model).[43]

Do valuation and satisfaction mappings satisfy the metaphysical realist property of Uniqueness? These mappings connect symbol with reality. For Putnam, Uniqueness is the view that there cannot be more than one complete and true description of Reality. There is a valuation mapping condition on propositional and first-order logics. It is that formulas in the language cannot be mapped onto two (or more) distinct truth values. This condition is not sufficient for Uniqueness. It is fairly easy to see. Consider the following sentence in propositional logic: 'If p then (if q then p)'. This sentence comes out true no matter what assignment of truth values one makes to the atomic sentences in it, for it is a tautology. Assignment of truth values to the atomic sentences and to the compound sentence 'If p then (if q then p)' respects the valuation mapping condition. Nowhere is a syntactical object assigned both truth values T and F. Nonetheless, there are *four* complete and true descriptions of Reality.[44] The four descriptions are ordered pairs $\langle T, T \rangle$, $\langle T, F \rangle$, $\langle F, T \rangle$, and $\langle F, F \rangle$. The valuation mapping *could* have assigned $\langle T, F \rangle$ rather than $\langle T, T \rangle$, or it *could* have assigned $\langle F, F \rangle$ instead of $\langle F, T \rangle$. No matter which pair it does assign, 'If p then (if q then p)' comes out true. Valuation mappings are compatible with four distinct and true descriptions of Reality.

In response, the anti-realist anti-computationalist might argue that these are four complete and true descriptions of *part of* reality, not Reality. For them, Reality is 'If p then (if q then p)' being true, period. In looking at Reality, we do not look at what truth values we assign to its parts. But this is a dangerous move. In criticizing our claim that propositional and first-order logic can violate Uniqueness, he will have to describe what is the Ultimate Reality—the very object that he contends is incoherent and that he vehemently eschews. He must show that on this conception of Ultimate Reality, how we conceive of its parts is irrelevant to how we conceive of the whole. That seems to be a crazy view, since it denies supervenience of reality on its parts.[45]

If not, he has to countenance Ultimate Reality having Ultimate Parts. Just as the whole of Ultimate Reality has a unique truth value, so must each of its parts. However, computationalism is not committed to there being only one unique assignment of truth values to the Ultimate Parts of the formula 'If p then (if q then p)', for it is compatible with four unique assignments of truth values to the Ultimate Parts. Propositional logic tabulates all the possibilities for Ultimate Parts, but says nothing (in fact, it can't say anything) about which one is the Truth and thus can say nothing about which reality is Ultimate Reality.

Take each of the theorems of propositional logic, their premises and antecedent derivations and express them as a conditional by making the theorem its consequent and its premises and antecedent derivations its antecedent. Each of these conditionals is a tautology.[46] They will evaluate to true no matter what truth values are assigned to their Ultimate Parts. Suppose that all the theorems of propositional logic describe the propositional structure of Ultimate Reality. Thus, whatever is the extent of Ultimate Reality, there are multiple truth value assignments to its Ultimate

Parts. On the assumption that its Ultimate Parts are part of Ultimate Reality (what else can they be?), there are multiple complete and true descriptions of Ultimate Reality. Thus valuation mappings are not sufficient for Uniqueness and so Uniqueness is not necessary for valuation mappings. Classical logic and computationalism don't satisfy the metaphysical realist property of Uniqueness.

Valuation mappings are not necessary for Uniqueness   It can also be shown that valuation mappings are not necessary for Uniqueness, though certain assumptions must be in place to do so. It is logically possible that there is one, and only one, complete and true description of Ultimate Reality under which there is a single assignment of two distinct truth values to a single atomic wff (in the language of propositional logic). How can we have Uniqueness without satisfying the valuation mapping?

Suppose that an atomic wff of propositional logic is assigned T and F as truth values. How do we understand that wff? Do we say it is both true and false? To make our point, we use Australian semantics, in which the lattice of truth values includes 'true-and-false' and 'neither-true-nor-false' as distinct and determinate truth values in addition to 'true' and to 'false'. Consider the liar sentence: 'This sentence is false.' If it is assigned two truth values *and* we have some means for avoiding contradictions built into the logic (typically, this logic will either be a paraconsistent logic or a relevance logic), then there will be (at the maximal Lindenbaum or Henkin construction) one, and only one, complete and true description of Ultimate Reality. Certainly, not everyone will find this example convincing. However, it does show that the valuation mapping is not necessary for Uniqueness—even though the conditions obtain only in deviant logics. Ruling out a deviant logic as a basis for computation is far from trivial, given the large corpus of work that has been done on connecting paraconsistent and relevant logics to a theory of computability.

There is an example from propositional modal logic in which uniqueness of the valuation mapping is not necessary for Uniqueness. Here, too, certain assumptions must be made so the example will work. Let one of the worlds in a modal model structure be inaccessible from the actual world. Assign to sentences in that world two different truth values. The structure of the world, as seen from the actual world, is unique. But the valuation mapping, in the modal model structure, has been violated—it fails to be unique.

Even in classical propositional logic, under suitable assumptions, it can be shown that uniqueness of the valuation mapping is not necessary for

Uniqueness. Suppose that a valuation mapping assigns both true and false to the atomic sentences of a classical propositional logic. Tautologies will evaluate to true no matter what the truth values of the atomic sentences out of which they are constructed—this is evident in the case of supervaluations. To get this result, we have to assume that only the truth value of Ultimate Reality, and not the truth values of any of its Ultimate Parts, counts. Thus, either the uniqueness of valuation mappings is not sufficient for Uniqueness or it is not necessary for Uniqueness. It depends on whether or not the Ultimate Parts of Ultimate Reality count in assessing the uniqueness of Ultimate Reality.

Thus, in relevant, paraconsistent, modal, and classical logics, under certain assumptions, uniqueness of the valuation mapping is not necessary for Uniqueness and thus Uniqueness is not sufficient for uniqueness of the valuation mapping. Thus, uniqueness of the valuation mapping is neither necessary nor sufficient for Uniqueness. We could also have run the same arguments in first-order logic on the notion of satisfaction. Since valuation and satisfaction mappings—which are essential for connecting a logic's syntax with its semantics—are neither necessary nor sufficient for the metaphysical realist property of Uniqueness, classical and non-classical logics do not have Uniqueness. So it is false that computations have it. This is significant, for Uniqueness is a necessary condition for metaphysical realism. Thus, since it is the case that computations do not satisfy Uniqueness, it follows that they are not committed to metaphysical realism.

Computationalism is not committed to Independence and Bivalence I will now show that computational functionalism is not committed to Bivalence and Independence. Bivalence is the view that statements are either true or false That is, there are only two truth values. Independence is the view that truth is independent of "what humans do or could find out."[47] If the underlying logic of a computational procedure is intuitionistic logic, Independence and Bivalence fail. Cognitive scientists worry about what kinds of logic capture cognitive activities. For instance, it is claimed that non-monotonic logics capture inductive reasoning. All non-monotonic logics are non-classical (they fail monotonicity), and some are intuitionistic (in the base logic). Intuitionistic and non-intuitionistic non-monotonic logics for inductive reasoning set the limits for what humans do or could find out about the world. But they are not independent of what humans do or could find out about the world. Intuitionistic non-monotonic logics also fail bivalence.

Recently, Dana Scott and his co-workers at Carnegie Mellon University devised a modal intuitionistic logic of computations that fits neatly into the program of denotational semantics. It bridges traditional mathematics (viewed in terms of ZFC set theory) and the algebraic objects—categories—that are the primary mathematical objects in domain theory (the bedrock of denotational semantics). This is a different example from the use of non-monotonic logics to capture inductive reasoning. Here the issue is the logic of computations. It is not about the logic of the processes computationally modeled. The modal intuitionistic logic of computations fails both Independence and bivalence.[48]

Whether computations or computational descriptions of cognitive processes satisfy the metaphysical realist properties of Bivalence and Independence is not a settled matter. The existence of non-classical logics underlying computations that do not satisfy these properties shifts the burden of proof onto Putnam's shoulders. He must show the *ultimate* logic of computations and/or of computational descriptions of cognitive processes is committed to Bivalence and Independence. To do that, he must now know that ultimate logic. But how could he know that *now*? What shape cognitive science will take in the future is (now) not known. In order to discharge the burden of proof, Putnam has to tell us what ultimate cognitive science will be like. If not, asserting that computationalism is a scientistic doctrine begs the question.

Computationalism is not committed to Correspondence   Correspondence is the view that truth is correspondence of sentences with facts or reality. Putnam thinks Correspondence is a deep philosophical prejudice that underlies indeterminacy and ontological relativity: "... we understand such notions as 'refers to' and 'corresponds to' *by associating these notions with Platonic objects* ('correspondences'). ... Once this assumption has been made ... then the entire system of competing philosophical theories and arguments unwinds itself with a sort of inevitability. But can we *avoid* this common assumption?"[49] To show computationalism is not committed to Correspondence, we argue that if human beings can avoid Quinean indeterminacy and ontological relativity by reasonable reasoning (as Putnam claims), then it is possible that computational systems can acquire the information needed to determine whether they inhabit the standard model or a non-standard model. If so, the computational system sidesteps ontological relativity and indeterminacy. For Putnam, Correspondence is sufficient for them. (This is how I read the passage quoted above.) Thus, they are implied by it. In that case, showing that they fail shows that Correspondence fails (by modus tollens).

I will show that indeterminacy and ontological relativity fail to be satisfied in a computational system by showing that the system can acquire information about what model it inhabits. If it has information that it inhabits the standard model, then it rules out that, for example, the term 'cat' refers to cat-slices, cherries, stars, and so on. A system committed to Correspondence can't acquire information needed to determine what model it inhabits, because the system is subject to indeterminacy and ontological relativity.

For Putnam, rational interpretation is used to determine what model (or Reality) a human being occupies. Using it, a human agent can acquire information that enables her to decide that her use of the word 'cat' refers to cats and does not refer to cat-slices, cat-flies, cherries, stars, and so on. If so, human beings sidestep indeterminacy and ontological relativity by using rational interpretation. But it is used to make judgments of warranted assertibility that are constitutive of epistemic semantic conceptions of truth. Epistemic semantic truth is not committed to Correspondence.

If it is shown that a computational system can engage in rational interpretation, then if the human beings who engage in it are not committed to Correspondence, it also follows that the computational system that engages in it is not similarly committed. But can a computational system formalize rational interpretation so that it can employ it? Putnam has argued that it cannot. He has employed several different kinds of argument. One is the use of the Gödel incompleteness theorems to show that inductive reasoning and all modes of inquiry into nature cannot be formalized. Another kind of argument is that essential properties of certain kinds of inductive reasoning can't be formalized, such as normal predicates (as opposed to abnormal ones, such as the predicate 'grue') or a prior probability metric used in Bayesian reasoning. In chapter 9 I will argue that these and other kinds of arguments that rational interpretation can't be formalized fail to be convincing. Here I will show how the argument against formalization of rational interpretation from the Gödel incompleteness theorems can be undercut.

Consider a computational system subject to Gödelian incompleteness. It cannot know the truth of its Gödel sentence. A human agent characterized by that computational system can't know whether it inhabits the standard model (in which its Gödel sentence is true) or whether it inhabits the nonstandard model (in which its Gödel sentence is false). Within the computational system, the only way the truth of a sentence can be determined is by a finitary derivation, so the human agent characterized by it can't know which model she inhabits. If we take the steps of the finitary derivation to be facts the agent has at her disposal to determine the model she inhabits, we have a form of Quinean indeterminacy. Let us see why this is so.

From within the computational system, there is no fact of the matter as to what model the agent inhabits. For this agent, knowing what model she inhabits is not just underdetermined; it is indeterminate, since there is no possible information, available as a proof line in a finitary derivation, that can decide what model she inhabits. Any information is a finitary derivation and thus can't establish the truth of the agent's Gödel sentence. If she adds her Gödel sentence, she is now characterized by a new computational system and the question of the model she occupies transfers to the new computational system, since there is now a new Gödel sentence for it.

But computable agents subject to Gödel's incompleteness theorems *can* know what model they inhabit. This is not a contradiction, provided we qualify 'know'. What is known about the model our agent occupies cannot be known with mathematical certainty. But it might be known in any other epistemic modality other than mathematical certainty or with less than mathematical certainty. As we have already seen, those who employ Gödelian incompleteness theorems in the mechanism debate have failed to appreciate that the epistemic modality for knowing within a formal system subject to Gödelian incompleteness is mathematical certainty. Achieving certainty (other than by mathematical means) and acquiring knowledge using a justificatory procedure that has less than mathematical certainty are options *not* ruled out by the Gödel incompleteness theorems, unless the methods used to secure knowledge with less than mathematical certainty or with certainty other than mathematical certainty are themselves Gödelizable.

Consider a computable agent subject to the theorems who employs reasoning systems some of which are not Gödelizable and who can determine by using the non-Gödelizable reasoning system the truth of her Gödel sentence, though with less than mathematical certainty or in another epistemic modality. She can know, with less than mathematical certainty, what model she inhabits. Now consider a human being not characterized by a computational system, who uses rational interpretation to determine the model that she inhabits. It is impossible for her to determine what model she inhabits with mathematical certainty (unless rational interpretation is infinitary and there is no evidence to think that it is). If she could do so, she would violate the Gödel incompleteness theorems, even though she is, by assumption, not characterized by a computational system. The only way to secure knowledge of a proposition with mathematical certainty is to derive the proposition in a system of finitary logic. Thus neither the computable agent nor the agent that has no computational description can determine what model they inhabit with mathematical certainty. If so, this places a fundamental constraint on rational interpretation. The information an agent acquires using it cannot be used to determine, with mathematical certainty, the model she inhabits.

If rational interpretation is used to determine the truth of a Gödel sentence with less than mathematical certainty, it is also available to a computationally characterized agent to do the same. Neither agent is committed to Correspondence, since both agents can distinguish between the standard and non-standard model and thus neither agent succumbs to the indeterminacy that arises in this limited setting. Notice that this is a relative consistency proof. If it is true that rational interpretation can determine the model a human being inhabits (with less than mathematical certainty), it is also available for a computationally characterized human being to do the same, but only if rational interpretation can be formalized and is not subject to the Gödel theorems.

But if rational interpretation can't be formalized because it is subject to the Gödel theorems, then any human mind that has no computational description can't use rational interpretation to establish, with mathematical certainty, the model it inhabits. But if it can't use rational interpretation to establish with mathematical certainty the model it inhabits, it must establish it with less than mathematical certainty or in another epistemic modality. But these procedures are also available to a human mind that has a computational description. It follows that if it is shown that rational interpretation can't be completely formalized because it is subject to Gödel's theorems, then Putnam is not able to conclude that human minds with no computational description can determine the model they inhabit by rational interpretation, but human minds with a computational description can't determine the model they inhabit by using formalized rational interpretation.

I conclude that there is no good reason to believe that a computational description of a human mind is subject to abstract Correspondence, or any of the other hallmarks of metaphysical realism. Cognitive science is not scientistic, even though it is naturalistic. To put things boldly: Naturalism does not imply scientism nor the kind of scientific realism Putnam thinks is committed to metaphysical realism.

Three Objections to the Claim That Computationalism Is Not Committed to Correspondence

Let us now consider three possible objections to the claim that computable agents can know, with less than mathematical certainty or in some other epistemic modality, what model they inhabit.

Objection 1: You have shown computable agents subject to the Gödel incompleteness theorems can know what model they inhabit with less than mathematical certainty. However, Putnam's permutation theorem formally captures indeterminacy and it applies to first-order logics too weak to express Peano arithmetic. The theorem is as follows: "Let L be a language with predicates $F_1, F_2, \ldots, F_k$ (not necessarily monadic). Let I be an interpretation, in the sense of an assignment of an intension to every predicate of L. Then if I is nontrivial in the sense that at least one predicate has an extension which is neither empty nor universal in at least one possible world, there exists a second interpretation J which disagrees with I, but which makes the same sentences true in every possible world as I does."[50] Doesn't it show that non-Gödelizable computationally characterized agents succumb to indeterminacy? That is, these agents can't determine the model (or world) that they inhabit.

Is I the interpretation of our sentences, or is J? The same sentences come out true under either interpretation, so we can't distinguish the interpretations in terms of which sentences are true in them. I picks out one model (or world); J picks out another model (or world). Since all such agents formalized within classical first-order logic (without Peano arithmetic) are syntactical constructions (at the computational level), they cannot reason about the models they inhabit outside the constraints of their syntax. But all the models (standard and nonstandard) of first-order logic are indistinguishable in terms of their syntax alone. Thus, all models are indistinguishable in terms of any computations executed within computationally characterized agents.

Response: That response can be countered in two ways. First, Edward Keenan has argued that Putnam's permutation theorem is false.[51] That is, the condition under which the formulas in the logic remain true in the permuted model is *not* that the interpretation function is nontrivial, but that the relations in the models are permutation invariant. Putnam takes a necessary condition for the permutation theorem to be that at least one predicate in the logic has neither non-zero nor universal extension. Keenan shows this is false. This is significant, since satisfying this condition is innocuous and is *prima facie* independent of permutation invariance of the models. He reformulates Putnam's permutation theorem in terms of permutation invariance: "An n-ary relation R over a universe E is permutation invariant iff f(R) = R, for all permutations f of E."[52] Since not every relation is permutation invariant, it follows that universal indeterminacy in a first-order language can't be inferred from the permutation theorem. More important, if it is required that all (or most) relations are permutation invariant in order for the permutation theorem to hold, then the theorem says nothing more than that where is indeterminacy (because of the permutation invariance of the relations) there is indeterminacy (because of the permutation invariance of the models of the theory). Put graphically, the point is "indeterminacy in, indeterminacy out." If a theory is subject to indeterminacy, then it is indeterminate. The question is: What relations are permutation invariant? The permutation theorem shows the same sentences are true under different interpretations. But that does not mean the truth of each sentence is established in the same way in each interpretation. Truth, for Putnam, is radically epistemic. Under certain epistemic conditions, we can verify that S is true. In different interpretations, we verify that S is true under different epistemic conditions. One can object that all the sentences that make up a verification of the truth of S are themselves interpreted either one way or the other and they come out true under both interpretations. But what the permutation argument does not prove is that the sentences that make up the verification of S under one interpretation are the same sentences that make up the verification of S under the other interpretation. If all the relations that underlie verification of the truth of S under one interpretation, as well as relations about the relations that underlie the verification of S, are not permutation-invariant, then there is a way for the computable agent to distinguish between the two interpretations. Second, if rational interpretation can be used to sidestep indeterminacy, then it can also be used by a computationally characterized agent, provided it is formalizable. Though the permutation theorem governs logical systems too weak to express Peano arithmetic, if rational interpretation can be formalized in such logics, computationally characterized agents can determine the model they inhabit by using formalized rational interpretation. One could argue that rational interpretation can't be formalized because if it did determine the model agents inhabit, it would violate the permutation theorem. But this move begs the question. Rational interpretation determines the model an agent inhabits in some way. It is left open that the way it's done is by exploiting the failure of some relations to be permutation invariant. To suppose otherwise is to beg the question against computationally described agents determining the model they inhabit.

Objection 2: There is a simple argument to show computationalism can't do what rational interpretation can that doesn't use either Putnam's permutation theorem or the Gödel theorems. In epistemic semantics, truth precedes reference. When it is known under what conditions a sentence is true, one thereby knows the referents of the singular terms in the sentence. But reference precedes truth in the semantics for first-order logic. The satisfaction relation can't be defined until assignment of references has been made. This difference accounts for why rational interpretation can be used to sidestep indeterminacy and ontological relativity and computationalism cannot.

Response: The objection does not provide any argument that it is because truth precedes reference in epistemic semantics that indeterminacy and ontological relativity can be sidestepped. Putnam has never shown how rational interpretation actually works in picking out the standard model from the non-standard model, or in showing that 'cat' refers to cats and not to cherries. He does say that metaphysical realism underlies Quinean indeterminacy and ontological relativity. We have shown that computationalism is not committed to metaphysical realism. Unless it can be shown Quinean indeterminacy and ontological relativity arise from the two independent sources, metaphysical realism and that truth precedes reference, there is no argument that computationalism can't sidestep them.

Objection 3: There is a dilemma for computational functionalism. Computable methods that prove, with less than mathematical certainty (or in another epistemic modality), the truth of their Gödel sentence are probabilistic and thus not conventional computations in the original style envisaged by Turing. In short, the price to be paid for immunity to indeterminacy and ontological relativity is that the classical picture of computation inherited from Turing must be replaced by a non-standard picture. This is a bad replacement. The import of Turing's conception of computability for the representational theory of mind is that it offers it the only plausible way to explain how truth is preserved in reasoning. Give up that conception of computability and you lose the raison d'être of the representational theory of mind.

Response: Not all human reasoning needs to be explicated in terms of a classical Turing model of computation, since not all of it is truth preserving.[53] It would be absurd to computationally model reasoning that is not truth preserving by reasoning that is. The classical Turing model works best where we engage in deductive reasoning with mathematical certainty. Where it needs to be altered is when we engage in inductive reasoning with less than mathematical certainty. There has been, within the last decade, a profusion of work on computable models of uncertain reasoning. The burden of proof falls onto the shoulders of the objector. She must rule out, as psychologically unrealistic or mathematically incorrect, computational models of uncertain reasoning that do not employ classical Turing-machine models.

Augmenting the representational theory of mind with probabilistic and non-monotonic computational models does not destroy its raison d'être. In Turing machines, we computationally model how deductive reasoning preserves truth by manipulating physical symbols in the right way. In probabilistic Turing machines, manipulations still guarantee that, within an error estimate, truth is preserved. By manipulating physical symbols within them, we are able to attain truth within the bounds provided by the error estimates.

Computational Growth

There is another source of growth in the size of the set of computational realizations of an arbitrary intentional state: computational growth. The computational models, computer architectures, programming languages and algorithms that are used in cognitive psychology are the means for increasing the number of disjunctions of the computational states realized in a computational reduction. We now show there are infinitely many computational realizations of an arbitrary intentional state by using computational growth. If true, this refutes SCS.

There are a number of different ways this can be done. For instance, one can argue there are infinitely many programming languages. If so, there are infinitely many different ways to realize an algorithm as a computer program. The same is true of computer architectures. It might be true of computational models, but that depends on how we individuate them.

Suppose we use a method for constructing trivial variants of any computer program. Given a fixed computer program in a fixed programming language, a fixed computer architecture, and a fixed computational model, we construct infinitely many variants of that computer program. The method to do this is well known: program padding. Take a fixed computer program (for an arbitrary intentional state) and pad the instructions. That is, either add to the instruction set inessential lines of code that are ignored by the compiler or lines of code that effect actions that do not affect the overall computation. Example of the latter type of padding: Line 5 in the program adds '1' to register R and line 6 in the program removes '1' from register R. Padding easily generates infinitely many variants of the initial computer program. This method of falsifying SCS does not jeopardize local computational reduction, since one can computably partition all the padded programs into the same equivalence class.

Putnam considers computational growth within the framework of Carnapian inductive logics.[54] Assume that the inductive logic we use is a non-negotiable architectural feature of human cognition. In Carnapian inductive logics there is a caution parameter. This parameter indicates how quickly or how slowly the inductive logic learns from exposure to sequences of data from its local environment. For example, if the learner is presented with the sequence 10100000000, will it guess that the next number in the sequence is 0, or must the learner be presented with the sequence 101000000000 before it guesses that the next number in the sequence is 0? There are also questions about how much weight to attach to analogy and to similarity and the issue of prior probabilities. How does a Carnapian inductive logic assign prior probabilities to the initial state of its local environment?

There are denumerably many values of the Carnapian caution parameter. Thus there are denumerably many inductive logics. Assume that different agents have different hard-wired caution parameters. Among all possible agents, actual and counterfactual, there can be infinitely many different values of the caution parameter. If so, there are infinitely many distinct computational states that realize an arbitrary intentional state. This falsifies SCS. Here is what Putnam has to say about the number of different computational states for varying caution parameters: "Computers that have to compute very different 'analogies' or employ very different caution parameters (caution parameters which can themselves be different mathematical functions of the particular evidence *e*, not just different scalars) may have totally different descriptions, either in the Turing machine formalism or in any other formalism. The number of states may be different, the state transition rules may be different, and there is no reason why either machine should have a table which can be embedded in (or even mapped homomorphically into) the machine table of the other [machine]."[55]

Even though there are nondenumerably many Carnapian inductive logics (the caution parameter can take on any real number in the interval $[0, 1]$), it is likely that almost all of them are not employed in computably negotiating a *local* environment. If we all inhabit the same place (or small set of places), why would Nature assign so many different caution parameters to different individuals? We might be able to computably partition caution parameters into a small set of equivalence classes in terms of the ecological requirements of local environments. Dry environments differ from wet ones, and perhaps this difference demands that different caution parameters be used.

Putnam says there might be intelligent beings who rationally project the predicate 'grue' and not the predicate 'green'.[56] But if the computationalist opts for a local reduction that takes in only human beings, such intelligent beings no longer enter our considerations. Putnam drops "all possible intelligent beings," and substitutes the local condition "all human beings" in a spirit of concession in EQUIVALENCE. There is work in cognitive science (such as the M constraint in linguistics) that shows it is unlikely we project grue-like predicates.[57] In the next chapter I will examine results in mathematical logic relevant to assessing if computational-growth-induced computational multi-realizations can be computably partitioned into a small set of equivalence classes.

Summary

The failure of SCS is a necessary condition for EQUIVALENCE. The latter argument is that the infinitely many computational realizations of an arbitrary intentional state cannot be computably partitioned into a small set of equivalence classes. If the number of computational realizations is not infinite, there is no need for EQUIVALENCE. Considerations based on radical Quinean meaning holism or on Quinean indeterminacy show that SCS is false. I called such considerations 'modes of content growth'. Falsity of SCS is also demonstrated by computational growth. I considered two modes of computational growth: padding methods and the continuum of inductive methods in Carnapian inductive logic. My view is that a content-growth refutation of SCS requires showing that rational interpretation cannot be formalized. Computational-growth refutations of SCS are less problematic for me than they are for anti-functionalists, since I believe that computable partitionings of computational-growth-induced computational realizations are possible.

Next I will critically examine EQUIVALENCE. I think there are two important errors committed in it. One is a fallacy of equivocation (on "rational interpretation"). The other is a failure to actually show that there is no computable partitioning of the infinitely many computational realizations of an arbitrary intentional state. The argument appears to be that because the infinite set of computational realizations is extraordinarily heterogeneous, there cannot be a computable partitioning of it.

I think the only argument Putnam has against local computational reduction, and against computational functionalism in general, is that rational interpretation can't be formalized. But I have not found any convincing reasons in *R&R* or in Putnam's other writings to think this is so. Computationalism has other problems, but I don't believe it suffers any of the problems Putnam claims for it.

7 Against Local Computational Reduction: The EQUIVALENCE Argument

Even if Putnam can show that there are infinitely many computational realizations of an arbitrary intentional state, this does not refute the program of computational functionalism. Suppose a computationalist shows that the infinitely large set of computational realizations can be packaged into a small number of computable equivalence classes, and that each equivalence class possesses a "class identity" that comports with cognitive science. If that is the case, there is a local computational reduction.

Putnam argues that a local computational reduction is not possible without the cognitive scientist occupying an Archimedean point. He accomplishes this by showing that any algorithm for rational interpretation is an infinitary algorithm and that only an infinitary being or a god could design or use such algorithms. 'Occupying an Archimedean point' is another way of saying 'has infinitary powers'. He makes several claims in EQUIVALENCE that really need to be argued if it is to succeed.

There is no argument that the infinite set of computational realizations of an arbitrary intentional state can't be computably partitioned into a small set of equivalence classes. What substitutes for the needed argument is an inference from the claim that there is an extraordinary diversity of the infinitely many computational realizations to the claim that they cannot be computably partitioned. Moreover, Putnam's arguments for the claim that rational interpretation cannot be formalized because inductive reasoning can't be formalized are circular. If one argues that inductive reasoning can't be formalized because determining a prior probability metric requires rational interpretation and that can't be formalized, the reasoning is circular if the point of showing that inductive reasoning can't be formalized is to show that rational interpretation can't be formalized.

The biggest difficulty EQUIVALENCE faces is the fundamental ambiguity in Putnam's use of 'rational interpretation'. There is rational interpretation as it is used by human beings in making synonymy judgments and coreferentiality decisions. Putnam has argued that this use of rational interpretation escapes Quinean strictures on synonymy. For instance, it can be used to distinguish auxiliary beliefs from meaning constituting beliefs.

If it can be shown that this kind of rational interpretation can't be formalized, the only option that is available for formalization is a notion of rational interpretation that depends on definitions of synonymy and coreferentiality. But any notion that requires such dependency will turn into an infinitary monster, because it will have to survey all possible theories of the universe and what is in it, all possible local physical environments and all possible theories of human rationality and inference patterns. Any algorithm for such rational interpretation will be an infinitary algorithm. But if it can be shown that the rational interpretation as it is used by human beings in making synonymy judgments and coreferentiality decisions can be formalized, a necessary presupposition for EQUIVALENCE fails. My aim here and in the following chapters is to examine various arguments that attempt to show that radical interpretation, as it is used by human beings, cannot be formalized. I contend that none of them succeed. If that is so, then the *R&R* case against computational functionalism unravels.

Partitioning a Large Set into a Small Collection of Sets

Suppose you wanted to show that you could not partition an infinitely large set of rocks into a small collection of sets, each of which has its own class identity. You would have to show that each rock is *sui generis* and that it does not share natural (non-Cambridge) properties with any other rock. It would be easy to use Cambridge or gerrymandered properties to show that groupings can be obtained. Take the first six rocks and classify them by the property "These are the first six rocks I selected."[1]

Putnam argues that the infinitely large set of computational realizations of an arbitrary intentional state cannot be computably partitioned into a small set of equivalence classes. To computably partition them into a small set of equivalence classes, he will have to argue that computational realizations of an arbitrary intentional state are *sui generis*. (If those features are common to all members of the set—of size K—of computational realizations of an arbitrary intentional state, that set will be an equivalence class with respect to those common features.) How does he argue for this claim? He does it by showing that an algorithm for rational interpretation must be infinitary because both the kinds and the amount of the information it must explicitly contain are infinitary. The idea is that the array of information is infinitarily wide ranging and infinite in amount, so that there is no computable partitioning of it. But simply because it is infinitarily wide-ranging and infinite in amount does not mean that there is no computable partitioning of it. As we shall see, Putnam categorizes the information into three distinct kinds: local environmental information, theories of the world and what is in it, and theories of human rationality and of inference patterns. I will argue that Putnam has failed to show that there can be no computable partitioning of this information.

There is another way to argue that an infinitely large collection of rocks cannot be grouped into a small set of equivalence classes: Assume that the collection of rocks you now have is not all the rocks there are. In the future, new rocks will be created and added to it. The idea is that even if you have been able to partition the collection into a small set of classes, you can't know what the future will bring. All future instances of rocks might be *sui generis*. Or they might have their own similarities but fail to resemble any of the current rocks. Putnam makes an argument of that kind. He contends that future successor linguistic communities will be as different from current linguistic communities as we are from primitive linguistic communities of the past, to which we are successors. We can't know, now, what future linguistic communities will be like. But an algorithm for rational interpretation must, according to Putnam, anticipate future linguistic communities. However, Putnam fails to consider a plausible option: that there is a parameter in the rational-interpretation algorithm in the form of a query to the user, asking for information about the current linguistic community. If so, when such communities come into being, the rational-interpretation algorithm will have access to information about them.

If there is no computable partitioning of the infinitely large set of computational realizations of arbitrary intentional states, there are no local computational reductions of intentional states. But just as damaging to the program of computational functionalism is the fact that one cannot understand the infinitely long disjunction of computational states without first understanding the intentional state they computationally reduce. The computational reduction cannot explain the intentional state, for the reducing state is an infinitely long disjunction. Since any genuine computational reduction must provide an explanation of the intentional state it reduces, the program of computational functionalism is bankrupt by definition if the reducing state must be explained in terms of the reduced state.

What EQUIVALENCE Shows and What Is Wrong with It

Putnam's project is to argue there cannot be a finite empirical definition of intentional states in terms of computational states: "... I am going to give principled reasons why a finite empirical definition of intentional relations and properties in terms of physical/computational relations and properties is impossible...."[2] This is how Putnam wishes to refute computational functionalism.

Putnam's project is too strong. He surely means that there cannot be finite *and* feasible empirical definitions of intentional relations and properties. If an empirical definition is finite but infeasibly long (suppose it contains $10^{1,000,000}$ clauses), it cannot be accepted as a reduction *for us*. Finite but infeasibly long empirical definitions of intentional relations and properties will do us no good whether we are psychologists or philosophers. They injure the prospects of local computational reduction. Putnam's project need not show that all finite definitions of intentional relations and properties are impossible, but only that some of them are impossible— namely, those that are finite and short. If there are no finite and short empirical definitions of intentional states, there cannot be local computational reductions of them (if computational definitions are finitary).

However, Putnam argues that *no* finite definition, whether short or infeasibly long, is possible. He argues this, I conjecture, to avoid a slippery slope. For instance, human beings now do not have the ability to appreciate a definition that has 10,000,000 clauses. But in the distant future, who knows? Genetic enhancements may give us the ability to appreciate it. If an algorithm is based on that definition, then in the future humans might be able to appreciate it. But if the algorithm is infinitely long, it is unlikely that future humans will have the cognitive abilities to appreciate it.

Let us assume that Putnam has already shown that there are infinitely many computational realizations of arbitrary intentional states (though in chapter 6 I argued that this is not so). So a computational reduction of an arbitrary intentional state will be an infinite disjunction of computational states, and it cannot provide a computational definition of intentional states. The possibility is still open that it can be radically reduced in size by computably partitioning the disjuncts into a small set of equivalence classes. The point of EQUIVALENCE is to show this cannot be done.

One source of the infinite size of a computational reduction of intentional states is computational growth. Two different machine models of an intentional state will give us two or more disjuncts. But why not abstract away from the details of the machine models? Putnam discusses a precise way of doing this: *"If* we can make this decision [that words W_1 and W_2 are synonymous—JB] and *we* are Turing machines, *then* the predicate 'word W_1 as used in situation X_1 is synonymous with word W_2 as used in situation X_2' must be a predicate that a Turing machine can employ: a recursive predicate or at worst a 'trial and error' predicate.... States of different 'machines' can lie in the same *equivalence class* under an arithmetical relation.... Moving from the requirement that the 'states' of speakers with the same reference ... be identical to the requirement that they be *equivalent under some equivalence relation which is itself computable, or at least definable in the language of computational theory plus physical system,* gives us enormous additional leeway."[3]

Putnam used synonymy determination (SD) and coreferentiality decisions (which are necessary for SD judgments) to refute single-computational-state functionalism. A computational reduction of SD will be an infinitely long disjunction of computational states. Both of these linguistic phenomena are used in EQUIVALENCE, where their connection with rational interpretation is exploited. Throughout *R&R* and elsewhere in his writings, Putnam claims that rational interpretation is necessary for SD and coreferentiality decisions. Rational interpretation is used in EQUIVALENCE in a pivotal way.

Putnam assumes that any algorithm for rational interpretation must be based on a definition of synonymy and a definition of coreferentiality. But to define these notions requires a survey of all possible theories of the universe and what is in it, all possible local environments, and all possible theories of human rationality and inference patterns. Putnam gives us good reason to think that this survey will contain infinitely many clauses. So a rational-interpretation algorithm will be based on an infinite amount of information. Putnam claims that this information is explicitly listed in the algorithm and that it cannot be computably partitioned into a small set of equivalence classes. Thus the rational-interpretation algorithm is infinitary, since it will contain an infinite lookup table containing all the information in the three surveys needed to define synonymy and coreferentiality. It is not a genuine algorithm, since it is not finitary. That is Putnam's point. The only formalization of rational interpretation is infinitary, and only a god could appreciate that algorithm. Metaphorically, Putnam tells us that to either use or construct a rational-interpretation algorithm one must occupy an impossible Archimedean point that only gods can occupy and that is for us a we-know-not-what.

There appears to be no argument that there is no computable partitioning of its infinitely many clauses into a small set of equivalence classes. A finitary partitioning would be the basis for a finitary computational definition of an arbitrary intentional state. It is not clear the no-computable-partitioning claim follows from showing that a rational-interpretation algorithm must contain (in an infinitary lookup table) an infinite amount of information of infinite diversity. It is at this critical point that an argument is needed that an infinite amount of information that is infinitely diverse can't be compressed into a small finite set. Certain kinds of finitary algorithms can't be compressed. This is well known from algorithmic information theory. There are well-known examples from α-recursion theory of infinitary algorithms that cannot be made finitary. The reason why there is no finitary reduction is that there is some essential step in executing it that requires an infinitary capacity, such as the ability to enumerate an infinite set. If all infinitary algorithms are incompressible, then from the fact that an algorithm is infinitary, it would immediately follow it can't be compressed. No argument would be needed that it can't be compressed.

But the infinitary lookup table in a rational-interpretation algorithm might be compressed (unless it is proved that it cannot), in which case the algorithm would not store an infinitary table but only a finitary one. To show that there are infinitary algorithms that can be compressed to finitary algorithms, I use as an example a BLOCKHEAD algorithm for addition that is infinitary but that can be given a finitary compression. That is, the infinitary BLOCKHEAD algorithm for addition can be reduced to a finitary algorithm for addition. Compression failure for rational-interpretation algorithms is not explicitly argued in EQUIVALENCE. It is argued that an algorithm for rational interpretation must be infinitary, but not that there is no finitistic compression of it. Since compression failure is the main aim of EQUIVALENCE, this is a serious omission.

The Central Problem in EQUIVALENCE

The central problem for EQUIVALENCE is that Putnam uses 'rational interpretation' ambiguously. It is because of his ambiguous use of 'rational interpretation' that he can motivate the conditions necessary for showing rational interpretation algorithms must contain an infinitary lookup table. Below I will distinguish his two uses of 'rational interpretation'. I call his first use 'rational interpretation$_1$' and his second use 'rational interpretation$_2$'. If he distinguished rational interpretation$_1$ from rational interpretation$_2$, Putnam would have to do additional work before he could show an algorithm for rational interpretation$_2$ is infinitary. He would first have to show that rational interpretation$_1$ cannot be formalized. We can best see the ambiguity and how it undermines EQUIVALENCE by making these eleven points:

1. Putnam has famously claimed that we are able to engage in SD and make coreferentiality decisions by exercising our capacities for rational interpretation, reasonable reasoning and general intelligence. (The principal idea of epistemic semantics is that we use rational interpretation to solve semantical problems, such as SD.)

2. Putnam says that a rational-interpretation *algorithm* must be based on a definition of synonymy and coreferentiality and that these definitions must be based on a theory of all human discourse, of all possible theories of the universe and what is in it, of all possible local environments, and of all possible theories of rationality and inference patterns.

3. Putnam's *reductio* of the claim that such a rational-interpretation algorithm is one human beings use is that it is infinitary and no human being can use an infinitary algorithm. This shows that rational interpretation as it is used by human beings for SD and to make coreferentiality decisions does not depend on a definition of synonymy and a definition of coreferentiality.

4. If the rational interpretation that human beings use to make coreferentiality decisions and for SD does not depend on using a definition of coreferentiality and of synonymy, then any formalization of that kind of rational interpretation will not require a dependency on those definitions.

5. If it is shown there is no formalization of this kind of rational interpretation, then the only other kind of formalization available is an infinitary one (described in EQUIVALENCE). But this rational-interpretation algorithm is based on conditions that no human being can satisfy and thus on conditions that no human being satisfies when using rational interpretation to engage in SD and to make coreferentiality decisions. Two of these conditions are that the rational-interpretation algorithm depend on a definition of synonymy and that it depend on a definition of coreferentiality.

6. The two conditions mentioned in the preceding item define a notion of rational interpretation$_2$ that human beings do not and cannot use. Only an infinitary being (or a god) can use rational interpretation$_2$, and an algorithm that formalizes it will be infinitary.

7. Rational interpretation$_1$ is what human beings use to make coreferentiality decisions and for SD. Whether there is a finitary formalization of rational interpretation$_1$ is an open question. Putnam argues (in various places) that there is no such finitary formalization, but I argue that his arguments are either refutable or unconvincing.

8. EQUIVALENCE is the claim that there is no computable partitioning of the infinitely large set of computational realizations of a computational reduction of an arbitrary intentional state into a small set of equivalence classes. If that is the case, there are no local computational reductions. But EQUIVALENCE follows from showing that formalizing rational interpretation$_2$ gives us an infinitary rational-interpretation$_2$ algorithm and that the algorithm cannot be given a finitary compression. (The latter is not argued for in EQUIVALENCE, even though it is necessary for its central claim.)

9. If rational interpretation$_1$ can be formalized and its formalization is finitary, then there is no need to consider rational interpretation$_2$, and thus there is absolutely no use for the argument EQUIVALENCE. Only if there is no formalization of rational interpretation$_1$ can we consider the prospects of formalizing rational interpretation$_2$ (which, Putnam argues, has an infinitary formalization).

10. If it can be shown there is no formalization of rational interpretation$_1$, it makes sense to consider rational interpretation$_2$ and EQUIVALENCE. If that cannot be shown, there is no argument that local computational reductions are impossible.

11. Rational interpretation$_1$ and rational interpretation$_2$ are distinct. They do not collapse because (according to Putnam) human beings successfully engage in SD and make coreferentiality decisions using rational interpretation$_1$. We could not do so if rational interpretation$_1$ depended on definitions of coreferentiality and of synonymy. But rational interpretation$_2$ depends on those definitions. So rational interpretation$_1$ is not the same as rational interpretation$_2$, or, contrary to Putnam, we do not successfully engage in SD and make coreferentiality decisions.

The central point is that no human now existing is able to appreciate infinitary definitions of synonymy and coreferentiality. Thus, if our abilities for SD and for making coreferentiality decisions don't depend on an infinitary definition of coreferentiality and of synonymy, the possibility that there is a computable account of those abilities remains open. Putnam must show that rational interpretation$_1$, as it is for humans now existing, cannot be formalized. I contend that there is no decisive argument for the claim. In chapter 9, I critically review several arguments Putnam makes that rational interpretation$_1$ cannot be formalized. Here, let us examine EQUIVALENCE carefully, looking at the conditions that make algorithms for rational interpretation$_2$ infinitary. It will be clear that human beings do not make coreferentiality decisions, engage in SD, and engage in rational interpretation$_1$ under those conditions. The question whether there is a way to compress the conditions raises the possibility of a finitary algorithm for rational interpretation$_2$. To sidestep the possibility that there is a finitary formalization of rational interpretation$_2$ (and if there is, EQUIVALENCE fails), Putnam must show there is no compression of the definitions of synonymy and coreferentiality and thus no compression of the infinitary lookup table in the rational-interpretation$_2$ algorithm. But he does not argue for the latter claim in EQUIVALENCE.

Marr's Computational Theory of Vision and Phenomenalism

Putnam compares his project with the Reichenbach-Carnap-Hempel-Sellars refutation of phenomenalism. In the latter, principled reasons were provided against phenomenalistic translation of sense-datum language into material-thing language, though the reasons do not constitute a strict mathematical impossibility proof. Putnam tells us that his argument can be viewed in the same way. It provides principled reasons, though it falls short of a strict mathematical impossibility proof.

But there is a disanalogy between phenomenalism and algorithms for rational interpretation. The sense data presented to us are exiguous with respect to their basic properties; that is why it was easy to show that the infinite disjunction of sense-data qualities could not be bundled into material objects unless one already had higher-level properties that could be used to construct the bundles. These higher-order properties allow us to compress the sense data. It is not apparent the computational realizations of rational interpretation algorithms are exiguous and lack higher-order properties.

Another problem for the analogy is that Marr's theory of computational vision can be viewed as a resurrection of phenomenalism.[4] Marr showed that visual sense data contain much more information than was imagined by Sellars (and by Hempel, Carnap, and Reichenbach before him). The beauty of Marr's computational theory of vision is that it shows how computations can extract that information and bundle it into objects. The computations play the role of higher-order properties necessary for bundling. The human eye can see stereoptically even when all the visual sense data have the same shape, size, and reflectancy. Sellars did not anticipate Marr. Putnam must do better. He must examine the work of computationalists that is relevant to his project. Much of my method is to point out such work, thus shifting the burden of proof onto Putnam's shoulders. Marr's computational theory of vision and its deep connection with the philosophical program of phenomenalism pragmatically justify this method.

Putnam's Epistemic Semantics and a Methodological Point

Putnam endorses and employs an epistemic semantics that, he believes, can capture synonymy and meaning and is immune to indeterminacy and ontological relativity. This explains why Putnam does not worry that Quinean meaning holism and Quine's arguments in "Two Dogmas of Empiricism"[5] appear to scuttle any prospects of a synonymy relation (as opposed to central practices in a linguistic community) that is semantically justified.

The core of Putnamian epistemic semantics is the family of notions: reasonable reasoning, rational interpretation$_1$, and general intelligence. These provide us with reasoning that enables us to distinguish between meaning-constituting beliefs and auxiliary beliefs—a distinction that is the basis of the synonymy relation. Reasoning, in turn, is a central component of interpretation theory. In Putnam's writings there is no real difference among the concepts of rational interpretation, reasonableness, and human rationality. But reasonable reasoning and the other notions—according to Putnam—are no less complex than our conception of what it is to be human. This provides Putnam with a reason for thinking that none of these concepts can be formalized.

If that is the case, no algorithms distinguish meaning-constituting beliefs from auxiliary ones. In critically assessing Putnam's project in general and EQUIVALENCE in particular, I do not proceed by finding problems for epistemic semantics and offering a semantics (such as informational semantics) that does not suffer from them. I argue that the project and EQUIVALENCE depend on demonstrating the nonformalizability of the family of notions. I show that the reasons for nonformalizability of the family of notions either commit logical errors or are unconvincing since they fail to take into account recent computationalist work. I don't endorse epistemic semantics. But my strategy is not to find internal problems for epistemic semantics. EQUIVALENCE and the project fail because the arguments for the nonformalizability of the family of notions fail.

Trivial or Psychologically Unrealistic Computable Equivalence Relations Are Easy to Find

Recall that one source of computational multi-realization of intentional states is computational growth. Can the set of realizations induced by computational growth be computably partitioned into a small set of equivalence classes? I will now address that question, using results obtained in the discipline of mathematical logic to undermine the claim that the question has a negative answer. First, however, let me provide a note of clarification. Trivial equivalence relations are easy to find. The conclusion of EQUIVALENCE is there is no computable equivalence relation over the set of computational realizations of a single, arbitrary intentional state. Here I add an important qualifier to that claim: There is no *non-trivial* or *psychologically realistic* computable equivalence relation over the set of computational realizations of a single intentional state. Though Putnam does not make them, these two qualifications are necessary, since it is easy to find trivial and psychologically unrealistic computable equivalence relations for the set of computational realizations of a single intentional state.

What is it that all the computational realizations of the content of arbitrary intentional states have in common? They are all states of some rational-interpretation algorithm. I claim there is a computable equivalence class: the equivalence class whose elements are defined by the property of being computational realizations of an algorithm for rational interpretation. Being an algorithm for rational interpretation is a monadic predicate, but it is easily transformed into a dyadic predicate. Let the relation Rxy mean that x is RATINT-related to y, where x and y are computational realizations of a rational-interpretation algorithm and 'RATINT related' means that x and y are computational realizations of the same algorithm for rational interpretation. It is easy to see that R is an equivalence relation. It is reflexive, since any computational realization is RATINT related to itself. It is symmetric, since any computational realization A RATINT related to B entails that B is RATINT related to A. It is transitive, since if A is RATINT related to B and B is RATINT related to C, it follows that A is RATINT related to C. This equivalence relation is computable, for determining that a given computational realization A is an element of a rational-interpretation algorithm is positively decidable—one simply runs the algorithm for every possible input and searches the set of computational realizations until the computational realization A is found.

We could define another trivial computable equivalence relation by letting x, y, etc. range over computer programs of a single rational-interpretation algorithm and defining R as 'x and y are both computer programs of a certain rational-interpretation algorithm'. Once we choose a representative member of the equivalence class as our exemplar, we then have a local computational reduction. It is easy to see it is trivial, but perhaps harder to see is it not psychologically realistic. It is trivial, because it uses a recipe that can be used to define a computable equivalence relation for any set at all, even for sets that are noncomputable and for which there are mathematical proofs that there are no computable equivalence relations definable over them. The equivalence relation is not psychologically realistic, since cognitive psychology is not interested in defining a relation that two computer programs for a rational-interpretation algorithm are indeed computer programs for a rational-interpretation algorithm.

Notice that the two equivalence relations I defined above falsify the conclusion of EQUIVALENCE. But they are both trivial and psychologically unrealistic, and thus they cannot be considered genuine local computational reductions of an arbitrary intentional state. However, Putnam is not right when he says there are no computable equivalence relations of the required sort. Rather, there are no non-trivial psychologically realistic computable equivalence relations of the required sort.[6]

Just as it is a truism that any two objects whatsoever are similar to one another in infinitely many distinct ways (and dissimilar to one another in infinitely many distinct ways), the same is true of objects that are members of equivalence relations. Any two objects are elements of infinitely many computable equivalence relations. (Similarity is not always an equivalence relation, since A can be similar to B and B can be similar to C, though A and C might not be similar at all. Thus, we cannot map all the similarity relations onto equivalence class relationships.) In fact, you do not need more than one object for an equivalence relation R, since aRa (reflexivity), aRa implies aRa (symmetry) and aRa and aRa implies aRa (transitivity) will be satisfied for some Rs. There are infinitely many distinct and computable equivalence relations R to which the object a belongs. Showing there are infinitely many distinct and computable Rs is a variant of a padding argument in computability theory used to show there are infinitely many distinct computer programs, all of which are padded variants of a single computer program.

The preceding shows that it is too easy to find computable equivalence relations, even when the class of objects over which the computable equivalence relations are defined is restricted to either those of a certain kind or those bounded numerically from above. If computable equivalence relations are easy to find, then EQUIVALENCE needs to argue that all the "easy-to-find" computable equivalence relations are trivial or psychologically unrealistic. It is hard to show that all the easy-to-find computable equivalence relations are trivial, since 'trivial' is a vague term unless it is defined in purely logical terms. But if 'trivial' is defined in empirical terms, vagueness arises. The same is true of psychologically unrealistic computable equivalence relations. One may not know that a computable equivalence relation is psychologically unrealistic until all of cognitive science is in place. If you try, now, to chart all the ways that cognitive science might go, in order to provide an estimate of how many of those ways rule out a computable equivalence relation to be psychologically realistic, you will be faced with an AE-logical problem. That is, you will need to prove the truth of the following:

(1) (For all computable equivalence relations x of kind K) NOT (There exists a psychologically realistic computable equivalence relation y of kind K) (R Computable x and kind K x, Computable y and psychologically realistic y and kind K y).

(Here R is an empirical relation of compatibility between x and y.) By quantifier negation, (1) is logically equivalent to (1*):

(1*) (For all feasible computable equivalence relations of kind K x) (For all psychologically realistic computable equivalence relations of kind K y) NOT (R Computable x and kind K x, Computable and psychologically realistic y and kind K y)

Sentence (1*) is of the logical type $(x)(y) \sim Rxy$. To determine the truth of a sentence of this type, one first looks at a single witness to x and then runs through each witness to y in order to show that for each pair $\langle x, y \rangle$ it is not the case that Rxy. If there are infinitely many witnesses to y, then for the first witness to x one will not be able to show, in a finite number of steps, that $\sim Rxy$. Notice that (1) and (1*) are just the first layer of complexity, since they hold only for computable equivalence relations of one specific kind. Adding another quantifier over kinds of computable equivalence relations creates a logical problem even higher in the arithmetical hierarchy than the problem expressed by (1) or (1*).

The point is that Putnam will have to solve very hard logical problems if he wants to show—before all the results of cognitive science are in—that there are no non-trivial and psychologically realistic computable equivalence relations for the computational realizations of rational-interpretation$_2$ algorithms. Let us waive these problems, since we want to find defects, if there are any, internal to EQUIVALENCE.

Mathematical Facts Confronting EQUIVALENCE

One way in which there can be infeasibly or infinitely many computational realizations of an arbitrary intentional state is by computational growth. For instance, we get different computational realizations of a given intentional state using different programming languages and different computer architectures. Later I will examine content growth, but here I point out that there is work in mathematical logic that shows that it is possible to computably partition into a small set of equivalence classes the computational realizations induced by computational growth. Some of this work shows that the idea of a god's algorithm for rational interpretation—that requires occupying an Archimedean point—is not as clear as Putnam takes it to be; some of it addresses computational realizations that are induced by content growth. Each mathematical fact I cite imposes a burden of proof on Putnam: he must show that EQUIVALENCE is not negatively affected by it. There are more mathematical facts than those I cite that are relevant to critically assessing the argument. My point is to show that there is much work relevant to assessing it he has not considered and so he cannot assert that it "fall[s] short of a strict proof, but [is] convincing."[7]

Any two computational systems are isomorphic
There is a general isomorphism theorem for all possible programming-language systems. The theorem tells us that any two programming-language systems can be mapped onto one another by an isomorphism.[8] This implies that it is arbitrary which programming language we choose to employ, since it is possible to computably "move" from any one choice of programming language to any other. We also know that isomorphisms preserve properties of the systems they map in both directions: all the properties of the source system are preserved in the target system, and all the properties in the target system are preserved in the source system. The isomorphism is also monotonically increasing, so we will not observe under the mapping parts of the source programming language being mapped into incompatible parts of the target programming language.

The isomorphism theorem justifies carrying results to programming-language system B when there are problematic features in programming language A. Its relevance to the issue of finding psychologically realistic and feasible computable equivalence relations (over all SD computational realizations) is that there might be an equivalence relation definable over the programming-language constructs available in one programming language that is not available in another programming language. This is not to say that the equivalence relation must be available *in* the programming language. Perhaps it can only be defined over the programming language in a meta-level language. Putnam has to show that there is no computable procedure that allows one to go from a programming-language system in which there are no computable equivalence relations definable over constructs within that language to a programming-language system in which there is a computable equivalence relation (either inside or outside the programming language) definable over those constructs.

Recall that one way of getting computational growth is by padding instruction sets. The isomorphism theorem gives us a good reason to lump all the padded instruction sets into a single equivalence class.

When computable, isomorphisms are polynomial-time computable

A remarkable set of theorems proved by Douglas Cenzer and Jeffrey Remmel beginning in the late 1980s shows that computable equivalence relations can be replaced by feasibly computable equivalence relations.[9] Cenzer and Remmel give well-defined mathematical conditions under which any computable equivalence relation is computably isomorphic to a polynomial-time equivalence relation with standard universe. By "standard universe," Cenzer and Remmel mean any one of the standard representations of the natural numbers, such as a binary or a tally representation. There are also well-defined mathematical conditions under which the computable isomorphism is itself polynomial-time computable. The significance of this work is that if an equivalence relation defined over computational realizations is computable, then there are well-defined conditions under which it is polynomial-time computable as well.

Cenzer and Remmel have also studied the isomorphism types of recursive linear orderings that are not recursively isomorphic to any polynomial-time linear ordering with the tally representation of the natural numbers. If it could be shown that a set of computational realizations exhibit a recursive linear ordering of that isomorphism type, then the computational realizations are not recursively isomorphic to a feasible recursive linear ordering. We have, then, two kinds of logical facts. One shows the conditions under which a computable equivalence relation is feasibly computable; the other shows the conditions under which it is not feasibly computable.

Bisimulations: A Tool for Establishing Modal Invariance

Bisimulations were largely unknown to philosophers in the early 1980s, when Putnam composed *R&R*. They originated with Johan van Benthem's work on modal logic.[10] Bisimulations provide an alternative way of describing equivalence relations between states (or possible worlds) of different models or between states within the same model. Suppose that there are two states in two different modal models. The two states are said to be bisimilar provided three conditions hold. In both states, atomic formulas truth-valuate identically, there is a forth mapping from one state (the source state) to the other (the target state) that preserves the structure of the source state in the target state—that is, preserves the structure of the R-relation between the source state and those states that can be R-reached from the source state, and there is also an inverse back mapping that preserves the structure of the R-relation in the target state in the source state. Bisimilar states have identical atomic information and matching transition possibilities.

Modal formulas cannot distinguish bisimilar states. This fact marks a profound difference between first-order formulas and modal formulas. All modal formulas, but not all first-order formulas, are invariant under bisimulation. Bisimulation is not mere preservation of properties across states of different models that one gets from a forth mapping; it is invariance of properties across states of different models that one gets if the forth mapping has an inverse, or back, mapping. Invariance properties are determined by mappings that are back and forth.

Bisimulations are used in logic and in programming-language theory. They are the optimal way to describe program equivalence for parallel and for distributed programs. It is highly likely the cognitive architecture of human cognition uses both parallel and distributed programs. Since one definite source of multiple realization of computational states is the prolixity of computer programs (in, particular, those which are generated by padding operations), and the computer programs are highly likely to be parallel or distributed, bisimulations are the tool to use to computably partition syntactically distinct computer programs into equivalence classes. Bisimulations are well suited to examine the multi-realization problem induced by computational growth, where the growth comes from the prolixity of programming languages.

If cognitive algorithms express modal concepts (such as possibility, necessity, belief, knowledge, awareness, . . .), bisimulations have a role to play in determining when different computational states are bisimilar. That is, bisimulations can also be used to examine the multi-realization problem induced by content growth. If some properties of intentional states are structural computational properties, bisimulations can describe their structure and determine when different computational properties are equivalent. One standard way to look at a computation is as a labeled transition system. A bisimulation provides a way to locally traverse labeled transition systems. Traversing labeled transition systems is to compute within the system. Bisimilar labeled transition systems are observationally indistinguishable—an automaton situated at a node in one labeled transition system that is bisimilar to another does know if it has been switched to the other system. If one determiner of mental content is structural computational properties, bisimulations determine computable equivalence relations over them. If so, bisimulations might be the tool used by a rational interpreter (at an unconscious level of mental processing) to, in part, determine synonymy relations.

Modal Conditions Defining Equivalence Relations

G. E. Hughes's work on how modal logics express equivalence relations and sub-equivalence relations in modal sentences is relevant to examining the multi-realization problem induced by computational growth.[11] Hughes found infinitely many pairs of conditions on arbitrary dyadic relations that have the properties of reflexiveness, symmetry and transitivity (defining equivalence relations). But when the pair is separated, neither condition has any of those properties. That is, condition A by itself, when imposed on an arbitrary dyadic relation, is not reflexive, symmetric nor transitive. The same is true of condition B. A dyadic relation is an equivalence relation when it satisfies both conditions A and B.

A corresponding problem arises in modal logic. There are infinitely many pairs of formulas each of which, by itself, when added to the minimal normal modal logic K, fails to yield any of the three characteristic formulas of the modal logic of equivalence, S5. But the pair of formulas added to K yields S5. Algorithms for rational interpretation$_2$ that employ classical or modal logic—and any algorithm can be rewritten as formulas in either classical or modal logic—might employ joint conditions of this kind: singly there is no equivalence relation, but together there is one. Suppose that computable equivalence classes defined by these conditions curtail either computational growth or content growth. Putnam cannot ignore such a possibility. Since there are infinitely many such pairs of conditions, he can rule out this possibility by either showing there is some logical condition that prohibits appearance of the pairs in the minimal normal modal logic K or in classical logics or else enumerate all possible pairs and show that those that yield a computable equivalence relation don't appear in any algorithms for rational interpretation$_2$. The latter task needs to be informed by psychological work, for we want the prohibition to be on psychological grounds, given that there is little chance it can be made on logical grounds. Enumerating infinitely many pairs is not something a finite human can do. In that case, the possibility there is a pair in the rational-interpretation$_2$ algorithm that yields a computable equivalence relation can never be eliminated. If so, the conclusion of EQUIVALENCE—there are no computable equivalence relations—must be emended. It reads: there are no computable equivalence relations, but it is possible there might be.

Although Hughes shows there are infinitely many such pairs of formulas, any of which can be added to K to get S5, that does *not* thereby scuttle the first opportunity above—ruling out the pairs by a logical condition. Since the pairs of modal formulas will have corresponding algebraically specified conditions, it is unlikely that there are infinitely many distinct algebraically described conditions. On the other hand, it is an open question how many distinct algebraically specified conditions there are, and thus an open question as to how many distinct kinds of basic pairs of modal formulas there are. Hughes analyzed the logical relations that hold between the infinitely many pairs. They are all related in a precise way. The first condition is expressed in a first-order sentence:

$$(x)(\exists z)(xRz \cdot (w)(zR^n w \rightarrow wRx)).$$

New conditions are obtained by increasing the value of n, which, in terms of modal formulas, reflects the iteration of modal operators.

Although, for one condition, increasing the value of n leads to a weaker formula (and thus a descending chain of formulas in terms of logical strength), for the other condition there is a logical relation between values of n only when $n > 1$ and $n^* \equiv n \mod(n + 2)$, in which case the formula with value n logically implies the formula with value n^*. It follows that the logical relations are complex enough to make the logical problem of finding pairs of formulas and ruling them out on logical, and not empirical, grounds intractable. That is, although all values of n greater than 1 that are related by $n^* \equiv n \bmod(n+2)$ can be dismissed if dismissed for the first value of n in the sequence, there are still infinitely many values of n that are not related in that way, and for which each formula with one of those infinitely many values of n will have to be examined on its own. Hence, ruling out computable equivalence relations by finding a logical property satisfied by rational-interpretation$_2$ algorithms will be an intractable task. If so, Putnam can eliminate the possibility there are pairs of conditions in rational-interpretation$_2$ algorithms that generate equivalence classes only on empirical grounds. He must examine psychological and linguistic data relevant to constructing the algorithm. If he believes—and this is what EQUIVALENCE claims—that rational-interpretations$_2$ algorithms require a god to construct them (for one must occupy an Archimedean point in constructing them), he will never know if there is a computable shortening of the algorithm, since he cannot, in principle, know what the algorithm will look like. I think this points out an important moral: When you argue that X has the property of being incomprehensible to human beings, but it is also true that if X had the property Y it would not be incomprehensible to us, your argument is greatly diminished in strength. The idea of a god's algorithm for rational interpretation is not as transparent as Putnam takes it to be in EQUIVALENCE.

If Putnam does respect psychological and linguistic data—and, as I argued in the preceding paragraph, he must respect that data—it can be shown that using that data to rule out the infinitely many possible pairs of formulas is a logically intractable task which a computable agent cannot accomplish. One easily tractable task has the following logical form: For all formulas such that it is F_1, there exists an F_2 such that F_1 and F_2 in K yields S5. We can find F_2 by counting the number of modal operator iterations in F_1. But since it is an open question whether there are other kinds of basic pairs of modal formulas enjoying the property Hughes studies, a search to find such pairs will be intractable, because it has the logical form (For all Formulas) $\lozenge$ $(\exists x)(\exists y)$(Formula$_1$x and Formula$_2$y and ((Formula1x and Formula2y) $\cup$ K = S5)), where K is the minimal normal modal logic. However, we might not know that a formula is F_1 until we find its F_2. It is this latter prospect that makes the problem intractable, for it has no recursively enumerable solution.

Hughes's paper also opens up the possibility of near-equivalence relations. For example, there is a system of modal logic that is weaker than S5, characterized by the class of frames in which the accessibility relation R is serial, symmetrical and such that if xR^3y, then xRy. This modal logic is not similar to any of the existing systems studied in the literature of the late 1970s. There are many more systems of modal logic like that. There may be feasibly computable near-equivalence relations, even though there are no feasibly computable strict equivalence relations. Just as there are infinitely many pairs of formulas of modal logic (and infinitely many corresponding conditions on dyadic relations) that make K into S5, so, too, there are infinitely many pairs of formulas of modal logic that make K into a modal logic weaker than S5, in which there are near-equivalence relations. This purely logical possibility means that a defender of EQUIVA-LENCE must examine the available near-equivalence relations and how they partition the set of computational realizations of arbitrary intentional states into near-equivalence classes. The issue is both empirical and conceptual. In the latter case, it is a question of what we are willing to accept as an instance of a local computational reduction. In the former case, it is a matter of what near-equivalence relations can do with the available empirical data.

Finite Model Theory and k-Universal Finite Graphs

There is an elegant theorem on k-universal finite graphs proved by Eric Rosen, Saharon Shelah, and Scott Weinstein.[12] To define a k-universal finite graph, we need to define the relation $\leq^k$ on structures of the same relational signature, where two structures have the same relational signature provided they have the same relations. Assume that all formulas in the language of A and B are restricted to no more than k distinct variables. Define $A \leq^k B$ if and only if for all existential formulas X in the language of A and B, if X is a semantic consequence of A, then X is also a semantic consequence of B. Existential formulas are obtained by taking the closure of atomic and negated atomic formulas of the language of A and B under the operations of existential quantification, conjunction and disjunction. A graph G is k-universal if and only if, for all graphs H, $H \leq^k G$. The definition shows that any graph that satisfies sentences in language L restricted to k variables, can be embedded in the k-universal graph, since the k-universal graph will also satisfy those sentences. What this means is that the k-universal graph can *duplicate* any result that can be obtained in any graph whatsoever (under the restriction that the graph satisfy formulas in the language L restricted to k variables). This is not a conservativeness result, since there may be formulas in the language of L that cannot be satisfied in a graph H, but can be satisfied in the k-universal graph G.

The duplication property is important in using k-universal graphs to think about EQUIVALENCE. No matter how hard you try, you can't stop G from duplicating the results in H. Let results in the language of H be computational descriptions of single episodes of rational interpretation$_1$ transposed into the language of graphs. We know there must be a finite number of sentences in any episode of rational interpretation$_1$. So there is a k-universal graph G that captures every episode of rational interpretation$_1$ registered by the collection of graphs H. Suppose that the k-universal graph G is the algorithm for rational interpretation$_1$. G either connects (in a network) all episodes of rational interpretation$_1$ or contains all the information needed in any given episode of rational interpretation$_1$ (as nodes in G) and the edges (in G) are relations between pieces of information. We should expect that the disjunction of the set of H_i programs defines the superprogram G—since G appears to be the union of all the H_is. However, that turns out *not* to be the case for G and all the H_is. The Rosen-Shelah-Weinstein theorem says the class of k-universal graphs is *not* definable by an infinite disjunction of first-order existential sentences with a finite number (k) of variables. What does this mean in the case of rational interpretation$_1$? If it turns out that the formalized sentences of all episodes of rational interpretation$_1$ are the formulas that can be obtained by closing the set of atomic formulas and negated atomic formulas (of the L^k fragment of first-order logic) under disjunction, conjunction and existential instantiation, then any algorithm for rational interpretation$_1$ is not definable by the infinite union of all the specific episodes of rational interpretation$_1$. Later we define a BLOCKHEAD algorithm for computing a function F. Briefly, it is an infinite or finite, though infeasible, list of ordered pairs of the form $\langle x, fx \rangle$. The Rosen-Shelah-Weinstein theorem shows there can't be a BLOCKHEAD algorithm for rational interpretation$_1$ (under the conditions elucidated above) that is defined in terms of the specific episodes of rational interpretation$_1$ that make it up.

We get a similar kind of result when we move to rational interpretation$_2$. When all the episodes of rational interpretation$_2$ can be formalized in the L^k fragment of first-order logic or the $L^k_{\infty\omega}$ fragment of the infinitary language $L^k_{\infty\omega}$, the BLOCKHEAD algorithm (captured by the k-universal graph G) is not definable as the infinite union of the H_i graphs that formalize (in the language of graphs) the specific episodes of rational interpretation$_2$. What this means is that there can't be a BLOCKHEAD algorithm for rational interpretation$_2$ that is defined in terms of the specific instances of rational interpretation$_2$ that make it up.

There are some k-universal graphs that cannot be reached by extending an (induced) k-subgraph of them. However, random graphs (defined by taking arbitrary graphs from the set of all graphs constructible over a set of points representing vertices of a graph) extend, with high probability, to k-universal graphs. If one starts with a random graph, rather than one constructed according to a rule (expressing a design requirement), there is a high probability that graph extends to one that is k-universal. Take a random graph. With high probability, it can be extended to G. In the case of rational interpretation$_1$, the algorithm for it can be reached by extending a random graph (made up of arbitrary formalized sentences that represent natural language sentences). A similar result holds for rational interpretation$_2$.

What do these results mean? Consider a world in which natural selection is the mechanism by which species evolve. Suppose that in this world human minds have a computational description and that there is a graph for rational interpretation$_1$ (or for rational interpretation$_2$). Over time, if there are sufficiently many random changes in the graph, it will extend to G. Nature does not have to design the algorithm expressed in G. Instead, random mutations that underlie the random changes in the random starting point graph will, with high probability, extend to G. This possibility eliminates the worry that Nature could not anticipate future episodes of rational interpretation$_1$ or of rational interpretation$_2$ (and thus could not design a BLOCKHEAD algorithm for either).

Logical Consistency and Thermodynamic Phase Transitions

In the early 1990s, an extraordinary relationship was uncovered between the structure of spin glasses (defined in statistical mechanics) and consistency properties of sets of logical formulas in propositional logic. Scott Kirkpatrick and David Selman[13] discovered that satisfiability for randomly generated Boolean expressions exhibits a sharp threshold behavior under certain well-defined conditions. Take a randomly generated Boolean expression with two variables in each clause. If the ratio of clauses to variables is less than 1, these formulas are almost always satisfiable. If the ratio is greater than 1, the formulas are almost never satisfiable. Kirkpatrick and Selman have generalized this observation to higher values of k and shown principled ways of characterizing size-dependent effects near a threshold (where satisfiability goes to unsatisfiability and conversely). What's the importance of this work for critical assessment of EQUIVALENCE?

There is—now—no good explanation of why there is phase-transition behavior in the satisfiability problem for Boolean expressions. One view is there are underlying structural properties both logic and Nature satisfy. Perhaps such principles manifest themselves at the intentional level in characteristic ways even though descriptions of them are in terms of either the computational level or the physical level. (Putnam accepts that the intentional is emergent from, and may even be supervenient on, the computational.[14]) Here is a conjectured example of how such principles manifest themselves at the intentional level in characteristic ways. Suppose that we judge linguistic expressions A and B to be synonymous. Suppose too that quite different sets of background beliefs, background theories, local environmental conditions, etc. are in effect for uses of A and B respectively. We judge them synonymous in part because of phenomenological scaling: sufficiently close to a threshold, systems of all sizes are indistinguishable (except that they undergo a change in scale). Though the 'system' of linguistic expression A, sets of background beliefs, etc. and the 'system' of linguistic expression B and background beliefs, etc. are different in size and in composition, the scaling effect manifests itself at the intentional level in the synonymy judgment.

Though a conjecture, it represents a kind of possibility Putnam can't overlook. In "Artificial Intelligence: Much Ado about Not Very Much"[15] he assures us he is not making *a priori* arguments against success in AI, but that he is "engaged in thinking about the real world in the light of the best knowledge available." The phase-transition phenomenon for satisfiability of Boolean expressions is knowledge that can't be overlooked in arguing that there is no finitary algorithm for rational interpretation$_2$.

Scott's Work on Partial-Equivalence Relations

Dana Scott provides a different approach to partial equivalence relations.[16] Like partial recursive functions, they are not defined over all elements. For instance, a partial-equivalence relation over the natural numbers is not defined for all pairs of natural numbers. He discovered that partial-equivalence relations are important tools for constructing models of higher-order logics (such as full higher-order dependent type theory) and for constructing categories of domains for programming languages that are natural and rich enough to include all the kinds of data types instanced in each kind of programming language. Although the category constructed in terms of partial-equivalence relations is rich and natural, there is a relevance problem: some of the partial-equivalence relations have nothing to do with the underlying topology of the space. The category is defined over topological spaces which are transformed by mappings—this is just a mathematical abstraction of the basic fact that computer programs are transformations of spaces of data points. Those data point spaces have a topological structure. Solving the relevance problem will probably mean limiting the kinds of partial-equivalence relations used to construct the category.

What is the significance of Scott's work for assessing EQUIVALENCE? There are more partial-equivalence relations than there are total equivalence relations, and they play an important role in the basic mathematical structure of computability. So there may be more possibilities for feasible computable equivalence relations over the complete set of computational realizations of arbitrary intentional states than Putnam originally envisaged. They may provide a way of partitioning multi-realizations induced by computational growth. And these possibilities are not vacuous. Partialequivalence relations figure centrally in a comprehensive mathematical theory of the semantics of programming languages. Since not all partialequivalence relations respect the data point topology of the category of domain semantics for programming languages, there is more to their use in domain semantics than just the fact that they are partial. These limitations show that not just any partial-equivalence relations will do the job and that, in turn, shows that they are not vacuous.

8 Rational Interpretation, Synonymy Determination, and EQUIVALENCE

Rational interpretation plays a major role in EQUIVALENCE. It is important to see how it connects with synonymy determination (SD) and with coreferentiality decisions. Let us consider a simple example Putnam employs as a concrete case of SD. We want to show that an English (E) speaker's use of the word 'cat' is synonymous with a Thai (T) speaker's use of the word 'meew'. Putnam tells us that the SD decision "can involve enormously many factors—can involve not only the speech dispositions of [E] and [T], but also the speech dispositions of other members of the linguistic communities to which they belong, and information about the microstructure and evolutionary history of paradigm 'cats' and paradigm 'meew'"[1] Suppose we can tell, on the basis of facts from biology, that the animals that E takes to be 'cats' and that T takes to be 'meew' are domestic felines. This need not prove that 'cat' and 'meew' have the same extension. 'Meew' refers to cat slices, if Thai has an ontology of temporal slices. Even if we discount this worry, there is another: that (for whatever reasons) neither E nor T might respect the scientific classification of animals. They might employ their own methods of classification. How can all this information be assessed in SD? Its successful assessment requires that one can make reasonable judgments about it. For instance, when is it reasonable to discount information about the ontology of cat slices and opt for personal classificatory systems? Are these forms of assessment computable?

The challenge of algorithmitizing SD is daunting. An SD algorithm must find maximal information about the belief systems of E and of T, the theories and inference patterns available to them, their local environments, and the societies to which they belong, and must use that information in making reasonable judgments. Putnam writes: "What is at stake, as Quine and Davidson have emphasized (not to mention European hermeneuticists such as Gadamer), is the interpretation of two discourses as wholes.... To interpret a language, one must, in general, have some idea of the theories and inference patterns which are common in the community which speaks the language."[2] So algorithms for SD must engage in rational interpretation. But Putnam thinks that rational interpretation can't be formalized—i.e., that there is no computational description of it. Consider the following argument:

P1 A necessary condition for SD is rational interpretation.

P2 There is no computational description of rational interpretation.

C There is no computational description of SD.

This argument is valid. P1 is true. Putnam has argued that P2 is true. If it is, then how can EQUIVALENCE claim that an algorithm for SD can only be understood by a god? (After all, if the argument is sound, there is no computational description of SD and thus no algorithm for SD.) Here we must distinguish between a finitary algorithm and an infinitary algorithm. In the classical computationalist picture, all algorithms are finitary, because human beings are finitary and the notion of an algorithm is modeled on how a human being would engage in a computation.[3] I have claimed that Putnam uses two notions of rational interpretation in EQUIVALENCE. There is rational interpretation that human beings use in SD and in making coreferentiality decisions. If this cannot be formalized, isn't that the end of the line for algorithmitizing SD? No, it is not. Putnam argues that if there are any algorithms for SD, they must depend on a definition of synonymy and a definition of coreferentiality. "Any theory that defines coreferentiality and synonymy," he says, "must, in some way, survey all possible theories."[4] He then argues that only an infinitary SD algorithm can satisfy this dependency. But human beings cannot use infinitary SD algorithms. Only a god or an infinitary mind can use them.

But if the rational interpretation that is formalized is infinitistic because it depends on a definition of synonymy and coreferentiality, then it cannot be that the rational interpretation human beings use in making coreferentiality decisions and in SD depends on a definition of synonymy and coreferentiality. If it did, then we would not be able to make such judgments, since we are not infinitary beings. We are finitary, and we do—according to Putnam—make such judgments.

Let us call a form of rational interpretation that human beings use in making SD and coreferentiality decisions and that does not depend on a definition of synonymy and of coreferentiality rational interpretation$_1$, and let us call a form of rational interpretation that is used in infinitary algorithms for SD and coreferentiality decisions and that does depend on a definition of synonymy and coreferentiality rational interpretation$_2$.

P2 in the above argument should be understood as asserting that rational interpretation$_1$ cannot be formalized. We can now understand the conclusion. It is that there is no computational description of an SD algorithm that uses rational interpretation$_1$. And we can say that there is no finitary or infinitary computational description of an SD algorithm that uses rational interpretation$_1$.

Let us carefully examine whether rational interpretation$_1$ can be formalized. How does Putnam use the conclusion of the above argument? Given that rational interpretation$_1$ cannot be formalized, any computational description of it must be a computational description of rational interpretation$_2$. Such descriptions occupy an Archimedean point. Putnam writes: "To ask a human being in a time-bound human culture to survey all modes of human linguistic existence—including those that will transcend his own—is to ask for an impossible Archimedean point."[5] In view of the nature of an Archimedean point, it follows that the infinitely many computational realizations of the contents of an arbitrary intentional state cannot be computably partitioned into a small set of equivalence classes.

Whether Rational Interpretation Is Necessary or Sufficient for Coreferentiality Decisions and Why It Matters

Making coreferentiality decisions is a necessary part of SD. Putnam speaks of coreferentiality decisions in EQUIVALENCE, so let us look at the connection between them and rational interpretation$_1$. Whether rational interpretation$_1$ is a necessary or a sufficient condition for coreferentiality decisions depends on how we understand his claims about the connection between them and it. For Putnam, objects and reference arise out of discourse. They are not prior to discourse. Knowing the conditions under which sentences are true—that is, epistemically justified—is knowing what singular terms refer to.[6] Epistemic justification involves reasonable reasoning.[7] The notions of being a justified, warranted, reasonable, or true belief are a family of similar notions.[8] If these notions could be explicated in computational terms, we would have an algorithm for rational interpretation$_1$.[9] So there is a family of notions—reasonable reasoning, rational interpretation$_1$ and general intelligence—used to determine when sentences are true and thus to determine what objects singular terms refer to.

Rational interpretation$_1$ is necessary for coreferentiality decisions, and so they are sufficient for it. The importance of this is methodological. Since coreferentiality decisions are sufficient but not necessary for rational interpretation$_1$, to show that there is no formalization of coreferentiality decisions would not be to show that there is no formalization of rational interpretation$_1$. On the other hand, to show that there is no formalization of rational interpretation$_1$ would be to show that there is no formalization of coreferentiality decisions, since the former is necessary for them.

Environment Totalism

Putnam asks what information is needed to make computable coreferentiality decisions.[10] His basic assumption is that any algorithm for making these decisions must be based on a definition of coreferentiality. He then asks what information any theory that defines coreferentiality decisions must employ. The amount of information required is staggering. The basic kinds of information can be divided into information about the environment, information about all possible theories of the universe, and information about kinds of rationality and reasoning patterns. Though that classification is rough, it follows what is said in EQUIVALENCE closely.

Putnam also tells us that we cannot make coreferentiality decisions about two words without rationally interpreting$_1$ the discourses in which they are used. Rational interpretation$_1$ of an arbitrary discourse requires use of a great deal of information. Since rational interpretation$_1$ is necessary for making coreferentiality decisions, any definition of coreferentiality must use that information. Remove that information and one can't make a coreferentiality decision. Thus a definition of coreferentiality must cite it. Since any algorithms for rational interpretation$_2$ depend on a definition of synonymy and of coreferentiality, we need to use that information to construct them.

Putnam takes us through his catalogue of kinds of information needed to engage in successful rational interpretation$_1$ of arbitrary discourses. He tells us that no one would be able to rationally interpret$_1$ a discourse in which terms such as 'quantum mechanical spin', 'negative charge', and 'inner product' occur without learning a lot of physics and mathematics. This is indisputable. However, Putnam asserts that three significant claims follow from this indisputable fact. These claims are bold and must be assessed critically. Do they really follow from the indisputable fact? What is their role in the argument structure of EQUIVALENCE?

The first significant claim that follows from the indisputable fact is "the assumption that in principle one can tell what is being referred to by a term used in an environment from a sufficiently complete description of that environment in terms of some standardized set of physical and computational parameters is false *unless we widen the notion of the speaker's environment to include the entire universe.*"[11] Let us call this claim *environment totalism.*

In other words, a computational description of the environment necessary for the successful rational interpretation$_1$ of arbitrary discourses cannot be anything less than a computational description of the entire physical universe. That is an extraordinarily large description, and it appears to stretch credulity to think that it could—or would—be programmed into a rational-interpretation$_2$ algorithm. How is this claim argued?

According to my earlier discussion of Putnam's treatment of the Bohr electron case, general intelligence is necessary for SD. It is used to determine that Bohr's use of the term 'electron' in 1900 is synonymous with his use of the same term in 1934, and it is used to determine that the term used at two different times has the same reference. But the difference between 1900 and 1934 is that Bohr held different theories at those times, and not that his local environment changed between 1900 and 1934. To argue for environment totalism, we need to consider cases in which local environments matter in making coreferentiality decisions and SD.

Putnam asks us to imagine a case of SD in which agents inhabit radically different local environments. Suppose that one term is used within a culture located on Mars and the other term is used within a culture located on Venus. Assume that each culture has a different theory in which the term occurs. To make the coreferentiality decision, we need to know the complete physical constitution of the local Martian and the local Venusian environments. Of course, that is not enough to determine that the two terms are coreferential. We will also need to know the two theories (in which the terms occur, respectively) are both approximately true in those environments. The reason why this is so is that reference in Putnam's metaphysics presupposes truth, not conversely.[12] From having to know whether the two theories are approximately true in their respective local environments, it follows that we might need to use more than just local information about the environments of the speakers to make coreferentiality decisions. We might need to use information about any part of the universe, since part of determining that a theory is true involves collecting data from distinct environments to confirm it. In a local environment, successful determination of the extensions of a term in a theory whose speaker resides in that environment may require obtaining information about any part (or power set of parts) of the universe.

This argument for environment totalism is not a statistical generalization over a random sample of local environments. Putnam is not generalizing over local, though randomly selected, environments of Mars and Venus. (It is not clear how we could get a random sample of all possible local environments.) If this argument were a statistical generalization, it would be open to the charge that environment totalism is secured at the expense of assuming that *any* rational-interpretation$_2$ algorithm must be prepared to encounter alien cultures inhabiting arbitrary parts of the universe. This is contrary to the spirit of local reduction and contrary to Putnam's concession that he will consider only human cultures. ("Let us begin by considering a somewhat less mind-boggling question. Can we hope to survey (and write down rules for interpreting ...) the reasoning and beliefs of all possible *human* beings and societies?"[13])

Environment totalism appears to deliver the conclusion of EQUIVALENCE. Doesn't it follow from it that information about arbitrary parts of the universe might appear in the computational realizations of arbitrary episodes of human rational interpretation$_2$? If that is the case, then in view of the extraordinary diversity of such information we could not computably partition it into a small set of equivalence classes. But that the requisite information is diverse does not entail that it can't be computably partitioned. I will argue that there are two hidden assumptions in the arguments for environment totalism, theory totalism and a rationality totalism that renders them ineffective in securing the conclusion of EQUIVALENCE.

Theory Totalism

The second significant claim that follows from the indisputable fact is as follows: "Any theory that 'defines' coreferentiality and synonymy must, in some way, survey all possible theories."[14] A slightly different formulation is: "To interpret a language one must, in general, have some idea of the theories ... common in the community that speaks that language."[15] Let us call this claim *theory totalism*.

Putnam provides a list of compelling examples to support this claim. He tells us that we could not learn what the word 'spin' refers to in quantum mechanics without learning quantum mechanics or what the phrase 'inner product' refers to without learning linear algebra. Certainly no one would dispute these examples. But trouble soon arrives. Given the word 'spin' in English and the word 'groph' in Sirian (spoken on the planet Sirius), how would a current speaker of English determine whether the two words are coreferential without learning Earthian quantum mechanics and Sirian quantum mechanics? Suppose we restrict ourselves to all possible theories proposed by human beings on Earth. Given the word 'spin' in English spoken in the year 2005 and the word 'spin' spoken in the year 8005, how would a current speaker of English determine the two words are coreferential without learning current quantum mechanics and the quantum mechanics (or the physical theory that supersedes it) of 8005? We can learn how to follow quantum mechanics, but how can we learn to follow a physical theory that we do not have? As Putnam says, "no human being can follow all possible mathematics, all possible empirical science, and so on."[16]

Let us pursue an analogy. We have seen that Putnam assimilates intuitive judgments of reasonableness to general intelligence, and that he approvingly cites Fodor's pessimism (expressed in *The Modularity of Mind*[17]) that general intelligence has a computational description. One reason Fodor is pessimistic as to whether general intelligence can be formalized is that one of its essential features—isotropy—is recalcitrant to formalization. Isotropy is the property of information unencapsulation: in fixing a belief, we might use any information whatsoever stored in our brains or capable of being accessed by some cognitive mechanism (such as inductive inference) implemented in our brains. Suppose that there are 10^{70} data points stored in the human brain. Any one of these data points might be needed for any given episode of belief fixation, for it is not the case (Fodor argues) that for each episode of belief fixation there is a precisely demarcated set of data points that are intrinsic to that episode.

It is easy to misread Fodor's definition of isotropy. Isotropy does not entail that all the data points stored in the brain or accessible to it *must* be surveyed or used in any given episode of belief fixation. Rather, it is the case that any data point *might* be surveyed or used—should the circumstances demand it. Thus, any algorithm for belief fixation need not explicitly list all data points stored in the human brain or accessible to it, nor need it have a subroutine that examines all data points stored in the human brain or accessible to it. On the other hand, there must be no architectural or algorithmic impediments in belief-fixation algorithms to using any particular data point. Should a belief-fixation procedure at a certain time need a certain data point, a mechanism must be available to retrieve it.

Does theory totalism misread the role of theories in algorithms for making our coreferentiality decisions in the same way Fodor's isotropy has been misread? We need to examine the surrounding text in which theory totalism is suspended. Putnam tells us that "a theory that figures out what people … are referring to when they speak of 'spin', and that decides whether the notion of 'spin' in terrestrial quantum mechanics is or is not the same notion as the notion of 'grophth' in Sirian Mootrux mechanics … must, in

some way, anticipate the processes of belief fixation on which the understanding of quantum mechanics (including the mathematics presupposed
by quantum mechanics) and Mootrux mechanics (including the mathematics presupposed by Mootrux mechanics) depends. Certainly such an
algorithm would have to do more than 'simulate' an ability that human
beings actually have."[18]

The term 'follow' is critical to the meaning of the above passage. Does
the meaning of 'follow' require that rational-interpretation$_2$ algorithms
explicitly list all possible theories about the universe? Putnam asserts that
a necessary condition on interpreting a discourse is being able to follow
it—that "one cannot interpret a discourse unless one can follow it."[19] This
makes good sense. It is incoherent to say that one rationally interpreted$_1$
the discourse but did not follow it. However, the threat of circularity is
imminent. What is it to follow a discourse? One response is that a necessary condition for following a discourse is to rationally interpret$_1$ it. It is
incoherent to say that one followed the discourse but did not rationally
interpret$_1$ it. Thus, we have a closed circle of notions. Can we break out of
the circle by making, for instance, understanding a *prima facie* necessary
condition on both rationally interpreting$_1$ and following a discourse? That
would put us in the odd position of saying that a necessary condition on
rational interpretation$_1$ is that the interpreter first understand the discourse
she subsequently rationally interprets$_1$. How does the interpreter come to
understand the discourse in the absence of rationally interpreting$_1$ it? In
short, it is not clear how to understand the use of the term 'follow' in the
critical passage in *R&R* cited above. We cannot tell if the requirement of
listing all possible theories of the universe in coreferentiality algorithms follows. Thus, it is not transparent that Putnam misreads theory totalism in
the same way isotropy is misread.

Let us focus on another claim in that passage. The algorithm must 'anticipate' the processes of belief fixation on which our understanding of quantum mechanics depends. What is the meaning of the term 'anticipate'?
Does it mean that the algorithm must explicitly represent those belief-
fixation procedures? If so, it must explicitly represent all the theories that
the belief-fixation procedure uses in making its verdicts. Since belief fixation can range over any subject matter at any time in the history of the
universe, all possible theories of the universe must be explicitly represented
in the algorithm. Or does 'anticipate' mean that there is some mechanism
that allows the algorithm to access any possible theory of the universe,
though without having to store it in a giant lookup table? (Presumably

this is how an algorithm would explicitly encode a large amount of information.)

On either construal of 'anticipate' there is trouble. The generation of all possible theories of the universe is not recursive; indeed, it isn't even recursively enumerable.[20] There is a computational difference between isotropy and theory totalism. All the information stored in the human brain can be recursively enumerated (sidestepping issues of neurophysiology and categorization and compartmentalization). All possible theories of the universe the human species can (now and in the future) propose cannot be recursively enumerated. It easily follows there can be no coreferentiality and no SD algorithms, since there is no way to recursively access all the theories.

The ease with which we can show that there can be no coreferentiality algorithms and no SD algorithms should make us suspicious of Putnam's requirement that a theory of coreferentiality must be able to anticipate all possible theories of the universe. Unless human beings have some infinitary capacity, they will not be able to enumerate all the possible theories. But we have no reason to believe that human beings have infinitary cognitive capacities. Theory totalism requires any algorithm for coreferentiality decisions have steps whose execution requires infinitary capacities. If that is so, it is not a finitary algorithm; it is an infinitary algorithm (defined in α-recursion theory).

However, Putnam tells us, ordinary human beings cannot survey all possible theories of the universe. This is to admit that human beings do not have infinitary cognitive capacities. Only an infinitary being—a god—could do so. An Archimedean point requires god-like infinitary capacities to inhabit. To survey all possible theories of the universe is to occupy an Archimedean point, and it is impossible for human beings to do that. On the other hand, Putnam claims, human beings can successfully engage in SD and in rational interpretation$_1$, and can make coreferentiality decisions. If that is the case, human beings do not survey all possible theories of the universe when they make coreferentiality decisions and successfully engage in SD and rational interpretation$_1$.

If we do not need to occupy an Archimedean point in exercising such abilities, why is it a requirement on algorithms that simulate these abilities? Not even Putnam can now interpret the utterances of future science, were he to hear them from an oracle. Why does he require algorithms for such abilities to possess that capacity? We need to go back to the crucial passage in which C2 is suspended. There we are told that no human being can follow all possible theories of the universe, and that any theory that provides definitions of synonymy and coreferentiality must survey all possible theories of the universe. Since Putnam assumes that an algorithm for coreferentiality decisions must be based on a definition of coreferentiality and that such definitions must be based on a theory of coreferentiality, algorithms must meet the theory totalism requirement, even though human beings cannot and do not need to meet it.

When we learn quantum mechanics, we employ a belief-fixation procedure that freely helps itself to educational resources, such as textbooks and solved problems. When we rationally interpret$_1$ the utterances of others, we avail ourselves of resources, such as what we know about the other person and what we know about the world in which we and the other person live. But in neither case do we actually use infinitely many distinct kinds of resources or infinitely much of any one kind of resource. Of the infinitely many kinds of resources, we might use any one; and from the infinite amount of any one kind of resource, we use some finite amount. Which resources we do use and how much of them we use is a matter of applying general intelligence. If human beings are allowed to use general intelligence or rational interpretation$_1$ in making such decisions, why must a machine (or an algorithm) not be allowed to do so?

The answer Putnam surely would give is that general intelligence and rational interpretation$_1$ are not formalizable. But the argument that they are not formalizable is mired in circularity. If a reason for thinking general intelligence cannot be formalized is that rational interpretation$_1$ cannot be formalized, then there is a circle. If it can be argued general intelligence cannot be formalized *without* presupposing that rational interpretation$_1$ cannot be formalized and *without* presupposing that SD and coreferentiality decisions cannot be formalized, then we will also have an argument that rational interpretation$_1$, SD, and coreferentiality decisions cannot be formalized.

If general intelligence and rational interpretation$_1$ can be formalized, then there are algorithms for SD or for coreferentiality decisions that do not have to satisfy theory totalism, environment totalism, and rationality totalism. According to Putnam, human beings can successfully negotiate SD and make coreferentiality decisions without knowing all possible environments, all possible theories of the universe, and all possible kinds of human rationality. Given that human beings can successfully engage in SD and rational interpretation$_1$ and make coreferentiality decisions, I contend that the Archimedean point is a red herring. Either these abilities are formalizable or they are not. If they are formalizable, then *R&R* does not refute functionalism. If they are not formalizable, Putnam refutes functionalism without using EQUIVALENCE, since the latter shows only that there is an infinitary capacity that human beings do not have and do not use in SD, in rational interpretation$_1$, and in making coreferentiality decisions. If human beings do not have these abilities, there are no intentional-level phenomena about which we can ask whether they can be computationally reduced. In that case, there is no longer any multi-realization argument of the kind Putnam envisages against computational functionalism, for there are no phenomena of which one can ask whether they have a computational reduction.

I will argue that Putnam has not successfully demonstrated non-formalizability of rational interpretation$_1$ and general intelligence. Before I do that, there are two hidden assumptions in the EQUIVALENCE argument that must be critically scrutinized. I claim that even if EQUIVALENCE is not a red herring, these hidden assumptions undermine it. They are tacit stipulations that are not explicitly argued for in the body of the argument, and they are essential for the argument's success, but they are false. Before we examine these assumptions, let us look at rationality totalism.

Human Rationality Totalism

Putnam contends that any algorithm for coreferentiality decisions must survey all possible kinds of rationality and all possible methods of reasoning. Let us call this claim *human rationality totalism*. (A method of reasoning provides us with a way of rationally interpreting the utterances of others. So we can type classify kinds of rationality by type classifying methods of reasoning.) One way of putting the requirement is as a question: "Can we hope to survey (and write down rules for interpreting, perhaps by 'successive approximation') the reasoning and beliefs of all possible *human* beings and societies?"[21] How we answer this question depends on how we answer three other questions: (i) How does a human being living in society A interpret the utterances of a human being living in society B (where societies A and B are contemporary human societies)? (ii) How does a human being living in society A interpret the utterances of a human being living in society B, which is a successor to A? (We are to understand the phrase 'B is a successor to A' in the following sense: "B is more sophisticated ..., has modes of conceptualizing and describing things which members of A cannot understand without years of specialized study."[22]) (iii) Is it coherent to suppose that we can—now—interpret the discourse of any possible future society in which any possible future human being might live?

To answer the first question, we need to know how Putnam views rational interpretation$_1$. Rational interpretation$_1$ is how we come to understand the discourse of other human beings. What does it consist in? Since algorithms for rational interpretation$_1$ would have to (as Putnam sees it) "formalize our entire conception of what it is to be human,"[23] it must consist in our entire conception of what makes us human and it must not include anything that does not make us fully human. This is not helpful, however. We get a better idea of what rational interpretation$_1$ consists in from Putnam's case studies, such as his case study of the 1900 and the 1934 Bohr electron. There he shows that general intelligence is necessary for rational interpretation$_1$. We have already seen that for Putnam there is a closed family of ideas: general intelligence, reasonable reasoning, rational interpretation, the point of view of humanity. Below, I will add to this family the normative notion of warranted assertibility.

We find a valuable clue as to what our judgments of reasonableness consist in when we are told that "the notions of being a justified or warranted or reasonable belief are not reducible to physicalistic notions."[24] We have a cluster of related notions: justified, warranted, and reasonable. They are normative, epistemic evaluative notions. Putnam cites two of his own works in a footnote to the preceding quotation in which he argues that these notions are not reducible to physicalistic notions. One of those works is "Reflexive Reflections,"[25] in which he provides a Gödelian argument that "being reasonable" cannot be reduced to a computational description. Demonstrative and non-demonstrative reasoning are employed in the activity of being reasonable, and they do not have a complete formalization. The other work is *Reason, Truth and History*.[26] There, the argument that the notions "justified" and "warranted" cannot be reduced to some computational description appeals to (i) Goodman's grue problem, (ii) the use in Bayesian reasoning of prior probabilities whose selection mechanism cannot be formalized, and (iii) the value-ladenness of these normative notions, which cannot be captured in a computational description. If "reasonableness" is normative, that spells trouble for the requirement on a reduction that it capture all the "phenomenological" laws of the reduced discipline. If there is no foothold in a computational description for normative properties, then computational reductions of rational interpretation$_1$ can, at best, be quasi-reductions.

In his Howison lectures, which post-date *Reason, Truth and History* by several years, Putnam tells us that we cannot computationally eliminate the normative. If there is to be a genuine computational reduction of the notion of "reasonableness," then it must be that there is a normative

component within the computational description. If there is no normative component, "if *all* notions of rightness, both epistemic and (metaphysically) realist are eliminated, then what are our statements but
noise-makings? What are our thoughts but *mere* subvocalizations? The
elimination of the normative is attempted mental suicide."[27]

But why should we think a computational description of reasonableness
must eliminate its normative character? Suppose that logical consistency is
a norm of human reasoning. It does not follow that a computational
description of logical consistency eliminates its normative component.
And if a diehard insists that the normative component must be explicitly
described (whatever that means), he can easily be accommodated by a computational description of the consistency requirement that uses deontic
operators in some deontic modal logic. The real issue is, again, whether reasonable reasoning can be formalized. Arguing that computational reductions fail to preserve the normativity of reasonable reasoning will not work
unless it can be shown that the computational reduction cannot completely formalize reasonable reasoning.

Let us pursue Putnam's definition of idealized warranted assertibility and
its connection with his epistemic definition of truth. If idealized warranted
assertibility is related to general intelligence, to reasonable reasoning, and
to rational interpretation$_1$, then the latter are reliable indicators of truth
(but not conclusive, since they are not idealized). Putnam's view is that
truth just is idealized warranted assertibility. What is that?

We are told that there are no general rules or universal methods that can
be used to determine conditions under which we justify arbitrary empirical
judgments. That is, we cannot survey the truth conditions for arbitrary sentences. But what is the source of this limitation? Since truth conditions are
just assertibility conditions, knowing what sentences are true and what
sentences are false involves exercising the capacity to make judgments of
idealized warranted assertibility. We cannot appeal to intuitions about
truth to construct a theory of ideal warranted assertibility—that would be
blatantly circular. That is, we cannot reduce idealized warranted assertibility to the more primitive notion of truth. So we can't locate the source of
the limitation that we cannot survey truth conditions of arbitrary empirical
judgments in metaphysically realist truth.

What, then, is the source of the limitation? I quote Putnam: "If truth
conditions and assertibility conditions are not surveyable, how do we learn
them? We learn them just the way Dummett thinks,..., by acquiring a
practice. What Dummett misses ... is that what we acquire is not a knowledge that can be applied as if it were an algorithm. We do learn that in

certain circumstances we are supposed to accept 'There is a chair in front of me' (normally). *But we are expected to use our heads.* We can refuse to accept 'There is a chair in front of me' even when it looks exactly as if there is a chair in front of us, if our general intelligence screams *'override.'* The impossibility (in practice at least) of formalizing the assertibility conditions for arbitrary sentences is just the impossibility of formalizing general intelligence itself."[28] That spells out, although vaguely, the relationship between idealized warranted assertibility and general intelligence. General intelligence provides the reasoning that is necessary for learning warranted assertibility conditions. Substituting the notion of reasonable reasoning for general intelligence, here is what we get: Reasonable reasoning is necessary for learning warranted assertibility conditions. Failure to formalize general intelligence signals failure to formalize warranted assertibility and idealized warranted assertibility. We can make the same substitutions for the remainder of the notions that are allied to general intelligence. What we see is that they are all normative, because of their intimate connection with warranted assertibility. They are also semantical, because of the connection of idealized warranted assertibility with truth.

We are now in a better position to look at different types of human rationality. Since rational interpretation$_1$ is the means by which we come to understand the utterances of members of our own and other societies, we can restrict the notion of 'kinds of rationality' to 'kinds of rational interpretation$_1$'. It would not be out of place to bring in decision-theoretic rationality as one kind of rationality that Putnam has in mind when he claims that an algorithm for coreferentiality decisions must survey all kinds of rationalities, because one way of unpacking rational interpretation$_1$ is in terms of decision-theoretic rationality. In the 1990s Putnam becomes mysterious about this family of notions.

In *Renewing Philosophy*, reasonable reasoning has become "the point of view of reason."[29] It appears to be utterly mysterious how it works in human beings. Putnam does not isolate any kinds of structural features—such as compositionality—that the point of view of reason satisfies. It is a "bare primitive" capacity. We know that there must be some capacity underlying our evaluation of counterfactual conditionals. What capacity is it? It is "the point of view of reason." We might have an intuitive handle on "the propositional attitudes in their everyday use." but it does not extend to the point of view of reason. It is odd that Putnam would elevate a cognitive capacity—described at the intentional level—to one which is wholly mysterious. Is the point of view of reason any *less* clear than a Master definition of Reference and Synonymy? A computational account of "the point of view of reason" would be invaluable, for it describes in clear and precise computational terms a mysterious capacity, about which Putnam can say that it is not formalizable and that it is the source of our intuitions on a host of interesting questions, such as the evaluation of counterfactual conditionals.

Thus far, we see that the reasonable reasoning necessary for interpreting the utterances of our contemporaries is what an algorithm for coreferentiality decisions needs. If it is not formalizable, then there cannot be such an algorithm. But we have no reason to conclude that there are so many different kinds of reasonable reasoning that we cannot computably partition them into a small set of equivalence classes. This does not advance us toward the conclusion of EQUIVALENCE, unless we show reasonable reasoning cannot be formalized. If so, as we have seen, we don't need EQUIVALENCE to refute computational functionalism.

Now let us turn to the second question: How does a human being living in society A rationally interpret$_1$ the utterances of a human being living in society B, which is a successor to A? (We are to understand "B is a successor to A" in the following sense: "There is a possible other society which is more sophisticated, which has modes of conceptualizing and describing things which members of the first society cannot understand without years of specialized study."[30])

If we acquire the resources to reason in the same way that members of a successor society reason, the question is whether those methods of reasoning are or are not formalizable. Pointing out that there might be successor societies that employ methods of reasoning to which we now could not even approximate cannot be used to show that there is no computable partitioning of methods of reasoning (and kinds of rationality). It cannot be used to show that, for no human agents can now approximate to those methods of reasoning. In that case, no human agents can now employ those methods of reasoning when they engage in successful SD or make coreferentiality decisions. And so algorithms for SD or coreferentiality decisions do not, now, need to survey those methods of reasoning. Where an algorithm formalizes whatever methods of reasoning human beings now use for successful SD or to make coreferentiality decisions, that algorithm is fully capable of doing those things. To point out that there are currently unknown and unknowable methods of reasoning and modes of rationality that successor societies might possess is a red herring. However the future structure of the brain changes from its current structure, both neurophysiologically and computationally, when it manifests methods of reasoning of successor societies that we now cannot even describe, the point is that evolution will be the means by which those neurophysiological and computational structures arise. Any current algorithm for rational interpretation$_2$ need not either anticipate or explicitly describe such structures. We certainly do not take it to be a failure of molecular biology that it cannot now either anticipate or explicitly describe genetic regulatory structures that evolution might give rise to in the future and for similar reasons we should not take it to be a failure of an algorithm for rational interpretation$_2$ that it does not either anticipate or explicitly describe methods of reasoning of possible future successor societies.

Now let us turn to the third question: Is it *coherent* to suppose that we can—now—rationally interpret$_1$ the discourse of any possible future society in which any possible future human being might live? It is incoherent to suppose we—now—can do this, since we do not now have the concepts, conception of human rationality, background beliefs, knowledge, etc. necessary for rational interpretation$_1$ of future discourses. Putnam agrees that we cannot interpret the discourse of any possible future society, but he assumes that any algorithm for rational interpretation$_2$, SD, or coreferentiality decisions must have that ability. Presumably this follows from the requirement that any algorithm for rational interpretation$_2$ depends on a definition of synonymy and coreferentiality and that any theory that defines them must explicitly take into account any possible future society.

I will argue below that there is no reason to think such algorithms must have that capability. But it is instructive to see why it is incoherent to impose this requirement on rational-interpretation$_2$ algorithms. I pursue the point because it is relevant to the question of how general the methods of reasoning that are used for making coreferentiality decisions and engaging in SD must be and of how general theories on which definitions of synonymy and coreferentiality are based must be. Putnam also explicitly connects global methods of reasoning, what it is to be fully human, and the variety of languages and cultures that we can successfully interpret.[31] Below, in a section titled "The Generality Constraint and Why It Is Psychologically Unrealistic," I will explore that connection and argue the supposition that any algorithm for rational interpretation$_2$ have this ability is incoherent.

Two Hidden Assumptions in Environment Totalism, Theory Totalism, and Rationality Totalism

The first hidden assumption is that all the information about all the local environments in the universe, all the possible theories we can construct about it, and all possible kinds of human rationality and inference patterns has to be *explicitly* represented in algorithms for rational interpretation$_2$, coreferentiality decisions, and SD. If this hidden assumption is true, then any such algorithms will have an infinitary component: representing an infinite amount of information explicitly in a data structure of some kind.

This rich diversity of information does not preclude computably partitioning it into a small set of equivalence classes. That is the second hidden assumption—it can't be computably partitioned into a small set of equivalence classes. If it can't be computably partitioned, then neither can the computational realizations of arbitrary intentional states, since these realizations will express that information (though no one realization will express all of it). Putnam owes us an argument. Just because an infinite set contains members that are radically different from one another does not mean that it can't be computably partitioned.

I will not deny that it is controversial to say that it's a hidden assumption in EQUIVALENCE that there is no computable partitioning of the infinitely many computational realizations of an arbitrary intentional state into a small number of equivalence classes. That is supposed to be the conclusion of EQUIVALENCE. But there are no premises in EQUIVALENCE from which it follows. Showing that an algorithm for rational interpretation$_2$ is infinitary does not show that there is no computable partitioning. We will see why this is so below.

Let us consider the first hidden assumption. What if it is not made? We then fail to show that algorithms for SD, rational interpretation$_2$, and coreferentiality decisions must be infinitary. We also show that these algorithms do not need, now, to have information about what will happen in the future. They do not, now, have to explicitly list forms of future human rationality or forms of future human societies or forms of future local environments. If so, the EQUIVALENCE argument fails.

But why should the assumption even be made? Why can't there be algorithms that have, for example, parameters for environmental information that is necessary to make coreferentiality decisions? Perhaps the parameter is in the form of a user query. It asks the user for information about their local environment. No local environmental information will be explicitly listed in the eternal algorithm, but at run time a small fragment of it will explicitly appear in the algorithm as it executes. But local environmental information *will* explicitly appear in computational realizations of the eternal algorithm. However, there is no need to computably partition those computational realizations according to the kind of local environmental information they contain, since all of them can be partitioned into the equivalence class marked by the property of being local environmental information.

Consider eternal algorithms for the acquisition of natural language. Such algorithms do not explicitly list all the sentences a speaker will encounter in any possible linguistic environment. No linguist thinks that such algorithms list all the sentences in English, French, Farsi, and so on. Even restricting what is learned to English datives, this is true. But the computational realizations of the algorithm will explicitly represent the datives encountered by the speaker in the linguistic environment she inhabits. We can classify them as instances of a parameter in the algorithm triggered by the linguistic environment. The use of parameters in the algorithm removes the need to make the first hidden assumption. These parameters also provide a natural way of computably partitioning the computational realizations of the algorithms.

On the opposite side, the first hidden assumption is too extravagant. It takes the first step in turning an SD algorithm into a BLOCKHEAD algorithm.[32] Such algorithms are (and are no more than) complete listings of input and output pairs for whatever function is computed. BLOCKHEAD algorithms are infinite lookup-table structures. Let us define a BLOCKHEAD algorithm for computing an arbitrary function F as follows: Take each ordered pair consisting of the domain element of F as first member and the range element of F as second member and linearly order them according to the cardinal size of the domain elements. This is an infinitary lookup table. For each query of the form 'What is the value of Fx?' posed to a BLOCKHEAD algorithm, it takes the number 'x' and does a search of the infinitary table of ordered pairs, looking for 'x' among the first members of the ordered pairs. When it finds 'x', it outputs the second member of the ordered pair, which is 'Fx'.[33]

For algorithms making coreferentiality decisions, their inputs would consist of the words whose referents are to be determined and the time, place, and occasion of the uses of those words. All theories, environments, and theories of rationality relevant to making the decision (and other features that can be omitted here) will then be determined by the input octet. Suppose that words W_i and W_j, times T_i and T_j, places P_i and P_j, and occasions O_i and O_j are input to the algorithm. The next step is to find the theories and environments that are relevant to deciding the referents of W_i and W_j. That is done by using the infinite lookup table. The entry for the ordered octuple $\langle W_i, W_j, T_i, T_j, P_i, P_j, O_i, O_j \rangle$ in the table will list all the theories and environments necessary for deciding the referents of W_i and W_j. This is a simplified model of the BLOCKHEAD algorithm for coreferentiality decisions. The point it illustrates is that BLOCKHEAD algorithms are nothing more than an infinite list of data points.

It is an important question whether the first hidden assumption necessarily makes algorithms for rational interpretation$_2$ into BLOCKHEAD algorithms. The assumption certainly makes any such algorithms infinitary and makes them impossible to implement in human minds in human beings now living. We, now, do not know the future. If we did know the future, we would occupy an Archimedean point. Let us factor out the issue about containing information about the future to simplify the discussion. If the first hidden assumption makes an infinitary rational-interpretation$_2$ algorithm into a BLOCKHEAD algorithm, then it does not follow there is no computable partitioning. Why is that? There can be a BLOCKHEAD algorithm for any computable or non-computable arbitrary function. But there are computable functions that have very short descriptions under which every ordered pair can be subsumed. For instance, 'the square of x' is an equivalence class into which all the squares of 'x' can be put. Some BLOCKHEAD algorithms can be replaced by algorithms with short descriptions and some can't. (For an example of a BLOCKHEAD algorithm that can be replaced by a non-BLOCKHEAD algorithm with a short description, see below.) The point is that it can't be inferred from being a BLOCKHEAD algorithm that there is no non-BLOCKHEAD algorithm with a short description.

'Infinitary' and 'BLOCKHEAD' are not necessarily coextensive properties of algorithms. Proving an algorithm is infinitary does not necessarily prove it is a BLOCKHEAD, nor does proving an algorithm is a BLOCKHEAD necessarily prove it is infinitary. If the first hidden assumption does *not* make rational-interpretation$_2$ algorithms into BLOCKHEADS, Putnam has to argue for it. And if the first hidden assumption *does* make rational-interpretation$_2$ algorithms into BLOCKHEADS, he must argue that there is no finitary algorithm for rational interpretation$_2$ that has a short description.

Not providing these arguments amounts to making a tacit stipulation that the conclusion of EQUIVALENCE is true. In that case, we get it by tacit stipulation. The same can be said about the second hidden assumption. To say that there is diverse information and that there is thus no way to computably partition it into a small set of equivalence classes begs the question. Not making any of these arguments just is to tacitly stipulate that there is no computable partitioning.

More seriously, in both cases making the tacit stipulation is to beg the question. The question is whether all the computational realizations of an arbitrary intentional state can be computably partitioned into a small set of equivalence classes. If in answering this question it is simply assumed that it is not so for three of the subtasks required for the computable partitioning —partitioning all possible theories, all possible environmental information and all possible kinds of human rationality—then the question has been begged. For each of the three subtasks, Putnam must argue there is no computable partitioning of the kinds of information they express. If the second hidden assumption is not made, then EQUIVALENCE fails.

A BLOCKHEAD Algorithm for Addition

It is important to see what a BLOCKHEAD algorithm looks like. I choose as an example one for adding natural numbers. It uses an infinite table consisting of every instance of adding natural numbers. Compare that with a finitary non-BLOCKHEAD algorithm for adding natural numbers that has a short description. You need to know the decimal representation of the natural numbers (but so does BLOCKHEAD), their well ordering, a table for adding the natural numbers 0 through 9, and rules for carrying numbers. The non-BLOCKHEAD algorithm for adding natural numbers is small. It does not require an infinitely large storage table. We could prove there is no non-BLOCKHEAD algorithm for adding natural numbers only if we could prove there is no finite rule for carrying. Here is a BLOCKHEAD algorithm for adding the natural numbers:

$$
\begin{array}{llll}
0+0=0 & 0+1=1 & \quad 0+2=2 & 0+3=3 \ \ldots \\
1+0=1 & 1+1=2 & \quad 1+2=3 & 1+3=4 \ \ldots \\
2+0=2 & 2+1=3 & \quad 2+2=4 & 2+3=5 \ \ldots \\
3+0=3 & 3+1=4 & \quad 3+2=5 & 3+3=6 \ \ldots \\
4+0=4 & 4+1=5 & \quad 4+2=6 & 4+3=7 \ \ldots \\
5+0=5 & 5+1=6 & \quad 5+2=7 & 5+3=8 \ \ldots \\
6+0=6 & 6+1=7 & \quad 6+2=8 & 6+3=9 \ \ldots \\
\vdots & & & \\
\end{array}
$$

$$n+0=n \quad n+1=(n+1)\ldots \quad n+3=(n+3) \qquad \ldots$$

$$\vdots$$

$$\omega+0=\omega \ \ldots$$

That completes the infinite lookup table (with an infinite number of omissions). For any finite or infinite n and m, you can find their sum by consulting the table. Find n by going down the table vertically and find m by going across the table, at the level of n, horizontally. At that location you will find $n + m$. Notice that the preceding instructions constitute a finite rule for finding the sum of n and m, for any n and m. However, that it is a finite rule is relative to the existence of an infinite lookup table.

Suppose someone argues that in an algorithm for addition of the natural numbers, all pairs consisting of the domain element as the first member and the range element as the second member must be explicitly listed. This requirement makes the algorithm a BLOCKHEAD algorithm. It is analogous to the requirement that algorithms for rational interpretation$_2$ explicitly list all possible theories of the universe, all possible environments, and all possible conceptions of human rationality.

Even though the BLOCKHEAD algorithm for addition of the natural numbers is infinitary (because it has an infinitary lookup table), it can easily be compressed into a finitary algorithm (by eliminating the infinitary lookup table). Imagine someone arguing the BLOCKHEAD algorithm for addition has no finitary compression because the ordered pairs of the form $\langle x, fx \rangle$ are quite different from one another. Even if they are right about the pairs, they are wrong about non-compression. The analogous case is an algorithm for rational interpretation$_2$ or for making coreferentiality decisions or for SD. That there is no finitistic algorithm for any of these must be argued. One can't infer non-compression, without argument, merely from the fact that there is an extraordinary diversity of information on which the algorithm operates.

Quasi-Reductions and Quasi-Definitions

Recall that theory totalism asserts that any theory which *defines* synonymy and coreferentiality is a theory of all human discourse and so it must survey all possible theories. Quine tells us there is no such thing as synonymy. If he is right, it follows there is no definition of synonymy. Putnam tells us that rational interpretation$_1$ is used for SD and to make coreferentiality judgments, even though there is no definition of synonymy and of coreferentiality. That is, there is no fixed and finitary set of necessary and sufficient conditions that defines synonymy and coreferentiality. Putnam frowns on the idea that there is a fixed set of necessary and sufficient conditions that provide a definition of a concept.

Why does Putnam saddle functionalists' attempts to algorithmitize coreferentiality decisions, SD, and rational interpretation$_1$ with the utopian task of giving a definition of synonymy when it is not likely that there is such a finitary definition? Why not give an algorithm for reasonable reasoning, an algorithm for general intelligence, and an algorithm for rational interpretation? These algorithms would simulate the reasoning used by human beings when they successfully engage in SD and make coreferentiality decisions. The short answer is that Putnam claims there is no formalization of them. We have seen that he employs Gödel's incompleteness theorems to argue that they can't be formalized. IN EQUIVALENCE he argues that they can be formalized, but the formalization depends on a definition of synonymy and coreferentiality and the consequence of using these definitions is that algorithms for them are infinitary and have no finitistic compression.

Putnam would agree that when we engage in (say) SD our practice does not depend on a definition of synonymy and of coreferentiality. We use rational interpretation₁, reasonable reasoning, and general intelligence. If these methods can be formalized, then there is an algorithm for SD and an algorithm for coreferentiality decisions. The line I take is that Putnam has not successfully argued the case that these methods can't be formalized. If he can argue that they cannot be formalized, then their infinitary formalization in EQUIVALENCE is the only option for formalization. But until he shows that these methods as they are used by human beings in making coreferentiality decisions and engaging in SD can't be formalized, we have little reason to accept the EQUIVALENCE option.

Even if functionalists *must* give a computable definition of synonymy in designing rational-interpretation algorithms, must the definition survey all possible theories of the universe, all possible physical environments, and all possible theories of rationality? I have already canvassed the possibility that there is a parameter in the algorithm for, say, data of the kind 'physical environment'. Let me waive that possibility now. I contend that there is a philosophical motivation for the condition that algorithms for rational interpretation₂ explicitly list all possible theories of the world, all possible environments, and all possible conceptions of human rationality. The motivation is that the algorithm employs an infinite list, which counts as a quasi-definition of synonymy and of coreferentiality. Thus the algorithm is a quasi-reduction of rational interpretation₂. To see this, we must examine Putnam's views on computational reduction. Chapter 5 of *R&R* contains a clear discussion of computational reduction. Putnam guides the discussion with an example of a classical reduction from physics: reducing temperature to mean molecular kinetic energy. The first condition that a successful reduction in the physical sciences must meet is that there is a law-like relation between the reduced and the reducing disciplines. This easily follows from Kripke's work on *a posteriori* identities.[34] Once we discover that temperature *is* mean molecular kinetic energy, then something, in some possible world, that has the epistemic earmarks of temperature, but is not mean molecular kinetic energy, is not temperature either. Since this is true for any possible world, there is some law-like relation between the temperature and mean molecular kinetic energy. They cannot be coincidentally identical in the actual world, though divergent in non-actual possible worlds. However, there could be a law-like relation between them in the absence of identity. Additional requirements must be levied.

A second requirement on a successful reduction in the physical sciences is that all the laws of the reduced discipline are approximately satisfied by the reducing discipline. The third requirement piggybacks on the second. It is that the reducing discipline explains everything that the reduced discipline explained, though (and here a normative term of evaluation must be employed) with greater clarity. Putnam contends that the second and third requirements separate reductions that are merely law-like from reductions that are identities.

An interesting quasi-reduction can be constructed that satisfies only the first requirement. An illustration of it is Putnam's example of a computable quasi-reduction of the reference relation. Putnam assumes that for each organism and for each situation in which that organism refers to something, there is a computational property that *uniquely* describes that situation. It is not hard to justify this assumption. Since the total number of organisms and the total number of times during which they refer to something will always be finite, find some coding of the situation into the recursive functions. The coding can be done in terms of four basic parameters: the speaker, the time of the utterance, the utterance, and the place of the utterance. The parameters generate unique computational descriptions of any situation in which reference occurs, even if two persons can occupy the same place at the same time.

The construction yields a disjunctive reduction that is a list and not a theory of reference. The list describes (once the recursive function uniquely characterizing a situation in which reference occurs is decoded into its parameters) who said what and what it referred to, on which occasion, and where it was said. The gigantic disjunction is not a genuine reduction of reference to computational terms, nor is it a genuine definition of reference in computational terms. It is a quasi-reduction. If reductions are to be taken as definitions, it is a quasi-definition.

Another point must be made about quasi-reductions. If the reduction is not just over all actual speakers and actual occasions of referring but over all possible speakers and all possible occasions of referring, then the disjunction will be infinitely long. In the actual world, in all of human history, there will never be more than a finite number of speakers and a finite number of occasions where referential acts occur. If we consider alternatives to how human history goes, there will be infinitely many possible but non-actual speakers and referential acts.[35]

I am now in a position to make a claim.

T: Theory totalism implies that a computational account of SD must have the form of a quasi-reduction and be based on a quasi-definition.

It is easy to see T is true. By the condition that the computational description of SD must be based on a definition of synonymy, and by the surveyability condition that each possible theory of the universe must be explicitly listed in the computational description of SD, the only definition we can have is a list of all possible theories of the universe (and environments and theories of rationality as well). If T is true, it follows the computational description of SD is not a genuine reduction and is not based on a genuine definition. T is compatible with Quine's view that are no definitions or reductions of synonymy. On Quine's view, quasi-reductions or quasi-definitions are optimal.

But Putnam believes one can give an account of synonymy at the intentional level. Such an account makes essential use of the reasonableness of reasoning or general intelligence or rational interpretation$_1$. If computational descriptions cannot formalize these methods necessary for SD, then they are optimally quasi-definitions. T drives a wedge between Putnamian epistemic semantics and computationalism. But it does so only if it can be shown there is no formalization of the methods human beings use to make coreferentiality decisions or to engage in SD. If that has been shown, then it follows from T that there are no genuine computational reductions and no genuine definitions of synonymy and reference. Optimally, there are quasi-reductions and quasi-definitions. Moreover, any algorithm that is based on a quasi-definition of the form mandated by T and is a quasi-reduction must be infinitary. That is, it must contain an infinite lookup table listing all the possible theories of the universe (and much else). But if there is no argument for the condition that a computational description of SD must be based on a theory of synonymy, T fails, since that is a necessary condition for T. Similarly for the surveyability condition, interpreted to mean that each possible theory of the universe must be explicitly listed in a computational description of SD: T fails if there is no argument for it, since it is a necessary condition for T. Finally, since theory totalism, environment totalism, and rationality totalism are each necessary for EQUIVA-

LENCE, if the arguments for any one of them fail, EQUIVALENCE fails. If theory totalism is successfully argued, then any algorithm for SD will be infinitary. In fact, it will be an infinitary algorithm that has an infinitary lookup table.

To summarize: I deny that there is an asymmetry between computational and Putnamian semantic accounts of SD. Computational accounts of synonymy succumb to T only if Putnam can demonstrate that there is no formalization of reasonable reasoning, general intelligence, and rational interpretation$_1$ necessary for SD and for making coreferentiality decisions. More troubling is the following: If Putnam stipulates the truth of the surveyability condition and the condition that computational descriptions of SD must be based on a definition of synonymy, then EQUIVALENCE fails. We have seen that the definition condition is an option only if there is no formalization of reasonable reasoning, rational interpretation$_1$, and general intelligence. And we have seen that it is the explicit listing of theories that makes the surveyability condition problematic, and that there are alternative possibilities for algorithms other than explicit listing. For example, query parameters can replace explicit lists. If there is no argument for either condition other than a stipulation that they are true, then, given there are alternatives to the conditions, such stipulations destroy the argument. If it is possible that either A or B is true, but not both, it will do no good to settle the matter to stipulate that A is true.

EQUIVALENCE concludes that there are no local computational reductions, because any algorithms for SD or coreferentiality decisions are infinitary, are non-compressible, and require information about the future. The latter follows from T, and I think T fails. But even if T holds, Putnam has not supplied an argument that it implies there is no computable partitioning of the set of computational realizations of an arbitrary intentional state.

Below I will show that arguments purporting to show that rational interpretation$_1$, reasonable reasoning, and general intelligence cannot be formalized are defective or do not provide convincing reasons. I have already shown that Putnam's Gödelian argument that general intelligence, rational interpretation$_1$ and reasonable reasoning cannot be formalized is defective. It will be necessary to consider other kinds of arguments that they can't be formalized. Although some of these arguments are well known and not readily answerable, neither are they considered definitive refutations, since there are too many cogent responses to them. In the case where the supposed refutations are not definitive, Putnam sustains, at best, only a mixed verdict on his project of refuting computational functionalism.

A No-Win Dilemma for the Computational Functionalist Based on an Equivocation on 'Rational Interpretation'

The point of this section is to show what kinds of arguments can be made when no distinction is made between 'rational interpretation$_1$' and 'rational interpretation$_2$' and what kinds of arguments can be made when a distinction is employed. To put it more bluntly: If one equivocates on 'rational interpretation', an anti-functionalist conclusion can be secured from an argument that is in the form of a dilemma.

EQUIVALENCE argues that any algorithm for rational interpretation$_2$ must use a definition of synonymy and coreferentiality, and that such a definition commits us to surveying all possible theories (about our universe and what is in it). The best one can do in designing the algorithm is to explicitly list all possible theories in an infinitary lookup table. This table (along with other infinitary tables for all possible local environments and all possible theories of rationality) gives us a quasi-definition of synonymy. In that case, the rational-interpretation$_2$ algorithm is, optimally, a quasi-reduction of rational interpretation$_2$. However, the rational-interpretation$_2$ algorithm is infinitary (and may be a BLOCKHEAD algorithm) and cannot be compressed into a finitary algorithm. There are no rules that all episodes of rational interpretation$_2$ share, nor are there any rules that subsets of those episodes share. This situation is tantamount to how Quine envisages SD. There are no rules that can be used in SD. Any perceived 'rule' is just a central practice that could be given up and so is not a genuine rule.

We can now formulate a dilemma for a computational functionalist.

First horn:
P1 If we formalize rational interpretation, then we are subject to Quinean strictures on synonymy.
C1 If we succeed in formalizing rational interpretation, then the anti-functionalist wins the mechanism debate.

Second horn:
P2 If we don't formalize rational interpretation, then we are immune to Quine's strictures on synonymy.
C2 If we don't succeed in formalizing rational interpretation, then the anti-functionalist wins the mechanism debate.

This is a false dilemma, since it omits a critical possibility. For Putnam, rational interpretation$_1$, reasonable reasoning, and general intelligence are used to engineer SD and coreferentiality decisions. If they cannot be formalized, there is no formalization of SD and of coreferentiality decisions.

If that is so, the only option is an infinitary formalization. This is how
EQUIVALENCE presents rational interpretation. The above argument
equivocates on 'rational interpretation'. Recall that rational interpreta-
tion$_1$ is what we use for SD and to make coreferentiality decisions. It does
not depend on a definition of synonymy and coreferentiality. Putnam
claims that it cannot be formalized. Rational interpretation$_2$ depends on
a definition of synonymy and coreferentiality, and any formal algorithm
for it is infinitary.

Let us eliminate the equivocation in the first and second horns above.

First horn:
P1 If we formalize rational interpretation$_2$, then we are subject to
Quinean strictures on synonymy.
C1 If we succeed in formalizing rational interpretation$_2$, then the anti-
functionalist wins the mechanism debate.

Second horn:
P2 If we don't formalize rational interpretation$_1$, then we are immune
to Quine's strictures on synonymy.
C2 If we don't succeed in formalizing rational interpretation$_1$, then the
anti-functionalist wins the mechanism debate.

We no longer have a dilemma, since different conceptions of rational interpretation appear in each of the horns. Moreover, the argument in the first
horn is invalid, for the real issue for computational functionalism is not
whether rational interpretation$_2$ can or cannot be formalized, but whether
rational interpretation$_1$ can or cannot be formalized.

We can easily see that even when the equivocation is eliminated there
are other possibilities. The dilemma is a false one, for we can add two more
arguments to it.

Third argument:
P3 If we succeed in formalizing rational interpretation$_1$, then we have a
rational-interpretation$_1$ algorithm for SD and coreferentiality decisions.
C3 If we succeed in formalizing rational interpretation$_1$, then the
functionalist wins the mechanism debate.

Fourth argument:
P4 If we do not succeed in formalizing rational interpretation$_1$, then the
only option is rational interpretation$_2$.
C4 Rational interpretation$_2$ commits us to the conclusion C1.

A clarification is in order. When I say "wins the mechanism debate," I
mean "wins the mechanism debate as it is framed by Putnam." There are

obviously many other ways to conduct the debate. Though the original dilemma is not explicitly stated in *R&R*, I conjecture that it would resonate with Putnam. There is a connection between EQUIVALENCE and Putnam's critique of Hartry Field's attempt to naturalize the reference relation. In his Locke lectures, Putnam argues that Field's naturalized definition of reference is nothing more than a list (in the form of a disjunction) and thus is a quasi-definition and so not a genuine definition. In his response to Field at the Chapel Hill Colloquium in the late 1970s, Putnam argues that the reference relation cannot be defined without a definition of rational interpretation$_1$, which "is inseparable from the analysis of either the normative notion of rationality, or from some such notion as Vico's 'humanity.'"[36] EQUIVALENCE echoes Putnam's response to Field. Putnam's argument that rational-interpretation$_2$ algorithms are infinitary non-compressible algorithms and thus not genuine computational reductions of rational interpretation$_2$ echoes his argument against a physicalist reduction of the reference relation.

The Generality Constraint and Why It Is Psychologically Unrealistic

For Putnam, a rational-interpretation$_2$ algorithm is *required* to survey all possible societies. because such algorithms must work for arbitrary societies and cultures. Otherwise, it would apply only to specialized cases and would not be a theory of rational interpretation$_2$ in general. Putnam says: "The reason that partial successes [of formalizing—JB] interpretation theory [such as Marvin Minsky's work in the early 1970s—JB] are always so limited is that any global success, any program for interpretation of sentences in a variable language, a variable theory, on variable topics and with variable presuppositions, would involve an analysis of the notion of humanity, or the notion (which in my view is closely related) of rationality. The function of limiting interpretation to a specific frame is to avoid having to tackle the totally utopian project of algorithmic analysis of these notions."[37]

Call the following condition the generality constraint on rational interpretation$_{1,2}$: The notions of rational interpretation$_{1,2}$ and of humanity apply to sentences in variable languages and variable theories on variable topics and with variable presuppositions.

The generality constraint can be used to formulate an argument.

P1　Human beings satisfy the generality constraint.

P2　No finitary algorithm can satisfy the generality constraint.

C　No finitary algorithm can engage in successful rational interpretation$_{1,2}$

This argument is valid. I contend that the first premise is false at best and (possibly) incoherent at worst. There is one way of showing that P1 is true, but it will show that P2 is false. The phrase "apply to" can be read as short for "would apply to if data of a certain kind is available to the human interpreter." A human interpreter cannot rationally interpret$_{1,2}$ the utterances of a speaker of Thai without knowing the words in Thai (and much more). But this information can be supplied to an algorithm for rational interpretation$_{1,2}$ as well. Indeed, without this proviso the generality constraint is not satisfied by human beings either. Consider a language that is invented in the future. We can easily explain why human beings cannot now survey future languages. We need—now—to have the data about those languages, but obviously it is not now available to us if those languages do not yet exist. The same is true of an algorithm for rational interpretation$_{1,2}$.

That rational interpretation$_{1,2}$ must work for variable languages and variable theories, as well as for variable topics and variable presuppositions, is a substantial philosophical and scientific claim. Are there *no* restrictions on the kinds of languages for which rational interpretation$_{1,2}$ must work? Are there *no* restrictions of the kinds of presuppositions for which rational interpretation$_{1,2}$ must work? I will show that there is a need for innate prejudices that place fundamental limits on the generality constraint.

Ugly Duckling Theory

Fodor famously argued that innateness plays critical roles in inductive reasoning, in language learning, and in concept learning. Nelson Goodman has argued for innate basic epistemological prejudices. Goodman's work is known collectively as "Ugly Duckling Theory."[38] An excellent discussion of it and its role in categorization theory can be found in Aaron Bobick's dissertation "Natural Object Categorization."[39] Bobick notes an ingenious theorem proved by Nelson Goodman (in *The Structure of Appearance*): that any similarity relations whatsoever between any objects whatsoever can be constructed, given the appropriate choice of logical primitives. Without restrictions on logical primitives, we can find any similarity relations we please. The theorem shows that there is a need for such restrictions, for finding any similarity relation is an odious (even absurd) prospect and must be avoided. What I wish to show is that rational interpretation$_{1,2}$, if it must work for variable languages, for variable theories, for variable topics, and for variable presuppositions, can place no restrictions on logical primitives. That is, the generality constraint is fully consistent with Goodman's theorem. Indeed, it is a form of it.

Goodman did not provide a rigorous mathematical proof of his theorem. That was done by Satosi Watanabe, and proofs of this kind became known as Ugly Duckling Theorems.[40] If each object shares the same number of properties with any other object, then we cannot categorize some ducklings as ugly and some as beautiful if numerical counting of shared properties is the basis of the categorization. The typical statement of Ugly Duckling Theorems is "Insofar as we use a finite set of predicates that are capable of distinguishing any two objects considered, the number of predicates shared by any two such objects is constant, independent of the choice of the two objects."[41]

It is easy to prove an Ugly Duckling Theorem for a small number of predicates. Suppose that we have two predicates. Without any constraints in place, any two arbitrary predicates logically generate a set of four distinct object types:

$$\{(P1 \cap P2), (P1 \cap \sim P2), (\sim P1 \cap P2), (\sim P1 \cap \sim P2)\}.$$

No restriction is placed on the number of objects available. The Ugly Duckling Theorem tells us that the number of properties shared by any two arbitrary objects is constant and that it does not depend on the choice of objects or on the number of objects. To show that, we must first determine how many different predicates are available. New predicates can be constructed out of the four basic object types by combining them set-theoretically. For example, combining the second and third object types by a set-theoretic union operation results in a higher-order property that is equivalent to the exclusive disjunction of P1 and P2. (This is easy to see. P1 aut P2 is logically equivalent to $(P1 \cap \sim P2)$ vel $(\sim P1 \cap P2)$.[42] Both of these sentences have the same truth table and are thus logically equivalent.) Since there are two predicates, there are 16 different ways of combining them, provided one includes a null predicate (false for all objects) and the identity predicate (true for all objects.)

These 16 properties have logical relations of implication, which can be captured in a lattice by the relationship of inclusion (where the least upper bound—the bottom—is the null predicate and the greatest upper bound— the top—is the identity predicate). The basic objects are determined by the four basic object types. We do not assume that there are equal numbers of each kind of basic object. To determine the properties that a basic object possesses, begin at the node—for example, $(P1 \cap P2)$—and follow all the upward connections from that node in the lattice. If there is some node above the four basic object type nodes which can be reached from two (or more) basic object type nodes, then each of those objects shares that property.

On the basis of symmetry considerations—the symmetry of the lattice—it can easily be shown that each object type shares four properties with every other object type. Thus the disturbing conclusion: any two arbitrary objects share the same number of properties, namely four. Each object is equally similar to every other object. Thus, there cannot be any means of classifying the objects via a categorization based on object similarity (which, in turn, is based on the properties shared by objects). If the object type (P1 ∩ P2) is a beautiful swan and the object type (∼P1 ∩ ∼P2) is an ugly duckling, it follows that the swan cannot be distinguished from the ugly duckling.

Goodman argued that placing purely syntactical restrictions on the properties is not enough to escape the Ugly Duckling Theorem. Another way of making the point is that we can't, on purely a priori grounds, privilege one property over another. There is a technical reason for this: redefining the basic object terms, but preserving logical structure between them, simply results in what were formerly syntactically complex properties now being simple and what were formerly syntactically simple properties now being complex. In short, we have merely redistributed the properties over the lattice structure in such a way that each object still shares four properties with every other object. Goodman argued only extra-logical information can derail Ugly Duckling Theorems. Bobick takes extra-logical constraints on categorization to be information about the local environment: "objects will tend to cluster along dimensions important to the interaction between objects (organisms) and the environment."[43] Avoiding a world in which all objects are equally similar to each other requires the world-maker to posit natural categories. These can be studied by the sciences, and one goal of foundational cognitive science is to study the nature of mental concepts and how they are responsive to these natural categories.

We are now in a position to critically examine Putnam's requirement on rational interpretation$_{1,2}$ that it work for variable languages, variable theories, variable topics and variable presuppositions. It is obvious that not all languages, theories, topics and presuppositions are created equal. There are some languages that human beings cannot learn. There are some theories that human beings cannot rationally interpret$_1$. There are some topics that are "conceptually invisible" to rational human beings and there are some presuppositions that would make language use incoherent. If rational interpretation$_{1,2}$ must work for an unconstrained choice of languages, theories, topics, and presuppositions, it, in effect, satisfies the conditions of the Ugly Duckling Theorem. It fails to make distinctions where natural distinctions are needed. We certainly need to distinguish between languages that are humanly learnable and those that are not. We certainly need to distinguish between theories that employ concepts that we are able to understand from those that employ concepts that we cannot understand. We certainly want to distinguish topics of discourse with which we are conversant because they involves aspects of the world with which we are acquainted from those with which we are not conversant because they involve aspects of the world that have not yet occurred and with which, therefore, we could not be acquainted.

If we have no argument that there cannot be a formalization of rational interpretation$_1$, then we would expect that the same morals we just cited for rational interpretation$_1$ hold when we consider the prospects of whether there are any algorithms for rational interpretation$_1$.[44] We also expect them to hold for rational-interpretation$_2$ algorithms. Recall that the point of finding a small set of computable equivalence classes over the set of computational realizations of a rational-interpretation$_2$ algorithm was to carry out a *local* genuine reduction. The restriction of rational-interpretation$_2$ algorithms to human beings *and* a small computable partitioning of the computational realizations would accomplish that task. However, by requiring that rational-interpretation$_2$ algorithms work for variable languages, variable theories, variable topics, and variable presuppositions is to require that the computational reduction be global, not local. It is inconsistent to force rational-interpretation$_2$ algorithms to conform to the conditions of the Ugly Duckling Theorem and to concede that rational-interpretation$_2$ algorithms are to be restricted to human beings in order to show that local reduction cannot work. This is taking away with one hand what the other hand delivers. It is also crazy, since there are natural restrictions that determine what kinds of languages, theories, topics, and presuppositions human beings can "cognize." Cognitive science studies such natural restrictions. Algorithms for rational interpretation$_{1,2}$ must explicitly code those restrictions. If they don't do so, then, whatever those restrictions are, they are clearly not algorithms for rational interpretation$_{1,2}$. By imposing the generality constraint on cognitive science, Putnam is saying, in effect, that we must ignore natural restrictions in evaluating computational reductions. He is also saying that rational interpretation$_{1,2}$ is required to do what is incoherent: to not make distinctions where they must be made and to make distinctions where they cannot be made. We know of languages that are not humanly learnable. Grammatical constructions in such languages could not be understood by human beings. Is Putnam saying that if we were to use rational interpretation$_{1,2}$ we would be able to understand those grammatical constructions? If that is so, it is a clear *reductio* of his generality constraint on rational interpretation$_{1,2}$. But if rational interpretation$_{1,2}$ is required to satisfy the conditions of the Ugly Duckling Theorem, that is the consequence that must be faced. Finally, if rational-interpretation$_{1,2}$ algorithms are required to *ignore* what cognitive science has told us about the natural restrictions imposed on cognitive systems, we can conclude that they are pseudo-science.

We can apply the morals of the Ugly Duckling Theorem to "the point of view of reason," a capacity Putnam takes all rational human beings to be endowed with.[45] Reasonable reasoning is reasoning in accord with the point of view of reason. Suppose that we understand that to mean that reasoning needs some bias in order to give it the proper direction. The notion of 'proper direction' is vague. One way to make it more precise is to use an analogy: In automated theorem proving, bias is introduced in derivations in order to eliminate derivations that do not proceed in the direction of the conclusion. Human reasoning has the potential to proceed in many different directions and thus end in many different conclusions. Many of the directions are irrelevant and wasteful. How do we know how to avoid them? One conjecture is that some bias is needed to move reasoning in a certain direction. One version of the frame problem in artificial intelligence is how to avoid courses of reasoning that move in irrelevant or wasteful directions. We humans solve that version of the frame problem. How do we do it?

If we were to take all courses of reasoning (from a given starting point) as equally acceptable, we could not solve the frame problem, though we would be in accord with the conditions for an Ugly Duckling Theorem. In this case, the theorem would concern derivational pathways and predicates that distinguish pathways. The theorem would say that, for a finite set of predicates that are capable of distinguishing any two derivational pathways considered, the number of predicates shared by any two such derivational pathways is constant, independent of the choice of the two derivational pathways. What does this have to do with the point of view of reason?

If the point of view of reason is something different from a bias in reasoning, then it is wholly mysterious what it is. But if the point of view of reasoning introduces biases in reasoning to solve, say, the frame problem, then it is not another name for rational interpretation$_1$. Since rational interpretation$_1$ must be in accord with the conditions of the Ugly Duckling Theorem (by Putnam's lights), and introducing a bias is inconsistent with those conditions, the point of view of reason is then inconsistent with rational interpretation$_1$. But rational interpretation$_1$, reasonable reasoning, general intelligence are a family of related notions for Putnam. So if it is the case that reasonable reasoning is reasoning that is in accord with the point of view of reason, there is a contradiction. Substitute any one of the other members of that family for reasonable reasoning and the contradiction is sustained. Thus the dilemma: either the notion of point of view of reasoning is a mysterious we-know-not-what or it is in contradiction with the family of notions—rational interpretation$_1$, general intelligence, and reasonable reasoning.

We can use Ugly Duckling Theorems to reach a strong conclusion: in enforcing the generality constraint on rational interpretation$_1$—and any algorithms for rational interpretation$_{1,2}$—Putnam is declaring, by fiat, there can be no *local* computational reduction. By 'local' I mean reductions that take into account the kinds of constraints that human cognizers must satisfy in order to have a cognitive mental life that does not satisfy the conditions of Ugly Duckling Theorems. Putnam's statement in *R&R* of the claim there are no local computational reductions is that there can be no computable partitioning of the infinite set of computational realizations of arbitrary intentional states into a small set of equivalence classes. But given his use of the generality constraint, what Putnam must mean is that there is no computable partitioning of the infinite set of computational realizations for arbitrary intentional states *satisfying the generality constraint* into a small set of equivalence classes. But given that satisfaction of the generality constraint implies globality, this statement says there are no global computational reductions, where by 'global' we mean that the computational reduction works for variable languages, variable theories, variable topics, and variable presuppositions. If so, Putnam does not have an argument that foils computationalism, since computationalists will not worry that there are no global computational reductions.

Ugly Duckling Theorems are quite general, applying to any rational cognitive system, whether it is realized in a human or not. EQUIVALENCE claims that no algorithm for rational interpretation$_2$ can satisfy the generality constraint without being a non-compressible infinitary or a BLOCKHEAD algorithm—thus occupying an Archimedean viewpoint. We can see the generality constraint as implying the Archimedean viewpoint. However, Ugly Duckling Theorems teach us that human cognitive systems must be biased in some way. Cognitive science teaches us the kinds of biases that are effective for human cognition. If we refuse to allow into cognitive science the natural constraints it teaches us human cognition requires, then, of course, we can prove that cognitive science is impossible. That, though, is hardly interesting. If we assume human cognition satisfies the generality constraint, we are making a fiction of human cognition. Ignoring Ugly Duckling Theorems is, in my view, a fatal error in the argument of EQUIVALENCE.

The burden of proof rests on Putnam's shoulders. He does have room for avoiding the harm Ugly Duckling Theorems inflict on EQUIVALENCE. Putnam can either show that the efforts of cognitive scientists to describe natural constraints on human cognitive mechanisms is for some reason futile—in which case he must still disarm the Ugly Duckling Theorem, though by other means—or show that the natural constraints on human cognitive mechanisms do not appreciably pare down the enormous multiplicity of possible languages, possible theories, possible topics, and possible presuppositions to which algorithms for rational interpretation$_{1,2}$ must reckon. In what follows I ignore the points made using Ugly Duckling Theorems and consider whether SD, coreferentiality decisions, and the family of notions consisting of rational interpretation$_1$, general intelligence, and reasonable reasoning can be formalized.

9 The Question of the Nonformalizability of SD, Coreferentiality Decisions, and the Family of Notions: Rational Interpretation₁, General Intelligence, and Reasonable Reasoning

If rational interpretation$_1$ cannot be formalized, there are no algorithms for it. Or, if there is an algorithm, it can optimally be either a non-compressible infinitary or a BLOCKHEAD algorithm, but then it is rational interpretation$_2$ that is formalized. (Recall that a BLOCKHEAD algorithm is an infinite or infeasibly long table consisting—in the case of rational interpretation$_2$—of, for all episodes of rational interpretation$_2$ in which human beings have engaged, are now engaging or will engage, the inputs to the episode and the output to that episode.) EQUIVALENCE argues that rational-interpretation$_2$ algorithms must be non-compressible infinitary or BLOCKHEAD algorithms and that they occupy an Archimedean point. But this conclusion of EQUIVALENCE can be secured only if it can be shown that there is no formalization of rational interpretation$_1$. If there is a formalization of it or if the arguments that there is no formalization of it are not conclusive, then it is left open that there are finitary non-BLOCKHEAD algorithms for rational interpretation$_1$ (that do not occupy an Archimedean point).

Let us now examine eight arguments proposed by Putnam that rational interpretation$_1$ can't be formalized.

(i) Gödelian arguments against the formalization of demonstrative reasoning. There are two strands here. The first is that first-order formalizable reasoning expressive enough for Peano arithmetic is necessary for formalizable rational interpretation$_1$. Such reasoning cannot, on Gödelian grounds, be formalized. The second strand is that formalized reasoning cannot formally survey itself, by Gödelian considerations.

(ii) Non-demonstrative reasoning that is necessary for rational interpretation$_1$, such as inductive reasoning, cannot be formalized, on two different grounds. One ground is Goodmanian, the other Gödelian.

(iii) Quinean indeterminacy—there can be no algorithm for synonymy determination, because there can be no finite and precise specification of the "correct" translation of one language into another. "The idea that *interpretive rationality can be fully exhausted by a finite set of criteria that we will actually succeed in writing down* is utopian on its face. But that is what Quine is demanding—that we succeed in writing down a set of criteria—before he will accept that we have succeeded in rationally reconstructing the notion of synonymy."[1]

(iv) Vico's view of rational interpretation$_1$ implies that formalizing it requires formalizing our entire conception of what it is to be a human being.[2]

(v) Radical Quinean meaning holism can be sidestepped by general intelligence (which can disentangle meaning-constituting from auxiliary beliefs), but general intelligence cannot be formalized.

(vi) The necessary globality of rational interpretation$_1$ and the necessary locality of computations.[3]

(vii) Twin-Earth considerations. A purely functionalist account of the mental lives of A and Twin-Earth A cannot determine when the referents of their uses of the word "water" have changed. However, A and Twin-Earth A can make the determination if they use rational interpretation.[4]

(viii) The infection problem that arises when stereotypes are taken as necessary for SD and which shows rational interpretation is "an essentially informal and interest-relative matter."[5]

The question "To what extent do non-formalizability arguments show that inductive reasoning cannot be formalized?" can be dodged here. Even if Putnam's arguments showed non-formalizability, it would be necessary to know to what extent inductive reasoning is non-formalizable. I don't think any of Putnam's non-formalizability arguments succeed, so I ignore this issue.

Let us now examine the eight arguments.

(i) Gödelian arguments show that rational interpretation$_1$ cannot be formalized

If it is shown that first-order reasoning strong enough to express Peano arithmetic is necessary for rational interpretation$_1$, a Gödelian argument can be used to secure the conclusion that rational interpretation$_1$ is not formalizable. I have already discussed why this kind of argument fails. Another kind of argument Putnam makes against non-formalizability of rational interpretation$_1$ is that it involves the ability of rational interpretation$_1$ to survey itself and that formalized reasoning cannot, on Gödelian grounds, survey itself. Thus rational interpretation$_1$ cannot be formalized. But I have also considered this kind of argument and shown that it fails.

There is more to be said, however. In his paper "Reflexive Reflections," Putnam writes that there is a deep philosophical problem for any theory of human cognition that offers a computational description of human cognitive competence.[6] Because of Gödelian limitations, we cannot justify, or even acquire, a complete computational description of our competence (in demonstrative and non-demonstrative reasoning). It is well beyond our cognitive powers, since any such description would involve either proving that our Gödel sentence is true or proving that the description is consistent. However, there might be other beings (for instance, the Alpha Centaurians) who do have the cognitive powers to acquire and justify the computational description of our competence. However, we now need a computational description of *their* competence, and they cannot supply it, to either us or to themselves, since they do not have the cognitive powers to do so, for the same Gödelian reason that we do not have the computational power to computationally describe our own competence.

Once again, other beings who do have the power to computationally describe the competencies of both us and the Alpha Centaurians must be found. The computational description of human cognitive competence is a gigantic disjunction $D_1 \vee D_2 \vee D_3 \vee \cdots \vee D_n$, where n must be, minimally, ω^{CK} (since the only being who could prove the Gödel sentences of all "lower" beings and their own as well is at the "Turing limit": a being who sits atop a nonrecursive ordinal pathway that marks the end of a transfinite autonomous progression of theories). Putnam claims that this disjunction does not address the question "What do all instances of interpretation have in common?" and thus cannot be a finite rule for rational interpretation$_1$. Thus, there is, on Gödelian grounds, no finite rule for rational interpretation$_1$. We can only appeal to the gigantic disjunction for a computational description of rational interpretation$_1$, but we are epistemically closed off from it. Even if we had epistemic access to it, we could not extract a finite rule for rational interpretation$_1$ from it, since there are infinitely many disjuncts and there is nothing that is common to all of the disjuncts.

The best we can do is simply write down all of the infinitely many disjuncts. But this is not an algorithm for rational interpretation$_1$. For one thing, it is not finite and the instructions in any algorithm must be finitary.

The preceding argument (from the last section of "Reflexive Reflections"[7]) is different from EQUIVALENCE. It is not that an algorithm for rational interpretation$_2$ must survey all possible future human societies in order to rationally interpret$_2$ arbitrary human discourses (an intermediate conclusion of EQUIVALENCE). It is, rather, that any computational competence theory of ourselves that includes a computational description of rational interpretation$_1$ must describe infinitely many different kinds of intelligent beings, and not just ourselves as we are now. But this computational competence theory cannot be formalized, insofar as to complete the computational description of our competence one must progress along a nonrecursive ordinal pathway and no finitary formalization allows such a move.

However, it is a rhetorical move to enlist the Alpha Centaurians (and other alien beings). The point about the infinite disjunction could be made locally: Human beings must acquire additional logical powers if they are to have the ability to computationally describe their own competence in demonstrative and non-demonstrative reasoning. We can replace the aliens by Gödel jumps of ourselves. That is, a Gödel jump of Arthur is Arthur enriched with a proof of his Gödel sentence or of his own consistency. The claim, then, is that a computational description of our competence in demonstrative and non-demonstrative reasoning will be an infinitely long disjunction of all of the Gödel jumps of our present selves, none of whose disjuncts have anything in common.

Two simple points I made in my discussion of Putnam's use of the Gödel theorems to refute functionalism undermine the above argument. One is that the competence description of ourselves can be accurate, but with less than mathematical certainty. We can use weak methods to describe our competence. If we do, then there is no longer any need to appeal to Gödel jumps of ourselves. A computational description of ourselves will not have infinitely many disjuncts, and so the argument that there is no formalization of it because to reach the end of the set of disjuncts one must follow a nonrecursive ordinal pathway no longer holds. The other point is that the justification of the computational description of our competence can be on less than mathematically certain grounds. Not only is it the case that the computational description is less accurate than one which is mathematically certain to be true, but the justification of that description is similarly less than certain. This should not occasion any worry that computational functionalism is thereby refuted. Why should we require that the computational description of ourselves be justified with mathematical certainty? It is impossible to do so, on Gödelian grounds. If we make the requirement of justification with mathematical certainty, the infinitely long disjunctive computational competence description will be the only computational description of ourselves. But we cannot justify that description of ourselves.

Is that a realistic requirement? We do not make it an epistemic requirement in biology that we know, with mathematical certainty, all of the field's pronouncements. Given that we know with mathematical certainty that we can't know with mathematical certainty the competence description of how we reason demonstratively and non-demonstratively, shouldn't that tell us that we must be content, in cognitive science, with justification that does not demand mathematical certainty? Isn't it *rational* to opt for justification with less than mathematical certainty when we know that we can never achieve justification with mathematical certainty? As philosophers we are interested in what human rationality consists in. Anyone who insists that we do what we know with mathematical certainty we cannot do has lost contact with human rationality. If cognitive science makes the epistemological demand that mathematical certainty is required for justification of any of its claims, then that must be argued for, since it is a very unusual, perhaps irrational, demand for any science.

(ii) Inductive reasoning cannot be formalized and is necessary for rational interpretation₁

The hardest problem is whether inductive reasoning can be formalized. Putnam has argued in different ways that inductive reasoning is non-formalizable. The important Gödelian argument for the non-formalizability of inductive reasoning has already been addressed—and dismissed. There are other arguments for the claim, two of which come from Nelson Goodman.

Grue
The first is Goodman's 'grue' argument.[8] 'Grue' names a color that is disjunctively defined: An object is grue provided it is green and observed or blue and unobserved before the year 2010. The empirical generalizations 'All emeralds are green' and 'All emeralds are grue' are equally confirmed by observations of green emeralds made before 2010. Before 2010, no grue emeralds can be observationally distinguished from any green emeralds.

What constraints can we impose on a system of inductive reasoning that will exclude grue-like empirical generalizations? Goodman contended that no purely syntactical constraints will do that job, and that the only way to distinguish genuine from grue-like properties is in terms of a history of past inductions. That we used 'green' and not 'grue' in the past gives us a reason now to use 'green'. But it could have been otherwise—in the past, we might have used 'grue' and not 'green', in which case we have a reason now to use 'grue'. Some take this to show that inductive reasoning cannot be formalized—i.e., that there are no syntactical or formal features of a formalized inductive logic that can be used to make the distinction.

My response to Goodman's 'grue' argument is quick and simple: Extra-logical knowledge is needed to solve the grue problem, and such knowledge is, more than likely, built into us by evolution. In linguistics, the M-constraint has solid empirical backing. The M-constraint rules out disjunctive concepts from our conceptual repertoire, and it fits computational accounts of both language learning and concept formation nicely.[9] It is not a logical solution to the 'grue' problem, but who would have thought the 'grue' problem is susceptible to such solutions? Innate metrics providing empirical constraints on computations do have explanatory value in a computational framework. That is one important lesson of Ugly Duckling Theorems. Deny this and you incur a burden of proof in the mechanism dialectic. Additionally, that algorithms for inductive reasoning can have access to extra-logical information is consistent with classical computationalism.

Ukuk

Another hard problem Goodman invented for inductive reasoning concerns Ukuk the Eskimo, a native speaker of Inuit. He enters Harvard's Emerson Hall, where until his entry no one has spoken Inuit. Before Ukuk enters Emerson Hall, "If a person enters Emerson Hall, that person does not speak Inuit" would have been a good induction. Obviously, it is severely undermined once Ukuk goes in. But *how* is it undermined? How do we decide that the induction "One does not lose one's ability to speak in one's native tongue when entering a building" overrides the induction "If one enters Emerson Hall, one does not speak Inuit?" That is Goodman's problem of conflicting inductions related to the grue problem (since green and grue hypotheses are conflicting statistical generalizations), but considerably harder, for the offending hypothesis is not expressed syntactically in the form of a disjunction.[10]

Putnam takes the Ukuk problem to show that inductive reasoning cannot be formalized in the absence of formalizing all of human nature. He thus makes a strong claim that inductive reasoning involves formalizing our entire conception of what it is to be a human being. (I will return to this claim in item vi below, where I will discuss Vico's notion of humanity and its connection with rational interpretation$_1$.) "I don't believe," Putnam writes, "that as a child I had any idea how often either of the conflicting regularities ... had been confirmed, but I would have known enough not to make the silly induction that Ukuk would stop being able to speak Inuit if he entered a building ... where no one had spoken Inuit ... it is not clear that the knowledge that one doesn't lose a language just like that is something we have an innate propensity to believe. The question that will not go away is *how much of what we call intelligence presupposes the rest of human nature.*"[11]

Ukuk is just one example of a general problem that some have characterized as a version of the frame problem: How do we acquire certain beliefs about the world that are not transparently beliefs that we were taught (for example, by someone else or by reading) or beliefs that are easily inferable from other beliefs? Typically, these beliefs are so commonsensical that they defy our efforts to explain their origins. No one taught us that great flaming pits do not materialize in thin air when we walk through our house, that hippopotami do not wear black lace stockings in the wild, or that East Orange was not nuked yesterday. How, then, do we acquire these beliefs? That is the problem. Putnam makes the point that there is no obvious way of telling whether the belief that one does not lose one's language when one enters a building is the product of an induction or is an innate belief. If we do not know how we acquire these beliefs, then we do not know how to formalize inductive reasoning, since we do not know how to formalize the adjudication of conflicting inductions (in virtue of our not knowing what the adjudication mechanism consists in).

Stalnaker's Point about Implicit Beliefs

In his article "The Problem of Logical Omniscience, I," Robert Stalnaker asserts that implicit beliefs are hard to characterize theoretically.[12] Are they beliefs that one has inferred from other beliefs physically stored in one's cognitive database, or are they beliefs that are stored in one's cognitive database and that are directly accessed? Stalnaker cannot see how cognitive science distinguishes these two possibilities. If there is, in principle, no way of explaining the cognitive mechanism by which these beliefs become explicit to the conscious mind, then cognitive science fails to explain a fundamental aspect of higher-order cognition.

Stalnaker's point about implicit beliefs does not indict computationalism. It is a call to philosophers and cognitive scientists to get clear about what is meant by a belief being implicit. If the notion of an implicit belief cannot be clarified, we shall have to reconsider whether to continue using it as an explanatory construct. Suppose that Putnam's cognitive-holism question ("how much of what we call intelligence presupposes the rest of human nature") derives from the Ukuk problem, because, given that there are different competing mechanisms for making implicit beliefs explicit, there is no way of telling what the true mechanism is without having a satisfactory definition of what is an implicit belief. This would not show that formalizing inductive reasoning depends on formalizing the rest of human nature. It would show that determining what is the true mechanism for forming explicit beliefs from implicit beliefs can't be done until we are clear about what we mean by an implicit belief. But that has nothing to do with formalizing inductive reasoning. Perhaps Ukuk is a problem only because we are not clear about what we mean by an implicit belief and because we are not clear we have not yet discovered the true mechanism by which implicit beliefs become explicit.

Ukuk, Inductive Reasoning, and Fodor's Version of the Frame Problem

Recall that for Putnam "the notions of being justified or warranted or reasonable belief" cannot be given a computational reductive analysis, because such an "algorithm would have to be as complex as a description of the 'general intelligence' of an idealized inductive judge."[13] Formalizing rational interpretation$_1$ is roughly equivalent to formalizing general intelligence, and that is roughly equivalent to formalizing inductive reasoning. Fodor has argued that the general intelligence needed to solve a version of the frame problem is just inductive reasoning—i.e., that a solution to the problem of formalizing general intelligence is a solution to the problem of formalizing inductive reasoning. In an important and neglected paper titled "Modules, Frames, Sleeping Dogs, and the Music of the Spheres," Fodor argues convincingly that frame problems are just the problem of induction "writ large."[14]

If we accept Fodor's claim, then the problem of whether any one of the family of notions consisting of general intelligence, rational interpretation$_1$, and reasonable reasoning can be formalized reduces to the question of whether inductive reasoning can be formalized. (I have already argued this, and it is implicit in *R&R* that this is so, but it is good to have an independent argument for the claim.) More important, if we conceive of the Ukuk problem as a frame problem, then showing that the frame problem cannot be formalized also shows that inductive reasoning cannot be formalized. Conversely, showing that the frame problem can be formalized also shows that inductive reasoning can be formalized. Lastly, showing that arguments that the frame problem cannot be formalized are bad arguments also shows that those arguments cannot be used to show that inductive reasoning can't be formalized.

It is easy to conceive of the Ukuk problem as a frame problem. We would like to show that certain truths persist even when the local environment changes. We would like to show that Ukuk does not lose the ability to speak Inuit when he enters Emerson Hall for the first time (and his location in his local environment changes). One version of the frame problem is how we determine that certain truths persist through local environmental changes. For instance, how do we determine that our address does not change when we retrieve our mail from our mailbox? In the paper cited above, Fodor argues that well-known solutions to this version of the frame problem do not work. One solution is known as the *sleeping-dogs strategy*. The basic idea is that one lets sleeping dogs sleep. How this advice can be fashioned into a formal tool is another matter. But Fodor contrives a property that resists the strategy: the fridgeon property. Something is a fridgeon at a given time if and only if Fodor's refrigerator is running at that time. This means that everything is a fridgeon when Fodor's refrigerator is running. Fridgeons suggest endless possibilities for things that change when events occur. Given any event whatsoever, everything changes when that event occurs. Since events are always occurring, everything is always changing. There are no sleeping dogs. The question is "On what grounds do we declare fridgeons to be illegitimate properties?" The fridgeon problem is closely related to Goodman's grue problem.

Fodor expresses pessimism that there are any forthcoming solutions to this version of the frame problem, for it is just the problem of induction.

Below I will look at some of the work that has been done in providing formal solutions to the frame problem. I will contend that there are promising avenues of work that Putnam will have to refute.

Method of Refutation: Push the Burden of Proof onto Putnam
There is a large body of literature—spanning the disciplines of philosophy, statistics, cognitive science, economics, artificial intelligence, computer science, and mathematics—on how to provide a formalization of inductive reasoning, either in part or in whole. For instance, in the literature on

non-monotonic reasoning (which formalizes inductive reasoning) one finds several competing models: different kinds of default reasoning, autoepistemic reasoning, different kinds of circumscription, closed-world assumptions, conditional logics, KLM (Krauss-Lehmann-Magidor) logics, and more. These formalizations of inductive reasoning supply structural syntactical principles that must be critically evaluated by anyone who claims there is no formalization of inductive reasoning.

In *Reason, Truth and History* Putnam claims that even if Bayesianism is an adequate computational account of belief revision (revising ones beliefs in the light of new information, which is reflected in the probability conditionals), there is no computational account of how we arrive at our initial probability estimates—that is, our "priors."[15] But Putnam's argument that inductive reasoning can't be formalized is circular: Inductive reasoning can't be formalized because there is no formalization of a prior probability metric, and there is no formalization of the prior probability metric since setting it up requires rational interpretation$_1$. But there is no formalization of rational interpretation$_1$ because there is no formalization of inductive reasoning. To break out of the circle, we need either a mathematical proof that the prior probability metric can be formalized or a mathematical proof that it cannot be formalized. For example, there is an interesting mathematical relationship between entrenchment orderings (priors, in Bayesian terminology) and revision/contraction functions that provide structural properties for belief revision (that is, for both expanding and contracting a set of beliefs).

Suppose there is a mathematical account of how we get a prior probability metric. What are the possible intentional-level consequences of such striking relationships? Structural relationships of this kind might explain, in new and startling ways (because it is a computational explanation where we least expect it) what to our eyes appear to be "the rest of human nature" or "what it is to be human." If you eschew such data, you cannot claim to have a winning hand in the mechanism dialectic. In particular, you cannot assert that there is no formalization of inductive reasoning.[16]

One thing we learn from frame problems is that solutions to them reveal how to collapse an infinite or infeasibly long list into a finite list or a small set of finitary rules. The first formulation of a frame problem, by John McCarthy and Patrick Hayes, dates from the late 1960s.[17] The problem is as follows: When we perform an action, some things change as a result of that action, but most things do not change. If we axiomatize the theory of actions and express the consequences of an action as what can be derived in first-order logic from the action axioms, all we have done is state explicitly what changes when an action occurs. But how do we prove statements about what does not change? Typically, an action axiom explicitly lists all the consequences of an action. Does that mean that we will have to list all the non-changes explicitly in order to reason about what does and does not change when we perform an action? That is infeasible. Solving the McCarthy-Hayes frame problem amounts to finding an axiomatization of action theory that allows us to infer by a finitary rule of inference, within some non-monotonic logic, what does not change when an action occurs. To solve this frame problem, McCarthy devised a formal mode of inference known as *circumscription*. This formal tool is a way of condensing a vast set of data into a finitary rule. Any one who claims that inductive reasoning cannot be formalized must critically examine the varieties of circumscription.

An Example from Computational Game Theory in Economics

Given the connection between rational interpretation$_1$ and inductive reasoning, we can also look at attempts to show human rationality cannot be formalized. Putnam criticizes the von Neumann-Morgenstern framework of expected utility theory (with its guiding idea that rationality is to be construed in terms of maximizing expected utility) and implies that the failure of that framework to capture human rationality is a symptom of a general malady: that there is no formal framework that can capture human rationality.[18] Much work has been done in this area since the 1950s, when the first cracks in the von Neumann-Morgenstern framework—the ones that Putnam cites as pointers to the general malady—were made by Daniel Ellsberg, Maurice Allais, and others. This is work that Putnam must examine.

The field of computable game theory has undergone explosive growth since 1985. For instance, Luca Anderlini and Hamid Sabourian have shown that under certain computability assumptions cooperation between agents is the only possible outcome of infinitely repeated games, and that under other computability conditions cooperation is the only way to secure a maximal payoff in finitely repeated games (even though there are other equilibrium conditions besides cooperation for those finitely repeated games).[19] We get computable constraints on cooperation, and perhaps we can define rationality in these terms, since it achieves a maximal payoff. We might also investigate how cooperation and maximal payoff can occur when we discount beliefs across and within linguistic communities. The point is that the literature on computational game theory, in addition to that on non-monotonic reasoning, can't be ignored in making arguments that inductive reasoning cannot be formalized and that human rationality cannot be formalized. The burden of proof shifts onto Putnam's shoulders. Not only must he show that the work in philosophy, economics, statistics, cognitive science, artificial intelligence, computer science, and mathematics does not show that inductive reasoning can be formalized; he also must show that it cannot, in principle, be formalized.

(iii) Quinean indeterminacy proves that rational interpretation$_1$ cannot be formalized

I addressed Quinean indeterminacy in chapter 6. There I argued that there is no reason to think that Quinean indeterminacy creates an asymmetry between rational interpretation$_1$ and algorithms for rational interpretation$_1$. Putnam contends that rational interpretation$_1$ can be used to determine what kind of world a human agent occupies: the standard model or a non-standard model. I argued that rational-interpretation$_1$ algorithms can be used to do the same thing.

Putnam uses Quinean indeterminacy to argue that rational interpretation$_1$ can't be formalized. "Neither Quine nor Chomsky," he writes, "expects *mechanical translation* to succeed. That is, neither Quine nor Chomsky expects us to find a set of criteria which will function as an *algorithm* to determine when one has correctly translated an expression of one language into another language. The idea that *interpretive rationality can be fully exhausted by a finite set of criteria that we will actually succeed in writing down* is utopian on its face. But this is what Quine is ... demanding—that we succeed in writing down such a set of criteria—before he will accept that we have succeeded in rationally reconstructing the notion of synonymy."[20]

My first response to Putnam's original reading of Quinean indeterminacy is that if rational interpretation$_1$ can be used to sidestep indeterminacy—as Putnam says it does—then it cannot consist in the application of a finite set of criteria. If the point secured by indeterminacy is that mechanical translation cannot consist in a finite set of criteria—and thus there is no finitary algorithm for mechanical translation—then that point applies to formalized rational interpretation$_1$ and to non-formalized rational interpretation$_1$. Recall that rational interpretation$_2$ depends on a definition of synonymy and of coreferentiality. That is why, if formalized, the algorithm for it is infinitary. But rational interpretation$_2$ unformalized cannot consist in a finite set of criteria. We can arrive at that view in two different ways. The first is that it depends on a definition of synonymy, and a theory of synonymy is a theory of all possible discourses. The second is indeterminacy.[21]

Indeterminacy applies equally well to rational interpretation$_1$. But rational interpretation$_1$ does not depend on a definition of synonymy. Nonetheless, by indeterminacy, neither formalized rational interpretation$_1$ nor unformalized rational interpretation$_1$ can consist in a finite set of criteria. Thus, an algorithm for rational interpretation$_1$ is infinitary, and the cognitive skill of rational interpretation$_1$ must involve infinitary cognitive capacities. But we do not have infinitary capacities. Thus, we cannot engage in rational interpretation$_1$, nor is there a finitary algorithm for it. As a consequence, Putnam cannot use Quinean indeterminacy to conclude that rational interpretation$_1$ can't be formalized. If he does, then he must agree that unformalized rational interpretation$_1$ involves infinitary capacities. In that case, it is rational interpretation$_2$. (Neither can he use it to conclude rational interpretation$_2$ can't be formalized, for the same reason.) Thus, either Putnam's original reading of Quinean indeterminacy is wrong or else there is a problem in the conception of rational interpretation$_1$.

A second response to Putnam's reading of Quinean indeterminacy is tentative. Suppose that we intend to add two positive integers. Kripke has shown there are no facts about our mental life and no criteria that single out addition from quaddition (and a host of other non-standard arithmetical functions).[22] Consider an algorithm for addition. Nothing in my mental life nor any criteria determine that my intentions single out this algorithm. But the algorithm provides precise criteria for addition. Consider an algorithm for quaddition. Nothing in my mental life nor any criteria determine that my intentions single out this algorithm. It, however, provides precise criteria for quaddition. That I cannot intend the addition algorithm over the quaddition algorithm does not mean that addition and quaddition cannot be formalized.

Consider algorithms for rational interpretation$_1$. There is nothing in my mind nor any criteria that determine that my intentions single out rational-interpretation$_1$ algorithms from non-standard rational-interpretation$_1$ algorithms. Similarly, there is nothing in my mind nor any criteria that determine that my intentions single out some non-standard rational-interpretation$_1$ algorithm from standard rational-interpretation$_1$ algorithms. But this is not a reason to think that rational interpretation$_1$ cannot be formalized. If it were, then it would also be a reason to think that addition cannot be formalized.

If we align Kripke's skeptical problem with Quinean indeterminacy, then we do not take the indeterminacy of sentences about addition in different languages to show that addition cannot be formalized. Moreover, arithmetic with addition—and no other arithmetical operations—is not sufficient for Gödelian incompleteness. But if it is true that addition cannot be formalized, then we get, by an analogue, the equivalent of the Gödel results in much weaker systems than Peano arithmetic! In fact, we get more. If addition is not formalizable, there are *no* truths of arithmetic that are provable, since there is no formal system in which we can erect proofs of those truths. (This is a somewhat loose way of talking. If addition over the counting numbers can't be formalized, we can't speak of a Gödel sentence for it, since a Gödel sentence only arises in a *formalized* system.)

The point is that Putnam's reading of Quinean indeterminacy has an absurd consequence, which is a *reductio* of it. Indeterminacy does not demonstrate that rational interpretation$_1$ can't be formalized. It only shows it is open to multiple readings (in the absence of additional knowledge, such as knowledge of which world—or model—we occupy). This second response to Putnam's reading is tenuous, since it depends on connecting Quinean indeterminacy with Kripke's skeptical problem. Kripke makes the connection, but not in the way it is done here.

(iv) Vico's view of rational interpretation$_1$ implies that formalizing it requires formalizing our entire conception of what it is to be a human being and that cannot be formalized

Putnam points out that rational interpretation$_1$ is holistic and that this view is echoed by Giambattista Vico: "As Vico put it, in interpretation we seek to maximize the *humanity* of the beings being translated. If this right, then the only criteria that we actually have for the 'content' of any signs, or sign-analogs, are our intuitive criteria of successful interpretation; and to *formalize* these would involve formalizing our entire conception of what it is to be human, of what it is to be intelligible in human terms."[23] What is our conception of what it is to be human? Here is a connection: "... the point is that *every* project for analyzing the notion of *interpretation* sooner or later involves recognizing that the analysis of the notion of interpretation is inseparable from the analysis of either the normative notion of rationality, or from some such notion as Vico's 'humanity'."[24]

I read the 'or' in the last quotation as meaning that the second notion (Vico's humanity) is the same kind of notion as the first (a normative notion of rationality). If so, we can speak of the normative notion of rationality and dispense with talk of formalizing our conception of what it is to be human. But does the functionalist gain anything in doing this? Putnam does not think so. His view is that "the theory of rationality is not separable from our ultimate theories about the nature of the things that make up both ourselves and the domains being investigated and ... even in a restricted domain, for example physics, nothing like precise laws which will decide what is and is not a reasonable inference or a justified belief are to be hoped for."[25]

It is rational interpretation$_1$ or general intelligence or reasonable reasoning that issues in reasonable inferences. If we have a formalization of any of these, then we have a formalization of rationality. Similarly, justified beliefs are beliefs that are rationally acceptable to us. In discussing his epistemic conception of truth, Putnam takes truth to be idealized warranted acceptability. But the notions 'rationally acceptable belief', 'warranted acceptable belief', and 'justified belief' come to the same thing. Each of these kinds of beliefs involves the exercise of rationality. Moreover, this exercise of rationality is the exercise of rational interpretation$_1$, of general intelligence or of reasonable reasoning. But in that case, determining that rational interpretation$_1$ cannot be formalized must involve more than just saying that rationality cannot be formalized or that reasonable reasoning cannot be formalized or.... Those kinds of arguments are circular. They have the form

P _____ cannot be formalized.
_____
C Rational interpretation$_1$ cannot be formalized.

Here the blank in the premise is filled in with one of the notions from the family of notions involving interpretation: general intelligence, reasonable reasoning, and so on. Here is a substitution instance of the above form.

P Reasonable reasoning cannot be formalized.
_____
C Rational interpretation$_1$ cannot be formalized.

Thus, if we have an argument that reasonable reasoning cannot be formalized, then we have an argument that rational interpretation$_1$ cannot be formalized. Suppose that it is objected that the notions in the family are distinct and cannot be identified. In that case, the above form is invalid. But in that case, for each one of the notions it must be argued *sui generis* that the notion cannot be formalized.

One way Putnam argues that inductive reasoning cannot be formalized is by arguing that rationality cannot be formalized and that the notion of rationality is necessary for any kind of inductive reasoning. But this argument requires that we can successfully argue the case that rationality cannot be formalized. If the argument proceeds by arguing that inductive reasoning cannot be formalized, it is circular. As we saw above, one way of arguing that inductive reasoning cannot be formalized is to argue that the notion of a prior probability metric that is reasonable or of a notion of projectibility of predicates that is reasonable cannot be formalized. But these notions can't be formalized because rationality can't be formalized. This reasoning is circular.[26]

If the case against computational functionalism depends on whether we can formalize our intuitive judgments about what is a reasonable prior probability metric or our intuitive judgments that privilege the predicate green over the predicate grue, then it is weak. Indeed, what do our intuitive judgments that a prior probability metric is reasonable employ? Certainly, reasonable reasoning or any of the other notions in the family. But then the question becomes "Is there an argument that reasonable reasoning cannot be formalized?"

Even worse, it is circular to argue in the following way: Inductive reasoning is necessary for rational interpretation, and the former cannot be formalized because there is no formalization of prior probability metrics. The reason why the latter cannot be formalized is that they involve rational interpretation and it cannot be formalized. This type of argument is circular, but Putnam appears to make it. Simply by bringing in such things as prior probability metrics does not provide an escape from the circle of notions, since it is necessarily tied to one or more of the notions in that circle. The effect of appealing to prior probability metrics, or to predicate projectiblity, is to enlarge the circle, but not to find a way out of it. If there is a mathematical theorem (that gives us mathematical certainty) that there is no formalization of prior probability metrics *and* that does not appeal to notions like reasonableness or rationality, then there is a way out of the circle. But now there are no such theorems.

I conclude that there is nothing special about the argument against the formalization of rational interpretation$_1$ from Vico's notion of what it is to be a human being. Since what it is to be human just is what it is to be rational, and what it is to be rational belongs to the family that includes rational interpretation$_1$, reasonable reasoning, and general intelligence, it is a fallacy of reasoning to assume one of the notions is non-formalizable in order to argue that one of the other notions in the family is also non-formalizable. The argument from Vico's notion of what it is to be human is not a new argument for the claim that rational interpretation$_1$ is non-formalizable.

(v) Radical Quinean meaning holism is sidestepped by general intelligence which cannot be formalized and which is equivalent to rational interpretation₁

We have already seen the use Putnam makes of general intelligence in his discussion of the Bohr electron case. General intelligence is closely related to rational interpretation₁, if not identical with it. One way this kind of argument against the formalization of rational interpretation₁ goes is to make that identification and then argue that general intelligence cannot be formalized. We have already considered the frame problem, which is used as evidence for the claim that general intelligence cannot be formalized. But this is not a conclusive refutation, since there are different views about what the frame problem consists in and there has been a great deal of work in the artificial intelligence community on ways to formalize the commonsense reasoning or general intelligence that is needed to solve a frame problem.

Anyone who argues that general intelligence cannot be formalized must work through this vast corpus of material and argue that none of the proposed formal solutions to the frame problem actually work. Furthermore, Fodor has argued that a version of the frame problem is the problem of how to formalize inductive reasoning. If he is right about this version of the frame problem, then the question is "Can we formalize inductive reasoning?" This is the question I considered above. In short, there is no new argument for the non-formalizability of rational interpretation₁ in the appeal to general intelligence.

(vi) Rational interpretation₁ is global and computations are local

Let us examine Putnam's argument that rational interpretation₁ is necessarily global and computations are necessarily local and thus rational interpretation₁ cannot be formalized because the globality property is non-formalizable. Be warned that 'local' and 'global' are not used to describe properties of computational reductions. The argument occupies a short paragraph in "Computational Psychology and Interpretation Theory." I have not seen it elsewhere in Putnam's writings. I call it GLOBAL1, and I quote it in full here:

The difference between functionalist psychology and interpretation theory is in part due to this: functionalist psychology treats the human mind as a computer. It seeks to state the rules of computation. The rules of computation have the property that although their interactions may be complicated and global, their action at any particular time is local. The machine, as it might be, moves a digit from one address to another address in obedience to a particular instruction, or to finitely many instructions, and on the basis of a finite amount of data. [This is just Turing's conditions on what a computor (Turing's term for a human making a computation) is allowed to do when computing a computable function.—JB] Interpretation is never local in this sense. A translation scheme, however well it works on a finite amount of corpus, may always have to be modified on the basis of additional text.[27]

Putnam defines the term 'global' in his criticism of Hartry Field's attempt to give a physicalist reduction of reference. Any physicalist definition of reference, he tells us, will "involve *interpreting the language as a whole* and not just individual signs (since what constitutes an interpretation of a theory that makes the theory rationally acceptable depends on looking at the *whole* theory), and is a relation whose very definition involves an analysis of rationality in its normative sense."[28]

Globality requires we look at the whole theory, not just at subparts of it expressed by individual sentences, or even individual signs, because we can't determine the objects a scientist is referring to without knowing what she *should* be referring to if her theory of those objects is to be epistemically acceptable and also a rational approximation to the truth. But we can't determine what she should be referring to without looking at the entire theory. Putnam takes it that explicating the normative 'should' requires one to provide an analysis of rationality in its normative sense. He elaborates what that analysis consists in. I call it GLOBAL2, and I quote in full here:

The reason that partial successes in interpretation theory are always so limited is that any global success, any program for interpretation of sentences in a variable language, a variable theory, on variable topics and with variable presuppositions, would involve an analysis of the notion of humanity, or of the notion (which in my view is closely related) of rationality. The function of limiting interpretation to a specific frame is to avoid having to tackle the totally utopian project of algorithmic analysis of these notions.[29]

It is disappointing how GLOBAL2 defines 'global'. The primary reason for this reaction is that we have already seen that Ugly Duckling Theorems can be used to show that globality in this sense is incoherent at worst and at best inconsistent with facts about ourselves (such as that there are languages that are unlearnable by human beings). But another reason is that this notion of global leaves it open that it can be computably realized. That is, Putnam must show that there is no formalization of the generality constraint or that there is no formalization of rational interpretation$_1$. If the latter is the case, there is no argument employing the notion of globality that can be non-circularly used to show rational interpretation$_1$ cannot be formalized. All we have is that there is no computational realization of globality (in the sense of GLOBAL2) because rational interpretation$_1$ cannot be formalized. But this cannot be used to show that rational interpretation$_1$ cannot be formalized! If the former is the case, then there is no argument that rational interpretation$_1$ cannot be formalized, because rational interpretation$_1$ itself had better not satisfy the generality constraint.

GLOBAL1 provides a different kind of definition of 'global': one based on the structure of computation. The basic idea is that computations are local because they cannot attend to information that is not immediately being "scanned." A Turing machine cannot attend to a '1' inscribed on a tape cell that is not now being scanned. A digital computer executing a sequential program (a non-parallel, non-distributed program) cannot attend to the contents of register j if it is now attending to the contents of register k. How should we define the contrasting term 'global'? Is it to mean that the digital computer can access multiple registers at the same time or that the Turing machine can scan multiple tape cells at the same time? Or is it to mean that the Turing machine can scan any tape cells, though not at the same time? Let us first define global in GLOBAL1 in the first sense: scanning multiple registers at the same time. Call this 'simultaneous multiple register accessing'. The problem is then one of simultaneous multiple register accessing.

Is the globality of rational interpretation$_1$ an ability to access multiple types of information? In rational interpretation$_1$ do we access all the information in our heads at the same time? Kantian syntheses work only for single objects. Should we expect that there is a Kantian synthesis of all available information in our heads when we rationally interpret$_1$ a discourse?[30]

If simultaneous multiple register accessing is what Putnam means by 'global', he encounters a serious difficulty. The problem of simultaneous multiple register accessing does not arise in computer architectures that allow parallel or distributed computations. In a parallel computation or in a distributed computation, two different registers are accessed at the same time, though by two different processors. At some point in a parallel computation, the information from two different processors is examined by a single processor. In a distributed computation, one processor A tells another processor B that it has finished doing task k and that the results of doing k can now be used by B. It does not matter whether we individuate the state of a parallel computation at a time when there are multiple processors executing instructions as a single state or as multiple states of the computation, since the latter set of states can be computably partitioned into a single state.

Suppose that the architecture of human cognition is parallel. Even if in a parallel machine we say that at a time there is a single global state of accessing several registers, do we say the same for the human mind modeled as a parallel processor? What motivates the decision as to how we individuate accessing states (or scanning states in Turing machines)? Is it mere stipulation? Or is it either philosophically motivated or motivated by cognitive science concerns? If the latter, whose concerns are taken as primary and why? The point is that there are a host of difficult questions waiting to be addressed by anyone who uses the GLOBAL1 definitions of 'local' and 'global'. Putnam must address them if he is to avail himself of arguing for the non-formalizability of rational interpretation using the GLOBAL1 definitions of 'global' and 'local'. Precisely defining 'accesses register . . .' and 'at the same time' (in the definition of simultaneous multiple register accessing) for both digital computers and human beings is where the real problems are located.

The problem for the argument against formalizability of rational interpretation₁ from the locality of computations is that GLOBAL1 definitions of locality do not provide a precise notion of locality in the context of computational functionalism. We will have to make difficult decisions about how to analyze the notion of locality as it applies to computationally reduced intentional states in such a way that we do not beg questions. But GLOBAL2 definitions fare even worse. They do not prohibit global computations, for one. But the other shortcoming is that they appeal to a normative notion of rationality and thus beg the question for the claim that rational interpretation₁ can't be formalized. GLOBAL2 analyzes the notion of globality as it figures in rational interpretation₁, while GLOBAL1 analyzes the notion of locality as it figures in computations. But GLOBAL2 does not provide a definition of locality as it figures in computations and GLOBAL1 does not provide a notion of globality as it figures in rational interpretation₁. There is a severe mismatch between the two definitions and for each definition, a serious lacuna.

Globality can be computationally cheaper than locality

Another definition of globality, one not considered by Putnam, is that global properties are defined over part or all of a computational system (taken at some level of abstraction). For instance, the number of registers in a computational system is a global property, since the entire computational system, considered from the hardware point of view, must be surveyed in arriving at an answer. The hard work will be in defining what a part of a computational system is, that naturally differentiates local and global surveys of the system. Given a solution to this problem, we could define GLOBAL1 globality in terms of this definition. I call this definition GLOBAL3.

One view is that global properties cost more to use in energy (or resources) than local properties. Perhaps one way of distinguishing rational interpretation$_1$ in global terms from local computations is that the former costs much more than the latter. The argument for the non-formalizability of rational interpretation$_1$ would go as follows: It is too expensive to implement rational interpretation$_1$ computationally, since it is a global property of any computational system. Local properties are less expensive, but rational interpretation$_1$ is not local and thus not formalizable, since the costs are so high that no human cognitive system could pay for them. I conjecture that this is an intuitively plausible way of how Putnam's argument in "Computational Psychology and Interpretation Theory" might go, given that the GLOBAL1 and GLOBAL2 definitions fail to secure his conclusion that rational interpretation$_1$ is non-formalizable. Since computationally infeasible algorithms are psychologically unrealistic, rational interpretation$_1$ is not formalizable, in the sense that there are no psychologically realistic algorithms for it.

Unfortunately, this kind of argument fails, in two different ways. First, problems that can only be solved by an algorithm that requires a large amount of resources to execute the computation typically possess a combinatorial property that accounts for the costliness of the computations. If a rational-interpretation$_1$ algorithm is computationally expensive, then *any* method for solving the problem will be as expensive, since any means of solving the problem must confront the intrinsic combinatorial property that makes solving the problem so prohibitively expensive. Second, in the literature there are technical results on GLOBAL3 definitions of 'local' and 'global' demonstrating global properties are computationally less expensive than local properties. For example, in their paper "Default Theories That Always Have Extensions," Christos Papadimitriou and Martha Sideri prove mathematically that for a special kind of default theory—a Krom default theory—it is computationally intractable (i.e., is an NP-complete problem) to determine that it has an extension.[31] That is, it is NP-complete to determine whether the Krom default theory provides a solution to a default problem.

Papadimitriou and Sideri contrast Krom default theories with theories for which the extension problem is computationally tractable—that is, is a problem in P, which is the class of tractable computational problems. They show that even severe 'local' restrictions on the syntax of the defaults in a Krom default theory do not ameliorate the NP complexity of the extension problem. However, GLOBAL3 global properties of graphs, such as the evenness or the orderability of the graph reduce the complexity of the extension problem to P. The point in considering GLOBAL3 globality and locality is that it appears to be the only definition that bridges the gap between locality in the context of computations and globality in the context of rational interpretation$_1$. It does this by using a notion of energy expense—that is, computational resources. But this move will not get Putnam any closer to his desired conclusion that rational interpretation$_1$ cannot be formalized.

There might be an argument that rational interpretation$_1$ can't be formalized using the idea of a distinction between local and global properties, but three obvious candidates for how to define the distinction fail to secure that argument. The burden of proof is on Putnam's shoulders to find a definition of local and global properties that does the work he wants.

(vii) Twin-Earth-style arguments show that rational interpretation$_1$ cannot be formalized

Twin-Earth-style arguments for non-formalizability of rational interpretation$_1$ are Putnam's invention, as are his Twin-Earth arguments for distinguishing narrow and wide mental content. His Ruritania argument shows that on a functionalist model of the mind, meaning-constituting beliefs cannot be distinguished from auxiliary beliefs. But if rational interpretation$_1$ can be used to make that distinction, then it follows that functionalist models of the mind cannot formalize rational interpretation$_1$. As we have already seen, the functionalist model Putnam employs in the Ruritania argument is so impoverished that it is scarcely credible anyone would think computational functionalism is thereby indicted. Moreover, one cannot conclude from the failure of one functionalist model to formalize rational interpretation$_1$ that all functionalist models can't formalize rational interpretation$_1$.

Why does Putnam think the Ruritania case shows that rational interpretation$_1$ cannot be formalized? He contends that the information provided by narrow mental contents is insufficient to make decisions about sameness of mental content unless it is augmented with the information that the terms about which the decisions have to be made either have the same mental content or not. That is, narrow mental content can't be used to determine that two terms are synonymous unless it is already known that they are synonymous. The Ruritania argument shows that this is so:

"It may be possible to give a complete functionalist psychology . . . without in any way solving the problem of interpretation or even the problem of . . . assignment of extensions. To have a description of how a system of representations works in functionalist terms is one thing; to have an *interpretation* of that system of representations is quite another thing."[32]

The Ruritanian word 'grug' means aluminum in southern Ruritania and silver in northern Ruritania. At some point, two speakers of Ruritanian, one of whom lives in the north and the other in the south, will mean different things by their use of the word 'grug'. But does rational interpretation$_1$ have access to the information needed to distinguish the wide mental contents of these two speakers? If it does not, how can it be used to show that the wide contents of northern and southern speakers using 'grug' differ? If the method of rational interpretation$_1$ has access to wide content information, it can distinguish the contents. Similarly, if a functionalist model has access to wide content information, it can distinguish the contents. The functionalist model that Putnam uses is deficient, for it has no access to information about the environment and thus no access to information needed to determine the extension of the word 'grug'. Its only reasoning ability is Bayesian updating of probabilities of its beliefs. Is it any wonder that it cannot assign an extension to the word 'grug'?

If you take away information about an agent's local environment, use an impoverished computational model of that agent, and then argue that the failure of the model to determine that 'grug' has changed its meaning over time in the mouth of an agent who lives in a certain part of Ruritania implies the inability of the model to distinguish meaning-constituting from auxiliary beliefs and consequently that it fails to formalize rational interpretation$_1$, you have only imposed avoidable handicaps on the computationalist. Give the model access to information about its local environment and give it reasoning abilities, and then see if the conclusion follows. The burden of proof is on Putnam's shoulders to show that it does. Putnam's claim that functionalism and rational interpretation$_1$ are incommensurate—that they have nothing to do with one another—also rides on the Ruritania argument. If that argument fails, then an important plank on which the incommensurability thesis rests is destroyed.

(viii) The infection problem for stereotypes shows that rational interpretation$_1$ cannot be formalized

One proposal Putnam has made for going about synonymy determination is to look at the extensions of terms and their correlated stereotypes. The latter are beliefs that all speakers are expected, though not normatively required, to have about a given word. He provides some compelling counterexamples to the claim that sameness of stereotype is necessary for the sameness of mental content. Attempts to explain away the counterexamples only reveal the magnitude of the what Putnam calls "the infection problem." Two different speakers may have the same perceptual prototype (which is a certain kind of stereotype) for grass, but may differ so much in other ways that it would be a mistake to say that they have the same mental content for grass. For instance, one speaker might have been raised in a place where all grass is synthetic, though visually indistinguishable from real grass.

One proposed remedy is to employ additional information to that of the perceptual prototypes, such as what Putnam calls "markers": the information that grass is a plant. But now we must determine when the two speakers have the same stereotype for plant. We began by asking what is the stereotype for grass and now we need to ask what is the stereotype for plant. This is the infection problem. In short, no matter what information—in the form of beliefs, linguistically expressed—is used to break the regress, that information will only continue the regress. The infection keeps spreading throughout the belief systems of the two speakers, but only if it is required that there are precise criteria that settle whether a word used in the mouths of each speaker has the same stereotype, and so has the same mental content (on the view that word synonymy is determined by extension and stereotype).

"In actual *interpretation*," Putnam says, "our policy is not to let infection go very far; i.e., for the purposes of deciding that [two speakers—JB] have the same notion of grass we may require that they both believe that grass is a plant *without* requiring that their notion of a plant be exactly the same. But this is already to accept the stance that interpretation is an essentially informal and interest-relative matter."[33]

The infection problem is really a problem about how to discount beliefs, which, in turn, is the problem of distinguishing meaning-constituting beliefs from auxiliary beliefs. Does it provide a new argument for the nonformalizability of rational interpretation$_1$? That rational interpretation$_1$ is essentially informal is a strong claim that does not follow from the infection problem. The reason why this is so is that Putnam thinks rational interpretation$_1$ can be used to distinguish meaning-constituting beliefs from auxiliary beliefs (though not infallibly) and can thus be used to solve the infection problem. But that does not show that rational interpretation$_1$

can't be formalized. It shows only that it is needed to solve the problem. If we stipulate that a solution to the infection problem is non-formalizable, we get the desired conclusion that rational interpretation$_1$, which is a solution to the infection problem, is non-formalizable. But this is not to make an argument for that claim; it is to get that claim by stipulation.

Appendix

The Form of an Algorithm for Rational Interpretation$_2$ as Demanded by EQUIVALENCE

EQUIVALENCE assumes that any algorithm for rational interpretation$_2$ must define synonymy and coreferentiality and that any definition of them must survey all possible theories of the universe and what is in it, all possible local physical environments, all possible modes of human reasoning and conceptualization, theories of human rationality, and more. But to make such a survey one must occupy an infinitary Archimedean point, and it is impossible for any finitary human being to do so. Thus, no human being could use or understand such an infinitary algorithm.

It is clear that normal human beings who successfully engage in rational interpretation$_1$ cannot make such a survey. It follows that rational interpretation$_1$ does not depend on a definition of synonymy and coreferentiality. Putnam contends that there is no algorithm for how we do it, because it involves (as do the related notions general intelligence and reasonable reasoning) inductive reasoning, which cannot be formalized. Given that inductive reasoning cannot be formalized, there is no algorithm for how we do rational interpretation$_1$. But that does not mean that there is no algorithm for how a god might do it. EQUIVALENCE shows how an algorithm for rational interpretation$_2$, which is for gods, looks. By "a god" we can mean a being that has the infinitary capacities needed to extensionally define synonymy and coreferentiality and/or can foresee the future. Another way of thinking about a god's algorithm for rational interpretation$_2$ is as a BLOCKHEAD algorithm: an infinite table listing every possible episode of rational interpretation$_2$, including episodes of rational interpretation$_2$ that have occurred, that will occur, and that never will occur. It is purely extensional. Thus, it provides a quasi-definition and not a genuine definition of synonymy and coreferentiality. Thus, it is a quasi-reduction of synonymy and coreferentiality and not a genuine reduction.

The following schema, which I call RATIONAL$_2$, lists the features that any infinitary algorithms for rational interpretation$_2$ must include:

Episode of rational interpretation$_2$ 1
Episode of rational interpretation$_2$ 2
$\vdots$
Episode of rational interpretation$_2$ n,

where each episode of rational interpretation calls up as subroutines schemata such as the following, which I call the TOTALITY SCHEMATA.

Examine possibly all the elements of the Cartesian product of
{all possible environments}
$\times$ {all possible theories—commonsense, scientific, philosophical, religious}
$\times$ {all possible societies}
$\times$ {all possible cultures}
$\times$ {all possible communities—which are subparts of societies which are not themselves societies}
$\times$ {for each i, all possible beliefs of the speaker$_i$}
$\times$ {for each j, all possible beliefs of members$_j$ (excluding speaker$_i$) of the linguistic community to which the speaker belongs}
$\times$ (for each k, j, all possible linguistic communities$_k$ and all possible beliefs of members$_j$ of linguistic community$_k$)
$\times$ {for each l, rationality type$_l$—where rationality types form a strict partial ordering from perfectly rational at one end to perfectly irrational at the other end}.

This schema for a god's rational-interpretation$_2$ algorithm must list all possible (actual and non-actual) episodes of rational interpretation$_2$. That is why Putnam says that using, constructing, or understanding it requires occupying an impossible infinitary Archimedean point. We cannot now know future episodes of rational interpretation$_2$ in societies whose modes of conceptualization are radically different from our own, nor can we know of possible but non-actual episodes in humanly possible but non-actual societies radically different from our own.

We can list the following initial segment of the function $f(x) = x^2$ (which is defined over the positive integers): 0, 1, 4, 9, 16, 25, 36, 49, 64, 81, 100. We know what the algorithm for computing that function looks like without having to continue listing the elements of the initial segment. On the other hand, we do not know what a god's algorithm for rational interpretation$_2$ looks like until we have completed listing all the elements of it—that is, until we have listed all present, past, and future episodes of rational interpretation$_2$. The reason we don't know what it looks like until we have done that is that there is no finite rule that will generate all the elements in the range of the rational-interpretation$_2$ function. That there is no finite rule to generate all the range elements is another way to express the conclusion of EQUIVALENCE. That is, if each episode of rational interpretation$_2$ is completely heterogeneous with respect to every other episode, there is no computable partitioning of episodes into a small set of equivalence classes.

Human beings living now (in 2007) cannot survey all future modes of linguistic existence, especially those which happen to transcend our own. "To ask a human being in a time-bound culture to survey all modes of linguistic existence—including those that will transcend his own—is to ask for an impossible Archimedean point."[34]

EQUIVALENCE and the Future of Cognitive Science

Let us suppose that EQUIVALENCE is sound. If so, it offers a troubling moral about the prospects of cognitive science. EQUIVALENCE argues that there can be no algorithm for rational interpretation$_2$, for to use the algorithm a human being needs infinitary capacities and to foresee the future of human existence.[35] Let us waive the requirement of infinitary capacities. Given that we can't foresee the future, in order to occupy an Archimedean point we would have to wait until all human existence had ceased.

Since we cannot now satisfy this requirement on using rational-interpretation$_2$ algorithms, we can't now describe a rational-interpretation$_2$ algorithm completely. Only at the end of human existence can that be done. This is not a claim that we will know that cognitive science is the correct theory of human cognition only when it is complete. Rather, it is a claim that cognitive science will become complete only after the end of human existence—only when the very last concrete episode of rational interpretation$_2$ has been added to the gigantic disjunctive list and there are no more that can be added. (The list is infinitary, but I waived the infinitary requirement in order to make my point.)

Since each concrete episode of rational interpretation$_2$ is *sui generis* and thus separate from every other concrete instance, the rational-interpretation$_2$ algorithm will not be complete until the last concrete episode is listed in it. EQUIVALENCE appears to be the only anti-functionalist argument (indeed, the only philosophical argument) that argues against computationalism (indeed, against any philosophical position) by asserting that we will not have a complete computationalist account of human cognition until after the end of human existence. Another way of making the same point is to say that cognitive science will not be complete until after all human life has ceased to exist.

Notes

Introduction

1. Hilary Putnam, "Minds and Machines," "Brains and Behavior," and "The Mental Life of Some Machines," in *Mind, Language, and Reality: Philosophical Papers, Volume 2* (Cambridge University Press, 1975).

2. Hilary Putnam, *Representation and Reality* (MIT Press, 1988). The book unites various ideas disseminated in talks, seminars, and papers in the early and mid 1980s. Participants in the talks and the seminars have told me that the manuscript was nearly complete during the summer of 1986, when Putnam hosted a National Endowment for the Humanities seminar in the philosophy of mind.

3. David Lewis was the first to articulate a local reduction response to the multi-realization argument. See his "Review of *Art, Mind and Religion*" (*Journal of Philosophy* 66, 1969: 23–35). Two subsequent important developments of local reductions are Berent Enc's "In Defense of the Identity Theory" (*Journal of Philosophy* 80, 1983: 279–298) and Jaegwon Kim's "The Myth of Nonreductive Materialism" (in *Supervenience and Mind* (Cambridge University Press, 1993)).

4. For a valuable and clear discussion of the different kinds of functionalism, see Jaegwon Kim, *Philosophy of Mind* (Westview, 1996).

5. Computational models are theoretical models of computations. The first computational model was the Turing machine. Invented by Alan Turing, it provided a mathematical answer to the question "What is it to compute a value of a function?" In early versions of computational functionalism, the computational model was either Turing machines, finite-state automata, probabilistic Turing machines, or probabilistic finite-state automata. These models are not used in cognitive psychology today, since they are psychologically unrealistic. Finite-state automata can't multiply, and Turing machines for even simple cognitive tasks (e.g., grammatically parsing sentences in natural languages) require too many internal computational states, violating the resource limitations of human minds.

6. David Lewis promoted this version of causal-theoretical functionalism. See his "Psychophysical and Theoretical Identifications," in *Readings in Philosophy of Psychology*, volume 1, ed. N. Block (Harvard University Press, 1980).

7. J. R. Lucas, "Minds, Machines and Gödel," *Philosophy* 36, 1961: 112–127.

8. There are two incompleteness theorems. The first says that there are truths of arithmetic that are not provable in a consistent first-order logic that can express arithmetic. The second says that a system of first-order logic that can express arithmetic cannot, if consistent, prove that it is consistent. The first theorem is an example of an independence proof. The truth of arithmetic cannot be proved in the system, nor can its negation. Gödel invented an ingenious coding method that coded the syntax of a formal system into arithmetical formulas. Using this method, formulas were able to refer to themselves. The unprovable Gödel sentence is a formula that says of itself that it is true but not provable. Mathematicians were not able to find a truth of arithmetic that was independent of first-order logic that could express arithmetic until the 1970s. Before that work, a philosopher might object to Lucas's argument by asserting that there are bizarre self-referential sentences that say they are unprovable truths but that there are no recognizable arithmetical truths they express. If that is so, then unprovable Gödel sentences are curiosities but are not worrisome for computationalists. The idea would be that the human mind does not deal with such curiosities, so it is not problematic that a Master Program of the human mind cannot prove them. (If the Second Incompleteness is appealed to, the previous worry disappears. The guiding idea is that if the program of the human mind can't be proved consistent, we have no rational grounds for accepting it as either a philosophical theory or a cognitive-science theory of the human mind.) Paris and Kirby showed in 1976 that an extension of the finite Ramsey Theorem is true but unprovable in that system. For an exposition of this work, see Jeff Paris and Leo Harrington, "A Mathematical Incompleteness in Peano Arithmetic," in *Handbook of Mathematical Logic*, ed. J. Barwise (North-Holland, 1977).

9. Roger Penrose, *The Emperor's New Mind* (Oxford University Press, 1986). This book spawned a cottage industry in how to use and misuse Gödel's theorems in philosophy. Penrose responded to much of this criticism in *Shadows of the Mind: A Search for the Missing Science of Consciousness* (Oxford University Press, 1994).

10. Hilary Putnam, "Review of Ernest Nagel and James R. Newman's *Gödel's Proof*," *Philosophy of Science* 27, 1960: 205–207; "Review of Roger Penrose's *Shadows of the Mind*," *Bulletin of the American Mathematical Society* 32, 1995: 370–373.

11. If a formal system is inconsistent, then any formula that is expressible in the formal language of the formal system can be proved in it. This is easy to show. An inconsistency has the form 'p and not-p', where p denotes any well-formed formula. By simplification, we get 'p'. By addition, we get 'p or q'. By simplification again, we get 'not-p'. By disjunctive syllogism, we get 'q'. This shows that it is important that a formal system or a computer program be consistent. But if either of them can express

arithmetic, it cannot prove that it is consistent if it is in fact consistent. That is what the Second Incompleteness Theorem tells us. That theorem makes more trouble for computationalism than the first one. If we cannot prove the consistency of a computer program for the human mind, we can't justify it as a computational description in cognitive science of how the human mind works. Similarly, we can't justify it as a philosophical description of the nature of the human mind. Moreover, unless it is shown or assumed the formal system that can express arithmetic is consistent, there is no Gödel sentence for it.

12. How long would it take a human being to visually scan every book in the Library of Congress? How long would it take a human being to carefully read every book in the Library of Congress? Suppose that the 3,348,992,922,557,457,576,868,687th line of code in the Master Program refers back to the 8,464,664,590,929,294,654th line of code. Would a human being find the connection? Suppose there are trillions of connections of this sort in the program. Would a human being find all of them?

13. See Putnam, "Reflexive Reflections," in *Words and Life* (Harvard University Press, 1994). Putnam's use of the Gödel theorems to refute computational functionalism first appeared in this paper. The paper, originally published in 1985, is based on a lecture Putnam gave in June 1984 at the annual meeting of the Society for Philosophy and Psychology, held at MIT.

14. Putnam, "Reflexive Reflections," in *Words and Life*.

15. Putnam, *Representation and Reality*, p. xv.

16. In proving his theorems, Gödel used methods of reasoning that are not susceptible to the theorems.

17. Edward Stabler, "Kripke On Functionalism and Automata," *Synthese* 70, 1987: 1–22. Stabler does not endorse triviality arguments, nor does he use them against computational functionalism. His target is Kripke's argument against functionalism.

18. EXPTIME is above NP in the hierarchy of complexity classes. P is below NP. P marks those problems that require a feasible amount of resources to solve. Problems in EXPTIME are even harder to solve than those in NP. Most mathematicians and computer scientists think that P is not equal to NP, but no one has succeeded in proving it. As of 2007, the Clay Foundation in Cambridge, Massachusetts is still offering a million dollars to anyone who proves the conjecture true or proves it false.

19. On Putnam's definition of what counts as a trivial computation.

20. Hilary Putnam, "Artificial Intelligence: Much Ado about Not Very Much," in *Words and Life*, pp. 391–402, 393, 401; *Renewing Philosophy* (Harvard University Press, 1992), chapter 1.

21. John Searle, *The Rediscovery of the Mind* (MIT Press, 1992), pp. 197–226.

22. W. V. Quine, "Two Dogmas of Empiricism," reprinted in *From a Logical Point of View* (Harvard University Press, 1965).

23. If meaning-constituting beliefs can't be distinguished from auxiliary beliefs, then meanings are holistic objects. Individuating meanings requires taking in all beliefs that are connected with a word, no matter how tangential. This view is called *radical Quinean meaning holism*.

24. The form of the computationalists' response to the multi-realization argument is as follows. P: It is possible there is a computable partitioning of the infinitely many computational realizations of an arbitrary intentional state into one equivalence class. C: It is possible there is a genuine computational reduction of intentional states into computational states. There are interesting questions about whether it is better to make a weaker claim—that there are a small number of equivalence classes rather than that there is one equivalence class—in the premise. I ignore these questions here, for I argue that (i) Putnam has not shown the possibility expressed in the premise above is not a genuine possibility and (ii) if there is a computational description of rational interpretation (or of general intelligence or of reasonable reasoning), there is a computable partitioning of the infinitely many computational realizations of an arbitrary intentional state into a small set of equivalence classes.

25. A computable partitioning provides a short computational description of any arbitrary intentional state. Since intentional states can be found for all forms of human reasoning, if there is a computable partitioning, for each intentional state, there is a short computational description of each intentional state instanced in human reasoning processes. Reasoning processes include deductive and inductive reasoning. Gödel's theorems show there is no computational description of a formal system that can express arithmetic and that can prove its consistency with mathematical certainty. No finitary being can do this, either. Thus there are no intentional states in a finitary being for such tasks. If so, there is no computational description and thus no worry that a computable partitioning of intentional states for deductive reasoning violates Gödel's theorems.

26. He also concludes that there are no finitistic algorithms for making coreferentiality decisions, for rational interpretation, for general intelligence and for reasonable reasoning.

27. Putnam, *Representation and Reality*, p. 89.

28. Ibid., p. 11f.

29. If so, the equivocation carries over to his use of "coreferentiality," "general intelligence," "reasonable reasoning," and "rational interpretation." Since my points hold for an equivocation on any of these terms, I discuss only the equivocation on "synonymy determination" in this introduction.

30. I argue that it does not follow from the assumption that an algorithm must survey all that information that it is infinitistic and able to foretell the future. It might

be the case that all the information can be computably partitioned. The conclusion of EQUIVALENCE is that there is no such partitioning. But the conclusion has to be argued for, by showing that the complexity of the information blocks partitioning into equivalence classes. Another reason for doubting the conclusion is that algorithms for synonymy determination might have parameters that get filled in when empirical data is available. We do not now know what future forms of rationality will be like. But that does not matter, if the algorithm has a parameter for forms of rationality.

31. This is true of both rational interpretation$_1$ and rational interpretation$_2$.

32. In "Model Theory and the 'Factuality' of Semantics," in *Words and Life*, Putnam says that "Quine writes as if there were a noumenal reality, and what his model-theoretic argument shows is that our terms have an infinite number of ways of being modeled in it. I argue that at least the naturalistic version of metaphysical realism land one in precisely such a conclusion as Quine reaches here—and I conclude there must be something wrong with metaphysical realism!" (p. 362)

33. Putnam, *Representation and Reality*, p. 107f.

34. Ibid., p. xv.

35. Why is it exactly analogous? If there is a computable partitioning, then arbitrary intentional states will have a short computational description. So the true nature of an arbitrary intentional state is given by some short computational description.

36. Putnam, *Representation and Reality*, p. xv.

Chapter 1

1. "Some Basic Theorems on the Foundations of Mathematics and Their Implications," in Gödel's *Collected Works, Volume 3: Unpublished Essays and Lectures* (Oxford University Press, 1995). Gödel's idea is much more subtly expressed than Lucas's subsequent elaboration of it.

2. J. R. Lucas, "Minds, Machines and Gödel," *Philosophy* 36, 1961: 112–127.

3. His target at the time was Roger Penrose, whose two books argued that computational functionalism is false because the Gödel theorems show there are things human beings can do in their mental lives that computing machines cannot do.

4. I use the phrase 'x is Gödel susceptible' to mean that Gödel's theorems apply to x. Similarly, 'x is not Gödel susceptible' and 'x is Gödel insusceptible' mean that Gödel's theorems do not apply to x.

5. Unless the epistemic modality in which the truths (the method of inquiry yields) are known is different from the epistemic modality in which the truths (the formalization of that method of inquiry yields) are known. I will address this below.

Although certain kinds of infinitistic beings can avoid the Gödel theorems, a finitistic being that has the ability to reason about elementary arithmetic cannot. This does not show, however, that if we are Gödel susceptible then we are finitistic.

6. "Some Basic Theorems on the Foundations of Mathematics and Their Implications," p. 310. Before the philosophical doctrine of functionalism was proposed (in the late 1950s), the view that the mind is a machine was known as 'mechanism'. Gödel's remarks are directed against mechanism.

7. David K. Lewis, "Lucas against Mechanism" and "Lucas against Mechanism, II," both reprinted in his *Philosophical Papers* (Cambridge University Press, 1999).

8. Penrose, *The Emperor's New Mind* (Oxford University Press, 1987) and *Shadows of the Mind* (Oxford University Press, 1994).

9. Putnam, "Review of Roger Penrose's *Shadows of the Mind*," *Bulletin of the American Mathematical Society* 32, 1995: 370–373. Putnam's review also appeared in the *New York Times Book Review* of November 20, 1994. (Apparently this was the first time a review appeared in a scholarly technical journal and in a popular newspaper.) Putnam blasted *Shadows of the Mind* (Penrose's attempt to defuse criticisms of his earlier resuscitation of the Lucas argument in *The Emperor's New Mind*). Putnam did not mince words. He called the publication of Penrose's book "a sad episode in our current intellectual life." According to Putnam, Penrose's argument rests on a simple mistake: "He mistakenly believes that he has a philosophical disagreement with the logical community, when in fact this is a straightforward case of a mathematical fallacy.... There is an obvious lacuna: the possibility of a program which we could write down but which is not 'simple enough to appreciate in a perfectly conscious way' is overlooked!" Moreover, Putnam does not think that Penrose has given a non-question-begging response to the problem: "To reject the possibility that such a formal system [the program is the length of the New York City telephone directory—JB] might simulate the output of a idealized mathematician (as involving something ... 'essentially dubious') is to give no argument at all—and most certainly not 'a very clear-cut argument for a non-computational ingredient in our conscious thinking.'" Penrose took the logical possibility of such a long program that computationally describes our ability in Peano arithmetic to be dubious. Putnam's response to this complaint goes right to the point: "Thus if the program is too complicated to appreciate in a perfectly conscious way, the resulting system will also be too complicated to understand, and there will be nothing 'essentially dubious' about the fact that we cannot prove its soundness."

10. I am deliberately refraining from introducing talk of the epistemic modality in which the proof of consistency is known in order to avoid confusion. Our aim here is to describe the error that Putnam found in the Penrose-Lucas arguments.

11. The same point can be made in terms of Peano arithmetic instead of the computer program used to characterize the finite machine: we can't distinguish between the failure of a finite machine to compute its own Gödel sentence and the failure of a

finitary human being—whom we hypothesize is not Gödel susceptible—to compute the consistency sentence for Peano arithmetic (which is logically equivalent to the Gödel sentence constructed within Peano arithmetic). Gödel proved that within a system of logic strong enough to express the truths of Peano arithmetic (a form of elementary arithmetic), there are truths that can be expressed within the logic, but that can't be proved in it. (The first incompleteness theorem) He also proved that the consistency of Peano arithmetic cannot be proved within the logic. (The second incompleteness theorem.) If one can prove the Gödel sentence for a system of logic, then one can prove that it is consistent. Similarly, if one can prove it is consistent, then one can prove its Gödel sentence.

12. I will not distinguish mathematical from logical certainty. I will simply use the phrase 'mathematical certainty' for the kind of certainty that provability in a system of logic secures. Issues about the reducibility of mathematics to logic and of differences between non-formal proofs and formal proofs will be largely ignored.

13. I use CON(PA) as an abbreviation for the sentence that expresses the consistency of Peano arithmetic.

14. Putnam has a valuable discussion of empirical mathematics in "Truth and necessity in mathematics," but his discussion is in service of a point about the revisability of mathematics in the context of the distinction between analytic and synthetic truths. The article is in *Mathematics, Matter and Method* (Philosophical Papers, volume 1).

15. The construction was first elaborated by Alan Turing in his epochal paper "Systems of Logic Based on Ordinals" (*Proceedings of the London Mathematical Society*, series 2, volume 45, 1939: 161–228).

16. I have not noticed this distinction made in the literature on Gödelian anti-functionalist arguments and critical discussions of them.

17. The phrases 'x is Gödel refuted' and 'Gödel refutation of x' mean that the Gödel theorems are employed in an attempt to refute x, where the variable 'x' ranges over mechanism, computational functionalism, functionalism and computationalism.

18. In "Reflexive Reflections," reprinted in *Words and Life* (Harvard University Press, 1994), Putnam carefully describes what he is doing as showing that his use of the Gödel theorems is intended to show that we can never be justified in believing the total computational theory for our prescriptive competence in proving theorems of mathematics. In fact, this is a version of the Gödel theorems.

19. Successful MGM arguments have little to say about whether the human mind is emergent from or supervenient upon a finitary machine, other than that if the human mind is supervenient upon it, the finitary machine cannot incorporate a finitary proof system. Emergence questions are notoriously thorny: infinitary capacities may emerge from purely finitary ones. Who knows? The mechanism of emergence is a black box. As I will argue later, it is unlikely that there is a successful MGM argument.

20. Do we have any reasons—empirical or otherwise—to think that human cognition employs infinitary processes? An infinitely long derivation requires of the prover that she write down infinitely many proof lines and of someone who follows the proof that she survey infinitely many proof lines. Is there any human being who has the cognitive capacities to do these things? The anti-mechanist who fashions an MGM argument must show more than that at least one exists and must show all normal human minds have this infinitary capacity when functioning normally.

21. We shall see that the other kind of use of the Gödel theorems—the epistemic use—is also confronted by these prospects.

22. Alonzo Church, *Introduction to Mathematical Logic*, volume 1 (Princeton University Press, 1956), p. 53f.

23. "Existence and Feasibility in Arithmetic," *Journal of Symbolic Logic* 36, 1971: 494–508. Work in this area exploded in the 1990s and continues to be an area of active research.

24. Parikh's work on "almost inconsistent theories" has spawned interesting work by Alexander Dragalin and by Alessandra Carbone on feasible theories.

25. An example of a cognitive ability that has been technologically enhanced is combinatorial search through a search space for a given mathematical problem. The four-color problem was solved by a computer, because it is infeasible for a human mind to search the space of possible solutions unaided by some technological enhancement.

26. William Reinhardt, "Epistemic Theories and the Interpretation of Gödel's Incompleteness Theorems," *Journal of Philosophical Logic* 15, 1986: 427–474.

27. Obviously, the schema is not so rigid that it allows only one computational model—Turing machines. If so, it would not hold any interest for the mechanism debate, since it is unlikely that human cognition is modeled, if it can be computationally modeled, by a Turing-machine model of computation.

28. However, it might be that the proof we are Turing machines is so long that it cannot be appreciated, in which case we do not have epistemic access to it, since it would never be written down.

29. Timothy J. Carlson, "Knowledge, machines and the consistency of Reinhardt's strong mechanistic thesis," *Annals of Pure and Applied Logic* 105, 2000: 51–82; Carlson, "Elementary Patterns of Resemblance," *Annals of Pure and Applied Logic* 108, 2001: 19–77.

30. Dan E. Willard, "Self-Verifying Axiom Systems, The Incompleteness Theorem and Related Reflection Principles," *Journal of Symbolic Logic* 66, 2001: 536–596.

31. In the mechanist literature the distinction between EGM and MGM arguments is not made, perhaps because the principal kind of anti-mechanist argument is an

MGM. In *R&R*, Putnam appears to use only MGM arguments. In his paper "Reflexive Reflections" (pp. 416–427) there is textual evidence of MGM and EGM arguments. For the former, we have the boldly italicized assertion that *"we always have the power to go beyond any reasoning that we can survey and see to be sound. Reflexive reflection cannot totally survey itself."* (p. 417) For the latter, we have two citations. The first: "Thus no formalization of human mathematical proof ability can both be sound *and* be such that it is part of human mathematical proof ability to *prove* that soundness." (p. 418) The second: "... even if we pretend that the Alpha Centaurians do have the description D [a computational description of our Chomskian competence—JB], the description of *their* prescriptive competence isn't D but, say, D*. And the description of beings powerful enough to find *that* out is D**." (p. 425) The question of whether Putnam employs MGM or EGM arguments depends on the use to which he wants to put them. His principal use is in showing there cannot be a formalization of the kind of reasoning we engage in when we rationally interpret discourse or when we make synonymy judgments. Thus, he needs an MGM argument, for he needs to show there is something we can do that no finitary computing machine can do: namely, rationally interpret discourse and make synonymy judgments.

32. Marr's view is quite attractive and makes the competence/performance distinction fairly precise. There are other ways of understanding this distinction. For Marr's discussion, see his book *Vision* (Freeman, 1980). It is available to the philosopher who endorses cognitive science as a philosophical theory of the human mind to do without a competence theory, though such a psychological theory could not be scientific, since performance profiles for human beings, without a theory of the nature of the commonalties and differences between those performance profiles (described by psychological laws grounded in a competence-performance distinction) would make cognitive science little different from the crudest behaviorism.

33. Putnam, "Reflexive Reflections," p. 417f.

34. Just how much less than mathematical certainty is tolerated in the epistemic justification of C? We will not allow guessing as a method of epistemic justification. Guessing does not have a degree of reliability greater than 50 percent (under relatively mild assumptions). However, between guessing and mathematical certainty there is much room for maneuver. We can learn from what we have: computational descriptions of cognition not Gödel susceptible could be used as exemplars for the standard of epistemic justification we should adopt for theories of cognition that are Gödel susceptible. This is sound methodology: there is no evident reason to suppose Gödel-susceptible descriptions of cognition must require more stringent epistemic standards than Gödel-insusceptible descriptions of cognition. (One example of this kind of sound methodology might be the use of probabilistic algorithms for cognitive processes that are justified in terms of their explanatory and predictive successes.)

35. Recall Gödel's disjunction: "Either mathematics is incompletable in this sense, that its evident axioms can never be comprised in a finite rule, that is to say, the

human mind (even within the realm of pure mathematics) infinitely surpasses the powers of any finite machine, or else there exist absolutely unsolvable diophantine problems of the type specified (where the case that both terms of the disjunction are true is not excluded, so that there are, strictly speaking, three alternatives.)" ("Some Basic Theorems on the Foundations of Mathematics and Their Implications," p. 310)

36. George Boolos, "Introductory note to 'Some basic theorems on the foundations of mathematics and their implications,'" in Gödel, *Collected Works*, volume 3, esp. p. 293.

37. Nathan Salmon, "The Limits of Human Mathematics," in *Metaphysics, Mathematics and Meaning, Philosophical Papers, Volume 1* (Oxford University Press, 2005), pp. 243–265. Remarkably, Salmon's paper has received virtually no critical attention. That is unfortunate, since it is arguably the best philosophical paper ever written on the use of the Gödel theorems in refuting mechanism.

38. Georg Kreisel, "Which Number Theoretic Problems Can Be Solved in Recursive Progressions on $\Pi(1, 1)$ Paths through O?" *Journal of Symbolic Logic* 37, 1972, no. 2: 311–334.

39. Ibid., p. 323.

40. Ibid., p. 323.

41. We would not take the application of *any* Gödel-insusceptible method toward proving the consistency of C to be epistemologically adequate. We would not be epistemically justified in taking the proofs obtained by any Gödel-insusceptible method to be epistemically justified.

42. There are many good textbooks available on this work. The classic is Hartley Rogers, *Theory of Recursive Functions and Effective Computability* (MIT Press, 1987).

43. For a good overview of reductive proof theory, see Solomon Feferman, "Does Reductive Proof Theory Have a Viable Rationale?" *Erkenntnis* 53, 2000: 63–96.

44. 'Short' is a vague predicate, but that does not matter for the point that we make. We do not have to make it precise to make our point.

45. If speed-up is bounded by a slow growing recursive function, then it might be that the program C^{n^*}, which is short, takes too long to reach. Even though the program is short, the amount of time it takes to get it is too long. Thus, an antifunctionalist trades the problem of C's being too long for the problem of the speed-up path's being too long.

46. Even if a method that proves CON(C) with less than mathematical certainty or in some other epistemic modality is Gödel susceptible, we still want to know whether the proof of CON(C) is epistemically justified. If it is, then we next look at whether a proof of CON(method that proves CON(C)) with less than mathe-

matical certainty or in another epistemic modality is epistemically justified. If it is, then we continue. Suppose the nth proof by the nth method of CON(Method$_{n-1}$) is epistemically justified and n is greater than 100. Wouldn't we be epistemically warranted in accepting the proof of CON(C) in that case?

47. I do not carry out this project in this work, because (i) all I need do here is to show the logical complexity of the problem facing anyone who proposes an MGM or an EGM argument and (ii) the project would itself require a book-length work.

48. The logical complexity of the problem of characterizing defeater chains in defeater epistemologies might be similar to the logical problem, in formal truth theories, of showing when a truth-predicate exhausts the true sentences. John Burgess ("The Truth Is Never Simple," *Journal of Symbolic Logic* 51, 1986: 663–681) shows that the recursive unsolvability of when the true sentences are exhausted (on any truth theory) is quite high. Perhaps it is the same in defeater epistemologies and that it is the same for the tangled chains problem MGM or EGM arguments encounter.

Chapter 2

1. The contrast is with strong methods: a method is strong if it proves CON(C) with mathematical certainty.

2. Putnam, "Reflexive Reflections," pp. 416–427. To date (2007), no one has responded to this argument, in spite of its critical importance in the mechanism debate. He first presented it at a Sloan Conference at MIT in June 1984.

3. Hilary Putnam, "Degree of Confirmation and Inductive Logic," reprinted in *Mind, Matter and Mathematics*, Philosophical Papers, volume 1 (Cambridge University Press, 1975).

4. Hilary Putnam, "Trial and Error Predicates and the Solution to a Problem of Mostowski," *Journal of Symbolic Logic* 30, 1965: 49–57.

5. David Kaplan and Richard Montague, "A Paradox Regained?" *Notre Dame Journal of Formal Logic* 1, 1960: 79–90. See also Richard Montague, "Syntactical Treatments of Modality, with Corollaries on Reflection Principles and Finite Axiomatizability," *Acta Philosophica Fennica* 16, 1963: 153–167.

6. Putnam, "Reflexive Reflections," p. 419.

7. Ibid., p. 419.

8. Ibid., p. 426, note 5.

9. Ibid., p. 419f.

10. In "The Gödel Theorem and Human Nature," an unpublished lecture delivered at a seminar on computer science and logic in Tel-Aviv in January 2005, Putnam

offered a new proof of his claim that dispenses with the assumption that one could be justified in accepting a mathematical falsehood. The proof in "Reflexive Reflections" needs this assumption in order to show that P cannot converge on the Computational Liar or on its negation. My criticism of PGA does not depend on making this assumption or on giving it up. In this chapter I will present and work with the assumption that one could be justified in accepting a mathematical falsehood.

11. A somewhat weaker assumption, that the formal system P is 1-consistent, will secure the same results.

12. Putnam, "Reflexive Reflections," p. 420f.

13. Richmond Thomason extended their work to belief predicates in his paper "A Note on Syntactical Treatments of Modality," *Synthese* 44, 1980: 391–395. For a discussion of the Montague-Kaplan and Thomason incompatibility results, see Nicholas Asher and Hans Kamp, "Self-Reference, Attitudes and Paradox," in *Properties, Types and Meaning, Volume 1: Foundational Issues*, ed. G. Chierchia et al. (Kluwer 1989), especially pp. 85–88.

14. Richmond Thomason, "Motivating Ramified Type Theory," in *Properties, Types and Meaning, Volume 1: Foundational Issues*, pp. 47–62, esp. 54ff.

15. Solomon Feferman, "Arithmetization of Metamathematics in a General Setting," *Fundamenta Mathematicae* 49, 1960: 35–92.

16. David Chalmers, "Minds, Machines and Mathematics: A Review of *Shadows of the Mind* by Roger Penrose," *Psyche* 2, 1995: 11–20.

17. Per Lindström, "Penrose's New Argument," *Journal of Philosophical Logic* 30, 2001: 241–250.

18. Ibid.

19. Under the view, held by Saul Kripke, that diagonalization is a way to show that there is a violation of the unrestricted comprehension axiom and that all of the paradoxes are violations of it.

20. In his famous paper "Is Justified True Belief Knowledge?" (*Analysis* 23, 1963: 121–123), Edmund L. Gettier argued that there are cases in which one has a true, justifed belief that is not knowledge. Theses cases rely on being justified in believing a falsehood.

21. Arthur Danto, "On Knowing That We Know," in *Epistemology*, ed. A. Stroll (Harper and Row, 1967).

22. Putnam, *Representation and Reality*, p. 11. Chapters 8 and 9 of the present volume include an extensive discussion of the notions 'justified', 'warranted', 'rational interpretation', 'reasonable reasoning', and 'general intelligence' and of the role of each of these notions in Putnam's refutation of computational functionalism.

23. For the proof that the theorems of G are preserved under exchange of Löb's schema for the counterpart of Thomason's fourth axiom, see Andreas Blass, "Infinitary Combinatorics and Modal Logic," *Journal of Symbolic Logic* 55, 1990: 761–778. Blass credits A. Macintyre and H. Simmons with the proof, citing their paper "Gödel's Diagonalization Technique and Related Properties of Theories" (*Colloquium Mathematicum* 28, 1973: 165–180), though the result is only mentioned there. Blass's proof is simple, and it involves only elementary derivations in G and the use of propositional logic. Here I give a slightly different version of it. The first step is to assume the tautology in G : $(\alpha \cdot L\alpha) \to \alpha$. Apply to this the derived rule of G, that "from $\alpha \to \beta$ infer $L\alpha \to L\beta$." Thus, we get that $L(\alpha \cdot L\alpha) \to L\alpha$. We now need to find a way to massage that formula into something which looks like $L\alpha \to L(L(\alpha \cdot L\alpha) \to (\alpha \cdot L\alpha))$. This can be done by propositional logic and a modal tautology. Using addition, we get $(L(\alpha \cdot L\alpha) \to L\alpha)$ or not-α. By commutation, we have not-α or $(L(\alpha \cdot L\alpha) \to L\alpha)$. Then, by implication, we have $\alpha \to (L(\alpha \cdot L\alpha) \to L\alpha)$. Finally, if $L(\alpha \cdot L\alpha) \to L\alpha$, then we also have, as a consequence, $L(\alpha \cdot L\alpha) \to (\alpha \cdot L\alpha)$. This is a inverse modal analogue of the theorem in propositional logic that a conditional whose consequent is a conjunction can be split into two conditionals, each with the same antecedent and where the left-hand side of the conjunct is the consequent of the first conditional and the right-hand side of the conjunction is the consequent of the second conditional. In classical propositional logic, it is invalid to infer $A \to (B \cdot C)$ from $A \to B$, but valid to make the inference in the converse direction. However, in normal modal systems, if $L\alpha$ follows from $L(\alpha \cdot L\alpha)$, then $\alpha \cdot L\alpha$ follows from $L(\alpha \cdot L\alpha)$. We can now apply the derived rule to $\alpha \to (L(\alpha \cdot L\alpha) \to (\alpha \cdot L\alpha))$ to get $L\alpha \to L(L(\alpha \cdot L\alpha) \to (\alpha \cdot L\alpha))$. Now use a substitution instance of Löb's schema $L(L(\alpha \cdot L\alpha) \to (\alpha \cdot L\alpha)) \to L(\alpha \cdot L\alpha)$. We now need another tautology in G, namely, $\alpha \cdot L\alpha \to L\alpha$. Apply the derived rule of inference to it, to obtain $L(\alpha \cdot L\alpha) \to LL\alpha$. We are now in a position to use propositional logic to get the promised result. It is a simple matter of two consecutive applications of hypothetical syllogism. The first application is on $L\alpha \to L(L(\alpha \cdot L\alpha) \to (\alpha \cdot L\alpha))$ and $L(L(\alpha \cdot L\alpha) \to (\alpha \cdot L\alpha)) \to L(\alpha \cdot L\alpha)$ to get $L\alpha \to L(\alpha \cdot L\alpha)$. Using this and $L(\alpha \cdot L\alpha) \to LL\alpha$, we get, by hypothetical syllogism, the promised theorem: $L\alpha \to LL\alpha$.

24. Putnam, *Representation and Reality*, p. 118.

25. Ibid., p. xv. See also the passage on p. 118.

26. We do know, from Kolmogorov complexity theory, that programs that output random sequences can be no shorter than those sequences. (Please note that a random sequence is not a random number.) If we could show that the outputs of a program that models human demonstrative and non-demonstrative reasoning are random, we could prove that the program is infeasibly long. This appears unlikely, since it is unlikely those outputs are random.

27. That is not to say that we can't use informal methods to prove CON(FORMAL SYSTEM). But these methods can eventually be formalized.

28. Putnam, *Representation and Reality*, p. 118.

29. Perhaps human minds implement genetic algorithms, which try out alternative modes of reasoning that transcend what we can formalize in the program of ourselves, with less than mathematical certainty. This might provide a means for human minds to springboard into stronger formal systems. It provides a computational explanation of how we can go beyond whatever we can formalize.

30. Putnam, *Representation and Reality*, p. 116f.

Chapter 3

1. Putnam, *Representation and Reality*, p. xv.

2. See Saul Kripke, *Wittgenstein on Rules and Private Language* (Harvard University Press, 1982), pp. 7–21.

3. Edward Stabler, "Kripke on Functionalism and Automata," *Synthese* 70, 1987: 1–22. Stabler is not arguing against computational functionalism in his paper. His target is Kripke's attempted refutation of functionalism. He describes, in detail, a triviality argument, in order to distinguish it from Kripke's argument against functionalism. Although I use the term 'Stabler-triviality' in this chapter, it is only to refer to Stabler's description of a triviality argument. Since it is the only rigorous and precise description of a triviality argument in the literature prior to *R&R*, and since it is different from Putnam's triviality argument in *R&R*, it requires critical scrutiny. Once again, Stabler does not endorse triviality arguments. He thinks it is difficult to find constraints that tighten up the definition of what it is for a physical system to physically realize a computation, but nowhere does he argue that the constraints can't be found. He also thinks psychology can find constraints that will tighten up the definition for use in cognitive science, even though these constraints will not tighten it up for use in computer science in general.

4. Stabler, "Kripke on Functionalism and Automata," p. 3.

5. PHYSYS abbreviates 'physical system'.

6. The physical system can be as small as one wants—a single elementary particle can trivially compute any function. Even a point-sized region of space-time can trivially compute any function. As long as there is a description D, which is counterfactually supported throughout T_i by physical laws, the interpretation function guarantees that the physical system, whatever its size, computes F. It is assumed the laws of nature do not change, and that the physical system will satisfy those physical laws throughout T_i. Even though it will only persist for a finite time T, if it did persist for infinitely many values T_i, it would compute all of the values of F. Thus, physical laws ensure that the counterfactual "If PHYSYS exists at T_i, it will compute F_i," is true. Below we describe a different counterfactual about computations that cannot be evaluated in S-triviality.

7. We could design an operating system that forces programs to compute range values only at odd times and to read domain values only at even times. This would be a foolish stipulation. It is doubtful that nature imposes such a temporal order on natural computations (if there are any).

8. But it is easy to mathematically define F by I in TRIV. One need only affix to the symbol 'F' in TRIV its mathematical definition. Obviously, it is not appealed to by I, so it is inert in TRIV. The problem is how to provide a mathematical definition of F in the definition of what it is for a physical system to compute a function F that is not inert.

9. John Searle, *The Rediscovery of the Mind* (MIT Press, 1992), pp. 200–226.

10. A trivialist is an anti-functionalist who employs triviality arguments to argue that computational functionalism is false.

11. If the physical states the world manifests are not contingent, but necessary, then there are no error conditions for a computation. But the physical states that the world manifests are contingent, not necessary.

12. Notice S-triviality allows the same physical state at T_i to simultaneously physically realize range values of infinitely many distinct functions (and to simultaneously physically realize errors for infinitely many distinct functions). The physical state can be at the intersection of infinitely many different trivial computation sequences. Or the physical state can satisfy many different descriptions at T_i. Notice that where a physical state satisfies different descriptions at T_i, there are different correspondences in which it figures. Each description, D, generates a unique correspondence. So it is possible that the same physical state at T_i computes both F(domain value$_i$) and an error in computing F(domain value$_i$). It all depends on what descriptions the physical state satisfies at T_i.

13. Since EXPTIME is well above NP in the complexity hierarchy (it is above PSPACE, which is above NP), that it is not equal to P does not tell us whether NP is not equal to P. For a good introduction to computational complexity theory, see Christos Papadimitriou, *Computational Complexity* (Addison-Wesley, 1994).

14. Ronald Fagin, "Generalized First-Order Spectra and Polynomial-Time Recognizable Sets," *SIAM-AMS Proceedings* 7, 1974: 27–41.

15. Let the physical system be the smallest possible physical object in contemporary physics and find a time interval during which none of its physical properties change. Divide that time interval into N moments, where N is the total number of computational states the physical system must enter so that it can compute any function. Or let the physical system satisfy a physical description that is always true of it. Then relative to that physical description, the physical system never changes. The supervenience base is the physical object relative to that description. Since the physical system always satisfies the description, the supervenience base never changes.

16. In classical propositional logic, variables eliminate the problem of explicitly writing infinitely many expressions to specify which propositional formulas are well formed. We say 'p and q' is well formed, where p and q are any well-formed formulas. We do not have to write: 'A and A' is well formed, 'A and B' is well formed, 'A and C' is well formed, etc.

17. Why do we need a second Turing machine that counts intermediate states in the universal Turing machine? Why not code the universal Turing machine to count its own intermediate states? The problem is that the coding is a computation that is like a subroutine. It has initial, intermediate, and final computational states, and these must also be counted, since they occur in real time (i.e., T_i), and it is real time that is used to partially individuate physically realized computational states in COMP. (The description, D, completes the individuation of physically realized computational states.)

18. Whether the containment is strict is an open question.

19. David Gale, "An Indeterminate Problem in Classical Mechanics," *American Mathematical Monthly* 59, 1952: 291–295.

20. In the preceding paragraph we examined a situation in which the physical state is fixed and the computational states vary. Here the computational state is fixed and the physical states vary. Both situations violate supervenience.

21. Ned Block, "The Mind as the Software of the Brain," in *Invitation to Cognitive Science: Thinking*, second edition, ed. E. Smith and D. Osherson (MIT Press, 1995), esp. pp. 398–400; B. J. Copeland, "What Is Computation?" *Synthese* 108, 1996: 335–359; David Chalmers, "On Implementing a Computation," *Minds and Machines* 4, 1994: 391–402.

22. Block, "The Mind as the Software of the Brain," p. 399.

23. John Searle, "Is the Brain a Digital Computer?" *Proceedings and Addresses of the American Philosophical Association* 64, 1990: 21–37.

24. Block, "The Mind as the Software of the Brain," pp. 399–400.

25. At the summer 2002 NEH Summer Institute (as reported by Barry Loewer).

26. It would be interesting to compare this proposal with holographic views of identity over time.

27. Block, "The Mind as the Software of the Brain," p. 399.

28. Searle, *The Rediscovery of the Mind*, p. 209.

29. Chalmers, "On Implementing a Computation," p. 393.

30. For a good discussion of why bisimulations are superior to isomorphisms, see Patrick Blackburn, Maarten deRijke, and Yde Venema, *Modal Logic* (Cambridge University Press, 2001), pp. 51–73.

31. There are issues in the metaphysics of realization, such as the basic kinds of objects that serve as realizers (do we allow in addition to physical properties, distinct physical individuals and distinct causal powers?) that I will not dwell upon, other than to note that we can adjudicate the metaphysics by determining what kinds of basic objects are needed to satisfy invariance (in addition to the basic kind of mapping). Another issue is that the physical system that physically realizes a computation must satisfy the laws of physics, but they are inapplicable to abstract computations that are physically realized. If that is so, there is structure in the physical system (satisfying the laws of physics) that is not mapped to the computational states. For instance, the physical system has to satisfy the laws of thermodynamics. Unless there are information-theoretic analogues of these laws that hold for computations, there is no computational structure into which the thermodynamic "structure" of a physical system can be mapped.

Chapter 4

1. Putnam, *Representation and Reality*, p. 121.

2. Ibid.

3. Whether this can happen in nature is an empirical question whose answer awaits an account of natural computation in objects. In biological computing, computations can occur across boundaries, such as the membrane of a cell. But in this case, the boundary of the membrane and the interior and exterior of it are all part of the physical system that does the computation. The cases we want to rule out are where we define the physical space in which computation occurs and then find that some computational states of that computation are physically realized outside the physical space.

4. On jump objects see Eli Hirsch, *The Concept of Identity* (Oxford University Press, 1982), p. 21, note 8. They were invented by Saul Kripke and first introduced in his fall 1978 Princeton metaphysics seminar on identity over time.

5. Giving a precise definition of this condition will not be easy, since we do not want it to include parallel or distributed computations.

6. Assuming that we do know that the physical system normally computes F(n). If we do not know that, then a theory of error will tell us nothing, since the theory of error presupposes that under normal conditions the physical system computes F(n). The point made here is that in trivial computations, without a theory of error, but knowing the physical system trivially computes F(n), we cannot say when either computational flows across boundaries or computational flow merges occur, whether there is an error in computation or whether another function has been computed.

7. Physically chaotic systems can exhibit such indeterminate behavior. Such physical systems arise everywhere in nature. There are other sources of discontinuity (which

may or may not be instances of chaos). For instance, classical Newtonian mechanics fails to determine unique predictions of experiments, even for simple physical systems, such as three steel balls of uniform size and mass moving down an inclined plane.

8. Putnam, *Representation and Reality*, p. 122f.

9. He says that though the theorem is restricted to finite automata, it also works when any other computational model is substituted for finite automata (and corresponding changes in the proof are made).

10. Ronald Chrisley "Why Everything Doesn't Realize Every Computation," *Minds and Machines* 4, 1995: 403–420.

11. Gale, "An Indeterminate Problem in Classical Mechanics."

12. Recall Putnam's example of the finite automaton that repeats the computational states A and B in his proof of his triviality theorem.

13. Recall that to obtain this value we need to have the values of the field parameters for each point that is inside the boundary of S at t.

14. Putnam, *Representation and Reality*, p. 123.

15. Discounting the physical indeterminacy problem in classical mechanics noted in the previous section.

16. A precise statement of the recurrence theorem is: Let $B = \{s \in S | s$ is not recurrent$\}$. Then B has measure zero. (B is a set of points in phase space that are not recurrent and S is a surface of constant energy whose measure or volume is finite.)

17. Putnam, *Representation and Reality*, p. 121.

18. Ibid., p. 123.

19. This assumes there are no other problems for the triviality theorem. But several problems were pointed out earlier in this chapter.

20. Putnam, *Representation and Reality*, p. xv.

21. Putnam, *Renewing Philosophy*, chapter 1; "Artificial Intelligence: Much Ado about Not Very Much," pp. 391–402.

22. Ideally, there are no versions of triviality to which Putnam can appeal in arguing his case against computational functionalism.

23. Putnam, "Artificial Intelligence: Much Ado about Not Very Much," p. 401, note 7.

24. The second condition is in force, because if the function finitely recursively approximated is defined over the reals, it might not be possible to construct a step function that exactly matches its behavior over some finite set of points. For

instance, it might be easy to come within ε of a finite set of range values of a discontinuous function over the reals, but impossible to exactly match that behavior. The accuracy level depends on, at least, the types of discontinuities the function exhibits and the nature of its differentiable behavior (i.e., how its nth-order derivatives, for all n, behave on the interval in question).

25. I use the acronym 'FRA' for both 'finitely recursively approximate' and 'finite recursive approximation'.

26. In defining SF-triviality, I fix the specified accuracy level. Otherwise it can be said that there are infinitely many specified accuracy levels (because the accuracy level can be specified with infinitely many significant digits) and thus infinitely many FRAs true of the human mind. In addition, different accuracy levels are not the same as some physical object trivially computing different functions.

27. Putnam, "Artificial Intelligence: Much Ado about Not Very Much," p. 393.

28. M. Carter and B. vanBrunt, *The Lebesgue-Stieltjes Integral* (Springer-Verlag, 2000), p. 24f.

29. Carter and vanBrunt, *The Lebesgue-Stieltjes Integral*, pp. 26, 27. Notice that in the definition of this step function the domain interval is closed on the left and open on the right. Recall that this condition is also imposed on interval states in Putnam's proof of his triviality theorem. That the construction of a step function and an interval state is similar reveals an important point: both triviality constructions of computations and FRA of functions by FRA require as inputs the function values (in FRA) or the full set of computational states (in computations). You cannot use triviality to compute a function value if its value is not already known. Similarly, you cannot use FRA to determine the behavior of a function on an interval unless its behavior on that interval is already known.

30. It is an alternative to the standard theory of computational complexity, that measures how hard it is to compute a function in terms of the time or space resources a computer uses in the computation. For a good survey of Kolmogorov complexity theory, see M. Li and P. Vitanyi, "Kolmogorov Complexity and Its Applications," in *Handbook of Theoretical Computer Science*, volume A: *Algorithms and Complexity*, ed. J. vanLeeuwen (Elsevier and MIT Press, 1990).

31. This is the theory of resource-bounded Kolmogorov complexity.

32. Putnam, "Artificial Intelligence: Much Ado about Not Very Much," p. 393.

33. Ibid., p. 401, note 8.

Chapter 5

1. Searle, *The Rediscovery of the Mind*, p. 209.

2. Ibid., p. 210.

3. The same point can be made by replacing 'brain states' with 'intentional states'.

4. Searle, *The Rediscovery of the Mind*, p. 212.

5. David Marr, *Vision* (Freeman, 1982).

6. For an elaboration of this notion of interanimation, see Hilary Putnam, *Pragmatism* (Blackwell, 1995).

7. Physical inscriptions (ink arranged in various shapes on paper pages) in Searle's book *The Rediscovery of the Mind* are the physical realization of the argument, but the argument itself is an abstract object.

8. On the classical conception of computability (the theory of computability accepted by the first observer), Rice's theorem asserts that all nontrivial computational properties are undecidable. This is a "law" of computability theory.

9. W. V. Quine, "Truth by Convention," reprinted in *The Ways of Paradox and Other Essays*, revised and expanded edition (Harvard University Press, 1976).

10. In his Princeton seminars on the nature of logic, Saul Kripke endorsed Quine's argument that the laws of logic are not true by convention.

11. Some might take Searle's views on the metaphysics of computation to be as follows. The laws of computability theory (and of computational complexity theory) are not observer relative, but that a physical system performs a computation governed by those laws is observer relative. Computations are abstract objects independent of the existence of observers, but that they are physically realized in a physical system is an observer-relative feature of that physical system. It is the physical realization of computations relation that is observer relative. If there were no human observers, there would be no way of metaphysically tying abstract computations to physical systems. If this is Searle's view, then it is equivalent to a triviality argument (that any physical object computes any computable function), since it is a human convention as to which computable function the physical object computes. What we have tried to show in the preceding paragraphs (in the text) is that Searle's views on the metaphysics of computation are much stronger and must be much stronger than the views expressed above (in this note).

12. Searle, *The Rediscovery of the Mind*, p. 210.

13. We earlier discussed whether isomorphisms are the appropriate kind of map between computations and physical realizations of them. Since computations are modal in character, bisimulations are probably appropriate. Isomorphisms are too strong, since they make the source and target mathematically equivalent. Bisimulations make the target and source modally equivalent. The point I make in the text with isomorphisms can be made just as well with bisimulations.

14. For instance, the supercoiling of DNA in nucleosomes in eukaryotic cells is dictated by the shape of the nucleus. In this case, its diameter determines supercoiling.

15. Suppose Hugh Everett's relative state formulation of quantum mechanics is correct. If so, when a universe branches into two (or more) universes after a measurement is made, each universe is observer relative on Searle's metaphysics. (Does that mean everything in it is observer relative?) The only universe that is not observer relative is the primordial one, before any measurements were made. As soon as a measurement is made, all successive universes are observer relative. This is either a *reductio* of the many-worlds interpretation of quantum mechanics or a *reductio* of Searle's distinction between intrinsic and observer-relative properties of the world. At the very least, the burden of proof is on Searle. He must recuse quantum physics from absurdity. He can do so by keeping his distinction between intrinsic and observer-relative properties and claiming that measured quantum-mechanical properties are not observer relative (it just looks that way to the observer!), but intrinsic features of the world. Or he can give up the distinction or he can revise it.

16. For a good exposition of the recursion theorem, the double recursion theorem and the n-ary recursion theorem, see pp. 36–48 of Carl Smith, *The Theory of Computability* (Springer-Verlag, 1993).

17. The full range of cases subsumed under standard semantic externalism might not be capturable in an application of the double recursion theorem, but the point is that at least one of the cases has been captured.

18. See Stephen Wolfram, *A New Kind of Science* (Wolfram Science Press, 2002).

19. Perhaps we can say there is a mathematical proof of the falsity of physicalism, since there are no physical causal connections between either mind that accounts for their mutual informational sensitivity. Or we could subsume the informational dependency to superluminal causation, as in some interpretations of the EPR experiment.

20. In this case, we have to idealize Trivialist. No human being could enumerate every physical object in the universe. On the other hand, since Searle does not say anything specific about how the act of interpreting a physical object as computing a function proceeds, it is open for us to allow Trivialist to make a blanket declaration: "I interpret all n physical objects in the world at time t as computing functions in accord with the n-ary recursion theorem."

21. Another problem for this case is that every physical object in the world at time t now carries information beyond what it carried at time t − 1. That each physical object carries this information is a consequence of Trivialist interpreting each of them as carrying it. However, carrying information requires energy, since it decreases the entropy of the carrier physical system. Where does this energy come from? By hypothesis, every physical object in the universe carries additional information at time t, even though no physical system experiences an increase in entropy at time t. So Trivialist must supply the energy. If so, Trivialist experiences an enormous increase in entropy. But this is absurd. Notice that respecting the laws of thermodynamics could

be used as an additional constraint on the definition of a proper physical realization of a computation. If an energy source is required for a trivial computation that is not also needed for an authentic computation, or if the user of a trivial computer system must experience an increase in entropy where the user of a computer system that engages in genuine computations does not, then there is a violation of the laws of thermodynamics. If an arbitrary object could trivially compute a single value of each of the infinitely many computable functions at a given instant, then it would require an infinite source of energy and the Trivialist would experience an infinite increase in entropy. This is absurd and is a reason to think thermodynamic constraints must be satisfied by any definition of what it is for a physical object to physically realize a computation.

Chapter 6

1. It need not be the physical brain that is the locus of the mind in different kinds of organisms that possess minds. In a different star system, a mind might be located in an organism's foot.

2. This category must be kept small. The exceptions category is the equivalent to errors in a physical theory and the smallness of the set of exceptions corresponds to the size of the margin of error tolerated for the purposes of epistemic justification of the theory.

3. Putnam, *Representation and Reality*, p. xii.

4. Ibid., p. xivf.

5. There are other kinds of local reductions. Restrict the class of architectures or the kinds of programming languages or the kinds of algorithms (modulo that solve a fixed problem). We can now devise 120 distinct local reductions. For instance, one local reduction is: restrict the class of physical beings, the class of architectures and the kinds of programming languages.

6. Jerry Fodor criticized epistemic semantics in "Language, Thought and Compositionality" (*Mind and Language* 16, 2001: 1–15.) Fodor claims it can't respect (because it can't implement) semantical compositionality, which is non-negotiable in psychology. Donald Davidson also thinks semantical compositionality is non-negotiable: "Knowledge of a general compositional structure remains essential to the understanding not only of language but of belief and all the other propositional attitudes." ("Reply to P. Pagin," in *Donald Davidson: Truth, Meaning and Knowledge*, ed. U. Zeglen, Routledge, 1999, p. 73)

7. It is not my goal to provide an argument that Quine's views about the analytic synthetic distinction are wrong.

8. Putnam, *Representation and Reality*, p. 132, note 5.

9. Ibid., p. 79ff.

10. Putnam does not make this distinction. But it is important, for one might reduce the disjunction length of a computational multi-realization to a small finite number but still have a colossal intrinsic sum size.

11. Putnam, *Representation and Reality*, p. 80ff.

12. Ibid., p. 75. Putnam discusses this problem extensively in chapter 1 of *Representation and Reality* and in his earlier essay "Computational Psychology and Interpretation Theory," in *Realism and Reason* (Cambridge University Press, 1983).

13. The extensions to the model Putnam considers (and shows to be deficient) are ones that have been proposed in the philosophical and psychological literature. He has done something valuable in showing what computational models will *not* work.

14. W. V. Quine, *Word and Object* (MIT Press, 1960), chapter 2.

15. This argument for showing there are infinitely many computational realizations of an arbitrary intentional state by Quinean indeterminacy does not appear in *R&R*. Although we will argue computationalism can avoid indeterminacy, suppose it cannot. Does it follow that there are infinitely many computational states realizing SD given indeterminacy? Consider two speakers A and B. A uses stimulus meaning 1 and B uses stimulus meaning 2. Suppose each uses the same algorithm for SD. A computational realization of A and B's utterances ("There's a house" and "Es gibt ein haus.") that does not identify their stimulus meanings will be a disjunction of two computational states: one state contains stimulus meaning 1 and the other contains stimulus meaning 2. But why can't we computably partition the stimulus meanings into a single computational state? That state is marked with a label 'stimulus meaning'. Any stimulus meaning at all can be in that state. Similarly, why not take all English speakers and put them into the same equivalence class labeled 'English'. Thus there is a disjunction of computational states whose length is bounded by the total number of natural languages and their dialects. This number is no greater than 200,000. Perhaps we can computably partition the natural languages by using linguistic criteria to create language families. We can reduce the 200,000 to less than 20.

16. Putnam, *Representation and Reality*, p. 14f.

17. Ibid., p. 75.

18. Putnam, "Computational Psychology and Interpretation Theory," p. 145.

19. For this discussion, see Putnam, *Representation and Reality*, pp. 12–15.

20. Putnam, *Representation and Reality*, p. 13ff.

21. Ibid., p. 12ff.

22. Ibid., p. 11ff.

23. Putnam, "Introduction: An Overview of the Problem," in *Realism and Reason*, p. viiff.

24. For the most part, I will use the notion of rational interpretation in conducting my discussion of the arguments SCS and EQUIVALENCE, although reasonable reasoning and general intelligence also figure in these arguments. Nothing hangs on this, however.

25. Jerry Fodor, *The Modularity of Mind: An Essay on Faculty Psychology* (MIT Press, 1983).

26. Putnam's example of radical charity is facetious, though. Cyril Stanley Smith joked to him that phlogiston is really valence electrons. It would take radical charity to declare those who used the term 'phlogiston' were really referring to valence electrons. See *Representation and Reality*, p. 13ff.

27. A dichotomy that is useful for diagnosing philosophical positions (but now discredited) is that between analytic *a priori* necessary and synthetic *a posteriori* contingent.

28. Putnam, "Computational Psychology and Interpretation Theory," p. 144ff.

29. Putnam, *Representation and Reality*, p. 107.

30. Ibid., p. 108.

31. See Putnam, "Model Theory and the Factuality of Semantics," p. 363ff.

32. "Quine writes as if there were a noumenal reality, and what his model-theoretic argument shows is that our terms have an infinite number of ways of being modeled in it. I argue that at least the naturalistic versions of metaphysical realism land one in precisely such a conclusion as Quine reaches here—and I conclude that there must be something wrong with metaphysical realism!" (Putnam, "Model Theory and the Factuality of Semantics," p. 362) See also "Realism without Absolutes," in *Words and Life*, p. 280ff.

33. Putnam, "Realism without Absolutes," in *Words and Life*, p. 280.

34. Putnam, "Introduction: An Overview of the Problem," in *Realism and Reason*, p. xiii.

35. Putnam, *Representation and Reality*, p. 110ff.

36. Putnam, "Introduction: An Overview of the Problem," p. xvi.

37. Ibid., p. xvii.

38. In classical logic, ontological relativity is a fact of life: different models of first-order logic may have different objects. How do we know that a referring term in the language picks out an object in one model, but not in the other model, if the sen-

tences that the referring term occurs in are true in both models? Classical logic employs a correspondence notion of truth that creates this problem.

39. Putnam, *Representation and Reality*, p. 107ff.

40. Putnam, "Model Theory and the Factuality of Semantics," in *Words and Life*.

41. Still, it is possible that computationalism sidesteps them and yet cannot provide a computational description of radical interpretation. Rather than just take it for granted that it can, I argue in chapter 9 that Putnam's arguments showing it can't are not convincing. In particular, his use of the Gödel incompleteness theorems to show it cannot fails and his other arguments come close to begging the question. For instance, his argument that rational interpretation can't be formalized since inductive reasoning can't be formalized goes in a circle. Inductive reasoning can't be formalized because prior probability metrics require rational interpretation, which can't be formalized.

42. For the algorithm, see any elementary text in mathematical logic. There are many computations that require logics intermediate between first-order and second-order logics, as well as second-order logics.

43. For a rigorous discussion of valuation mappings, assignment of references conditions, and satisfaction conditions, see Richard L. Epstein, *The Semantic Foundations of Predicate Logic* (Oxford University Press, 1994), chapter 4.

44. In fact, there are infinitely many such descriptions, since the descriptions of Reality in terms of truth values are really equivalence classes of all of the situations, state of affairs, . . . that come out true or that come out false.

45. Or he could give a Parmenidean argument that ultimate Reality has no parts, but that would be hopeless.

46. This follows from Jacques Herbrand's Deduction Theorem.

47. Putnam, *Representation and Reality*, p. 107.

48. See Steven Awodey, Lars Birkedal, and Dana Scott, "Local Realizability Toposes and a Modal Logic for Computability," *Mathematical Structures in Computer Science* 12, 2002: 319–334.

49. Putnam, "Introduction: An Overview of the Problem," p. xiii.

50. Putnam, *Reason, Truth and History*, p. 217f.

51. Edward L. Keenan, "Logical Objects," in *Logic, Meaning and Computation*, ed. C. Anderson and M. Zeleny (Kluwer, 2002), esp. pp. 151–154.

52. Ibid., p. 151.

53. B. Jack Copeland, Peter Kugel, and C. Calude have urged us to extend the classical conception of computationalism to embrace non-computable methods. But

even discounting the introduction of non-computable methods into computation-alism, the proliferation of relevantist, non-monotonic, probabilistic, and linear logics since 1975 complicates what should count as a classical conception of computationalism.

54. Putnam, *Representation and Reality*, p. 83.

55. Ibid.

56. Ibid.

57. I will discuss this work in chapter 9, where I will examine the arguments that rational interpretation cannot be formalized.

Chapter 7

1. Cambridge properties are relational properties that do not satisfy or figure in any known physical laws. For instance, wherever you are right now, you have the rela-tional property of being a certain distance d from the Eiffel Tower.

2. Putnam, *Representation and Reality*, p. 79f.

3. Ibid., p. 85.

4. Marr, *Vision*, chapters 2 and 3.

5. W. V. Quine, "Two Dogmas of Empiricism," in *From a Logical Point of View* (Har-vard University Press, 1982).

6. Using the term 'trivial property' suggests a result from recursion theory that might be recruited to shed light on EQUIVALENCE. Rice's theorem can be invoked to give a quick argument for what EQUIVALENCE concludes. The theorem is that all non-trivial properties of the recursively enumerable sets are undecidable, where a property is defined to be trivial if it is either universally true or universally false. If a property is non-trivial, then there is some recursively enumerable set satisfying it and some recursively enumerable set not satisfying it. It tells us we cannot use a non-trivial property to recursively separate sets. All of the computational realizations of an arbi-trary intentional state are recursively enumerable, since each one is an output of the algorithm for computably describing that intentional state. By Rice's theorem, we cannot computably partition this set of computational states into equivalence classes, for whichever non-trivial property we use to make the recursive separation. Thus we have the conclusion of EQUIVALENCE without having to argue, as Putnam does, that all rational-interpretation$_2$ algorithms are necessarily infinitary. But Rice's theorem has a fatal defect in this context. Suppose your task is to partition beliefs, modes of inference, scientific theories, . . . , into equivalence classes. It is clear there will be borderline cases and indeterminate cases. In the former, a given belief, for instance, might be equally well assigned to two different equivalence classes. In the latter, there is no equivalence class to which it belongs. If an algorithm did not simi-

larly declare borderline and indeterminate cases, it would not accord with human judgments about SD and coreferentiality decisions. Rice's theorem allows for accord, for it shows that any computable partitioning is undecidable. But that it allows for accord does not mean accord will be obtained. This is an empirical issue. Since we now do not know what an algorithm for either SD or coreferentiality decisions looks like, it is premature to invoke Rice's theorem in arguing for or against EQUIVALENCE.

7. Putnam, *Representation and Reality*, p. 80.

8. See Carl Smith, *A Recursive Introduction to the Theory of Computation* (Springer-Verlag, 1994), p. 31ff.

9. Douglas Cenzer and Jeffrey Remmel, "Feasible graphs with standard universe," *Annals of Pure and Applied Logic* 94, 1998: 21–35.

10. J. van Benthem, Modal Correspondence Theory, Ph.D. thesis, University of Amsterdam, 1976. For a good discussion of bisimulations, see Blackburn et al., *Modal Logic*, pp. 64–73.

11. G. E. Hughes, "Equivalence Relations and S5," *Notre Dame Journal of Formal Logic* 21, 1980: 577–584.

12. Eric Rosen, Saharon Shelah, and Scott Weinstein, "k-Universal Finite Graphs," in *Logic and Random Structures*, ed. R. Boppana and J. Lynch (DIMACS Series in Discrete Mathematics and Computer Science, Rutgers University, 1997).

13. Scott Kirkpatrick and David Selman, "Critical Behavior in the Satisfiability of Random Boolean Expressions," *Science* 264, 1994: 1297–1301.

14. Putnam, *Representation and Reality*, p. xiii.

15. Putnam, "Artificial Intelligence: Much Ado about Not Very Much," p. 402.

16. Dana Scott, "A New Category? Domains, Spaces and Equivalence Relations," draft of April 19, 1998, Department of Computer Science, Carnegie Mellon University.

Chapter 8

1. Putnam, *Representation and Reality*, p. 85.

2. Ibid., p. 86.

3. For a discussion of why the definition of computability is relative to a human being, see Wilfried Sieg, "Mechanical Procedures and Mathematical Experiences," in *Mathematics and the Mind*, ed. A. George (Oxford University Press, 1994). Although Turing defined computations relative to human beings, that does not make computations observer relative.

4. Putnam, *Representation and Reality*, p. 87.

5. Ibid., p. 89. If it is the case that predicting all future modes of human linguistic existence requires more than infinitary powers, only an omniscient infinitary god can occupy an Archimedean point. If infinitary powers include, by definition, the ability to predict all future modes of human linguistic existence, then all infinitary beings can occupy an Archimedean point.

6. Hilary Putnam, "Introduction: An Overview of the Problem," in *Realism and Reason*, Philosophical Papers, volume 3 (Cambridge University Press, 1983), p. xviff.

7. Putnam, *Representation and Reality*, p. 115ff.

8. Ibid., p. 11ff.

9. Putnam, "Computational Psychology and Interpretation Theory," in *Realism and Reason*, p. 150ff.

10. The same points hold for computable SD. The primary emphasis in EQUIVA-LENCE is on coreferentiality decisions, though this is probably done for the sake of brevity.

11. Putnam, *Representation and Reality*, p. 87.

12. Ibid., p. xvi. Putnam first argued this in his John Locke lectures, collected in his book *Meaning and the Moral Sciences* (Routledge, 1978).

13. Putnam, "Why Functionalism Didn't Work," in *Words and Life*, p. 456.

14. Putnam, *Representation and Reality*, p. 87.

15. Putnam, "Why Functionalism Didn't Work," p. 455.

16. Ibid., p. 456.

17. Fodor, *The Modularity of Mind*, p. 119ff.

18. Putnam, *Representation and Reality*, p. 87.

19. Ibid., p. 87.

20. This is easy to prove. Suppose we can arithmetize any possible theory of the universe—this is just a simplifying assumption necessary to determine the $N \times N \times N \times N \times \cdots \times N$ (k times) cardinality of the set of all possible theories of the universe. Let a possible theory of the universe be a function from natural numbers to natural numbers. The domain of the function is a Cartesian product of the natural numbers, $N \times N \times N \times N \times \cdots \times N$ (k times), and the range is a natural number, N. For each k, there are $2^{\aleph_0}$ k-place partial functions. That is an extraordinarily large cardinal number (whatever it happens to be, since we do not have a solution to the continuum hypothesis). Among all of these partial functions are the $\aleph_0$ many recursive functions. There is, however, no recursive enumeration of the set of total

recursive functions—this is a theorem in computability theory. Restricting theories of the universe to just those which are computable (whatever that means) is no help at all. So on either construal of the word 'anticipate', the required task is not computable.

21. Putnam, *Representation and Reality*, p. 88.

22. Ibid., p. 89.

23. Putnam, "Computational Psychology and Interpretation Theory," in *Realism and Reason*, p. 150.

24. Putnam, *Representation and Reality*, p. 11.

25. Putnam, "Reflexive Reflections."

26. Putnam, *Reason, Truth and History*, chapter 8.

27. Putnam, "Why Reason Can't Be Naturalized," in *Realism and Reason*, p. 246.

28. Putnam, "Introduction: An Overview of the Problem," in *Realism and Reason*, p. xviif.

29. Putnam, *Renewing Philosophy*. See chapter 3, especially pp. 47–55.

30. Putnam, *Representation and Reality*, p. 89. A pedantic point: Putnam's definition of 'successor society' implies that a successor society cannot be a Gödel-jump successor society. That is, B is not a society in which members can prove, with mathematical certainty, the Gödel sentence generated in the predecessor society A. For, no member of A could, even with years of specialized study, prove their own Gödel sentence with mathematical certainty. Thus we must rule out, as a reason why no current human being can survey all possible future societies, that a future society is successor related to a present society as a Gödel jump.

31. Putnam, "Computational Psychology and Interpretation Theory," in *Realism and Reason*, p. 152.

32. Ned Block invented the name 'BLOCKHEAD' for algorithms that are nothing more than lookup tables. If there is a computational description of human intelligence and the algorithms for it are BLOCKHEADS, then human intelligence is somewhat stupid.

33. If the input to the algorithm consists of a string of letters from an alphabet, the ordered pairs $\langle x, fx \rangle$ can be ordered lexicographically.

34. Saul Kripke, *Naming and Necessity* (Harvard University Press, 1980), esp. pp. 35–38.

35. Which infinity is not an issue. In some possible worlds there are gimmel-5 fissions of a single individual into gimmel-5 individuals. If the disjunction is infinitely long, its cardinality does not matter.

36. Putnam, "Computational Psychology and Interpretation Theory," in *Realism and Reason*, p. 151.

37. Ibid., p. 152.

38. Nelson Goodman, *The Structure of Appearance* (Houghlin-Mifflin, 1951). See also chapter X of Goodman, A *Study of Qualities* (Garland, 1990).

39. Aaron Bobick, Natural Object Categorization (Technical Report 1001, MIT Artificial Intelligence Laboratory, 1987). See chapter 2, titled Natural Categories.

40. Satosi Watanabe, *Pattern Recognition: Human and Mechanical*, JohnWiley and Sons, 1985.

41. Bobick, *Natural Object Categorization*, p. 23.

42. 'Aut' is exclusive disjunction (P1 or P2 but not both). 'Vel' is inclusive disjunction (P1 or P2 and possibly both).

43. Ibid., p. 27.

44. Putnam wants algorithms for rational interpretation$_2$ to depend on all possible theories of the world, all possible environments and all possible conceptions of human rationality. We are not familiar with most of the items in each of these categories. Our practice of rational interpretation$_1$ does not depend on knowing all of the items in each of these categories. Showing why we can't satisfy the generality constraint not only explains why rational interpretation$_1$ can't depend on a definition of synonymy and coreferentiality. It also shows why algorithms for rational interpretation$_2$ are incoherent as well—they violate Ugly Duckling Theorems.

45. Putnam describes "the point of view of reason" in chapter 4 of *Renewing Philosophy*.

Chapter 9

1. Putnam, "Model Theory and the Factuality of Semantics," in *Words and Life*, p. 364.

2. Putnam, "Computational Psychology and Interpretation Theory," in *Realism and Reason*, pp. 149–152.

3. A terse paragraph in "Computational Psychology and Interpretation Theory" introduces this idea, and there is an illustration of it in Putnam's discussion of Field's project of a physicalistic reduction of reference. See the second full paragraph on p. 150 of "Computational Psychology and Interpretation Theory."

4. Putnam, "Computational Psychology and Interpretation Theory," pp. 144–147.

5. Ibid., p. 147f.

6. Putnam, "Reflexive Reflections," in *Words and Life*, p. 424f.

7. Ibid., p. 424f.

8. Nelson Goodman, *Fact, Fiction and Forecast*, fourth edition (Harvard University Press, 1983).

9. See, for instance, Robert Berwick, *The Acquisition of Syntactic Knowledge* (MIT Press, 1985), p. 249ff.

10. Goodman, *Fact, Fiction and Forecast*, p. 92ff.

11. Putnam, in "Artificial Intelligence: Much Ado about Not Very Much," in *Words and Life*, p. 398.

12. Robert Stalnaker, "The Problem of Logical Omniscience, I," in *Context and Content* (Oxford University Press, 1999), pp. 241–254.

13. Putnam, *Representation and Reality*, p. 11.

14. Jerry Fodor, "Modules, Frames, Sleeping Dogs, and the Music of the Spheres," in *Modularity in Knowledge Representation and Natural Language Understanding*, ed. J. Garfield (MIT Press, 1987), pp. 25–36.

15. Putnam, *Reason, Truth and History*, pp. 188ff.

16. For a discussion of nonmonotonic approaches to formalizing belief revision—both belief expansion and belief contraction—see chapters 14–16 of Grigoris Antoniou, *Nonmonotonic Reasoning* (MIT Press, 1997).

17. Patrick Hayes and John McCarthy, "Some Philosophical Problems from the Standpoint of Artificial Intelligence," in *Machine Intelligence*, volume 4, ed. B. Meltzer and D. Michie (Edinburgh University Press, 1969).

18. Hilary Putnam, *The Collapse of the Fact/Value Dichotomy and Other Essays* (Harvard University Press, 2002), pp. 78–95.

19. Luca Anderlini and Hamid Sabourian, "Cooperation and Effective Computability," *Econometrica* 63, 1995: 1337–1369.

20. Putnam, "Model Theory and the Factuality of Semantics," p. 364.

21. If one reads Quinean indeterminacy as showing there can't be a definition of synonymy (and this is how Quine reads it), then either it does not apply to rational interpretation$_2$ or it shows there can't be any such thing as rational interpretation$_2$. I will not pursue this point.

22. Saul Kripke, *Wittgenstein on Rules and Private Language* (Harvard University Press, 1982).

23. Putnam, "Computational Psychology and Interpretation Theory," p. 150.

24. Ibid., p. 151.

25. Hilary Putnam, "Philosophers and Human Understanding," in *Realism and Reason*, p. 201.

26. There are no conclusive arguments in the literature that either prior probability metrics can't be formalized or that there is no formal solution to the grue problem.

27. Putnam, "Computational Psychology and Interpretation Theory," in *Realism and Reason*, p. 150.

28. Ibid., p. 151.

29. Ibid., p. 152.

30. There is a temptation to interpret Fodor as taking this view in *The Modularity of Mind*, since it is suggested by the wording in the second part, though Fodor has said privately that this was not what he had in mind.

31. Christos Papadimitriou and Martha Sideri, "Default Theories That Always Have Extensions," *Artificial Intelligence* 69, 1994: 347–357.

32. Putnam, "Computational Psychology and Interpretation Theory," p. 150.

33. Ibid., p. 147f.

34. Putnam, *Representation and Reality*, p. 89.

35. Suppose that it is true our sun will go nova in 4 billion years. Then the end of human existence—unless we vacate this star system—is 4 billion years from now (unless something else ends it before then such as, for example, the evolution of human beings into a new biological species). On the other hand, if the sun doesn't go nova, then human existence will continue, and new forms of rationality, cultures, societies, etc. will appear in the far-off future. Need we take into account in the construction of a rational interpretation$_2$ algorithm what might but will not happen in a possible but non-actual, future? That is, need we take into account counterfactual forms of human rationality, cultures, societies, and so on? If so, then waiting until the end of human existence to catalogue all of the forms of human rationality, societies, cultures, etc. will not be sufficient for the construction of a rational-interpretation$_2$ algorithm. Satisfying the counterfactual forms of human rationality, societies, cultures, etc. requirement can't be done at any time between now and the heat death of the universe, since there may be in principle obstacles in the way of describing the counterfactuals. A new form of rationality that would arise if the universe did not expire in heat death might be wholly alien to us because we cannot see it is an authentic form of rationality given our current forms of rationality. The point is that even if we wait until the end of human existence and have infinitary powers, we still might not be able to occupy an Archimedean point if occupation of it requires us to describe the counterfactuals about forms of human rationality, societies, cultures, etc.

Index